The Study *of* Photography *in* Latin America

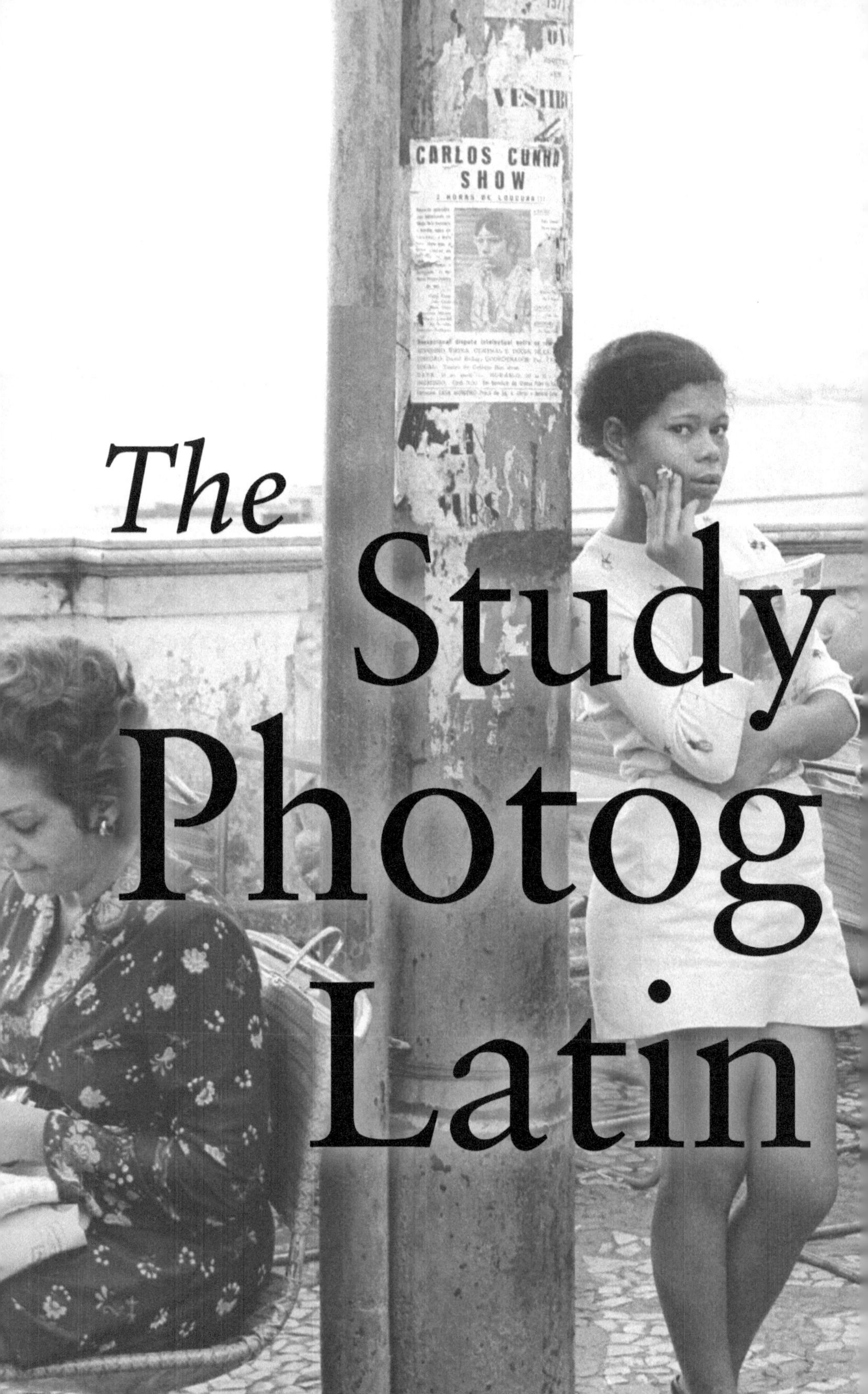
CARLOS CUNHA
SHOW
The
Study
Photog
Latin

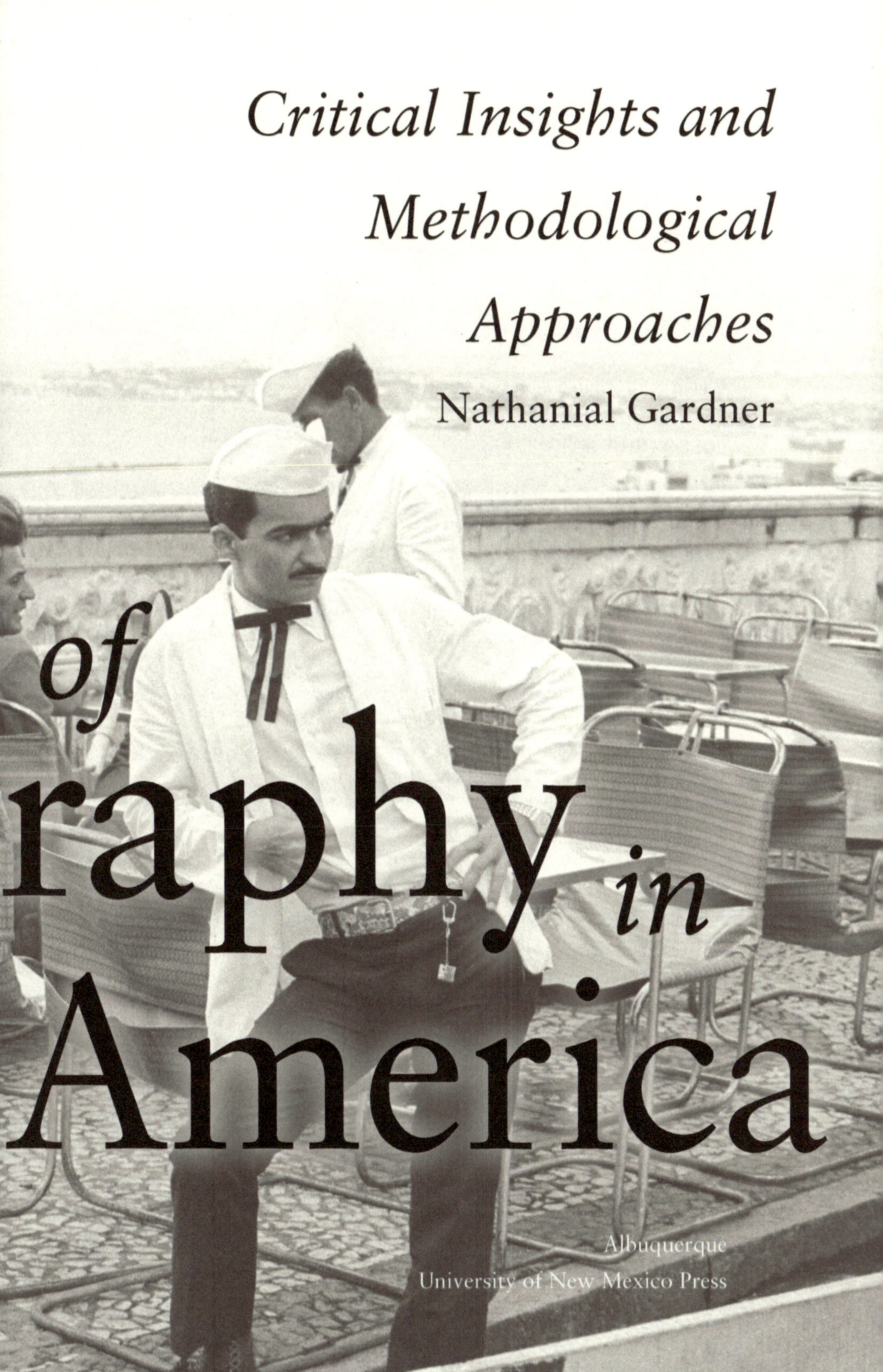

Critical Insights and Methodological Approaches

Nathanial Gardner

of raphy *in* America

Albuquerque
University of New Mexico Press

 Published 2023
Printed in the United States of America

First paperback printing 2025

ISBN 978-0-8263-6448-7 (cloth)
ISBN 978-0-8263-6810-2 (paper)
ISBN 978-0-8263-6449-4 (e-book)

Library of Congress Cataloging-in-Publication data is on file with the Library of Congress.

Founded in 1889, the University of New Mexico sits on the traditional homelands of the Pueblo of Sandia. The original peoples of New Mexico—Pueblo, Navajo, and Apache—since time immemorial have deep connections to the land and have made significant contributions to the broader community statewide. We honor the land itself and those who remain stewards of this land throughout the generations and also acknowledge our committed relationship to Indigenous peoples. We gratefully recognize our history.

Cover illustration Sem título (Untitled), Bahia, Brazil, 1972. Boris Kossy. ©Boris Kossoy.
Designed by Isaac Morris
Composed in Akzidenz, Sabon

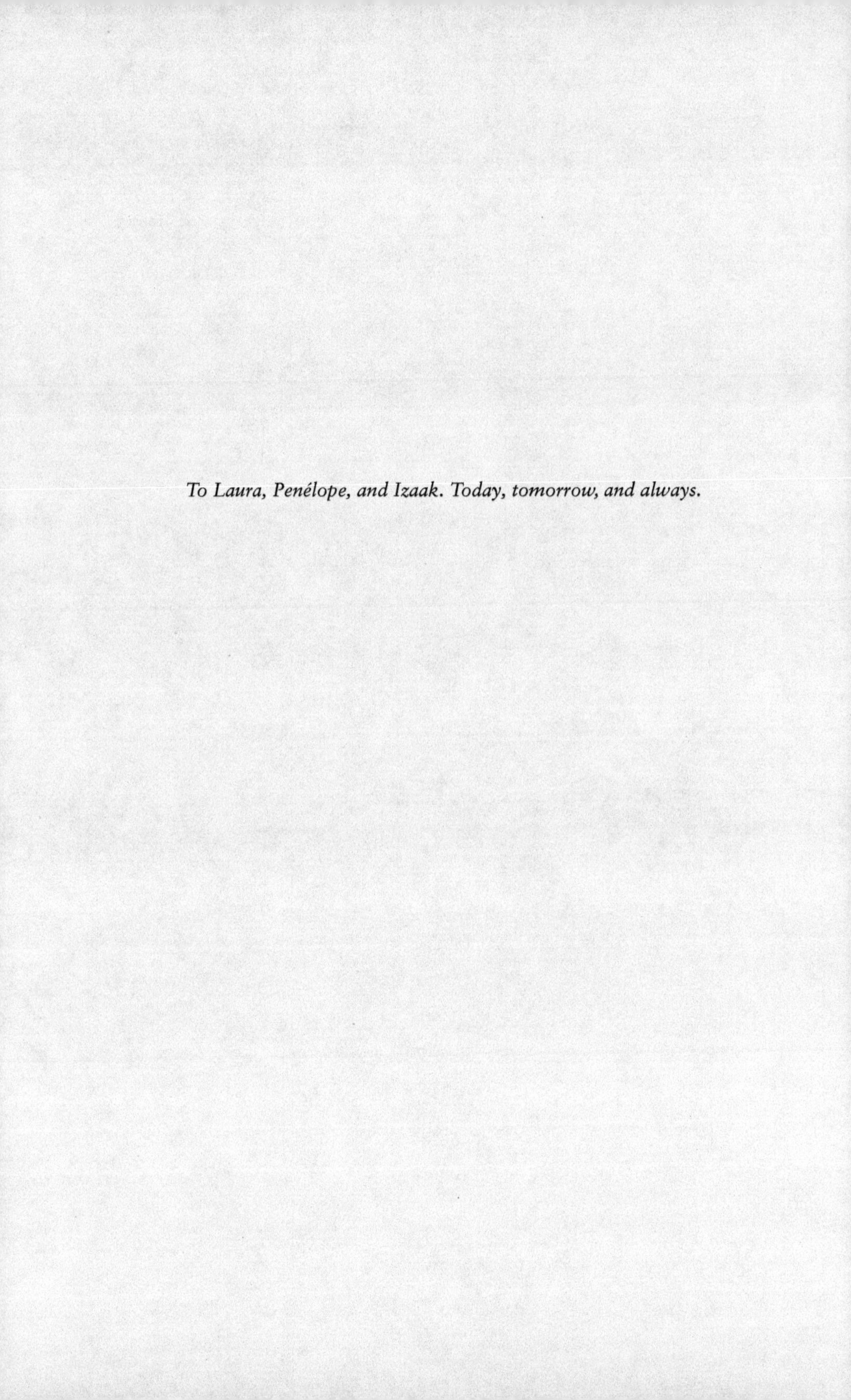

To Laura, Penélope, and Izaak. Today, tomorrow, and always.

Contents

Illustrations

Introduction

IN RECENT YEARS, Latin American research on the history of photography has revealed that this region has played a more important role in the development of photography than previously thought. The Brazilian scholar and photographer Boris Kossoy, for example, revealed that Hercule Florence, a Frenchman residing in Brazil, made an independent discovery of photography in 1832. In his history of the inventor and his work, *The Pioneering Photographic Work of Hercule Florence* (2017), Kossoy cites the physical remoteness of the Frenchman as one of the reasons why Florence's findings were not included in the canonical narrative on the discovery of photography. Indeed, the distance between Latin America and economic and cultural centers of power in the north has long been a source of gaps in the knowledge of what occurs within the vast and varied regions of its southern neighbors. Helping to bridge that void in the growing field of visual studies in Latin America is one of the aims of this study.

In this book, I analyze the study of photography that is currently taking place in Latin America and interact directly with recent scholarship, artists, and other key developments in the field. I respond to a lack of unified knowledge of the practices and the development of the study of photography in Latin America and focus on established scholars there who research photography produced in that region. In most cases, scholars are affiliated with universities and other research institutions in Latin America. To a lesser extent, this book profiles independent scholars who are striving to become established in the field. Two of the scholars whose work is studied are not of Latin American origin (John Mraz from the United States and Anne Girard de Marroquín from Switzerland) but are exclusively based in Latin America. I uncover the different research strategies, challenges, and opportunities that have arisen in Latin America as the study of photography develops there. This narrative evidences the evolutionary paths that the study of photography has taken in Latin America and provides specialist guidance that will allow for a more successful navigation through the field of the study of Latin American photography. I identify and explore key thoughts and ideas that have influenced the study of photography in Latin America and underline important research productions there. This book also indicates future avenues of research and research tools that can be useful to the study of photography from that area of the world. The purpose is to form an image of the ample range of research topics that this field has generated and to facilitate an increase in the academic dialogue on these subjects, promoting intellectual exchanges between Anglophone and Latin American countries.

Recognizing the challenges of writing on photography (Nochlin xiii), it is valuable to mention what this book is not. This study does not focus on scholars located outside of Latin America (regardless of their origin) who research Latin American photography (which is the intended topic of a future project). Though this book contains elements that reveal the history of Latin American photography, it is not a history of Latin American photography. And while a wide range of countries has been included, certain geographic omissions are evident. In some cases, this has been due to inaccessibility of information in certain countries. In other cases, a lack of response from those I approached impeded coverage. Future editions of this study will surely fill in these gaps.

The chapters that follow center on individual scholars, their work, and examples of the visual narratives to which their work is connected. The photographs that accompany each chapter connect to the research of the scholar in focus. Each chapter provides visual samples of scholars' academic interests and offers a wide range of photographs, most of which have not been included in scholarship on Latin American photography in English. After discussing my methodology, I explore foundational topics that relate to the study of Latin American photography. These include considerations on the photographic canon, thoughts and ideas that influence analytical approaches, and the prevalence of documentary photography in the study of photography in Latin America. While I include examples from across Latin America, some of those that I analyze with greater depth are from Mexico. This choice reflects the strong development of the study of photography in that country and my research expertise.

Methodology

This book began as a simple question: How is photography studied in Latin America? In searching for the answer, I soon realized that while there were important experts on the study of photography throughout the region, there was no specific center where they were all located nor a book or a study that offered a broad-ranging answer. As I searched, I discovered that the field there is young and dynamic. Most of the researchers featured in this book are academic pioneers. While the majority are academics working in the field of social sciences, none of them are in departments that strictly study photography. As I considered my initial findings, I concluded that in order to help scholars in the English-speaking world discover what type of research on photography was being undertaken in Latin America, the best way to make this knowledge evident was to conduct primary research on those directly involved in the field. I began by charting a geographic map of the Latin American scholars who study photography throughout Latin America, and I approached them and their research to learn more.

Hence, the chapters that follow are the product of hours of intentional and thoughtful dialogues on the study of photography in Latin America with leaders in the field. To create uniformity between the chapters and to embed common threads that allow for meaningful comparisons, we agreed prior to our conversations that we would touch on a range of relevant topics. Notwithstanding, we also allowed for the intellectual exchanges to flow into other areas. The purpose of that freedom was to make evident the unique interests, challenges, and opportunities each scholar faces. This enables the reader to observe and appreciate some of the differences between the areas where they work.

These conversations were recorded, transcribed, and reviewed by me and the participants. Unclear points were further discussed and clarified. The evolving drafts were agreed on as they developed with each one of the scholars (as was the final version).

As I searched for the right presentation of this information, I decided that I would adopt a style that permits each one of the participants to speak for themselves. This allows for the discussion to be dynamic and engaging. Because one of the intentions of this study is to facilitate the creation of new connections between the English-speaking world and Latin American scholarship, my direct approach is designed to encourage engagement with the academics, their work, and the environment and context in which it is created.

Another key goal in the creation of this study was to enable scholars to share photographs that connect different aspects of their research. Therefore, each one of the chapters contains photographs (selected by the scholars themselves) that have direct links to the scholarship that they produce. In some cases, the photographs are mentioned explicitly, and in others, the photographs are referred to only indirectly. This broad collection of photographs, aside from representing the photographic interests of the scholars that have been showcased, foregrounds many lesser-known archives and photographers. The photographs are part of the bridge to the new knowledge and opportunities this study offers, as are scholars' recommendations for further reading at the end of each chapter.

As I conceived this book, I concluded that understanding the work of the experts though direct contact with them would enable more direct access to the field. I also wanted to show that the field is different across Latin America due to varying levels of support and materials as well as the separation of academic communities that focus on the study of photography. I wanted to encourage readers to observe that in Latin America this field draws on a wide range of experts, while offering a way of bringing them together. Although all of them are leaders in their local contexts, and some are well known beyond their local borders, others are still growing beyond regional recognition. Yet they are all connected by the common thread of the study of photography, and while this volume connects the reader to them, it also connects these scholars to each other, offering a broader view of the study of photography in that area of the world.

In deciding who to include, I began by identifying the leaders in the field in different countries. Brazil and Mexico stand out for creating the most scholarship and having the largest number of strong institutions dedicated to Latin American photography and its study. This is the reason this book includes several leading academics from both countries. As references within the other chapters evidence, the Brazilian and Mexican scholars are already reference points among other scholars in Latin America. The Centro de Fotografía de Montevideo (Uruguay) also proved key in creating my selection as their international conferences on photography and open-access publications helped me begin to identify other outstanding scholars in countries such as Uruguay, Chile, and Argentina, as well as confirming my choice of scholars in Brazil and Mexico. Reading the work of these academics led me to identify others in countries where the scholarship is gaining traction and having an important impact, such as in Peru and Bolivia. It also helped me consider who to attempt to include as I looked at Central America and the Caribbean. The work of the London-based researcher Ileana Selejan also helped me to identify the Central American scholars to consider for inclusion. In Central America, experts work in greater isolation than those in countries where the study of photography in Iberoamerica has broader bases, but including their work helps to offer a fuller view of the region. Initially, I identified several Caribbean scholars that I hoped to include in this study. However, these individuals did not respond to my offer to share their views and experiences. Overall, I am confident that this book captures a broad spectrum of the study of photography in Latin America that includes experts from established fields and emerging ones and has been successful in showing the diversity within the field, the uniqueness of different areas, and the ample variety manifest in the scholarly outputs this region is bringing forth.

After reviewing the field of researchers and their scholarly outputs and selecting individuals whose academic production was significant and who were willing to engage with me in a series of critical encounters, the primary research began. In some cases, these discussions took place in person across different locations within

Latin America; in other cases, modern technology assisted these scholarly interchanges. Indeed, even ten years ago, it would not have been possible to write this book in the same way I did. Digital platforms, email, and other communication channels allowed for deep, engaging, and continued encounters with scholars as well as direct access to their research and their colleagues.

The chapters in this book contain common themes. This is not a coincidence but a result of my constant and attentive curatorial work. I wanted to demonstrate the origin of the scholars' work in the field of photography studies as well as the threads that unite them. Most entered their field of scholarship through serendipitous means. Some of them enjoy the support of strong academic institutions, while others forge ahead more independently. Likewise, I strove to emphasize the texts and scholars that have influenced their work as well as provide an understanding of their research agendas and how they have uniquely contributed to the study of photography in Latin America. These conversations offer a sense of the methodologies, discoveries, and unique contributions these scholars offer to the field. I also attempted to foreground their challenges as pioneers. Most have forged their own way in the field and have experienced their work being questioned and even disregarded at first. However, I am quick to underline how, with perseverance, their research has now come to be highly regarded in this growing field. Bearing in mind the growing number of studies in the United States, Canada, and western Europe on the study of photography in Latin America, I was also keen to know what advice they have for those outside of Latin America who desire to read and research that region from afar with greater insight, confidence, and relevance. Indeed, I undertook and designed these critical conversations with the goal of building a bridge between their work and the scholarly work on Latin American photography that occurs outside of Latin America as well as connecting their studies to each other. A desire to share this information with the widest number of people in a variety of fields in the academic world and beyond motivated me to publish the book in English (though I am increasingly convinced that publications of the same in Spanish and Portuguese would also prove to be fruitful). In the interest of emphasizing the primary research that was essential to the creation of this book, I have referenced secondary research only where it naturally enriches the text so that what we already know does not overshadow the voices of the scholars but rather underscores connections and enhances our understanding of what is being presented.

Canon

Latin American photographers are underrepresented in the world canon. A search through commercially produced books on photographs that are of canonical value indicates their exclusion. A brief sample indicates that two photographers from Latin America surface repeatedly: Sergio Larraín and Manuel Álvarez Bravo (Lowe). The value of both photographers is unquestionable in terms of form, technique, and content. Already achieving international reputations during their lives, Álvarez Bravo and Larraín were also well-known to key members of the modern visual canon in the West. Álvarez Bravo was Henri Cartier-Bresson's lifelong friend who accompanied him during his time in Mexico and exhibited with him in 1935 at the Palacio de Bellas Artes and the Julien Lévy Gallery in New York (Hopkinson 10). This led to André Bretón inviting Álvarez Bravo's photography to grace the catalog of the International Surrealist Exhibition held in 1940 in Mexico City, the event for which his iconic photograph *La buena fama durmiendo* was produced (Kismaric 33–35).

While Manuel Álvarez Bravo worked from his home country of Mexico, Sergio Larraín lived abroad in the United States and in western Europe for several years before retreating to life marked by simplicity and isolation in his native Chile. His international contacts led to his photography being seen by Henri Cartier-Bresson and an invitation to join the Magnum cooperative. Sergio Larraín would remain an active member over the course of four years during his European residence as well as having associated Magnum status for several years after returning to Chile (Sire 25–26).

In academic texts that include canonical photography, Latin American photographers do not have a much stronger presence than in commercial publications. A brief survey of them reveals important considerations regarding the presence of Latin American photographs in the photography canon written from the northwestern region of the global north. *The Photograph as Contemporary Art* draws on examples from photography from the United States and western Europe (Cotton). Abigail Solomon-Godeau's *Photography at the Dock* includes photographers from Europe or the United States. Newhall's *The History of Photography*—a book born from his foundation-building MoMA exhibition *Photography: 1839–1937* that is credited with being the beginning of the serious study of photography in the United States—features only three photographs linked to Mexico. Two are from Edward Weston's Mexican productions and another is from his Italian student Tina Modotti.[1] Though some might debate her place as a Latin American photographer, Modotti is the only arguably Latin American photographer in the collection (though she lived in Mexico for approximately a decade in total, she strongly identified with Mexico during her first stay, and all of her significant photographic output took place over her first seven years there) (Argenteri 45–138). Her one photograph included in Newhall's book is only reminiscent of Mexico in its name: *Tehuantepec: The Mother and Child* (142). In that photograph, she draws on the ubiquitous mother and child iconography that is abundant in Christianity. Though the photograph Newhall includes does exhibit a slightly experimental approach to the image, Modotti leaves the mother's head out of the frame. Of Weston's seven photographs in Newhall's book, the two photographs taken in Mexico are of nature (184–85). The trunk of a single palm tree from Cuernavaca and another photograph titled *Cloud, Mexico* are excellent representations of Weston's interest in natural forms and aesthetics (Mora 10, 13, 22). Nonetheless, they are images that could have arguably been produced in any location and are not specific to Latin America. It could also be suggested that Weston's Latin American locations in Newhall's book are irrelevant, since he was known for believing location and time to be secondary qualities to his photographs (Mora 19). Other scholars use another of his photographs taken in Mexico to exemplify his work: *El excusado* (Newhall *Supreme Instants* plate 25; Stack "An Appetite" 135–39), but Weston's idea with that image was to raise questions on form, function, and beauty (like Duchamp's urinal to which it is contrasted) (Solomon-Godeau 2–3). There was nothing particularly Mexican about the photograph because the toilet he photographed obeyed the same physical design as the rest of the Western world. Hence, this image also has very few Latin American references, aside from its Spanish title and the location where he took the photograph.

Some Latin American photographs are present in certain narratives on the photographic canon. Fred Ritchin's essay in *The New History of Photography* mentions the tendency of the then young photographers Pedro Meyer, Graciela Iturbide, and Sebastião Salgado to produce photographs that have strong documentary qualities (609) but only includes one Latin American photograph in his brief discussion of his works: Salgado's *Gold mine in the Sierra Pelada* (611). In this piece, Ritchin is reflective of his notable interest in photography in Latin America. Further evidence of this would come to fruition in his and Carole Naggar's subject-specific book *Mexico Through Foreign Eyes*.

Though Latin American photography has only a small impact on academic works from the field of photography studies produced in Anglophone countries, discussing this impact reveals important trends. In *Images of History*, Robert M. Levine encouraged historians and anthropologists to use photographs in their scholarly writings on Latin America due to photography's ability to show patterns of behavior and "disclose realities" (*Windows on Latin America* 6). The fact that Cartier-Bresson and Tina Modotti promoted Manuel Álvarez Bravo's work bode well for Mexico's most celebrated photographer. But, even though *The Family of Man* exhibition circulated widely within Latin America, he was the one Latin American photographer in it and in the exhibition catalog (Steichen; Sandeen "Guatemala").[2] In the exhibition catalog that has sold over four million copies (Sandeen *Picturing an Exhibition* 40), one of the Latin American photographs included depicts a simple and recent grave, graced only with a wooden cross and a minimalist decoration of wire and paper to create a dome and cross-like temporary structure that is placed over the grave. From a death-facing culture such as Mexico's (Lomnitz), the organizers made a logical (even stereotypical) visual selection to represent one of the stages of life shared by humanity.

Consider Latin America's thin coverage in books such as *The Art of Photography 1839–1989*. This information-rich volume that studied photography's first 150 years of production does include some Latin American references (Wolf and Weaver). However, some detective work is required to uncover their Latin American connections. Weston's photographs of forms and foreigners in Mexico (Tina Modotti and D. H. Lawrence) speak of Weston's presence in Latin America but follow the techniques that he was developing both before and after his sojourn in Mexico (Newhall *Supreme*; Conger *Weston in Mexico* 36). Cartier-Bresson's photograph of prostitutes (Wolf and Weaver 278) is one of the several photographs used to illustrate his oft-referenced "decisive moment" that the expert photographer must know how to hunt and capture. Susan Meiselas's 1970s photographs from the Nicaraguan Revolution are also included in a section on photography and conflict (429–31). Even so, I would argue that Wolf and Weaver's inclusion of such images has less to do with an interest in Latin American revolutions and more with the fact that the color photographs were used to represent them, an avant-garde move that Meiselas would be obliged to defend (Meiselas 116). Ian Jeffrey's recent book, *How to Read a Photograph*, has a Manuel Álvarez Bravo photograph on its front cover and features his work over an eight-page section illustrated with ten of his photographs. He is the only Latin American photographer featured among the one hundred–plus canonical photographers included. In the brief texts linked to the photographs, the author establishes important connections to other photographers featured in the same book such as Paul Strand, Edward Weston, and Henri Cartier-Bresson. Thames & Hudson's *The Photograph as Contemporary Art* features many photographs from artists around the globe (including Africa, the Middle East, Eastern Europe, and Asia) but only one photo from a Latin American—the Mexican artist Gabriel Orozco, who experiments with a wide variety of artistic mediums, including photography (Cotton 116–17). The 2015 Thames & Hudson *Dictionary of Photography* suggests that an increase in focus on Latin American photography is on the rise, and further details will improve our understanding of this panorama more fully (Herschdorfer).[3] This brief survey helps reveal that when Latin American photographs are included in non-specialist books on photography, their work normally accounts for less than 1 percent of the images used, and those included are generally men who have strong connections to western Europe or the United States.

The role of Latin American photography in books about the history of photography or with a canonical view of world photography remind us of the lessons from the case of Hercule Florence. Since its inception, the writers of photography's history tend to have their eyes on Europe and the United States. Latin America does appear in the world canon of photography. However, Latin America most often gains its presence as it has been seen by foreigners in these latitudes as has been evidenced by foreign photographers. This has foreseeable consequences: viewers of these images begin to become accustomed to viewing Latin America as it has been portrayed by foreigners, travelers and otherwise. Such was the case of the former French schoolteacher turned photographer Désiré Charnay who the French government sent to Mexico on a reconnaissance mission as France considered its possibilities of colonial expansion there (and later in other areas of the world such as Java and Madagascar) (Rosenblum 127). Hugo Brehme, who had a talent for capturing poverty and danger with beauty, produced timeless Mexican images that became one of the early standards for picturing Mexico. Breathtaking though many of his photographs are, they focus on a picturesque image of Mexico that does little to capture social reality.[4] Images from these narratives on photography tend to employ Latin America as a location used by foreign photographers as they continue to build their photographic projects, be they portraiture (Toomey), abstraction (Weston), social movements, or conflict (Mesilas; Klich). However, though Latin America might have been an important stage in the development of their visual narratives, they often form part of artistic projects that neither began nor finished during their time in Latin America. This region's incorporation into the world canon of photography appears to be highly dependent on first-world connections, be they through foreign photographers who sojourn there or via photographic exhibitions, publications, or collections in the northwestern region of the global north. In every case, visibility within that sphere is fundamental. While the examples of Manuel Álvarez Bravo and Sergio Larraín were contemplated earlier in this regard; the example of the Brazilian photography of French extraction, Marc Ferrez, helps to solidify this point. Born to a French father in Rio de Janeiro in 1843, Ferrez studied during his youth in Paris and trained with the German photographer Franz Keller. Interested in photography as art, his landscape photographs are among the best in South America (Rosenblume 127), breaking with typical portrayals of that time (Burgi; Marc Ferrez, "ims.com.br"). His work won prizes in the 1882 *South American Continental Exhibition*, and the *Exhibition of the Century in Pennsylvania* in 1876. The quality of his photography earned him the only gold medal for a photography submission to the 1904 World's Fair exhibition in St. Louis, Missouri. Surely, Rio de Janeiro's then status as capital of the largest Latin American country and the flow of information from north to south helped promote his work. His participation in international contests and the fact that the Brazilian emperor Dom Pedro II was a patron of his creative projects granted him access to the means and promotion to achieve visibility further afield. One example of this is the fact that after he won in the 1904 World's Fair exhibition, the J. Paul Getty Museum acquired some of his photographs. His presence in that collection led to a single image of Ferrez's Brazilian natural landscape photographs to be incorporated in the *World History of Photography*. That same book also includes four paragraphs on Latin American photography in a section on realism in photography since the 1950s. In a book that focuses on the world history of photography, the seven photographs that accompany this brief mention of Latin American photography underline the documentary nature of photography in Latin America (Rosenblum 537–39). Likewise, though it does not name the event outright in the body of the text, this book draws on and indirectly references the 1978 colloquium on photography in Mexico City, *Hecho en Latinoamérica*, that marks the beginning of the serious study of photography in Latin America. This is a noteworthy event, not only because it is one that brings together Latin American photographers and critics for the first time, but also because it allows them to have a stronger notion of what Latin American photography looks like. Their book/catalog, which shares the same name as the event itself, forms an information-rich source of photographic production and vision. Though it was not an overt topic of the colloquial or its exhibition catalog, the results of this event suggest what Mauricio Lissovsky has also mentioned: the need for a Latin American canon (this volume, 200).

Modestly named *Primer Coloquio Latinamericano de Fotografía* (The First Latin American Colloquium on Photography) at that time, this large event brought together Latin American photographers in a way that allowed them to debate the nature of photography, its role in art, and concrete examples of technique and practice. Historically situated during a time of social movements, political and ideological struggles, and military dictatorships, this event was a strong symbol of solidarity during a time of effervescence in Latin America (Rojo; Markarian, Zolov, and Carrara; Cronin; Volpi; Robinson). Headed by Pedro Meyer, the newly formed Consejo Mexicano de Fotografía sent out a call for images and for direct participation from across the American continent, inviting Argentina, Brazil, Chile, Colombia, Cuba, Ecuador, United States (Chicanos and Puerto Ricans), Guatemala, Mexico, Panama, Paraguay, Peru, Puerto Rico, Uruguay, and Venezuela. In their invitation, they solicit a broad sample requesting photographs from "among its entire geographic region and variety of concepts" (11). The canonical effort manifests itself clearly. They then explain that a selection of these images will form part of a large exhibition with the option of all participants allowing their work to form a part of the permanent collection of the Instituto Nacional de Bellas Artes, the center for art in Mexico, underscoring the seriousness of the collection and strong government support of the project. Photographers from across Latin America met between the 11th and the 19th of May 1978 in Mexico City to listen to papers presented and debate the state of photography in Latin America as well as participate in different master classes given by photography experts from Latin

America (Monroy "Conversation"). The success of the first meeting in terms of participation and ideas shared would generate a second meeting in Mexico City in 1981 and a third colloquium in Havana, Cuba, in 1984 with their own talks, exhibitions, and catalogs (Consejo Mexicano de Fotografía *Hecho II*; Carreras). Each of these events would help to solidify a sense of Latin American photography as a field of study and practice.

Though the call for participation in the event invited photographers to send a wide variety of images, after the selection of the photographs, the organizers made the following observation regarding some of the common features of the submissions received:

> the rejection of an alienating and unjust society; the denunciation of exploitation, margination and colonization; a rupture with conventional aesthetic models; an impulse toward a reaffirmation that recognizes in concrete things an unexhaustible [*sic*] quarry of creativity; a conscious reading of the geographic and ethnic peculiarities in order to place them, within the image, in levels of signification; the beginnings of new interrelations, new orders to conquer greater scope and complexity; a contempt for superficial description that do not tend to reveal man's relations to his social and natural space; a neatness of execution that demonstrates a capacity to see and feel. (Carreras 28)

While reflecting social and academic interests in Latin America from that time, the extensive description carefully details the documentary nature of the photography that was received and its intense focus on visions of Latin America that move past the images of the tropics and exoticism often promoted abroad. Indeed, while the introduction drew on Diego Rivera's comments that highlight photography's ability to capture life in a way akin to Diego Velázquez's paintings (17) as well as the important role that Edward Weston played in the entrance of modern photography in Mexico, it was the work of his student Tina Modotti that was more clearly underlined. This is significant because the approach in her later phase of photography could be easily described as documentary. Quoting her essay "Sobre la fotografía – On photography" published in the magazine *Mexican Folkways*, the introduction of the book/catalog sets to one side the debate as to whether photography is an art (suggesting that it is one). Instead, it uses Modotti's words to underline photography's ability to successfully record life in an objective manner, an ideal tool for the artist intent on creating a documentary record (18–19).

The text *Hecho en Latinoamérica* and the photographic archive that it generated as part of its legacy (now housed in the Centro de la Imagen in Mexico

City) can be read as a project with a canonical outlook. It contains 170 pages of photographs (sixteen of them in color) and uses a broad visual spectrum. These images clearly establish Argentina, Brazil, and Mexico as countries with strong photographic bases regarding the work undertaken at that time, bases that continue to bear strong fruit in the present as reflected in this study. One aspect of *Hecho en Latinoamérica* that offers excellent insight into the inner workings of the photographers and their visual production are the "notas de autor" that the participants provide. In them, like Tina Modotti's essay referenced in the introduction of the same book, the photographers are afforded the opportunity to explain their methodology, influences, and their initiation into the field of photography along with their worldview and artistic intentions. This personal information allows the photographs to be read with a distinctively Latin American outlook, enabling them to stand out from previous external views of this area of photography and letting those that encountered these materials to begin to understand the Latin American vision associated with their photographs. The "Notas de autor: Testimonios" section manifests a wide variety of self-taught talent and a high level of civic engagement. Photography is described as an element to be put to the service of the people. It evidences a pragmatic approach to photography and its role in society, underscoring the usefulness of documentary photography. It is this view of photography in Latin America, which helps to inform the *World History of Photography* and its influence, that is still detectable. Seen in its wider context, *Hecho en Latinoamérica* emphasizes the notion that to become noticed by those that write the world canon, local canonical texts are important. Evidence of the canonical vision in the 1978 colloquium was in the 2018 exhibition at the Centro de Fotografía de Montevideo that revisited the event on its fortieth anniversary. That event underlined how the Mexican gathering played a key role in establishing a regional visual identity and weighed up the results of this collective project, underlining the challenges that Latin American photography faced at that time.[5] The second colloquium (held in Mexico City in 1981) and third colloquium (held in Havana in 1984) built on the momentum created by the first event. Those beginnings started to form the network of creators and critics that exist today.

When reflecting on the creation of a Latin American photographic canon, it is important to consider some of the challenges to creating one. These are not just geographical, but also cultural and social. Indeed, one of the questions raised by the 1992 Houston Fotofest *Image and Memory* was if a uniform Latin American identity exists. They suggested that it does not: "There is no such thing as Latin American identity" (5). Their conclusions reflect those of many others: that a single Latin American identity does not exist but that there are unifying threads that go beyond linguistic commonalities and create solidarity and identity between them (Parkinson Zamora 295–97). Though the existence of a Latin American identity has been a topic of debate for centuries in Latin America (Toro; Salomon; Beezley), the photographs gathered in *Image and Memory* and other collections show that photographs can create a narrative that reflects the Latin American experience by replicating its unity and diversity. Nonetheless, as this study on Latin American photography evidences, notwithstanding the past efforts to bring together Latin America on the subject of photography and find their communality, it is imperative to remember Latin American scholars' different approaches and interests as well as the difficulties that they face in accessing material from their sister countries (Pedro Querejazu, this volume, 144; and Ana Mauad, this volume, 189). Even so, academics strive for community and scholarly dialogue, look forward to frequent and increasing exchanges of research findings, and explore and take advantage of opportunities for further collaboration (Maria do Carmo Rainho, this volume, 217). One of the indications of a shared sense of Latin American identity is the desire to create theory from Latin America that can be applied to Latin American photography (Ariel Arnal, this volume, 85). However, what an analysis of the study of Latin American photography also suggests is that for a Latin American canon to fully form and be recognized, one of the logical steps to take would be for each country to write their own history of photography (Mauricio Lissovsky, this volume, 198). Efforts to do this are underway. For example, with over 600 photographs from across the full spectrum of techniques and time periods, *160 años de fotografía en México* is a significant catalog of producers and productions (Treviño). A brief chronology of important events relating to photography in Mexico suggest creators and institutions that have been key to the growth of photography in Mexico.

In Uruguay, Magdalena Broqueta's coordinated history of photography and its social uses in Uruguay *Fotografía en Uruguay: Historia y usos sociales* volumes one and two creates a unifying vision of the growth and use of photography in this South American country. The careful balance of texts and images in these two books reveals an extremely rich history of photography in Uruguay that draws on the knowledge of many experts and archives, suggesting many avenues of research and opportunities to the reader. A privately owned and operated cultural center in Guatemala City, La Fototeca, is currently writing a history of photography in Guatemala in the twentieth century (Girard, this volume, 93). In Costa Rica, *La mirada del tiempo: Historia de la Fotografía en Costa Rica 1848–2003* creates an important context for photography in this country while emphasizing creators and unveiling those who were not recognized previously (Vargas). These books work to establish the necessary bases for the study of photography locally and provide the steppingstones to make further research into the Latin American canon a greater reality.

Institutions

The link between books on photography and the exhibitions on which such texts are based has played an important role in building our shared knowledge of photography. Consider Beaumont Newhall's *The History of Photography* that was based on a series of photographs that were exhibited in the New York Museum of Modern Art. His retrospective, *Photography: 1839–1937* (March 17–April 18, 1937), looks back over almost a century of production and technique. It was the first major exhibition on photography at the MoMA, and it also marked the beginning of a department dedicated to photography there. The execution of a book that taught photography, and the slides from the exhibition that could also be purchased to accompany it, created a key catalog of visual images that helped cement the modern photographic canon because it facilitated the teaching of photography in institutions of higher learning. The influence of the MoMA on the formation of society's shared visual outlook extended even farther with Edward Steichen's 1955 exhibition *Family of Man*. His work not only created a vision of human solidarity from over two million photographs that he received from around the globe (Steichen 3), but it also incorporated over five hundred photographs from sixty-eight different countries united under the very specific message of fomenting peace and understanding. This and successive projects that have grown out of *Family of Man* have helped to shape the shared visual outlook held in the East and West. This is due in part because Steichen designed it to promote a oneness among humanity by focusing on precultural society with a defined focus on East-West relations during the Cold War period (Hurm; Mason; Sandeen "*Family of Man* in Guatemala"; Lunghi; Turner). The visual responses to *Family of Man* are a testament to the canonical impact that it has created. The nine million–plus visitors who saw the 1955 exhibition in thirty-eight different countries were able to absorb this visual narrative, bringing key visibility to specific photographs and their creators (Sandeen "The International Reception" 345). The catalog that accompanied it enabled further discussion in academic and other higher learning forums as well as lent important longevity to the project. Its continual reprinting shows the perennial interest in the narrative and suggests the power of institutions to create visual archives that remain a part of our debate on the visual. Eric Sandeen's article underlines both its impact and its difficulties in Latin America. For example, he argues that "Guatemala showed tensions that would become apparent as the exhibition moved beyond the East–West axis that was USIA's [the United States Information Agency] primary concern into an unstable, North–South terrain of Third-World nationalisms and post-colonial movements" ("*Family of Man* in Guatemala" 127–28). Though Sandeen's article makes no mention of this aspect of the exhibition, of the fifteen photographs from Latin America that are part of this specific visual narrative, eight countries are covered (Guatemala, Cuba, Bolivia, Colombia, Puerto Rico, Peru, Brazil, and Mexico). Mexico features six times.[6]

While some of the other photographers have undeniable ties to Latin America, like Gustave Throlichen and Marcos Chamudes, the Latin American photographers comprise less than 1 percent of the photographers whose work was part of the visual discourse: the previously mentioned Manuel Álvarez Bravo and, possibly, his wife Lola Álvarez Bravo.[7] Reflecting on this exhibition emphasizes two important factors: the key role that institutions can play in creating a visual corpus that creates a shared outlook and the relative absence of Latin American photographers in many of those discourses in English-language publications. Since the emergence of those two MoMA events and artistic productions just referenced, three institutions have begun to play an important role in the promotion, development, and study of Latin American photography in Latin America: El Centro de la Imagen in Mexico, El Instituto Moreira Salles in Brazil, and El Centro de Fotografía de Montevideo in Uruguay. These pathfinding institutions are forming archives, events, and productions that are key in the construction of the photography canon in Latin America.

The Centro de la Imagen, located in Mexico City, arose directly from the Primer Encuentro de Fotografía Latinoamericana. The Consejo Nacional para la Cultura y las Artes (CONACULTA) founded it in 1994 as a research institution for the conservation and study of Latin American photography. It inherited the photographic archives from the two colloquia organized by the Consejo Mexico de la Fotografía and other events as well as the photographs from other exhibitions held by CONACULTA. At the time of writing, it has more than 8,000 printed images, 5,000 documents, 300 exhibition catalogs, and 3,000 books by more than 760 authors from 28 countries, most of which are located in Latin America. Centrally funded, this institution is currently located in what is known as the Ciudad de las Artes in Mexico City (along Avenida Balderas in the Historic Center of the Mexican capital). It hosts photo exhibitions with artists that participate from across Latin America. The academic and monographic journal it edits, *Luna Cornea* (supported by the Consejo Nacional para la Cultura y las Artes), was launched in 1993 with an inaugural issue on the patriarchal figure in Mexico's photography: Manuel Álvarez Bravo.[8] Other publications, such as *Bienal de Fotografía*, *Festival Foto México* and the competition Premio Nacional de Ensayo sobre Fotografía foment academic dialogue and critical discussion on photography on both national and international levels (Carreras 209–11).

The Instituto Moreira Salles (IMS) is the most important institution dedicated to photography in Brazil. One aspect of this institution that sets it apart from the others mentioned here is that it is a private foundation dedicated to the arts, with a special focus on photography. With centers in three cities—Rio de Janeiro, São Paulo, and Poças de Caldas—the IMS houses the largest collection of photographs (over two million) in Brazil. Outstanding in its range, the collection contains classic images such as those of Marc Ferrez as well as contemporary photographers and others such as Thomaz Farkas, a known contemporary of Paul Strand and Edward Weston. It has both general and specialized archives that are open to researchers. The IMS continues to purchase archives, collections, and newspapers so that it can promote their academic study to any scholar with interests in photography. To this end, it collaborates with public and private universities and institutions at home and abroad. Its photography library contains more than thirty thousand dedicated volumes on the topic and is one of the most complete in Latin America, drawing on publications from all over Latin America and the world. It, too, has an academic journal dedicated to the study of photography, *Serrote*, which also includes scholarly discussions on art, literature, and culture in addition to exhibitions and permanent collections open to the public.

The Centro de Fotografía Montevideo (CdF) began with the specific focus of accumulating and overseeing the Uruguayan capital's photo archives as it expanded this subject-dedicated archive. However, it soon widened its vision to all Latin America with the clear objective of promoting reflection and critical thought on Latin American photography's themes and social intentions in addition to documenting and conserving its photographic heritage (Carreras 213). To that specific end, the CdF regularly hosts Las Jornadas, international seminars and conferences on the topic of Latin American photography. These events bring together regional and international experts on photography whose seminars and presentations are free and open to the public and are openly transmitted on the internet to facilitate diffusion and encourage participation from all over Latin America and the world. Not only do they have a dedicated library on Latin American photography with over 2,500 books and archives (and over 180,000 photographs), they also continually expand their collection of Latin American photography dedicated to both historical and contemporary photography. One area that distinguishes the CdF from other institutions is its publishing agenda on the topic of photography in Latin America. Their publications have adopted the same free and open-access ethos as their seminars and expositions. Designed to overcome some of the limitations that scholars in Latin America face (heavy importation duties for materials, lack of access, large distances), at the time of writing their publishing house has produced sixty-three volumes on Latin American photography in open-access format.[9] Importantly, their emphasis on republishing classic texts on photography in Latin America that have gone out of print, such as José Antonio Navarrete's *Fotografiando en América Latina: Ensayos de la Crítica Histórica*, facilitates the creation of an accessible Latin American corpus that could be used in ways similar to *The History of Photography* and *Family of Man*. Furthermore, they focus on books that help to shape the debate on Latin American photography (i.e., the third Coloquio sobre la Fotografia Latinoamerica held in Havana) and continue to renew critical dialogue via its collaborative research projects and exhibitions.

Key differences between the influences of these institutions and the power that MoMA and other Western institutions in the northern hemisphere exercise will continue to exist in the future. The MoMA, the Louvre, el Museo del Prado, and the Victoria and Albert Museum (to name only a few) command strong canonical voices that reflect social, economic, and cultural power that have been centuries in the making and have key connections to economic and political power. Photography's incorporation in their collections has given these institutions an authoritative voice with global infrastructure and an attentive audience that will continue to reinforce that structure. Many important collections and serious archival efforts in photography in Latin America are comparatively new. Like puzzle pieces that fit together and form a larger and clearer image, the formation of the Latin American photography canon will be shaped by the writing of many micro- and macrohistories that, notwithstanding, will be able to enjoy the progressive politics of our times: greater inclusion and participation can be part of its continued formation (Osborne; Brunet; Roei; Conrad Murray). New technologies are proving capable of providing solutions to difficulties that have kept Latin American researchers isolated in the past, enabling visibility of their work. New conferences and colloquia will help to provide and stimulate critical reflection as well as visual theory created in Latin America that can be used to analyze their photography, increasing their capacity to read themselves on their own terms.

Theory

One of the points that emerges from a review of the study of photography in Latin America is a lesser reliance on critical theory in comparison to other scholars who study photography in other regions of world (Lear; Levine "*Image and Memory* Review"; McCormack). In some instances, this is because, methodologically, theory is used as the scaffolding that initiates and builds analytical discussion that has been taken down at the conclusion of the study (Gardner 470). The wide variety of fields from which the scholars write may possess a role in this too. However, there is also a theoretical explanation for the softer focus on theory in the scholarship on Latin American photography in Latin America. Some scholars base their approach on the Brazilian/Czech philosopher Vilhém Flusser's ideas that argue that texts (in this case theoretical texts) can get in the way of understanding images by making the images that reflect our world less transparent (Finger 103). Hence, scholarly discussions often do not focus on texts, but rather on the visual. This approach can be explained as a strategy to avoid what Flusser describes as "textolatry" and foments critical engagement with photographs in a way that the discussion of theory does not become the first order of priority (Finger 103).

Alternatively, Louis Parkinson Zamora's essay "Quetzalcóatl's Mirror" leans on another argument that offers reasons why focus on theory related to the study of photography is not prevalent in Latin America. She outlines that the visual medium is key to the representation of culture and identity in Latin America precisely because of the strong visuality in their culture as well as the medium's ability to represent individuals and "everyday materiality of place and everyday actions of people" (293). Additionally, Parkinson Zamora argues that the classic and highly influential theorists of photography (Barthes; Benjamin; Sontag) "assume a universal modern western context" (363). She argues that those assumptions work well when applied to North American and European contexts within which they most often operate. Nonetheless, she adds, "when we attempt to apply these theories to Latin America, they are more often inadequate because they do not address the diverse traditions that conjoin in Latin American visual representation." Zamora Parkinson argues that "to assume that Latin American photography is no different from that of Europe or the United States is to ignore Indigenous and baroque ideas of the images that still condition ways of seeing [in Latin America]" (363). To this I would also add that those approaches do not take into account societal relationships with modern Western cultural production and power relations that help to generate those theories. Recent writings on the translation of visual imagery align with this thinking. They suggest the observers should not assume that photography speaks a universal language and that greater efforts are needed to understand photographic production from other areas of the world. Likewise, this method of understanding photography clarifies that other sets of critical tools are needed to successfully engage with foreign visual narratives as fundamental rules and visions apply that are unique to different areas of the world (Soutter 334). Among the most prevalent topics within the study of photography in Latin America is what this area can tell us about history and historical processes. These approaches focus strongly on the uncontemplated and additional information that photography can offer and strive to reveal how the visual is able to advocate and propose a more complete vision of Latin American society and culture.

Susan Sontag argues that the analogy of Plato's cave can be used to describe society's relationship to photography. Though *On Photography* suggests that we are still in Plato's cave, looking at images (photographs) without ever arriving at the true nature of the world in which we live, she also suggests that we need to leave and go beyond the cave (as one of the prisoners did in Plato's analogy in *The Republic*). Sontag proposes that though the viewers of photos see the images, they do not understand the social, political, and economic intentions with which they were made; hence, the true meanings of the narratives are not yet revealed to us. Latin American academics have taken this as a theoretical starting point and have left the proverbial cave to investigate the social, political, economic, historic, and other intentions with which the photographs were created. They go beyond the shadow of the image to bring those that engage with their research an expanded understanding of what the photographs represent and to reveal significant meaning that we can extract from them. These scholars recognize the traces of the real in the photographs they research (Currie 286). Their work offers access to greater context and encourages the viewer to avoid hasty conclusions. The aim of their research is to help others leave the proverbial cave described in *On Photography* as well. Their scholarship acknowledges the flawed images of the real in photography, but it also recognizes the merit in seeing the real within this form of representation and analyzes the elements in photography's constructed narratives.

Latin American photography scholarship often considers the physical productions of photography, an approach that has links to theory and the importance of origin. Walter Benjamin argued that in the mechanical age of reproduction, the only element of a photograph that cannot be reproduced is what Ariella Azoulay later described as the "photographed event" (*Civil Imagination* 25): the original photograph's presence in time and space; not be confused with—though an integral part of—the "event of photography" (Azoulay *Civil Imagination* 26). For this reason, a study of the context of the creation of the photograph—the social forces that created it, the history of the creator, the intended purpose of the photograph, and other related avenues of investigation—are all part of revealing the uniqueness of the original. This type of research, inspired by Benjamin, can lead to revelations regarding the origin or political outlook of a photographer because, as Manuel Álvarez Bravo taught Graciela Iturbide when she was still his student, "everything in life is political" (Iturbide *Eyes to Fly* 9). Benjamin's writings lead the researchers to the singularity of a photograph that the scholar can unveil with his or her work (106). To focus on what is unique to the original photograph is to reveal its context, which leads to a greater understanding of the forces that shaped it, not only in terms of its artistic creator, but also in terms of the social forces that conditioned the context within which it was formed. This is one of the areas in which Latin American scholars enjoy an advantage because they are more closely aligned with local cultural forces and understand their nuances and because they have greater unfettered access to the archives and other historical sources. This enables them to create the context "as they are nearer its unique existence at the place where it happens to be" (Benjamin 106). Additionally, as suggested by Benjamin, chemical and physical analysis is a core component in the discovery of the individuality of the photograph. For example, this information enables us to ascertain if a method was avant-garde or not, if the creator (and his or her mastery of technique) was excellent or poor, or if he or she worked with or against the grain (Monroy, this volume, 57). Benjamin's writings on context, and the fact that as photographs are reproduced they generate new reactions and engagements with them, are also relevant to how Latin American scholars approach the study of photography. Their focus on contexts creates new ways of seeing photographs, just as when the researchers interpret historical photographs in light of new political emphasis as Sussy Vargas does as she uncovers the gender and race inclusivity in the narrative of the German photographer Hans Wimmer working in Costa Rica.

John Berger's insights into Walter Benjamin's writings on photography in

Ways of Seeing remind us that photographs can be experienced in many settings thanks to their ability to be reproduced. As Berger reflects on art, he reminds us, like Benjamin, of the importance of context. Diverse contexts will read photographs differently (12). These theoretical considerations have important implications for images that were produced in Latin America by visiting foreigners. Consider Edward Weston and Tina Modotti's example. Both worked in Mexico. Their photography was exhibited in Mexico City in the gallery Aztec Land (Mora 65). Edward Weston interacted with the Mexican intelligentsia and was strongly interested in their opinion of his work (Weston *Daybooks Mexico* 6). However, Weston's work was mostly reserved for the American public and the international Western public that frequent the large and important galleries in the United States that he courted with great interest both before and after his Mexican sojourns (Warren; Wilson). During her life, Tina Modotti's work was made for Mexicans and shown in Mexico (perhaps excepting her collaboration with Weston in Anita Brenner's book *Idols behind Altars*). Her solo exhibition at the Universidad Nacional Autónoma de México underlines this difference and encourages Latin American readings of her photography. When reflecting on this it is useful to ask: How does her work change as it moves away from its context of creation and its intended audience? The fact that Tina Modotti produced in Mexico for Mexicans has generated a greater amount of interest in her work within Latin America than in Weston's oeuvre. This suggests that Berger's ideas on context also guide interests. He proposes that just as going to the original location where artwork is located will help the scholar understand the work with greater depth and appreciate its uniqueness (Berger 12–15), Latin American scholars develop a greater understanding of this local contact in relation to photography. Indeed, as those closest to the source, they are arguably the best equipped to undertake this type of analysis.

As Latin American scholars construct greater levels of understanding of the subtleties of the original context, their connectedness to the native environment leads to photography being read with local nuances. This includes reading them via history, biography, technique, and social implications in lieu of reading them through the prism of foreign theory. Consequently, it also means that they do not join in the international debate on theory with the same frequency. However, the connectedness and application of their research permits deeper understanding of direct application and the use of photography to rewrite important local histories, such as in Cora Gamarnik's study of the Malvinas/Falkland Islands conflict from the perspective of the photographs of this event in her article "El fotoperiodismo y la guerra de las Malvinas." The same applies to John Mraz's work as he rewrites the visual history of the Mexican Revolution or that of Boris Kossoy as he inserts Hercule Florence into international visual history (Kossoy *Hercule Florence*; Mraz *Photographing*). They reveal how photography helps us to reread visual signs like the deconstruction of the myths behind the "Adelita" photograph from the Mexican Revolution that converted a woman who was most likely a food vendor into the iconic *soldadera* image from the Mexican Revolution after it was mislabeled in Gustavo Casasola's *Historia Gráfica de la Revolución* (Mraz *Photographing* 240–44). This line of research enquiry uses Benjamin and Berger's notions on the importance of context to return to the site of the photograph and interrogate it with relevant sociological and historical tools to arrive at new conclusions that evidence how careful and inquisitive use of photographic archives can realign historical narratives when erroneous aesthetic appreciations have steered them off-course. Drawing on Berger as well, academics in Latin America make use of the connecting "corridor" of individual experiences when viewing photographs (Berger *Ways of Seeing*, Episode 1). The linkage between the present and the event captured photographically is used as scholars write about events from the past. It creates a connection that is unparalleled in the written archives and offers them direct access to the unintended capturing of historical content that photographs possess. The photos link them to these events, and the visual documents are examined to see what new information and insights they might offer our understanding of life and history in Latin America. Often, the lesser-heard voices of history (i.e., children, women, minorities) can give their version of events precisely due to the inclusive nature of photography, pointing to the intrinsic value of the visual in creating inclusivity. In this regard, the study of photography in Latin America is, and has been, notably progressive and democratic.

Roland Barthes's insights regarding *studium*, *punctum*, and photography's ability to contain traces of the past have been vital to Latin American scholarship. Academics there make specific use of studium and its ability to reveal what creates interest in a particular photograph. They also study our relationship to the camera and how we adopt new positions and behaviors for the camera (or a potential camera as later suggested by Azoulay) (*Civil Imagination* 21–27). While Barthes is mentioned sparingly on the carte de visite research in Latin America, the influence on how a camera conditions us physically and socially (both in the past and the present) is particularly evident in research on photography in Latin America (Bartra; Lissovsky *Escravos*). Photographs are especially useful in revealing microhistories of social classes that have received little attention from official macro versions of history (i.e., slaves and sex workers) (Lissovsky *Escravos*; Massé). Current photographers such as Maya Goded develop these topics that continue to be of interest to Latin American and international researchers of the visual in Latin America (Gasiorowski).

Without directly using the term, Barthes uses photography to reveal microhistory from his mother's life. It is the lens through which he offers his reader a glimpse of the personal (6–7). Photography's ability to reveal intimate details of daily life, everyday objects, events, and activities makes it a medium par excellence to construct microhistory. These microhistories can be the reconstruction of the individual photographer's life and work, such as Rodrigo Moya (Arnal, this volume, 84), Enrique Díaz (Monroy, this volume, 56), or Tomás Zanotti (Girard de Marroquín, this volume, 92), or the *fueginos* in Southern Chile (Leiva, this volume, 148). These studies can also be used to highlight neglected but key events, such as la Guerra de la Triple Alianza (Broquetas, this volume, 176). It has the capability to offer us clearer views of individuals like women, such as the *autoviudas* studied by Rebeca Monroy, or foreign immigrants, such as Hans Wimmer as studied by Sussy Vargas or Robert Gerstmann as studied by Pedro Querejazu. Photographs can also uncover insights about remote locations, such as Quetzaltenango (Girard de Marroquín, this volume, 89), or offer gendered readings of history (Vargas, this volume, 115).

Barthes's underlining of the signifiers within photographs also informs research in Latin America. Armed with local knowledge, these images reveal their meanings to their readers (*Camera Lucida* 34–40). The undeniability of the occurrence of events in front of a camera that Barthes emphasizes, and the photographs' concrete traces of real events, are highly attractive to scholars as they are pieces of the visually tangible past that allow for interrogation. These evidences of events form the bedrock of the studies on documentary photography and on history while lending strength to the critical arguments often found in Latin America. Likewise, the photograph's connections to actual occurrences allow scholarly studies on them to enjoy a strong sense of permanence and uncover new perspectives as new voices are included. The signifiers, and the fact that "they have been," also lead researchers to ask what photographs can provoke, showing how they can be agents of history as noted by Alberto del Castillo and others (*Fotografía y la construcción de un imaginario*).

Additionally, Barthes reminds the reader of the essence of what cannot be dismissed when considering photography: the actual presence of the object, person, and setting that was captured photographically (*Camera Lucida* 4–7). This appeal of what is irreducible about photography is especially valuable to those who wish to underline the evidence within a photographic image. Notwithstanding society's understanding of the potential to manipulate the photographic message, the veracity linked to the photographic image remains strong (Price 96). The notion that the photographic voice cannot be dismissed nor ignored is key to those who are writing against the grain of colonialism. The concept of photographic presence is essential to those who wish to foreground the voices of women, children, the Indigenous, immigrants, and the marginal. The increasing democratic power of photography (increasing because—as predicted by Benjamin—as reproducibility is facilitated, the number of producers increase) ("The Work of Art" 108) leads to more photography narratives that are independent of sovereign powers (Azoulay *Civil Imagination* 17). These narratives not only index events and information that may have been forgotten or ignored, they are also key to obtaining a more ample and inclusive understanding of Latin America's culture and history. As pointed out in *Photography: A Critical Introduction*, photographs possess key links to the real (Wells 79); those "this-has-been," in Barthes's words, contain vital connections to presence that are maximized by Latin American photography scholars.

Sontag's writings remind the reader of the ethics of looking and of our need to do so. Her thoughts on voyeurism have been presented by critics and scholars in Latin America and beyond as evidenced by the critical reactions to Daniela Rossell's *Ricas y Famosas* that I will explore later (Medina; Vargas "Genio y figura"; Villoro "Ricas, famosas y excesivas"; Gallo). Barthes's illustrations from *Camera Lucida* have been influential on scholarship in recent times. The photographs he uses underline the role that strategically placed photo agencies such as Magnum and Aperture play in what the world sees of Latin America. During the 1970s and 1980s, the focus was on conflict in Central America by photographers such as Koenwessing on assignment from the developed world (Barthes 22–24). In recent years, Pablo Hernández Hernández raises questions regarding these photography agencies and how they photographically portray Central America and contribute to how the world sees this area (as one of conflict). This is because widely circulated narratives use photographic illustrations taken by international photographers who focus on conflict and other representations of violence who, unlike local photographers such as Pedro Valtierra (del Castillo; Arnal), do not present the same nuances. Sontag argues that photography's authoritative voice, its incorporations into the systems of knowledge and its overseeing and indexing of processes, events, locations, information, and individuals imbues it with a power that makes this medium essential. Essential, not just because it is needed for the stability of social structures, but also for the economic wellbeing of our modern society (Sontag 178–80). To this end, Latin American scholars of photography show how images can take back power, the power of representation, and how that representative force can influence our outlook in ways that are not true to reality (referencing back to the analogy of Plato's cave). Their research enables the reader to contemplate how photography is a democratic process in that it belongs to many people who are outside the structures of power. This is true especially in our age of the inclusion of the auteur in photojournalism. Not only does it give citizenship and representation to foreigners who make their life within Latin America's border, like the Mexican Tomás Zanotti in Guatemala (Girard), the Italian Luigi Gismondi in Bolivia (Querejazu), or Palestinians in Honduras (Coleman); it also enables alternate power structures and their influences on photographic production to become visible. This is evident in the work of Roberto Gerstmann in Colombia and Bolivia. Published by the same Parisian publishing house and of similar quality as *Bolivia* and *Chile*, his book on Colombia was commissioned by the National Bank (Banco De La República) and the National Federation of Coffee Growers (Federación Nacional de Cafeteros de Colombia) and evidences an intense focus on order and progress. Universities, modern cities, state-of-the-art technology, and even an early airport are part of a visual outlook designed to inspire foreign and local confidence as a boon to investment and industry.[10] An extensive economic report by the director of Colombia's National Bank, Gustavo Otero Muñoz, suggests a healthy balance sheet to accompany the figures (7–33). Visual semantics are no less important, but they employ slightly different rhetoric. Indeed, the only color photograph from the book features two pink orquidea flowers in full bloom—symbolic, perhaps, of Colombia's potential in terms of seduction and tropical beauty. Gerstmann's work on Bolivia, similar in terms of style and technique, has a completely different focus. Imposing mountains, quiet and sleepy cities, and empty village pathways exhibit little (or no) technology at all (109). The Indigenous are pictured close-up in exquisite Native dress (55). Poverty or scarcity are captured in ways that show dignity without concealing lack (79). Images of children suggest a future that focuses on individuals, not economic power or potential for foreign investment (123). His book *Chile*, which appears to be an independent project, offers a similar outlook and style. Gerstmann's images always exhibit a mastery of technique, but when made to his own tastes, they show him to be a humanist. Other details reveal further aspects of his work that invite contemplation. He calls himself Roberto Gerstmann in this earlier text on Bolivia (1928), suggesting the outlook of an immigrant in the process of assimilation, unlike the later Colombian text (1951) that provides his name in German, which might have been used to suggest the prestige of a foreign documentary. There does not appear to be any official sponsor of his Bolivian work or an investment-orientated introduction. Here, Gerstmann is simply a committed photographic artist so focused on the perfection of his photographic projects that his work companions described him as obsessive (Gerstmann *Bolivia* 3). While Sontag's writings remind us that photography reveals social structure (59–60; 88–89), Latin American and other scholars also reveal the powers at work behind photographic vision and how this vision can mold the narrative. The intellectual thrust behind Latin American research on photography finds echoes in Jong-chul Choi's recent essay "Photo-Graphy," which argues that photography scholars have been successfully venturing outside Plato's cave for some time (103). Sontag's thoughts provide starting points that allow individuals to successfully question power narratives; for example, Gamarnik's article "El rol del fotoperiodismo en la construcción de la democracia en Argentina (1983–2002)" investigates the central role of photography in the building of democracy in Argentina between 1983 and 2002. She argues that analysis is possible because of photography's ability to refer to actual events and provide reliable evidence that was key to holding citizens and leaders accountable for their actions. Indeed, the photographic proof offered by journalists was deemed to be more reliable than what came from official authority figures and for that reason gathered more democratic support. This further confirms documentary photography's links to reformist projects that promote liberal social values (Price 110).

Archives

The prominence of the archive as a topic that Latin American photography scholars actively foreground deserves attention. Concerns regarding the creation, upkeep, and access to archives are paramount among them. Many raise a voice of warning regarding their underfunding, need for organization, and poor physical condition while they emphasize the high historical and social value of their contents. Having understood that "without users a depository (of photographs) does not function as an archive but rather as a private collection" (Azoulay "Lethal Art of Portraiture" 216), they encourage archive-user growth and engagement with materials. Ariella Azoulay's article "Photography Consists of Collaboration" offers additional insights regarding why archives are vital to photography scholars by describing the role of photography in society. She underlines photography's capacity to work against sovereign power when that force attempts to erase or modify the past. She also argues that photography's ability to make sovereign history incomplete means that it can be used to undermine presumed facts presented by regimes or attempts to obliterate or rewrite history according to their political outlooks (196). Likewise, the inability of the sovereign power to control photographic discourse means that photographic archives are sources of information that are more community based and "make present that which classified documents mean to hide" (197). Given Latin America's authoritarian regimes, social conflicts, and civil wars that have occurred since photography became commonplace in Latin American society, the role of the photographic archive is key to understanding what official versions of history have not yet been included, have been purposely made invisible, or have been simply forgotten. Hence, we observe the Latin American scholar's concern for photographs as archives of information and the need to value and protect photographic archives as a primary source for understanding Latin America's past.

Louis Parkinson Zamora suggests Latin American photography has a twin: Latin American narrative ("Quetzalcóatl's Mirror" 303). Roberto González Echevarría's *Myth and Archive: A Theory of Latin American Narrative* evidenced how, from colonial times to the present-day, Latin American literature has drawn on archives to create its narratives. Though González Echevarría explored anthropological and historical documents to establish his argument, you need not look far to observe how visual archives have become a key source of information for Latin American narrative. Indeed, they can change how we envision this region. *Tinísima* by Elena Poniatowska exemplifies this. It draws on Edward Weston's *Daybooks*, interviews with noteworthy figures such as Lupe Marín and Manuel Álvarez Bravo, as well as Tina Modotti's works in order to portray Modotti's life and the creation of iconic photographs such as *El excusado* (188) or the Modotti nude, *Tina en la azotea* (111; 398). The creation of Tina's photography is also portrayed in the novel. However, and building on González Echevarría's ideas, Poniatowska does not only draw on photographs to illustrate her chapters or provide fodder for anecdotes within the narrative. She researched numerous archives in Europe, Latin America, and the United States to gather photography that creates a counternarrative that depicts a specific visual narrative about Tina Modotti, including her influences, her legacy, and how she is seen by others in Mexico and abroad. The visual narrative evidences the ability of photography to reach beyond the scope of the novel and focuses on the rise of Modotti as a canonical photographer. To do so, this visual argument employs carefully selected images to suggest Modotti's photography legacy in Mexico (via her early influence on Manuel Álvarez Bravo and her promotion of him to Edward Weston) and it exhibits photographs both known to the photographic world and those previously unknown. *Tinísima* also draws on photography to show how the art of her mentors and promoters—her husband Robo, Hollywood media, Diego Rivera, and Edward Weston—objectified Modotti in their representation of her. Those archives portrayed her as a femme fatal, a muse, and a sexual body to be conquered and explored; however, Poniatowska also employs photography to strongly suggest that Tina is an agent. The written narrative details her political commitment as a constant, but the photographs in the novel also testify that Mexico is her artistic muse and an important source of her creative power. The visual narrative suggests that her true legacy is her Latin American photography. It does this in part by showing those directly affected by her work, Manuel Álvarez Bravo and Gerda Taro, and implies that it influences Los Hermanos Mayo, Robert Capa, and Chim Seymor—patriarchs and matriarchs of documentary photography in the twentieth century both within and without Mexico. Using photography and explaining its context strongly suggests Tina's work is influential on these key artists and puts her in the position of visual matriarch on the world stage of photography, evidencing photography's ability to reorient historical and cultural dialogues and focuses. Hence, Poniatowska's historical novel and its artistic and documentary photographs argue that photographs and their respective archives present alternate narratives on Latin America to which we should pay close heed. They evidence that photography can provide a powerful supportive narrative or a counternarrative accessible to those who are visually literate. Photographs supply traces of people, events, and ideas that allow the viewer to convincingly grasp history and its narratives in different ways as well as link text to image as documentary photography frequently does.

As postcolonial countries engage with photographs and their ability to expand our comprehension of the historical, social, and cultural with the information that they contain, it is natural that the scholars of these materials identify their locations and contents. It is also entirely consistent with this outlook that they express deep concern for archives that need further attention as well, that they describe their acquisitions of archives (Girard, this volume, 94), or the lengths they go to acquire or consult archives, or that they show the efforts of their institutions to preserve and promote photo archives (Broquetas, this volume, 168; Rainho, this volume, 206). As these archives are (re)constructed, the history of Latin America is expanded and restored as the micro- and macrohistories captured by visual creators intertwine to create a stronger, denser, richer material with which to weave the fabric of their national narratives. Time and close contact with the materials and contexts through which photographic materials are created form the key elements the experts featured here suggest for those who desire to engage appropriately with and interpret the archives' contents.

Processes

One of the key concerns of the study of photography in Latin America is connected to the actual photographic process. This interest in the mechanical process aligns with Benjamin's suggestion that chemical and physical analysis can reveal information linked to the unique original ("The Work of Art" 106), one of the areas on which photography scholarship in Latin America centers. In *After Photography*, Fred Ritchin shows that process, especially more recent processes in the fast-moving development of the visual image, are an active part of current debates within visual studies. This he does within the general context of photography, not specifically considering digital turns in Latin America that are revolutionizing the way we are able to interact with Latin American photography and its archives. The recurring focus on photographic processes in Latin American scholarship on photography evidences the diverse fields from which the scholars have come and their direct contact with the physical processes of photography as part of their education. In most cases, there are straightforward explanations for this. For example, most scholars began as participants in the creative process of photography before they started to delve beneath the surface of the image in search of greater meaning and connection. This approach frequently leads to greater depth in terms of technological processes as part of the critical discussion on photography in Latin America. This means that critical engagement on technique and conservation, in addition to revealing insights into historical processes, is frequently a natural product of the fieldwork of many of the researchers. One example from the study of photography comes from Rebeca Monroy's work on Enrique Díaz: *Historias para ver*. Studying the technical processes and providing the date of his 1921 experimental photograph *El Ángel de la Independencia* is what proves that his photograph was not only avant-garde, but also that it predates the arrival of Russian photography that was thought to have entered Latin America via Spanish Civil War refugees, Los Hermanos Mayo, Russian cultural ambassadors, and Russian film (this volume, 64). Hence, the technical data Monroy provided with her research gives the needed evidence to rewrite visual history in Latin America. Anne Girard's work shows how old processes are being resurrected to revive the past, connecting the past and the present for scholars and the wider public through physically recreating the processes of Latin American visual history (this volume, 97). Sussy Vargas and Magdalena Broquetas's work on the technical processes of the photographic archives allows them to identify the biological forces that literally consume Latin America's visual history. They use this insight to know how to detain advancing deterioration and physically restore photographs while underlining the value of conserving them so they can continue to benefit researchers and others. Indeed, the challenge to conserve, preserve, and interpret Latin America's visual patrimony is one of the manifest interests among scholars in this region. This interest in conservation underscores the value of photographic archives in Latin America and the role they play in opening new avenues with which to understand history and culture.

Maria do Carmo Rainho has raised concerns about the influence that photographs made by foreigners in Latin America has over the native production of Latin American images by its own residents. These concerns are connected to images of Latin America promoted abroad. While photo agencies such as Magnum and Aperture have played fundamental roles in the incorporation of Latin American photography into the world canon, when an analysis of the images used to represent this region are scrutinized with greater depth, questions begin to arise regarding the type of photographs that are promoted. Jean Paul Brandt's recent interview with the Chilean photo historian Luis Poirot underlines how Magnum showed little interest in Sergio Larraín's work that portrayed Latin America without poverty and misery. Brandt quotes that the agency was only interested in "exoticism in Valparaiso and the vagabond children [in Chile]" ("Conversation"). Emphasizing our previous points, research into archives is key to uncovering these connections because they reveal a wider body of images. For example, Magnum's focus on Larraín's work came to light when his biographer Angès Sire attempted to access his photography on the beauty found in the flora and fauna of northern Chile. Magnum apparently showed no interest in that area of his photography and was unwilling to allow her contact with their holdings of Larraín's work in that area (Brandt). Though it is a critique based on personal testimony (and does not appear to acknowledge the work that Larraín undertook as he reported undercover on organized crime in Italy) (Sire 218), we should not casually dismiss the fact that his currently promoted work features the exotic, the poor, the mysterious, the underprivileged, violence, or crime. As recent studies on the Magnum archives such as

Reading Magnum bring to light, this agency often reported on conflict and documented wrongs that need addressing, yet this was also counterbalanced with their use of portraiture, everyday life, geography, and celebrity culture. Even so, this vision from Latin America is less developed. However, when considering the images used in large projects that have a tendency to form visual canons, patterns of visual focus regarding Latin America begin to emerge; exoticism, conflict, poverty, and mystical images become the order of the day just as we see in literature (Hoelscher; Fuget and Gómez; O'Bryen). Indeed, just as photography's sister, literature, has evidenced, magic or other heightened emotions are what come to be expected, indeed required, of Latin America—a phenomenon that cultural critics have warned against (Said 374). Because many of the Anglophone studies of photography tend to profile "photography" as could be described as Euro-American photography, when photography from other areas of the world is exhibited, it tends to "foreground 'cultural' dimensions of practice" (Pinney 142). This is exemplified in the repeated usage of Manuel Álvarez Bravo's *La buena fama durmiendo* as a standard showpiece of Latin American photography within canonical writings on photography in English or the growing abundance of Frida Kahlo's photographs as examples of Latin American culture. This imagery, however, has very little relation with the study of Latin American photography in Latin America, which has a strong focus on documentary photography. Documentary photography provides a counter-reading: an alternate vision that includes a multiplicity of voices. The fact that much of documentary photography is connected to written texts expands this vision to other mediums that can be studied in tandem.

As suggested by Maria do Carmo Rainho, it can be the case that the local image-makers with desires to fulfill market needs willingly produce photographs that align with the visual outlook demanded from outside Latin America. Recent photographic studies from Latin America have shown that while some photographers are interested in using their craft to build visual documents based on authenticity, others are keen to employ the picturesque as is evident in an episode retold by Eleazar López Zamora, the founding director of the Instituto de Antropología e Historia Fototeca. In it, he shares details from an episode between the Mexican photographers Mariana Yampolsky and Flor Garduño.

Mariana Yampolsky, confused by the clothing worn by a person in a [Flor] Garduño photo, asked her to which Indigenous group the fellow belonged. Garduño evidently replied, "Oh Mariana, you're so naïve. I just grabbed those old rags out of my closet and dressed him up in them" (Mraz *Looking* 222–23).

Given the popularity of Garduño's work (such as *Witness of Time*) in mainstream venues in the United States and Europe, the previous quote suggests that a Latin American visual imagery that obeys foreign visual demands for the exotic and picturesque exists, raising questions on the promotion of foreign visual outlooks in Latin America. Pablo Hernández Hernández and Maria do Carmo Rainho's research suggests that further discussion is needed on Latin American photography as this vision and its promotion and reception can be used to arrive at conclusions regarding how Latin America is conceived by others and what implications this has on foreign and domestic visual conceptions of that area (this volume, 212).

The Documentary

Research has shown that photography in Latin America does not always follow the same pattern of foreign gazes. Ana Mauad has deftly evidenced that concerned photographers there, such as Evelyn Genevieve and Sebastião Salgado, have produced visual narratives on Brazil that show what she called "shared patterns of visual outlook" (Mauad "O olhar" and "Concerned America"). Both visual essays by the two photographers show a nuanced reading of the economic, political, and social landscape of the northeast of Brazil that had little or nothing to do with foreign conceptions of that region. These independent projects have led to both photographers producing remarkably similar visual essays on life in northeast Brazil, notwithstanding the fact that more than four decades occurred between the creation of their respective visual projects. The success of their narratives and their willingness to defy mandates, together with their eagerness to operate independently, shows that different work exists and captivates audiences.

Documentary photography in Latin America offers important lessons connected to its origins there. Hercule Florence's work asks important questions regarding art and technology. As a printer, inventor, and businessman, Florence discovered the photographic qualities of silver nitrate on paper in his attempts to create a faster and more economical way of reproducing documents such as labels, diplomas, and his own writings (Kossoy "Hercule Florence" 5). His application of photographic processes engaged with the documentary in a very literal sense. Though he was successful in creating the photographs and in coining the word *photographie* years before the word photography was adopted into English, the lack of technological resources and a supportive sociocultural context meant that his photography experiments were eventually abandoned for other printing methods and more economical pursuits (Kossoy "Photography in nineteenth century" 25). Photography's lack of practical usage and the remote location of the discovery led to it being forgotten for many years. Consider, on the other hand, the invention of photography in Europe, which arose as a product to satisfy the desire of industrial Europe's growing middle class for a visible register of possession available then only via art (Wells

"Thinking About Photography" 13). The market demand for paintings and art that recorded personal history (and vanity)—portraits of oneself, of one's property, and of other objects of beauty or science—inspired inventors to create mechanical reproductions of the visible image. The overt artistic focus of the first European photographs (that reproduced still life, portraits, and land and cityscapes) imitated the art of the period and found an immediate demand and acceptance among the scientists and technology aficionados of the day (Marbot 15–17). While it has not always been the case, early photography prospered when it copied the beauty and prestige found in other art forms and offered its visual recordings to an audience willing (and able) to purchase them.

Early photography masters such as Manuel Álvarez Bravo experimented with reality and fantasy. This is observable in his photograph of the false landscape, *Arena y pinitos* (Kismaric 41), and in Lola Álvarez Bravo's photomontage, *El sueño de los pobres II* (Debroise 233).[11] However, scholars in Latin America have not entered as deeply into the debate regarding the real and the imagined within photography in Latin America as in other areas of the world. As noted, when discussing the 1978 Mexico City colloquium on photography and the interpretations of the photographic body it produced, documentary photography is widely studied in Latin America. While prominent critics such as Abigail Solomon-Godeau have argued that all photography has a degree of documentary quality because of the way in which it captures images (*Photography at the Dock* 169), certain photography falls more deeply in its terrain. Latin American scholars recognize that images have a special claim on the real precisely because they represent the everyday experience with which we are familiar and enjoy "a special relationship to real life and a singular status with regard to notions of truth and authenticity" (Price 80). Price reminds us that travel photography, war photography, and photojournalism in particular are documentarian in nature (77), and these topics feature strongly within the body of Latin American scholarship on photography. Consider travel photography. In Latin America, this type of photography is abundant. Daniel Hernández-Salazar's *Para que todos sepan* is an example of internal and international travel photography combined with concerned and protest photography produced in his native Guatemala. This photography project documents the civil and political unrest throughout Guatemala in recent decades as well as the international tour of Hernández- Salazar's protest image *Ángel de la memoria* through key sites that represent culture, power, or conflict remembrance. Enrique Bostelmann's visual testimonial *América: Un viaje a través de la injusticia* is composed entirely of travel photographs from within Latin America and was brought into Martin Parr's *The Protest Box* collection. This move suggests its relevance to the world canon on protest photography witnessed through travel and underlines how documentary photography is frequently linked to reformist political projects.[12] Photography studies has also underscored the need for other technologies that provide support for these visual productions. On occasion, this emphasis focuses on how new visual equipment allows photographers to capture the world differently. In other instances, it is connected to the ways in which the photographs arrive at the locations where they take new images. For example, Pedro Querejazu helps us understand the importance of the role of the train, which enabled Martín Chambi to travel about Peru quickly and undertake his photographic assignments and explorations more rapidly.

As academics in Latin America explore documentary photography, they show how photography is inclusive, underlining lesser-understood events and reminding us of the role of those who are not always included in the macro-narratives of history (Kossoy; Leiva). Understanding and analyzing photojournalism has been central to the field of photography studies in Latin America. Indeed, its internal photojournalism often rewrites much of the rest of the world's reporting on Latin America precisely because local photographers who are concerned with the present and future of their county are the ones who do this. To that end they offer a visual narrative that mediates the local context from within (Arnal *Rodrigo Moya*; Mraz and Vélez; del Castillo Troncoso *Rodrigo Moya*). Alberto del Castillo's *Ensayo sobre el movimiento estudiantil* on the photography from the 1968 Mexican student movement demonstrates photography's ability to sway public opinion. His research analyzes a wide range of photographs that includes private and public photography, censured and self-censured photographs, and government-promoted and independently produced images of those events. This generous visual sample of the events of the 1968 student movement creates a new narrative that counters the official narrative, showing how the visual can forge renewed avenues of understanding and reveal new insights. Though the official/government version of the events of 1968 in Mexico are now generally discredited (Sloan), the photographs from journalists during that time period remind us that clearer readings of the events were there from the beginning. Indeed, they are among the best sources of knowledge of those events precisely because, unlike writing and other mediums of expression, sovereign powers are unable to control photography and its resulting narrative (Azoulay *Civil Imagination* 24–25). Photographs played a vital role in changing the public's opinion of the Partido Revolucionario Institucional (PRI) government, and, as manifest through the critical reactions to Daniela Rossell's documentary photography of the rich in Mexico, this trend continues. The visual narratives that provide new insights into Latin American history can often provide small details that create powerful counter arguments. One example helps to clarify this. One of the most sought-after narratives of the Tlatelolco massacre is *La noche de Tlatelolco*, an experimental journalistic text that is composed mostly of interviews, public documents, and photographs that were given to Elena Poniatowska after the massacre on October 2, 1968. The images were provided on the condition that they remain anonymous because at that time it was dangerous to speak out (Poniatowska "Letter"; Moyle). They remain anonymous over a half-century later. Countering government reports in newspapers that the victims (including military victims) were only few in number, a close-up photograph featured in *La noche del Tlatelolco* shows numerous shoes that were abandoned in the plaza: metonymic for the large number of students who never found their way home after that fateful night in October (xxvi). A cutline from the English translation of the same goes a step further in its visual analysis and notes that the shoes photographed were mostly women's, adding an obvious, though relevant, gendered reading of the image (*Massacre in Mexico* 192).

Cora Gamarnik's usage of photography to retell Argentina's invasion of the Falkland Islands proves to be a helpful example of the usage of photojournalism/nature photography to offer further insights into a key historical event in Latin America. Her article "El fotoperiodismo y la guerra de las Malvinas" reveals that a nature photographer who was coincidentally on the island (not the intended photojournalist sent with the invading troops) clandestinely captured the images of the invasion that were later used by the international press. While not an amateur photographer, this case reminds us of the increasing role of amateur photography and photographers who are not photojournalists in the formation of documentary narrative (Price 95). This specific case of the use of photography to understand historical events evidences a natural evolution of the genre when considering that the documentary should cover the everyday events of life and should be a natural way of incorporating nonhegemonic voices into historical narratives. These photographs can be read as visual narratives that escape the control of sovereign power and emerge from past positions of silence to ones of self-fashioning and nation-building. Gisela Cánepa Koch offers one exploration of this process in *Imaginación visual y cultura en el Perú*. Her coauthor of another volume, Ingrid Kummels, reminds us that documentary photography regularly features motifs from Indigenous and other marginalized Latin American peoples—another element meriting further exploration within Latin American photography. She describes how photography enables marginalized peoples to overcome what Kummels calls in *Transborder Media Spaces* the "visual divide" that existed in the past. All of this is possible thanks to the active role that amateur photography takes in new documentary narratives.

Thanks to the presence of amateur photography, photojournalism and documentary photography have the capacity to be genres that are more inclusive—allowing vernacular photography to enter the research efforts alongside well-established professionals. Mauricio Lissovsky argues that this phenomenon should increase as the field of the study of photography becomes even more established in Latin America (this volume, 202). So, we can see that photojournalism lends itself naturally to approaches that involve a mixing of visual narratives from different origins, which facilitates a more inclusive vision of events that approach the study of photography from other perspectives. Latin American scholars' interest in this type of photography suggests a more inclusive view of the capture and composition of texts that represent Latin America.

Susan Sontag's writings regarding voyeurism, the ethical dilemmas of capturing of pain and suffering, and the aestheticizing of the same are not strongly debated within Latin America (though it is making some headway among scholars who write on Latin American photography from without) (Gasiorowiski *Photographing the Unseen*). Perhaps this is because, as recognized by D. L. Strauss, to represent is to make aesthetic (9). Whenever you represent you transform, you filter, you reshape, and all are recognized qualities of photographic representation. The absence of this debate could also be because Latin American scholars appear to be more interested in understanding the meanings behind the images and what relations they have to social change and movement. More recently, Parvati Nair's study of Sebastião Salgado defends his visual outlook that received heavy criticism outside of Latin America. Nair underlines how Salgado is less concerned with critics and more concerned with developing his humanistic projects (150–58), an ethos shared by many Latin American photographers. Recent photographic theory also responds to such critics by arguing that the viewing of photography that documents suffering or injury can be a civic exercise instead of a purely aesthetic experience (Azoulay *Civil Contract* 14)—a tenet long held within Latin American scholarship on photography. Indeed, approaching documentary photography as a civic exercise is often the outlook applied by scholars when engaging with documentary photography produced in Latin America. This is most evident in the scholarship on war and conflict photography there.

The relationship between documentary photography, war, and conflict is of special interest to Latin American scholars. Pablo Hernández Hernández debates the role Susan Meiselas's photographs of the Nicaraguan Revolution have taken in the shaping of the world's view of Central America (this volume, 102). One of Ariel Arnal's most significant research projects, *Atila de tinta y plata*, focuses on identifying the different portrayals of Emiliano Zapata within the Mexican press during the Mexican Revolution. Arnal's research not only allows us to observe the visual strategies the photojournalists use as they work but also rewrites an important part of the visual history of the Mexican Revolution by deflating popular myths regarding Zapata and restoring authorial voice to those who represented the Mexican Revolution with photography while it was occurring.

While war and conflict as social movements are present among Latin American scholarship, quotidian images of poverty and violence in Latin America are not the particular focus of scholars. This is an important insight because, though scholarship on war and conflict grows out of these death-facing cultures, the scholarship does not tend to be death-focused.[13] In a different focus that allows us to see how Latin America approaches photographic critique, while poverty and suffering captured by photographs are not hotly debated, photographic portrayals of wealth can cause a critical reaction. In 2002, the relatively unknown (though politically connected) Mexican photographer Daniela Rossell published her book of photographs, *Ricas y famosas*. Her photographs display the extreme wealth of the rich (though not actually famous) Mexican women in a variety of domestic settings, flaunting their material goods to obscene (and kitsch) extremes. *Ricas y famosas* caused an outcry among many sectors of both foreign and domestic society as even those who were not normally photography scholars wrote what could be described as Barthes-inspired semiotic analysis of the codes of corruption (and simply poor taste) in Rossell's photographic narrative. This particular instance evidences how the exhibition of unbridled power and wealth can provoke heated debate on the ethics and impact of viewing excess. Documentary photography continues to bring forth unique and revelatory reactions within Latin America. Research intent on revealing excesses of power has a history in that region, and it has delved into the debate on how the government tried to control the role of photography. One example of this is explored in the magazine *Rotofoto*, which was critical of the Mexican government (Debroise 188–91; Mraz *Nacho López* 39–41).

A significant quantity of research on photography in Latin America is related to restoring the voice to those who have been ignored or eclipsed by the achievements or self-promotion of other narratives. Microhistory is a strong focus of many of the photography scholars in Latin America. In many cases, the producers of documentary photography have come into focus. Monographs and microhistories on photographers such as Nacho López, Enrique Díaz, and Héctor García have come to light (Mraz *Nacho López*; Monroy *Histories para ver*; Ortiz Monasterio *Escribir con luz*). The sensitive documentary photographs of Hans Wimmer, Mariana Yampolsky, Max T. Vargas, and Martín Chambi reveal their work and the context within which they labor, underscoring their excellence and that of their contemporaries. Much of this work proves that known key photographers were not isolated phenomena, but rather products of the combined energies of their time as Pedro Querejazu suggests. Latin American researchers have shown a growing number of European photographers whose visual narratives did more than simply reinforce colonial power or provide for the tastes of the exotic or the Other that European or United States markets demanded of Latin America (Maria do Rainho, this volume, 213). For example, the Tomás Zanotti archive reveals an ample range of portraits showing Quetzaltenango society in ways that are unparalleled in the written records. Hans Wimmer's photographic record of Puerto Limón in Costa Rica adds depth and texture to our vision of a multicultural society in Latin America that is known for its Afro-Caribbean influence brought by the United Fruit Company from neighboring countries (Putnam). To the well-known image of that particular region of Costa Rica Wimmer adds the influence of the Italian and German immigrants as well as those from India, Turkey, and China in addition to the Talamanca Indians from that region. Wimmer's visual narrative that Sussy Vargas's research rescued from his forgotten (and miraculously spared) archive gives visual voice to those who have been eclipsed by the larger narratives that center on the imperialist effects of the United Fruit Company—a major theme in the story of Central America. The documentary photographs in Latin America enable researchers to see the lives of the marginal and glimpse past the shadows in Plato's cave to appreciate the greater context the research and the photographs afford their viewers.

John Mraz

Benemérita Universidad Autónoma de Puebla

I Discovered How I Wanted to Do History

MY ENTRY INTO the world of photographic analysis was somewhat serendipitous. My dissertation in history was on the representation of history in Cuban cinema, so I presumably would have continued working in cinema here in Mexico. However, the story really goes back to 1971, when I made my first audiovisual: "The History of Mexico as Seen by the Muralists." At the time, I was moving directly into doctoral studies from a BA program at the University of California, Santa Barbara. I got slides of the murals from the art library, which I put together with music and some texts by Octavio Paz and Carlos Fuentes. It was probably pretty bad, but I had discovered how I wanted to do history.

I went on from there to codirect several Super-8 films in the early 1970s: *Coming Apart: America in the 60s*, *Cracks in the Wall: America in the 50s*, and *Todo es más sabroso con . . .*, a film essay on the continuing neocolonialism in Mexico. At that moment, I decided: This is what I am going to do—I'm not going to do anything else. I was in intellectual history before, but once I had found what I really wanted to do, I put all my eggs in that basket.

I was a mature student and had spent several years in the labor market before I went to the University of California, Santa Barbara in 1967. I worked hard and I got very good grades. I studied first with a very conservative professor in Portuguese Empire history, focusing on Brazil. It was through my work with him that I got directly into the PhD program in 1970. That year a Chicano professor, Jesús Chavarría, arrived in the History Department and founded the first Chicano studies center in the United States. Charismatic and intellectually stimulating, he was my only real academic mentor.

I decided to focus on Latin American history through film and chose a thesis topic based on La Decena Trágica: Mexico City's ten tragic days in February 1913. The dissertation was to be a history told through documentary film footage and photographs. I used the idea of split-brain theory—the experiments showing that one side of the brain reads words and the other images—to defend the project, arguing that we should do history with both sides of our brains. I also asserted that a film could portray the experience of the time better than the written word and thus would be an important way to represent the pressure on the populace of Mexico City to accept Victoriano Huerta's dictatorship. I marshalled other theoretical justifications as well, stimulated in part by Hayden White's groundbreaking notion that all histories are just narrative forms.[1] However, the project was stopped short by the director of the History Department's graduate program who said: "You are not going to make a laughingstock of this department." Thus, in 1975 I was granted a Regents' Fellowship, a terminal MA degree, and was told to disappear.

I discovered that the University of California, Santa Barbara (UCSB) had excellent library holdings on Mexican topics when I was a student. It was there that I first saw the albums produced by the Casasola Archive, began to make historical documentaries with other graduate students, and cocurated an exhibit of historical photographs. I became more and more deeply involved in what could be called the "visual turn." At that time, a lot of visual experimentation was occurring at the University of California and California State University: Paul Vanderwood and Brad Burns were writing on cinema; Carlos Cortés, Leon Campbell, and Patrick H. Griffin were making films. All of them, especially Paul, were supportive of my struggle to do history with modern media.

My conviction that I would use images to teach history became stronger through the first courses I gave while at UCSB. I had a night class at Ventura Community College in 1974–75. The class went from 8:00 p.m. to 11:00 p.m. and was composed largely of adults—firemen, secretaries, policemen, housewives—who would come in after working all day. The very first night I got up to lecture from behind the speaker's podium, as my professors did, I saw their eyes began to drop like shutters. So, I decided that starting with the next session we would first talk about the assigned reading, then go and get some coffee. On returning to the classroom, I turned out the lights and showed them slides while reading accounts such as letters from prisoners in Andersonville during the US Civil War, for example. They loved it. From that point, it became my method for teaching history because it offered the possibility for students to interact with something they could see for themselves as well as hear participant accounts, instead of having to listen to a professor expound on topics with which the students really had no way of interacting.

Although I had been ejected from the UCSB history doctorate program, Jesús Chavarría had been talking to David Sweet, a history professor at University of California, Santa Cruz (UCSC), who thought my work on using photos and film to do history sounded interesting. In 1975, I went up to Santa

Cruz to talk with David about the possibility of continuing my studies there. During my visit, I met Julianne Burton, who was just becoming a big name in the study of the New Latin American Cinema. David and Julianne made the pitch to the graduate school that I should be admitted in history, although there was no graduate program in that discipline. The graduate dean argued that I would never finish the dissertation or amount to much of anything in the academic world (fortunately, I only learned of this afterward).

However, I was supporting my application to UCSC with published texts. New history journals with an interest in modern media were appearing. I had published an article on the Cuban film *Lucía* in *Film & History*, and another on how to make historical films in *The History Teacher*. Having articles accepted for publication was unusual for graduate students during that period. That experience taught me something I always emphasize when talking with young professors and graduate students who want to work in modern media, citing Bob Dylan: "To live outside the law, you must be honest." If you are doing something new, you have to produce more than scholars who are following beaten paths in order to convince your peers that you are not a fraud, an implication that was applied to me during my graduate studies.

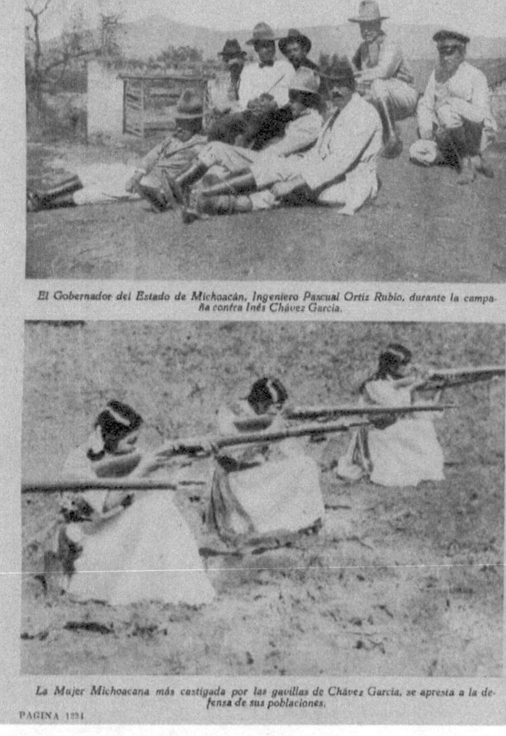

Figure 1.1. Photographs of women engaged in self-defense training and of Constitutionalist leaders in Michoacán, February 1914. J. Guerrero. Gustavo Casasola, *Historia gráfica de la Revolución, 1900–1940*, cuaderno 13, 1942, p. 1224.

After a year at UCSC, I gave up the film project, after one of the professors I had asked to serve on my committee replied intelligently, "I have never made a film. How could I judge the research of a film project?" I finally settled on the representation of history in Cuban cinema as a dissertation topic. I spent five years at UCSC, mainly in film studies. The person I worked with most closely was Janey Place, one of the first in the United States to get a doctorate in cinema studies. She worked on visual style and helped me find a method for my madness. I finally finished my dissertation in 1986, while I was living in Mexico, and it was based largely on the method of visual analysis I learned from her.

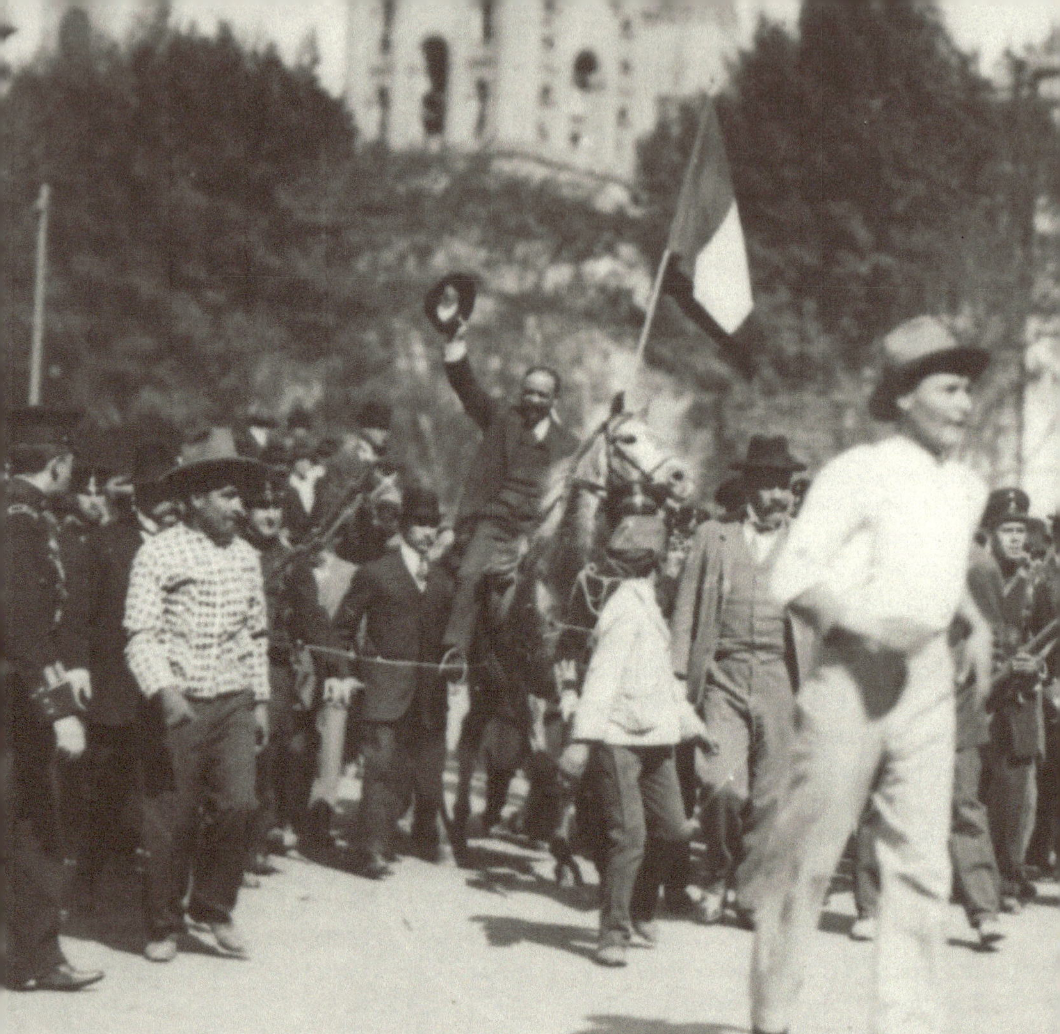

Figure 1.2. President Francisco I. Madero arrives at the National Palace on the first day of the Tragic Ten Days, Mexico City, February 9, 1913. Gerónimo Hernández. Inv. #37276, Fondo Casasola, SINAFO-Fototeca Nacional del Instituto Nacional de Antropología e Historia (INAH).

I left UCSC and moved to Berkeley in 1980, but I had not yet finished my dissertation, and had little or no opportunities for a job. I kept my hand in filmmaking, filming the hotel and restaurant workers' strike in San Francisco, as well as acts in solidarity with the guerrilla in El Salvador for a leftist video collective "Grand Illusions." My day job was making ethnographic video for a multiethnic research project with the National Institute of Education. I met Eli Bartra while she was visiting the Bay Area, and when the opportunity to join her in Mexico presented itself, I went to live there. My background in visual media was enormously helpful for me in getting my first employment in Mexico, which was in television. This is another thing I often emphasize to students: working in visual studies can open up many opportunities beyond teaching, and perhaps more interesting ones.

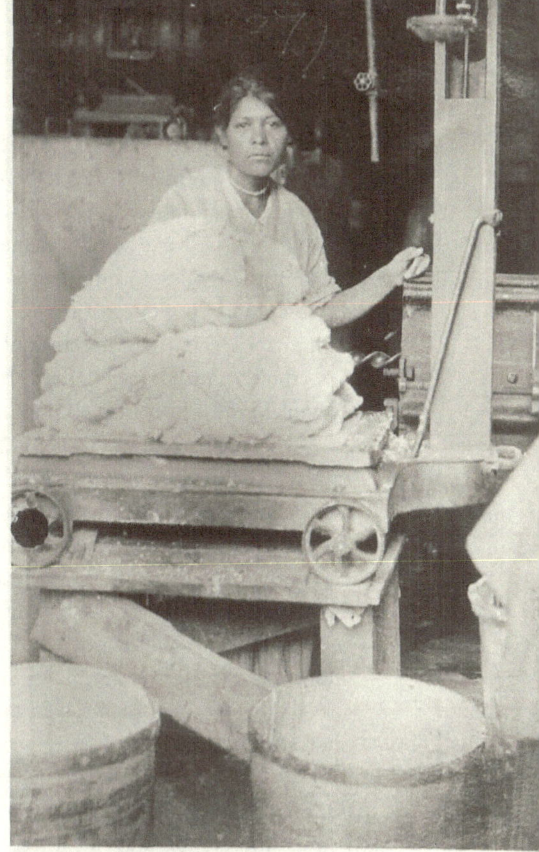

Figure 1.3. Nixtamal worker, Calle de Degollado, Mexico City, December 6, 1919. Juan de Beraza. Ramo de Trabajo. 172:12, Archivo General de la Nación.

Many of my research opportunities in Mexico have been linked to photo archives. Photo archives are very important in Latin America, and they vary from country to country. Mexico is somewhat unique because during the Mexican Revolution *historias gráficas*, picture histories, were being produced right in the middle of the revolution. Then, in 1921, Agustín Víctor Casasola began publication of his huge photo documentary project on the revolution. Hence, I think that we are more photography-oriented in Mexico. There have always been these huge volumes of photographic history to consult, which serve as catalogs if nothing else. They are national picture encyclopedias. I do not think that exists to such a degree in many other countries.

Another important factor is that Mexican governments spent money to acquire and conserve archives such as the Casasola or the Hermanos Mayo. The collections have been important in fomenting much development on the study of photography outside the field of art history. Moreover, photographers themselves have been very collaborative with academics. There are large and active communities of photo historians here that I will mention later. There are also institutions like the Escuela Nacional de Antropología e Historia, the Instituto Mora, and the Benemérita Universidad Autónoma de Puebla, where people acquire doctoral degrees in the field of photo history. This same type of activity occurs in Brazil in the Laboratorio de Historia Oral y de Medios that Professor Ana Mauad directs at the Universidade Federal Fulminense.

In 1982, I acquired a position at the Centro de Estudios Históricos sobre el

Movimiento Obrero Mexicano (CEHSMO). Meeting CEHSMO's founder and director, Enrique Suárez Gaona, was my first experience with what I call Mexico's "enlightened administrators." I had applied for a job in publications, but when he saw my resume, he appointed me *coordinador de historia gráfica* and provided me with the money to buy photos from archives, the equipment to copy them, and assistants to work with me. I also curated an exhibit, continuing to work with images from the standpoint of a historian. I was using them in terms of the ways their "transparency" offered the opportunity to do visual social history. For example, I did a historical ethnography on nixtamal workers in 1919.[2]

In 1982, incoming President Miguel de la Madrid dismantled CEHSMO. Enrique encouraged me to take the photo archive with me when I left, as it would only be mothballed. Soon after, I met the rector of the Universidad Autónoma de Puebla (UAP), Alfonso Vélez Pliego, who was another visionary. He suggested that I bring my project on the visual history of Mexican workers to Puebla. In 1984, I started working for the Centro de Investigaciones Históricas del Movimiento Obrero at the UAP. It was then that I began studying the photos by the Hermanos Mayo, not only in relation to workers' history, but also to the brothers themselves as authors of working-class photography and photojournalism.[3]

Although I was concluding my dissertation on Cuban film, I was also thinking of working with Mexican cinema, taking copious notes on the pictures I saw on television and in theaters. However, one of the problems of studying cinema in the 1980s was that you had to watch film on its own time, when it was available to be shown, and there was a fixed place to show it. Photographs, however, you can look at in your own time. Around 1988, Eleazar López Zamora, the founding director of the Fototeca Nacional, invited me to write a book on whichever of their archives interested me.[4] That is one of the incredible things about working in Mexico: some myopic bureaucrats may shut you out, but there are enlightened administrators who will nonetheless invite you to do projects for their institutions.

I accepted Eleazar's invitation and chose to write a book about the photojournalist Nacho López (Ignacio López Bocanegra). Until then, I had only seen photographs as a useful tool to teach or write about history, or as something that belonged to the art world—something on the margins. I had not yet conceptualized photography as the center of the visual world—now the hypervisual world—and it is!

A lot of life is being in the right place at the right time and knowing how to take advantage of that and doing the work to make things happen. With the invitations I received and the support offered to me, as well as my researcher's position, which gave me time for my projects, I moved increasingly into photography. I am fortunate that I did because in Mexico there is a large and vibrant community of individuals studying photography and struggling with how to advance its investigation. Informal and formal seminars, like the *Seminario de Fotografía* under the direction of the Instituto Mora and the Instituto Nacional de Antropología e Historia, have been taking place since the mid-1980s and continue today. It is much more exciting than other visual fields, such as art or film, because we are inventing the methodologies as we carry out projects, and there is a great deal of sharing, of generosity. I saw photography as a very open and dynamic field, but the invitations were also an important stimulus. Among others, I was invited by Pati Mendoza, director of the Centro de la Imagen and also a visionary, to curate an exhibit on the new photojournalism of Mexico in 1996, and then by the INAH director to curate the national exhibit on the centenary of the Mexican Revolution in 2010. At the time, I was also writing regularly about photography in *La Jornada Semanal*, a weekly magazine supplement to the newspaper *La Jornada* that everybody in Mexico read in the early 1990s. That enabled me to be a public intellectual in a way that would have been difficult as an academic in the United States.

Over the last four decades, there have been huge advances in the study of photography. In history, the changes have been enormous; over the last fifteen years or so excellent historians have begun writing seriously about photography, rather than just using photographs as illustrations. Of course, this new attention to photography is occurring across all of the disciplines. The sciences have been much more open to photography than any of the humanities. Visual anthropology also has a long bibliography in Mexico, and to a certain extent elsewhere. In Brazil, for example, young historians are now doing very solid work in photography. I think that it is part of the hyper-visual world in which we live and has to be incorporated. The great universities like Harvard, Yale, Oxford, the Sorbonne, or UNAM do not have positions for people who are using photos to undertake studies in the humanities or the social sciences. Where positions do exist, at Princeton, for instance, they are usually in history of art.

For a long time, I thought that the history of photography was a subdiscipline of the history of art, but I was disabused of that idea during a UNAM doctoral defense. A woman had written a brilliant PhD thesis on Winfield Scott, based on photo archives. She was pursuing her degree in the Art History Department because there was nowhere else one could study photography in the UNAM. The woman had gone through archives in the United States and Mexico, constructing an excellent thesis.[5] When the time came to decide if she should be awarded honors for her dissertation, I argued that we should give her that recognition, but the art historian denied it, saying, "No, because she did not prove the aesthetic value of the photos." I started laughing and explained that those photos were taken to sell real estate and tourism in Mexico and had little aesthetic value.

All of a sudden, as we say in Mexico, *Me cayó el veinte* (figuratively, "the penny dropped"), and I finally got it. I suddenly realized that the history of photography is not a subdiscipline of art history. To be generous, I would say that only 5 percent of photographs ever made were taken by artists. What are we to do with the rest? How are we going to study family photography, photojournalism, landscape photography, organizational photography, imperial photography, subaltern photography, revolutionary and postrevolutionary photography, Indianist and Indigenous photography, photography of and by workers, or the photography produced by companies for their own purposes? The list will become even longer as we define the different genres or functions of photography, and every area will need its own methodology for analysis. My sense is that we need to develop rigorous approaches to this hyper-visual world and that students want the different disciplines to allow them to pursue analyses of visualities. I think that those are the big changes, and I would have to say that the transformations have occurred in terms of concrete projects more than theoretical speculation.

The real advances have been made in histories such as those done in the United States and Europe by Alan Sekula, Sally Stein, Chris Pinney, Peter Hales, Deborah Poole, James Faris, Martha Sandweiss, James Krippner, and Parvati Nair, among others.[6] Among the important scholars in Latin America are Rebeca Monroy, Patricia Massé, Alberto del Castillo, Fernando Aguayo, Rosa Casanova, Carlos Alberto Sampaio Barbosa, Daniel Escorza, Ariel Arnal, Miguel Ángel Berumen, Magdalena Broquetas, José Antonio Rodríguez, and Samuel Villela.[7] A few general works by historians also contribute, for example, Boris Kossoy, Robert Levine, Ana Mauad, and Peter Burke.[8]

Influencing Ideas

With regard to theory, John Berger is essential, as are Walter Benjamin and Gisele Freund. *Ways of Seeing* by John Berger changed the way I thought about images, as did Walter Benjamin.[9] Both Benjamin and Siegfried Kracauer were in the Frankfurt School, where they argued against the notion of conceiving photography only as art.[10] They see photographs from another perspective; for example, Benjamin asserted that in David Octavius Hill's 1846 photos of Newhaven fishwives, there is something that cannot be silenced and will never consent to be reduced completely to art (Benjamin "Little History").[11] Those writers are among the thinkers who revolutionized how we understand photographs.

José Antonio Navarrete's *Fotografiando en América Latina* has been important to me. He writes about the development of photographic studies, arguing that there are essentially two schools. One comes out of art and is basically formed by Beaumont Newhall, who mounted the first important exhibit of photography in an art museum when he curated *Photography: 1839–1937* for the Museum of Modern Art in New York. Newhall and Nathan Lyon produced 250 slides from that exhibit, and those images became the devices for teaching photography around the world because they were available for purchase. This was long before photographic books were circulating extensively outside of research universities. That was part of how art history became established as the way to study photography, via the interests and investments of museums, art galleries, collectors, speculators, and art history departments, which relegated the study of photography to the realm of art history. Then there is the whole other line, which comes out of the Frankfurt School, with Siegfried Kracauer, Walter Benjamin, and Gisèle Freund, who wrote the first PhD on photography as a social form in 1936 at the Sorbonne in France.

Methods

My methodology for analyzing photographs is to separate them into genres; and, from there, find out what have been the various functions they have served. Further, I emphasize contextualization and comparison. Contextualization is fundamental to the study of photography. I like to paraphrase Alan Sekula who, writing in the 1980s, asserted that a photo on its own means nothing. It only begins to mean something within a discursive context.[12] Once, after a lecture I gave at the University of Cambridge, an academic there commented that my work was good on contextualization, and I thought: "What else is there?" We can also understand how the photographic is created by comparing photos. I will detail an example of this later using the *piropo* (catcall) photos by Nacho López and Ruth Orkin. We might say that contextualization is the study of how photographic meaning is generated from without, by the contexts often provided by written texts, while comparisons show us how it is produced from within the photo itself.

I try to emphasize that the concrete work that is out there, for me, is much more important than theorizing. Fernando Osorio is a leading conservationist here in Mexico on Latin American photography and founder of the Fotobservatorio del Patrimonio Fotográfico Mexicano. We have spoken to each other often regarding how to separate photos within this massive photographic body. He studied at the George Eastman Museum of the University of Rochester and introduced me to the idea of classifying photos via the functions that they serve. In my most recent book, *History and Modern Media: A Personal Journey*, I analyze the genres of photojournalism, Indianist, revolutionary, and leftist photography through studying the different functions photographs have served within those genres.

I believe that Roland Barthes and Susan Sontag's theoretical approaches are still suggestive, but I think the work of Vilém Flusser and his idea of "technical images" is fundamental today.[13] He described the world as having moved through three phases. The first was a visual phase; the second was a textual phase created by the invention of lineal writing; and, with the invention of photography, we are now moving into another visual phase. This new visual phase is going to be very different from the first phase because of the technical processes we now have and the credibility these images enjoy. It is all changing so rapidly with digitization and the Internet and social media that you must look now to scholars such as Fred Ritchin, who I think has certainly written some of the best books about the new visual world.[14] Ariella Azoulay is also an important theoretician.[15] I believe that technical images show us the world as scenes rather than processes. A photograph is not a narrative: you read it very differently from the way you read lineal texts. You do not read a photograph left to right or right to left, or top to bottom. You read a photograph as a whole unit, and you discover elements in it. It is a very different way of thinking. As Flusser says, it is "image thinking" rather than "writing thinking."

The comparative approach to analyzing photographs requires that you have significant experience with images, a large catalog of pictures in your head. This kind of analysis allows you to ask, "How does this photo convey meaning?" For example, if we want to understand how Nacho López photographed the piropo—the catcalls men give to women in the street—we can compare his depiction to a similar image: one by Ruth Orkin. Nacho's photo of a beautiful woman walking in Mexico City in front of a group of men who "compliment" her is shot from a low angle.[16] This angle gives her power—she is delighted to receive the piropos the men direct toward her. You can see López's intention by comparing his photo to the high-angle shot by Ruth Orkin of a woman in Italy being besieged by her "admirers."[17] In Orkin's photo the woman is trapped by the men and the buildings that loom over her; the high angle reinforces the offensiveness of the catcalls. Both are "directed photos," indicating explicitly the intention of the photographers, but it is only by comparing the two that you can talk about the meanings each creates.[18]

Fundamental Errors

In my experience, literary scholars do not usually have large image archives in their heads that would permit them to compare photographs. Instead, they are frequently steeped in postmodern theory that informs much of their analysis. I think it is a fundamental mistake to import literary theory to talk about photography because it focuses on a completely different medium. Moreover, it is often obscurantist, and I always remember what Nietzsche said regarding the difference between those who are profound and those who wish to appear profound: those who are profound express themselves in the clearest way possible so you can see to the depths of their profundity, whereas those who wish to appear profound express themselves in the most obscure ways so that you cannot see that they have no profundity.[19] Flusser is not easy, but he is worth breaking your teeth over. I am not sure that is true of literary theory as it is applied to photography. Walter Kaufmann, a leading translator of Nietzsche and Hegel into English, wrote that having to work very hard to understand a theorist can make you think that the author has a lot to say, though that is not always the case.

I believe that every discipline must develop a visual side. A friend of mine in literary studies at the University of Washington, Cynthia Steele, said to me that every time a position opens in her department, there is a fight between whether it will go to a literature scholar or somebody in film studies. What do the students want? They want film. There is perhaps the false idea that film is easier. In reality, films are very difficult to analyze because they are fundamentally a visual medium. Photography is even more difficult because it offers no narrative. However, I think that the top students choose to study the visual because they recognize its fundamental role in the world we live in today.

In the United States and Europe, scholars from literary studies are beginning to dominate the study of photography. On reviewing my own bookshelves, I discovered that half of my English-language books on photography were written by literary studies academics. It is they who review manuscripts for publication and the books eventually published, and they will probably soon be editors of series on photography. How do they review histories of photography? They ask: Where is Derrida? You did not cite him, so it must be that you have no theory. This emphasis on theory leads to misunderstandings of our tasks. For example, a reviewer of my book *Photographing the Mexican Revolution* criticized my concern with establishing the photos' authors, decrying my ignorance of the critique levied by theorists Abigail Solomon-Godeau and Geoffrey Batchen about borrowing from art history auteurist principles. However, the whole focus of my book was to end the myth that Agustín Víctor Casasola and his family had made all the photos of the revolution in his archive, and to establish who had made them, and for whom. In the midst of a revolution, you are on one side or the other, so every army had its own photographers. In that book, I rewrote the photographic history of the Mexican Revolution, but the only thing the reviewer saw was the absence of theory.

Furthermore, historians and art historians have a very different approach to theory. I read theory. I reread Nietzsche all the time. I read Flusser and theoreticians from the Frankfurt School and photographic theory of scholars such as Sekula, Solomon-Godeau, and Azoulay, among others. We historians use theory as a scaffolding to construct a house. Once it is built, we take the scaffolding down. We do not mention the theorists who have inspired us to write the kind of history we did. Why should we? Theory is important in opening up new questions, leading you to conduct research that you might not have done otherwise. It is not there to be applied like a grid. Flusser calls this "textolatry": idolatry of the text. That period in history is over. We need new thinkers who are interested in the visual.

The tricky thing about the visual is that it looks so easy. People think that anyone can take photographs and that anyone can analyze them. Janey Place told me a story about the visual style analysis work she conducted during her PhD studies at UCLA. She argued to her thesis director that there is a visual hint of a romantic relationship between John Wayne and his brother's wife in John Ford's famous film *The Searchers*. He said that was nonsense. So, Janey showed the film to him without sound, demonstrating how the wife touches John Wayne's coat in an endearing way. She proved her point, and her thesis director then said, "But that's obvious!" Well, yes, it was obvious, but only once he was shown it. That is what is difficult about visual analysis. It looks easy, but the moment that you have to sit down and really write in a rigorous way about photography, nothing is easy at all.

Any discipline that teaches you to look carefully at an image is important. The elements that create meaning in photography—the angles, the focal planes, the illumination, and so on—are relatively limited, but all is mediated by the content of the photos, and the understanding of content is always context-bound. There are contents whose meaning would be very apparent to Mexicans but not at all apparent to someone who did not have the experience of living in Mexico.

I am not saying that people in literature cannot do good work. Mike Weaver, who came from literary studies, did a wonderful job as editor of the journal *History of Photography* at Oxford University from 1991 to 2000. However, rather than focusing on postmodern theory, with which he was well acquainted, he emphasized ways in which to learn to look carefully at a photo. Mike could take a photo and suggest multiple meanings for the image. I think that researchers could use their literary training to search among those alternative readings. One wonderful thing about an image is that everybody is going to read it from their own personal history—their class, gender, race, age, and experience with images—and they bring all that when they look at it. The very act of interrogating photographs helps us become visually literate. The world is controlled today through media. If people cannot decipher the messages that are being put into their heads through images, they enter their heads as mere ciphers that stimulate consumption and manipulate our sexuality, and consequently, our love lives.

Those of us who are working on visual culture face difficulties unique to our studies, from finding good reproductions or having them made, to securing the rights to publish them, to convincing the publisher that the story can be most effectively told with images. All these steps require time, energy, and

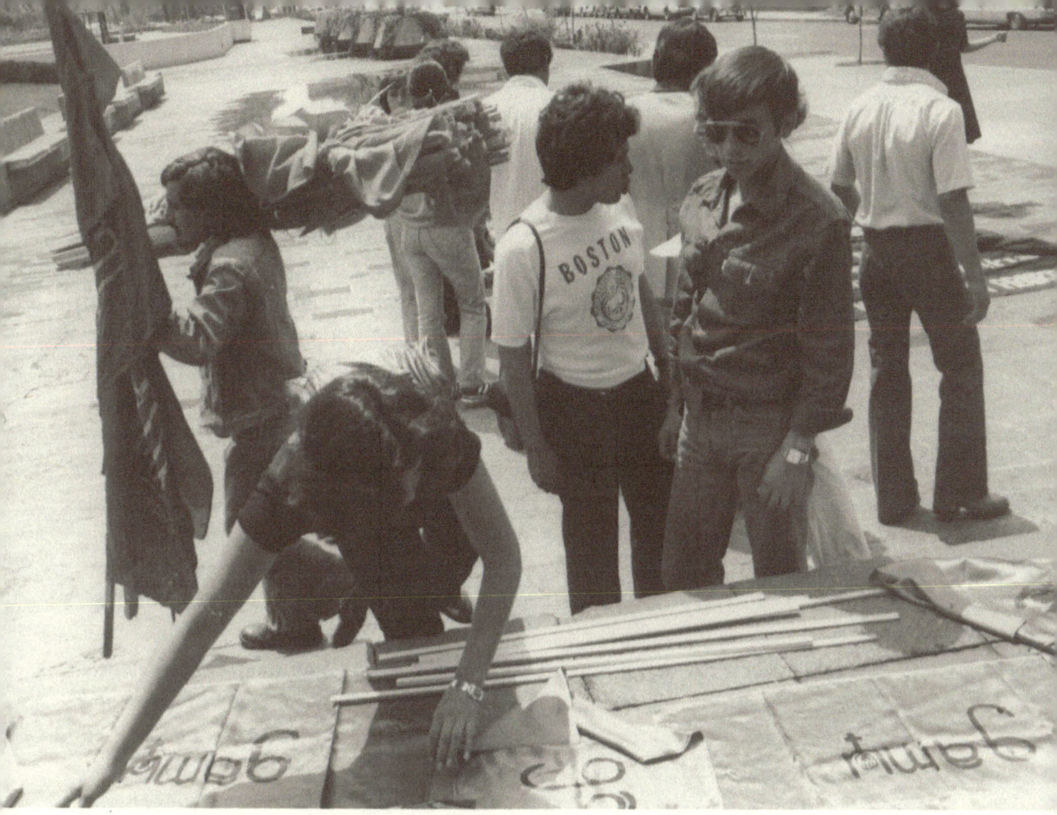

Figure 1.4. Preparations for a protest march against Mother's Day, Mexico City, May 8, 1980. Hermanos Mayo. Archivo General de la Nación, Fondo Hermanos Mayo, Concentrated Section, Manifestación de mujeres.

money, but we must be willing to struggle to include the maximum number of images possible. In the end, the visual must become visible.

The great thing about photography is the way in which it documents the mundane. Nobody writes about the mundane. Nobody paints the mundane. But a photo automatically captures the mundane. In Mexico, I often show a photograph of preparations for a feminist protest there in 1971. A man in the center of the photo is wearing a T-shirt from Boston University, which I use to demonstrate the "Americanization" of Mexican culture.[20] I pose a situation and a question: "You are a historian in the year 2050. What do you find in this photo that is a significant commentary on Mexican culture?" Mexicans very rarely identify the T-shirt. They simply do not see it. I do not think even the Mayo brother who took the photo intended to capture that. He was just taking a photo of the preparations for the march, but the image is a significant testimony to neocolonial culture.

Anyone who is considering studying photography in a scholarly way should start by looking at many photographs and be systematic about how they do so. I would try to learn what is important in a photograph. How can I find that in other photographs? How can I begin to extend my possibilities for talking about a photograph by comparing it to other photographs? How does a photograph's meaning change as it moves across different contexts? That to me is the most important thing. I would not spend my time reading postmodern literary theory, or semiotics, or psychology of perception, and I would be wary of most visual theory in terms of learning how to analyze photographs.

Those readings are not going to tell you how to look at a photograph. The only way to learn how to look at a photograph is to look at many photographs, talk to photographers, and study the contextualization. One of the most important strategies would be to become a photographer yourself. Despite the fact that I would learn a lot by taking photographs, my position is in history, and you can't photograph history—you can only photograph the present. Hence, I focus on writing about photography, but I prefer to express my artistic side by making movies when I can.

I do not think that it is at all easy to write about photography intelligently. You can see those who try to do so in their work. You can see them struggling to find ways to speak rigorously about photographs without taking refuge in some highfalutin theory that does not really say anything about photographs.

My first thought is that you should "just do it," just do your study. Before Nike appropriated it, it was the title of Jerry Rubin's classic book from the 1960s: *Do it.* Years ago, I was teaching in the United States and a graduate student approached me and said, "I really want to make films, but I have to finish my dissertation." To this I replied, "If you want to make films, then start making films. Don't wait."

Once you have done a proper visual analysis often people think it is obvious and easy, but it is not. To study the visual, you must break your teeth over really drawing out of those images everything you can. I think of my poor graduate student Ariel Arnal who wrote a brilliant master's thesis on the images of Zapata between 1910 and 1915 in the newspapers. The thesis became a legend and was photocopied by just about everybody. When he was going to write it, I told him: "Don't just look at the cutlines in the newspapers and draw your conclusions from that. You are working from photography; you have to study the visual representations of Zapata." It took him years to do that, and he had to come up with his own system of doing it. He later told me: "There were times when I really hated you, but you were right. It was something that had to be done." The problem is explaining to historians in language that they can understand because historians are very obdurate, very resistant to new ways of doing history.

One way of explaining the dilemma I am describing is to see it as a translation problem. How do we translate for these people so that they can understand what it is that we are trying to do, and that we are trying to do it with rigor? How can you explain to historians that you are not a fraud? You face very real challenges when you are doing new things. Even today, there are historians who do not understand what I am trying to do, nor the importance of it. They have not yet comprehended that we live in a post-literate world: a hyper-visual world.

One piece of advice I give to students is to tell them to find something that they love because they are going to be doing it all the time. That is the difference between being an intellectual and a scholar: an intellectual is someone who never stops learning and thinking. If you get to do what you want to do, you want to do it twenty-four hours a day. If you are a scholar, you will put in your eight hours a day and then hang up your satchel. I really think that I would have been a very mediocre historian had I not discovered the visual. I am sure that I would not have received invitations from institutions such as Oxford and Princeton had I done normal history because I would not have brought something new. Younger scholars and individuals who want to move into this field must find ways to translate what they are saying into concepts understood by others so that those people can comprehend what it is that they are researching as well as its importance.[21]

Selected Publications

Mraz, John. *Looking for Mexico: Modern Visual Culture and National Identity*. Duke University Press, 2009.

———. *Nacho López, Mexican Photographer*. University of Minnesota Press, 2003.

———. *Photographing the Mexican Revolution: Commitments, Testimonies, Icons*. University of Texas Press, 2012.

Mraz, John, and Jaime Vélez Storey. *Uprooted: Braceros in the Hermanos Mayo Lens*. Arte Público Press, 1996.

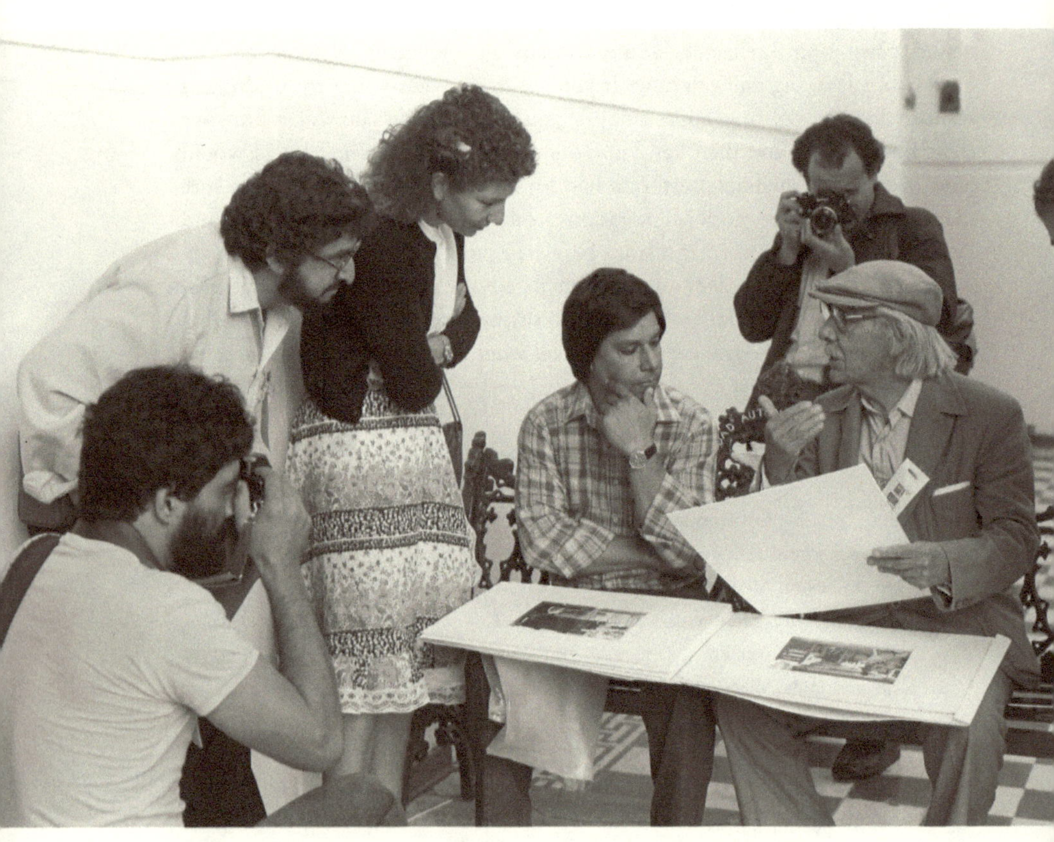

Figure 2.1. Manuel Álvarez Bravo at the 1978 Photography Colloquium in Mexico City. Rebeca Monroy.

Rebeca Monroy Nasr

Instituto Nacional de Antropología e Historia (INAH)

I STUDIED VISUAL arts at the Academia San Carlos, which was the national school of fine arts at the Universidad Nacional Autónoma de México. One of the peculiarities of this school is the fact that it is closely linked to social movements, and I learned how to become a part of those movements through photography. The fact that Academia San Carlos was located in the city center helped it become a part of this milieu. When I started studying at San Carlos in the late 1970s, there were several social movements in the country and most of them had their nexus in Mexico City. I was drawn to photography precisely because I did not know how to draw. Before studying art, I had spent a brief amount of time studying Marx and Engels along with other important thinkers in the field of political science. I was looking for an artistic medium that allowed me to express my ideas quickly, and photography seemed like it would do what I needed. We all wanted to engage with our social reality to work for a better world, and I found I was able to use photography to express myself well. As students, we would watch meetings and marches all the time. I started to work with photography to capture and display all the social movements that I felt were important. At that time, some of the more important topics that caught our attention were the considerable levels of unemployment, unions that were not defending their workers correctly, and the high levels of corruption in society.

When I entered the world of photography in 1978 there were already some important people whose writings were helping us understand the medium better, including Claudia Canales, Eugenia Meyer, Rita Eder, and Néstor García Canclini. I soon began to study them. Additionally, I was lucky enough to receive a Nikon FM for my birthday. It was a present from my father. Thanks to this equipment and my different work and school experiences, I began to learn all the techniques I needed. I began by being Jorge Acevedo's assistant. I cleaned his cameras and helped him to mix the chemicals to develop his photographs. He helped me to get a job working afternoons at the Dirección de

Monumentos Colonials at the Instituto Nacional de Antropología e Historia and to learn how to take documentary photographs. In the morning, I would study at San Carlos. At that time, I thought that I could use my camera to help others understand the social movements and how photography could be used to recover a sense of Mexican history. 1978 was also a watershed year for me because it coincided with the Consejo Mexicano de Fotografía y el Primer Coloquio Latinoamericano de Fotografía. Therefore, it was an important time to be a photographer, researcher, or art critic linked to Mexican photography.

It was a period when a lot of us were all caught up in the world of photography. At that time, Jorge Acevedo, Alicia Ahumada, and Pedro Hiriart had a small darkroom in a closet in their house in General Plata en Mixcoac. That darkroom produced pure magic. Everyone was caught up in taking photographs and participating in social movements. It was an excellent time to work in alternative cultural production because so much was going on. Many of the young students from that period went on to be important leaders in literature, theater, music, and the world of women's rights. However, that period also had its challenges. There were very few places to work. I spent a lot of time doing public exhibitions. We did many of them on the street or in parks like the Alameda in downtown Mexico City. We used to hang our work from cords in these public spaces. We also worked in the university's new Acatlán campus, which had just been opened. We felt like our work was making a difference and reaching people. We published some of our work on the marches and meetings as well as portraits of the leaders of these movements in the magazine *Punto Crítico* in 1978 and 1979.

Over time, I began to be more professional. I published in the magazine *¡Siempre!* thanks to Antonio Saborit. I participated in personal and collective exhibitions. My first collective exhibition was in the Escuela de Diseño y Artesanía with Rubén Pax. Then I did a show in La Casa del Lago in Chapultepec, and it was very successful. They were very intense times, when we were trying to use our knowledge of visual arts to help support the social movements in Mexico.

The Consejo Mexicano de Fotografía was an important response to the growth of the role of photography in society. You could see it everywhere: documentary work, journalism, the writing of history, and even photograph analysis. For that same reason, the Consejo Mexicano de Fotografía became very important because it brought a wide and diverse group of photographers together socially, culturally, and politically. Unlike other associations from before, it was able to show how photography formed a part of visual memory, and it generated a large amount of support throughout Latin America. It enjoyed plastic, aesthetic, artistic, and historical support. The Consejo Mexicano de Fotografía brought together many important historians, art critics, art historians, social scientists and photographers who were becoming professionals.

They put together exhibitions and began to organize the Bienal de Fotografía that took place in 1980. Those events were the beginning of our conferences in Latin America on the study of photography. Critical thinkers and photographers came from all over Latin America, including Cuba, Brazil, Argentina, the United States. It had a huge impact. After attending the conference, I decided that I no longer wanted to be a photojournalist. I wanted to do more.

Shortly after my exhibition *Aquí se construye el Distrito Federal* in the Casa del Lago, I began my BA thesis under the direction of Armando Torres Michúa. He taught art history and art criticism at the Escuela Nacional de Artes Plásticas in the UNAM. He was a Marxist who had a very solid theoretical base. He would make all his students read *Das Kapital* and Arnold Hauser's *Historia social de la literatura y el arte*. He made us read Nicos Hadjinicolaou and his positive-negative analysis of images from an ideological perspective. He taught us to read history and theory on the classics of art history. At that time, no one had written the history of photography in Mexico. The book/catalog of the exhibition *Imagen histórica de la fotografía en México* helped me to understand how to use our materials and our history, and it indicated new directions the study of photography in Latin America could take. I began to think that I would like to work in that field and that then was the time to do so. That book helped me to realize that there was much to be written on photography in Mexico. At that time, there were mostly just some articles in *Artes Visuales del Museo de Arte Moderno*. Facing such vast and virgin territory, I began to work with what little there was to form the ideas for my thesis.

Around that time, Carlos Jurado had published his book *El arte de la aprehensión de las imágenes y el unicornio* which helps us to think about the history of photography, and it teaches you how to work with and make photographs in different ways. For example, his book teaches you how to take photographs with a cardboard box and how to do photography with other household items. This book has been key to how I see and work with photography.

Armed with that information, I decided to teach a class on alternative technologies and photography. I made my cardboard boxes to be used as cameras, organized my notes, and I went off to the outskirts of Mexico City: Ciudad Nezahualcóyotl. There I taught a class to both children and adults. I wanted to help the popular classes and work with marginal communities. It was a very productive and enjoyable time. It was very moving to work and teach there, and it allowed me to move forward with my desire to do something documentary and aesthetic. I wanted to share what I had learned with others. It was during this time that I met photographers such as Pedro Valtierra, Javier Hinojosa, Alicia Ahumada, David Maawad, Marco Antonio Cruz, Jorge Acevedo, and Agustín Estrada. They were all very dedicated photographers whose work had already had an impact. After working with them, I began to become interested in the theoretical side of photography. In February of 1982, I successfully took an exam at the INAH to secure a place as a cultural object photographer in the Department of Archaeological Records. It was there that I encountered Carlos Jurado's work on Xalapa. I discovered that he was not only teaching students and writing about alternative technologies. He was also trying to create a degree in photography at the Universidad Veracruzana. At the same time, the visual artist Laura González Flores was working on her bachelor's thesis on photography. After being Carlos Jurado's student, she made some beautiful cyanotype photographs that won some competitions and went on to study photography with academic rigor (González Flores *Fotografía*).

At that moment there was no real degree in photography at the Escuela Nacional de Artes Plásticas at any level. There was no real systematic form of knowledge in the field of the study of photography at all. To learn how to work with photography I had to work with Armando Torres Michúa who taught me how to historicize and write art criticism. Since there were very little theoretical platforms to work with, I thought that I could probably write my thesis using the art history methodology. I worked toward a master's degree under the direction of Dr. Aurelio de los Reyes. He used very unconventional methods to explore and work in art history, but his work was very good. It was this experience that convinced me that I wanted to study the history of photography in the future. I also undertook a doctoral degree thanks to Dr. Aurelio de los Reyes. For my doctoral thesis, I worked on the photographer Enrique Díaz Reina who I had learned about thanks to Mariana Yampolsky who was undertaking a project with his photographs. Enrique Díaz's archive is in the Archivo General de la Nación (AGN) and contains over a half a million of his negatives. The AGN had asked Yampolsky to curate an exhibition on his work at a time (in the 1990s) that Enrique Díaz was virtually unknown. Mariana Yampolsky showed me the archive and its wonderful qualities. Enrique Díaz has excellent work in many different areas: social, political, and aesthetic. Most of his work held at AGN are negatives that he had ordered and classified himself. In them, you could see women from the 1920s, plays, workers, actresses, portraits of politicians and artists, social life, political and religious conflicts, cultural objects and urban discourse, as well as architecture (*Historias para ver* 365). *Historias para ver* was my second book on his work. My first was my thesis: *De luz y plata: Apuntes sobre tecnología alternativa en la fotografía.*

I worked hard to find a way to advance from being a photographer at the INAH to being a researcher there. At that time, there was a possibility of changing my contract from that of a technician to a researcher by developing and executing a research project. I submitted a project on Enrique Díaz. By that time, Yampolsky had finished her exhibition *Bailes y balas* that we showed at the AGN itself. Mariana Yampolsky let me write part of the exhibition catalog. My project on using photography as a historical source was accepted by the

Dirección de Estudios Históricos, and I studied my MA and PhD in art history within the Facultad de Filosofía y Letras in the UNAM. I was able to use my technical knowledge on photography as I wrote about art theory and aesthetics. I was able to apply these fields to my knowledge of photojournalism and documentary photography. These areas of learning helped me to put together the story of Enrique Diaz's professional life as a photographer. To do so, I used many sources: negatives, photographs, glass negatives, acetatos, cameras, his paperwork, his work diary, and information I gathered from periodical libraries, his work colleagues and his photo agency that began back in 1920, *Fotografías de la Actualidad.* His body of work is excellent for forming a visual chronicle of urban life in Mexico.

Methodology

Experience has taught me that the more tools you have as a researcher, the better. I have acquired different methodologies on social art history and traditional art history as I have worked through different projects. I learned how to understand social art, poetics, aesthetics, plastic elements and techniques, art criticism, communication theory, reception theory, psychoanalysis theory, many different areas of art theory, among all the different fields that I have come to draw upon. As a student, I opted to remain aloof from the many different political groups around, avoiding aligning myself with any one party. I decided that it was more important to do and circulate good work, be it mine or that of my colleagues, than to tow a political line.

One of the research questions that has driven my work has been: How do photographic development processes influence work? This led me to ask which art methodologies were capable of interfacing with photography or not. It also led me to ask what social theories could be used to understand art more effectively. I concluded that there was no single way to study photography. You can be very eclectic with photography because, in many ways, the tools you use depend on what you want to know. Those with a documentary approach will want to know some things and will use certain tools; others will employ different tools to discover other pieces of knowledge. The one area that is relevant to virtually all scholars who want to work with a series of photographs is to have a complete comprehension of their context and creation.

El Gordo Díaz: Many Ways of Working

I am very passionate about my work with Enrique "El Gordo" Díaz. Some historians have classified him as a "reactionary"; but I say that, even if that classification is correct, reactionaries need to be studied too. His work has given me a corpus on which to center my attention. It allowed me to understand him, photography,

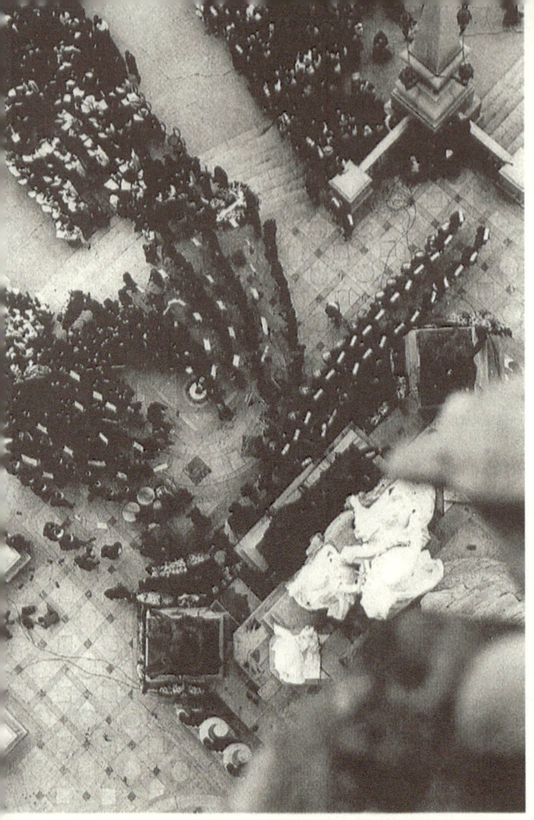

Figure 2.2. Concierto en el Ángel de la Independencia (Concert at the Ángel de la Independencia), Mexico City, 1921. Enrique Díaz Reyna. Archivo General de la Nación.

and Mexican society. He was the illegitimate son of a Lebanese immigrant, and he was very different from your average Mexican. He had great talent and many redeeming qualities. He was very self-motivated. He was an entrepreneur, inclusive, a hard worker, profound, and determined. He wanted to be someone, to be known. He felt the need to compete with the Casasola institution. He wanted his work to get covers, to make a clear impact. He worked as a regular photographer, then as a news photographer, and later as a photo essayist. Others such as Nacho López and Héctor García followed in his footsteps and worked his lines. My experience with photography helped me to see these distinctions and to identify his place in the history of Mexican photography.

I think that the fact that Mariana Yampolsky was a foreigner helped her to see Enrique Díaz's work in a new light. She considered other photographers, but she saw other ways in which he was doing new things and how he was a trendsetter. I think that the fact that Yampolsky was from the United States and that she knew about art from her father helped her to detect traits in certain photographers that others could not see. Maybe because she was not originally from Mexico she was able to see certain things in Mexico that we natural Mexicans take for granted or overlook. It was a bit like Edward Weston and his ability to find beauty in sombreros, homemade toys, or other Mexican faces or objects. Being an outsider can have its advantages because you seem to acquire a different taste for certain things. Yampolsky's critical eye was finely tuned, and it helped her to detect details others would have not seen or perhaps would set aside to work on more famous individuals like the Hermanos Mayo. I saw what she had collected from Enrique Díaz's archive, and I agreed that Díaz had something special. He is one of the forerunners of the new photojournalism in Mexico that began in the 1930s. Díaz made an important mark in the 1940s when the illustrated magazines were at their peak and during the 1950s when photography was being consolidated and being put to political use. I decided that I would focus on his work from the 1920s and 1930s because that was the part of his work that had been studied the least.

I wrote a small biography on Enrique Díaz for the book *Bailes y balas* that Yampolsky put together. While I was doing that, I discovered that Enrique Díaz had covered the María Teresa de Landa case. That woman had been Miss Mexico in 1928, and in 1929, she became what we call in Mexico an *autoviuda*, a "self-made widow." She was one of a number of women in the 1920s who had killed their husbands because they had been cheated on or suffered emotional or physical abuse. María Teresa de Landa had won the title of Miss Mexico in 1928 and then went on to represent Mexico in a beauty pageant that took place in the United States. When she returned, she married a general named Moises Vidal, and after less than one year of marriage to him, she found out that he was already married to another woman (also named María Teresa, last name Herrejón) who was suing them both. They were both going to go to jail for bigamy. When she read this in the newspaper, she grabbed his revolver and shot him five times. He died in his living room. Aurelio de los Reyes has studied the phenomena on the autoviudas (*Siglo XX: La imagen*) and he does so from the perspective of art history by using images in the press and considering their legal, cultural, and political repercussions.

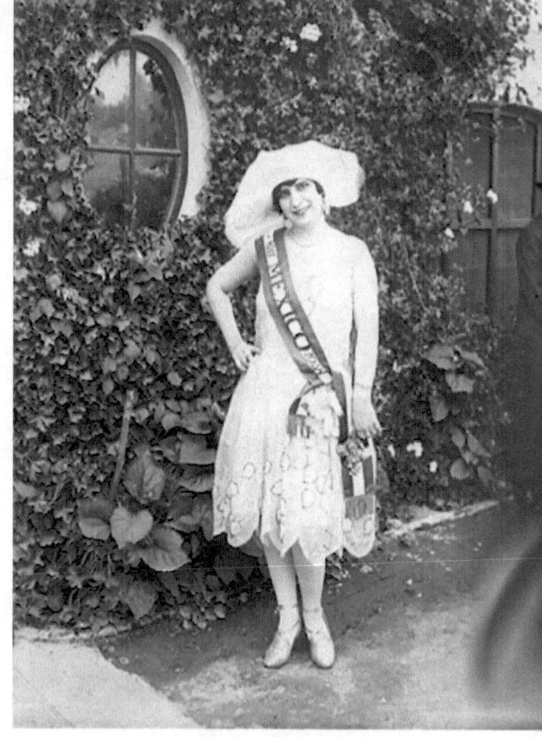

Figure 2.3. María Teresa de Landa el día que ganó como Miss México (María Teresa de Landa on the day she won the title of Miss Mexico), May 17, 1928. Enrique Díaz Reyna. Archivo General de la Nación.

I also decided to work with this topic. Díaz's photographs allow for a reading that includes topics such as gender, society, politics, and a little bit of everything really. That specific collection is very rich in information. The María Teresa de Landa story is a fascinating one for postrevolutionary Mexico that allowed me to speak about beauty pageants from that period: how they worked, who participated, where the events took place, what they represent, and how these events fit within gender and women's studies. I was also able to study de Landa's husband. Because he had belonged to the military, I was

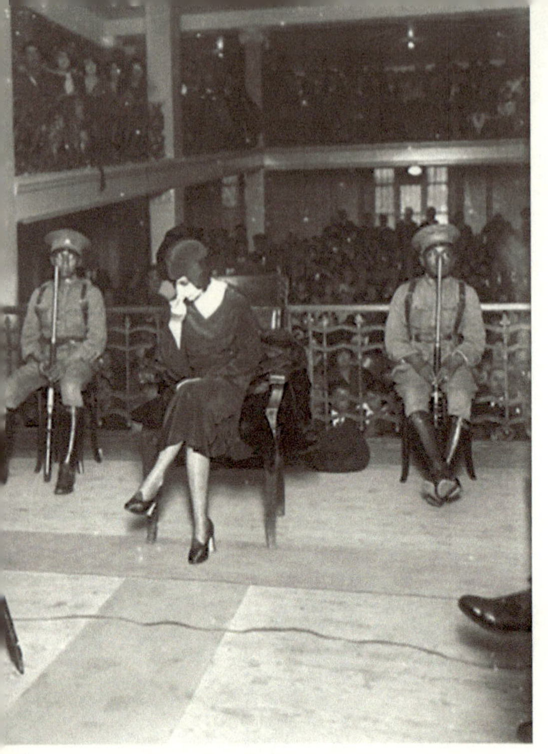

Figure 2.4. María Teresa de Landa en el juicio en su contra por matar a su bígamo esposo (María Teresa de Landa at the courthouse awaiting her trial for having killed her bigamist husband), November 1929. Enrique Díaz Reyna. Archivo General de la Nación.

able to research his military file. I discovered that he was a counterrevolutionary who had done some dastardly work. He had fought against the Zapatistas, the Carrancistas, and the Constitucionalistas. It was an extremely interesting story full of subtleties that showed how the military fought against the civil state and against modern women. The visual narrative rested on two important images that Enrique Díaz took. One was taken the day she won the Miss Mexico contest, and the other was taken the day that she went to trial. Her trial was the last trial by jury in Mexico. It took place toward the end of December 1929, and a new penal code began to be enforced in January of 1930. This change took place in part because none of the autoviudas were ever found guilty.

The María Teresa de Landa research required me to work with the images in the Mexican press. I consulted the *Excélsior* because it was the newspaper that sponsored the beauty pageant. I was able to study the announcement of the event, the advertisements, the use of coupons in order to vote in the pageant, the interviews with the contestants, and other aspects of the event. I also studied two other newspapers: *El Universal* and *El Nacional*. The newspapers featured both of the photographs that I mentioned earlier, and it was easy to see where the research was leading. Between the newspapers, the Enrique Díaz archive, and the Casasola archive I was able to obtain all the visual material I needed. Several of Díaz's students, including Dr. Luis de la Barreda, Francisco Pérez Arce, and Gerardo Monroy Alvarado, were able to fill in gaps with the oral history that they provided during their interviews. I could not have written this study with only the pictures. While they were important, I needed a variety of sources to write the full history in my book-length study. Hence, you can see that Enrique Díaz's work has given me an ample amount of source material.

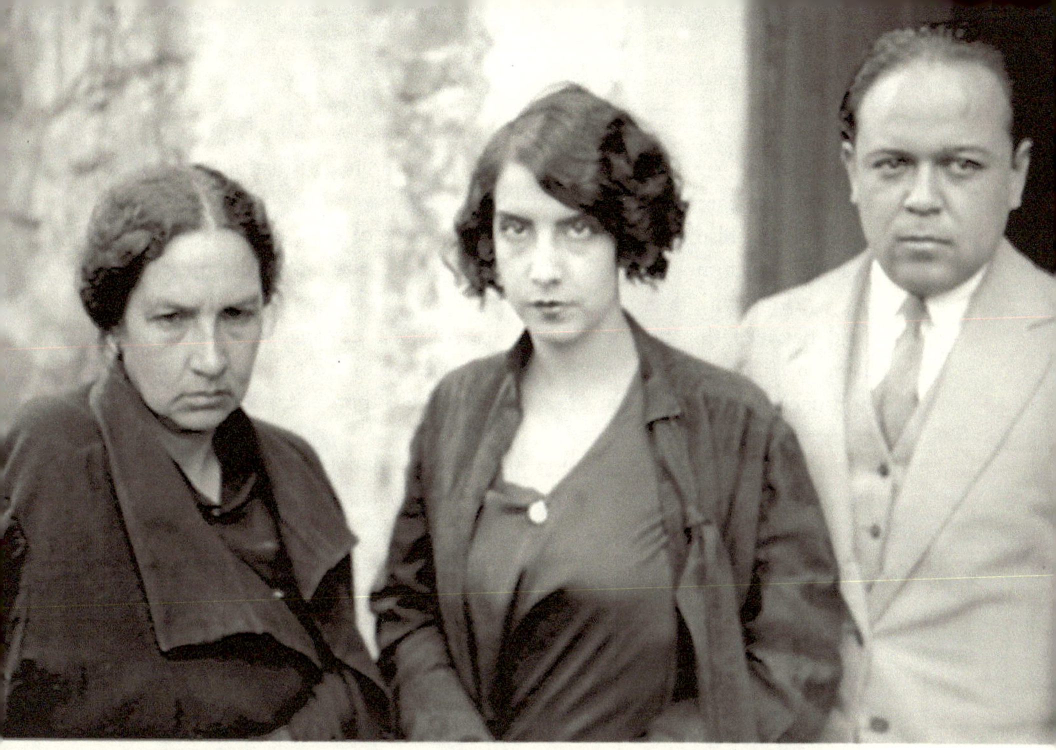

Figure 2.5. María Teresa de Landa con su madre cárcel de Belen antes de su juicio (María Teresa de Landa with her mother outside Belen Jail awaiting her Trail), 1929. Enrique Díaz Reyna. INAH.

Theory

I read a lot of theory, but more than filtering all of my research though one line of theory or being some strict disciple of some theorist in France, England, the United States, or even Latin America, I decided to analyze the material that I encountered, and I identified the appropriate ideas that apply to each set of information. I have worked with art history. That field has offered me many tools. I tend to work in the area of microhistory. This gives me a methodology to work with and a basic framework to build each subject. I make a strong effort to say something new with my work. I love cultural history, the social nature of culture, and the cultural elements in the social aspects of society. Roger Chartier's ideas have helped me to develop those ideas with clarity and have given me the added perspective that I need to undertake that kind of research. Boris Kossoy's texts, Peter Burke's *Eyewitnessing*, Barthes's *Camera Lucida*, and Phillipe Duboise's *El acto fotográfico* have given me tools to think about how to study semiotics in photographs. I use terms such as *el punctum*, *el índice*, and *lo denotative* and *connotativo*, *diacrónico*, and *sincrónico* in my analysis. Personally, I think that using semiotics to study photography makes perfect sense because many of the ideas from the texts I just mentioned blend well with research tools from art history. However, I tend to use art history, comparative history, visual history, the history of the gaze, and intertextual readings much more in my analysis. I think they are more relevant when you are working with documentary photography or press photography. You must read between the lines when you are studying newspapers and magazines. Being a critical reader is of vital importance. You need to adapt the analytical approach to every different situation; one single approach will not give you the best results.

I have also worked on other projects not related to Enrique Díaz. One of those was on Ezequiel Carrasco, a photographer whose work covers periods just before and after Díaz. Carrasco covered La Decena Trágica. I called my book on his work *Revista de Revistas, Ezequiel Carrasco: De las balas de bronce a las de plata.* Carrasco's work allows me to reveal how photojournalists functioned during the Mexican Revolution. While the technology at that time would not allow him to take the kind of photographs that he might have wanted to (he seemed to have a taste for photographic images that involved movement), a lot of his images appear to evoke cinema in their approach. I have also studied social movements during the 1970s and the 1980s like in my book *Con el deseo en la piel: Un episodio de fotografía documental mexicana a fines del siglo XX.*

Lessons I Have Learned While Working with Photography

I approach photography through social history. You need to avoid reading photographs by supposing what emotions might have been present at the time the image was taken. Contextualization is key to avoid speculations and error. I think that Ana María Mauad's advice to "write the photograph's biography" is very useful (*Como nascem as imagens?*). If you are looking at a group picture for example, you need to see what happened to the group. Where did its members go? You need to apply social history and work with outside sources as well. Comparative history is useful too. How and why was the group photo taken? What happened during the moment of the photo? What social forces were in play? If a news reporter took it, what newspaper did he or she work for, and what do we know about the publication venue? How often did the news reporter publish with that publication? Who worked with him? Such questions are very useful. For example, when Enrique Díaz worked for the magazine *Todo*, he worked with a man who used the pseudonym Gliebb, which is supposed to mean "bread" in Russian. Gliebb was a dedicated militant whose real name was Jorge Piñó Sandoval. Hence, a relevant research question to ask is, what type of work did Díaz do when he worked with Gliebb? Well, he did a lot of work on women during those times in the 1930s. Gliebb worked with table dancers, ticket sellers, women who sold beer, and he even covered Amelia Earhart when she came to Mexico. Therefore, knowing Gliebb's work is relevant to understanding Gliebb's contact with Díaz and his influence on him.

There are other relevant questions to develop as well. How did Díaz develop his visual style? I study his techniques, both the formal ones and the informal ones. I look at the camera he uses, how he touches up his photographs, how he frames his images, where he publishes them, and I consider his formal techniques. I study how the photographer treats his visual subjects. For example, Díaz showed a lot of empathy when he photographed children. He was very forward with his camera. He has very few photographs taken from side views. In most of his work, Díaz is facing his subjects. All these details help you to identify a photographer's style.

You must decide if a photographer was a good or a bad photographer and be able to support your evaluation with evidence. There are bad photographers who create excellent visual documents, but you need to be able to say why his images are good or bad. If the photographer worked with an editor, you want to know who the editor was because his or her viewpoint is critical to understanding how the work was portrayed. Perhaps most importantly you need to know what was photographically possible when that photograph was taken. This has important implications as well because you can fall into many traps if you do not.

Traps

There are many pitfalls to avoid when you are analyzing photographs. When I am teaching my students, I always remind them: "You have to put yourself in the photographer's tripod." You need to know how the photographer worked and what was possible when he or she was working. You cannot hold a photographer who was working with glass negatives and a camera with bellows to the same standards that you would a photographer with access to today's digital technology. You must understand the cultural environment in which he was working as well. There are many social forces at play. You need to understand what the photographer was trying to achieve with his work. You want to be able to empathize with the situation of the creator and the moment of his creation. A "bad photographer" just may have had many more social factors at play that limited what was possible.

Putting yourself in the photographer's tripod and knowing the context is vital. There was one time when I presented at a small conference. I spoke about a photograph of the Ángel de la Independencia on the Avenida de la Reforma in Mexico City. It is a black-and- white image that has lots of little black-and-white squares in it that remind the viewer of a chessboard. It was taken from high above, looking down from the point of the view of the angel at the top of the monument. It was taken in 1921 during a concert that was part of the events to celebrate the monument's centenary. When I showed the image, a member of the audience commented that the image was insignificant. However, if you understand the context of the photograph, you soon realize that person could not have been more wrong. The image in question was very important because it anticipates the Soviet visual style that had still not arrived in Mexico. I showed that the image arrived before the film *El Gabinete del doctor Caligari* or the cultural and political influences brought to Mexico by the Russian Ambassador Aleksandra Kolontái. Hence, Mexico was still unfamiliar with Soviet cinema, and this picture proves that this style was already in Mexico prior to these events. Previously, scholars thought that it came to Mexico along with the Soviet influences I just mentioned or with the Hermanos Mayo who came as Spanish Civil War refugees. Therefore, knowing the context enables you to rewrite Mexico's visual history by proving that images with bird's-eye and worm's-eye views are already in Mexico in 1921.

So, it is so important to know places and dates and to study many different photographs. This allows you to place an image and say why it is important or not, or why it is ahead of its time or not. Reading images is like reading poetry. You need to read many of them before you can get a feel of how to do it. You must dive into the visual work and really saturate your mind with it. You must ask yourself questions and determine who is imitating whom. This is what helps you to separate the unique from the mundane, and the good from the bad. There are photographers whose technique is 100 percent on point but whose ideology is very conservative and vice versa. You must avoid snap judgements because they can often take you down the wrong path.

I always give my students a few recommendations.

> Do not judge or label photographers or their images.
>
> Only write what is sensible and that which is certain.
>
> Become very familiar with the historical period in which you are working and develop an in-depth bibliography.
>
> Put yourself in the photographer's shoes.

There is much work to be done. Many photographers merit our attention. There are many photo documentarists: Rodrigo Moya, Héctor García, Enrique Bostelmann, Enrique Bordes Mangel, and the Casasola Dynasty to name just a few. Los Hermanos Mayo and Enrique Díaz have incredible work yet to be studied. There are many women too. María Santibañez from the 1920s; María Amparo Hernández took some incredible nude photographs for magazines in the 1930s. These creators are just some of the Mexicans. There are many Cubans who merit our attention as well: Mayito, Korda, and Mario García Joya to name just three. The list goes on and on.

The study of photography in Latin America is still very new. Brazil and Mexico are leading the field right now. At the Escuela Nacional de Antropología e Historia (ENAH) in Mexico there is now a postgraduate degree in image and national history. There is not another one like it in all of Latin America. The Universidad Nacional Autónoma de México now has a massive collection of photographs and historical documents. There are now over one hundred completed postgraduate dissertations on photography and history in the UNAM. We now have academics such as Claudia Canales, Eugenia Meyer, Rita Eder, and Néstor García Canclini who are beginning to write a theory of photography for Latin America. Researchers like myself are the second generation here, and the third generation is now well prepared for the research yet to come. Personally, I see a bright future ahead.

Our seminar series in Mexico City, "La mirada documental," seems to have grown every time we meet. It is very rich and has many projects to develop and stories to share and cultivate. There is no specific methodology or ideology in the group. It is not like painting. You do not have to affiliate with a specific school to belong. Everyone researches according to the material they have and the method they feel is most appropriate. As a group we work well together; this academic harmony helps us to progress in our different endeavors and to publish and produce with positivity.

Selected Publications

Monroy Nasr, Rebeca. *Con el deseo en la piel: Un episodio de fotografía documental mexicana a fines del siglo XX*. Universidad Autónoma Metroplitana (Unidad Xochimilco), 2017.

———. *De luz y plata: Apuntes sobre tecnología alternativa en la fotografía*. Instituto Nacional de Antropología e Historia (INAH), 1998.

———. *Historias para ver: Enrique Díaz fotorreportero*. IIE-UNAM and INAH, 2003.

———. *Revista de Revistas, Ezequiel Carrasco: De las balas de bronce a las de plata*. INAH, 2010.

Alberto del Castillo

Instituto Mora

Photography and the Emergence of the Modern Concept of Childhood

I BEGAN STUDYING the history of photography as part of my doctoral studies at El Colegio de Mexico. On that occasion, I used photography to study the emergence of the modern concept of childhood in Mexico. I was fortunate enough to publish my doctoral dissertation as the book *Conceptos, imágenes y representaciones de la niñez en México*. Dr. Solange Alberro, an important specialist in cultural history and mentalities in Mexico, headed my dissertation committee. Over the course of my PhD (1995–2001), I was able to discuss my findings on many occasions during a postgraduate seminar series that Dr. Alberro held with myself, Erika Pani, Elisa Speckman, and Claudia Agostoni. It was a real privilege to listen to their critical insights and their ideas, since these women are some of the most critical minds in the country. Thanks to a scholarship, I was also fortunate enough to be able to go to the New School University in New York and work under Professor Deborah Poole. That experience was particularly important because it granted me access to a completely new set of bibliographical material than what I had found in Mexico at that time.

In my doctoral dissertation I make photography my central focus, and I use it to analyze the rise of scientific thought related to childhood. At the same time, I also study the shift in photographic expression concerning children. To do so, I studied family albums from the second half of the nineteenth century, carte-de-visite postcards from the Porfirian era, and the first police and news reports that included photographs of children. My body of work ranged from the mid-1800s to the 1920s (including the Mexican Revolution). Covering that time period meant that I needed to include documentary photography, which contained a density and profundity that was much greater than the stereotypical picturesque and folkloric images that were commonly found in Mexico from that era. Photographic expression linked to children became one of the topics of documentary photography during the Mexican Revolution. As the Mexican

Revolution advanced, the raw nature of the subjects that circulated among the visual public became increasingly palatable to them, and over time, this changed how politics was projected and understood.

My research required several years of gathering and studying materials that traced cultural history from that period. This placed me in contact with photographic expression and the evolution of photographic images from the second half of the nineteenth century until the 1920s in Latin America. I found it necessary to review the international history of photography and how it depicted Mexico as found in the international press and from the Mexican newspapers during those years. Hence, I studied the photographs that were part of the news reports on the Mexican Revolution. In this sense, my first book can be viewed as one that interfaces with the predominant paradigms related to the history of photography in Mexico at that time. My book also applies Deborah Poole's ideas regarding visual economy in the Andes to a Mexican context. Likewise, I dialogue with ideas from international photography scholars such as Mike Weaver, Anne Hammond, Nikolas Rose, and Vivian Zelizer to connect my work to the global discussion on photography and local photography scholars (such as John Mraz, Néstor García Canclini, and Ricardo Pérez Montfort) whose work helped me to understand how my study could find local application.

Social History and Photography in Mexico

I have used photography as a focal point for my academic discussion on several topics. During the past fifteen years I have written on social history and photography from the second half of the twentieth century. This work attempts to understand how we can use photography to enter into new discussions with other texts written by scholars who publish on Mexico and Latin America during this increasingly complex historical period. If you study this time period, one of the events you must analyze is the 1968 Mexican student movement. This was a series of popular protests that has become one of the most important events in Mexico's recent history. These protests intended to create a grievance against the state of law during a period of the Mexican political system when the state was functioning without the proper level of checks and balances between the executive, legislative, and judicial powers.

I was working within this historical frame of reference as I tried to analyze photography's different uses and movements during the second half of the twentieth century. This meant that I had to work with several different sources that produced what we know from that time period: the photographs that were published in illustrated magazines and newspapers. This type of narrative is key as you study photography because it became the counter-dialogue to the official discourse that independent photographers such as Pedro Meyer, Héctor García, Rodrigo Moya, Manuel Álvarez Bravo, and Enrique Bordes Mangel offered. To this corpus you must also add the visual narrative that the Mexican state's intelligence agencies created during this period. This last narrative was ordered by those in power in the Mexican government to follow and persecute the young dissidents.

This research required the study of a visual corpus of approximately ten thousand images to draw my new conclusions. I wanted to focus on the leading images whose discourse supported those main ideas that would enable me to speak about how these images fit within the historical narrative. I wanted to use them to underline some of the problems with the previous historical concepts on a variety of subjects. These considerations included the visual representations of youth and their political connections or the appropriation and usage of urban spaces as part of the new way in which they understand and exercise citizenship.

Mexico's 1968 Student Movement and Photos

One of the issues that I found myself discussing as I wrote about this topic involves the images' production and how their meanings transformed as the photographs entered different contexts. There is a very relevant example that helps us understand this point. Pedro Meyer took a photograph of the student movement activities during August of 1968. This picture features two young women in a play that symbolizes the death of the Mexican political system. As they cry out in the photograph, other students carry a coffin behind them. However, that same photograph became the cover image for Elena Poniatowska's watershed book *La noche de Tlatelolco* (published in English as *Massacre in Mexico*). This book is, without a doubt, the most influential book on the 1968 student movement that was ever published. It became a bestseller that was based on interviews with the members of the Consejo Nacional de Huelga who were in the Lecumberri Prison in Mexico City and with many other members of the public. This book is considered essential reading by my generation and continues to be read by thousands of students in the whole country while remaining a key historical reference point to this day.

This widely disseminated visual coverage and its linkage to such an important narrative has led to a shift in how the public read the photograph. Instead of being happy and casual as it was in its original context, its subsequent linkage to the grimness of the student massacre on October 2, 1968, has changed the photograph's meaning. It shows you how the interpretation of an image can be drastically modified when you link an image to a text that is intended to process recent history and form a model for understanding it. It obliges us to read the image in a way that coincides with the meaning of the text. Personally, I think that understanding this specific usage of photography and how it changes our perception of it is one of the most important ways in which we can study the history of photography. Unlike art history, which is anchored to very conventional concepts, this type of reading (that photography allows) enables us to trace a broader understanding of social phenomena and the concepts within which they occur.

One of the specific challenges that I have faced is on the other side of my research agenda. In this case, it is related to my work with Zapatismo and Pedro Valtierra's iconic photo of the Indigenous X'oyep women who were confronting soldiers from the Mexican Army on January 3, 1998, in order to defend their lands. This event occurred only ten days after the terrible Acteal massacre in Chiapas during which a group of paramilitary soldiers murdered forty-five men, women, and children who were praying in a small church. They did this with support from the governing Partido Revolucionario Institucional (Institutional Revolutionary Party; PRI) at that time.

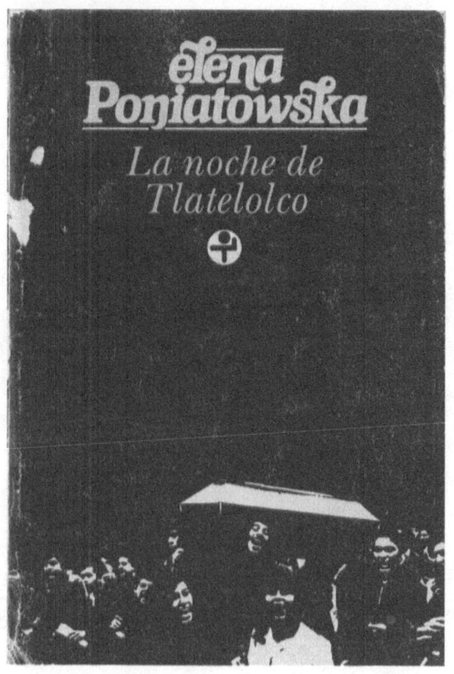

Figure 3.1. Cover of *La noche de Tlatelolco* by Elena Poniatowska, Ediciones Era, 1971.

The Mexican newspaper *La Jornada* published Valtierra's photograph of the X'oyep women, and just a month later, it received the famous Rey de España prize. This prize turned the photograph into a key global image on Zapatismo. In response to this, I wrote a book on Pedro Valtierra's images in his personal photo archive in order to understand the prize-winning photograph. The archive to which I am referring is found in the photo agency Cuartoscuro in Mexico City. Part of my context-building exercise for this book were my interviews with Valtierra and some of the editors and journalists who worked directly with his photography. I also consulted with several writers and intellectuals that have referred to Valtierra's famous photograph of the X'oyep women. Some use the image as a symbol of Indigenous resistance. Others use it as an example as ideological extremism. Still others employ the image to praise the Mexican Army's actions because they resisted the women without violence.

Context Is Key

I was interested in the different readings or interpretations that this image has provoked to justify different political projects. Among those who have referred to this photograph is Elena Poniatowska, who underlines the need to see these photographs as a type of resistance mechanism that the women show in the face of military oppression. This opinion is vastly different from that of Rafael Cardona who worked closely with Ernesto Zedillo's government in Mexico at that time. He stated that the photograph evidenced the Mexican Army's extreme tolerance, arguing that this quality was what set them apart from the Central American military who surely would have massacred the same Indigenous women in parallel circumstances.

A further testimony was that of Subcomandante Marcos himself who gave a keynote speech on the photograph to the Escuela Nacional de Antropología e Historia students in March 2001. He agreed with Elena Poniatowska's reading of the image, which of course reinforces the idea that this image is one of the most important visual icons of the Zapatistas. My analysis of these processes in my book helps us observe that it is important to consult many sources before declaring concrete and academic conclusions about an image.

Photo Essays Reveal Microhistories

In 2013, I began researching Marco Antonio Cruz's photographic trajectory because he is one of the most important photo documentarians in present-day Mexico. He has more than forty years of professional experience that began with newspapers and left-wing weeklies connected to the Communist Party in the 1970s. Later, he was one of the founding members of the photography department in *La Jornada*, a newspaper of substantial influence in Mexico. *La Jornada* itself and Antonio Cruz's photographs in that publication were constantly an emblem of Mexico's intelligentsia during the 1980s. After that venture, Marco Antonio Cruz created his own photo agency: *Imagenlatina*. He has been the author of several of the most important photo essays in recent years. For example, his essay "Cafeteleros" shows you the precarious conditions in which Mexicans and Guatemalans work as they harvest coffee beans in Chiapas, Mexico. His photo essay "Habitar la oscuridad" is an amazing narrative on blindness in Mexico that led Antonio Cruz to work with the blind over the course of seventeen years. In the essay he shows us how these individuals adapt to their personal circumstances, resist oppression, and face daily adversity. The photographer does this with immense documentary rigor and with artistic beauty that has rarely been seen in Latin American photography in recent years. I think that he is one of the most important photographers to have appeared since the 1968 Mexican student movement. An analysis of his life and work enables us to place him within the best of Latin American photojournalism in the 1980s and the very political and aesthetic world of the photo essay, where the use of symbols and documentary images can speak to the reader in unique ways.

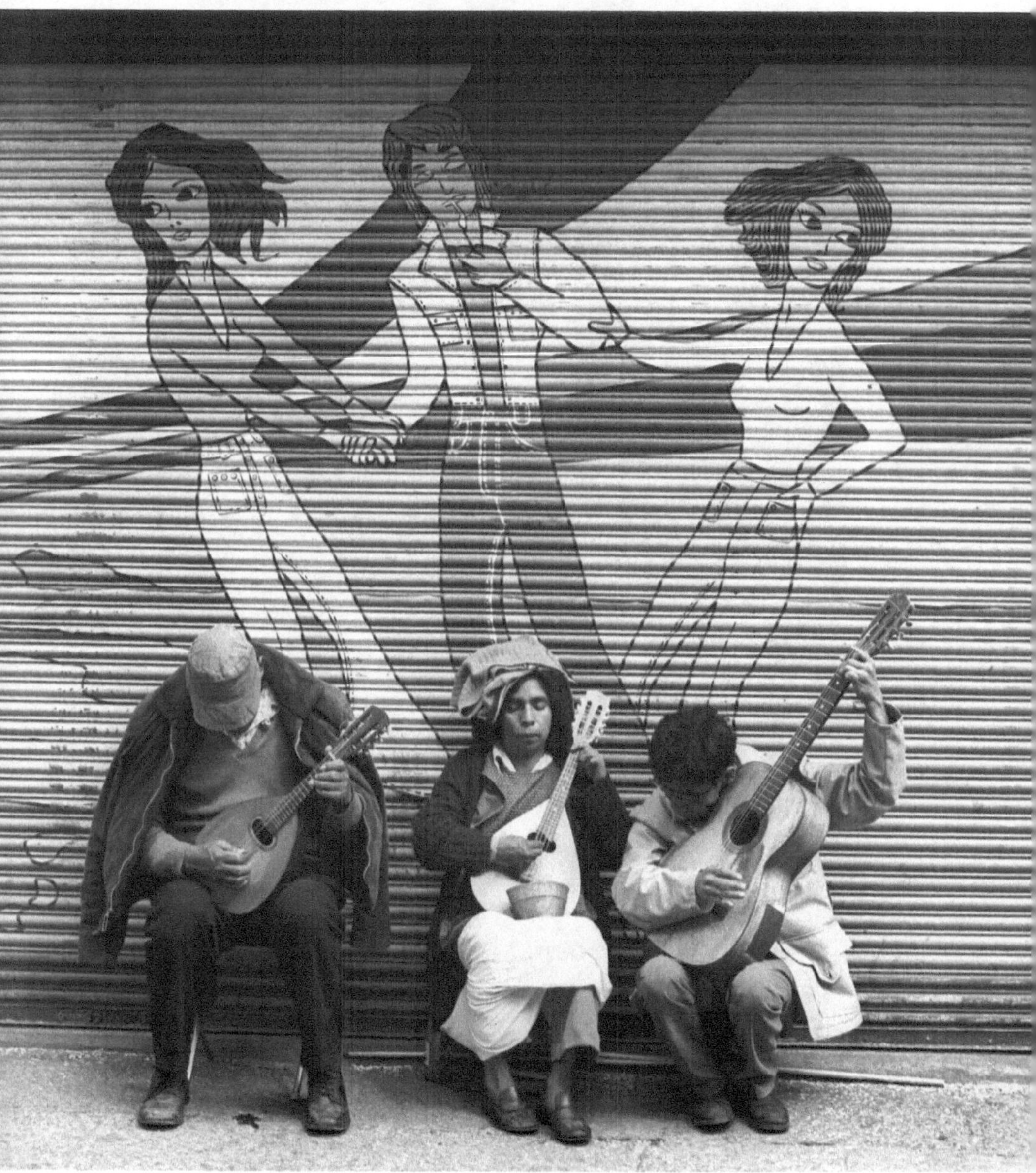

Figure 3.2. Tres músicos ciegos (Three blind musicians), Puebla, Mexico, 1977. Marco Antonio Cruz. Archivo Fotográfico.

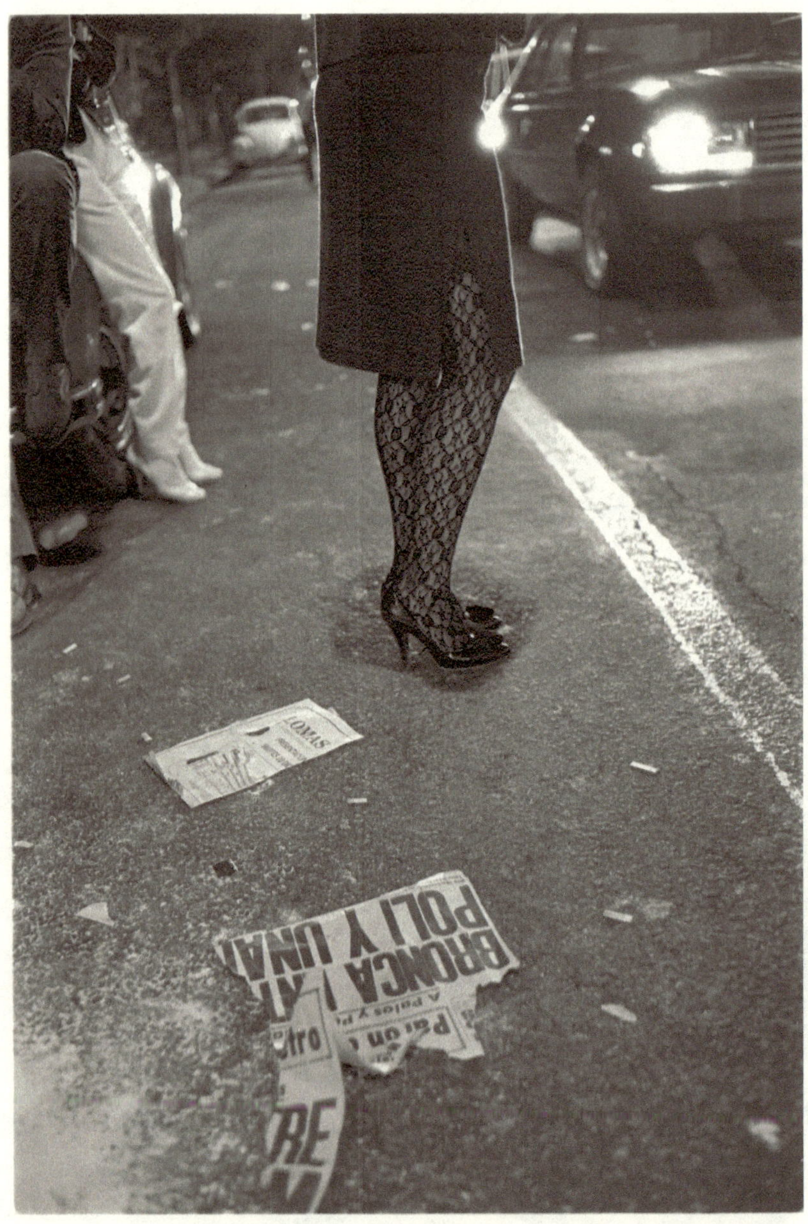

Figure 3.3. Sexoservicio, Río Panúco, Col. Cuauhtémoc (Sex worker, Río Panúco, Col. Cuauhtémoc), Mexico City, 1986. Marco Antonio Cruz. Archivo Fotográfico.

Museums, Photography, and Academic Study

There is a very important relationship between the museum and academic study here to emphasize. I reflect on this in some of my writing on photography in Latin America. In my case, this has been a very natural process. The material I work with leads me to dialogue and work with material in museums. Each one of my recent projects over the past fifteen years has allowed me to produce a museum exhibition that I have shown in different locations, increasing its impact.

In the case of the 1968 student movement, I have worked with the subject of different photographic viewpoints that consider the topic and how these images have constructed different visual outlooks on that period of history. This has led me to create a hierarchy and select a visual universe that is much wider than before and to think and discuss with new generations of students who are interested in Mexican politics. I have found that sometimes they don't have clear notions of the events from the 1968 student movement because they are from a different historical period. They tend to look back over this period the same way my generation looked back over the Mexican Revolution and its leaders, such as Pancho Villa and Emiliano Zapata. This distance I am mentioning is very significant when it comes to research because as researchers attempt to obtain rigorous and objective conclusions it is important that they are not connected to the militants of yesteryear who tend to impose their points of view. These young researchers tend to uncover a richer field of analysis, characterized by certain doubts and uncertainty.

The Future

In recent years, I have worked to bring the image of other photographers such as Rodrigo Moya, Pedro Valtierra, Mariana Yampolsky, and Marco Antonio Cruz to the foreground by curating several exhibitions on their work. It has been a challenge to reconstruct the right viewpoint on their work. I try to take these exhibitions to different student communities such as the Escuela de Antropología e Historia, the Universidad Nacional Autónoma de México, the Centro de la Imagen, or the Universidad Autónoma Metropolitana in Iztapalapa. By doing so, I am trying to expose these photographer's images to a wide and diverse audience while being able to take our discussion on these important photographers to public spaces.

These experiences have provided me with an immense amount of feedback and have helped me to adopt other narrative strategies as well as different ways to share my research on history with new readers and members of the public. Recently, I have been working with other curators on an exhibition in the Universidad Nacional Autónoma de México's Centro Cultural Universidad

Tlatelolco, which is right next to the Plaza de las Tres Culturas in Mexico City: the site of the October 2, 1968, student massacre. Because I have been a postgraduate thesis director as a part of my academic work, I have been able to help new generations observe how this critical distance has been able to play a fundamental role in the construction and the positioning of other historical themes within Mexican and Latin American photography in our recent history. My work with photography also forces me to work in ways that are oblique and tangential to the official history that is normally promoted. Violence and drug trafficking in Mexico are becoming important themes in the writing of our recent history. It will occupy an increasing amount of the young historian's time as they attempt to contextualize the effects of this trade. The work of photographers such as Marco Antonio Cruz and Fernando Brito will help with that labor. This new generation of historians will need to contextualize the growing tide of violence in Mexico and build civilized paths of analysis that enable us to visualize other horizons that are less pessimistic than the present reality for our Mexican society, which appears to be trapped in a spiral of violence and destruction.

Selected Publications

del Castillo Troncoso, Alberto. *Conceptos, imágenes y representaciones de la niñez en México, 1880–1920*. Instituto Mora/COLMEX, 2006.

———. *Ensayo sobre el movimiento estudiantil: La fotografía y la construcción de un imaginario*. Instituto Mora, 2012.

———. *Fotografía y memoria: Conversaciones con Eduardo Longoni / Alberto del Castillo Troncoso*. Fondo de la Cultura Económica, 2017.

———. *Las mujeres de X´oyep: La historia detrás de la fotografía*. Conaculta, 2014.

Ariel Arnal

Universidad Iberoamericana

History and Photography

I BECAME INTERESTED in photography at a young age. I have always liked it, both as an activity and as a product. However, when I realized I am a terrible photographer, I decided to spend more time writing about photography. My introduction into the field of the study of photography began while I was at the Universidad de Barcelona where I was studying my undergraduate degree in history. I had moved from Mexico to Barcelona when I was sixteen. I finished high school in Spain, and I was completing my undergraduate degree there. In 1988 John Mraz came to my university, and he gave a presentation on visual history in Latin America. After the event I went up to him and told him that I was interested in working in his field of research. In turn, he invited me to return to Mexico to work with him. That was exactly what I did once I finished my history degree. Back in Mexico, I began to work as a researcher. I joined a group of scholars who worked at the Fototeca Nacional de Pachuca in Hidalgo, Mexico. Eleazar López Zamora (the Fototeca's director) and John Mraz coordinated the group. At that time (in the early 1990s) Mraz, López, Zamora, Juan Carlos Valdez, Margarita Morfín, Mariana Figerela Mota, Patricia Masé, and Gina Rodríguez all belonged to that group of researchers. López Zamora would teach us how to work with the material, how to treat it physically. John Mraz helped us find our scholarly approach to the material. After working with that group for a while, I started a new job at the Instituto de Investigaciones en Ciencias y Humanidades en Puebla at the Benemérita Universidad Autónoma de Puebla. I worked there for ten years. At first, I researched in the area of photography and architecture because in Barcelona I had earned a diploma in photography and architecture. However, after a few years in Mexico, I began to study the topic of historical photography and documentary photography with greater intent, and I began my master's degree at the Universidad Iberoamericana in Mexico.

Even though I finished my degree in 2001, I did not publish my master's thesis on the photographs of Emiliano Zapata as the book *Atila de tinta y plata* until 2010 so that it would coincide with the centenary of the Mexican Revolution.

My PhD had some unexpected challenges. Though I studied it in Puebla with John Mraz as the head of my dissertation committee, my studies from Spain were not officially recognized in Mexico. In the end, these difficulties led to me finishing my doctoral degree at the Universidad de Tarragona, Spain in 2015. Originally, I was going to focus on Walter Reuter.[1] I had even done some splendid interviews with him because his memories about what he had done during the Spanish Civil War were extremely lucid and full of useful information. However, just as I was about to begin my PhD, he died, and his personal archive closed for several years (as well as the possibility of working with it in the short term). Since that material was no longer an option, I decided to write my doctoral dissertation on the representations of historic memory as they were presented in the film *La batalla de Chile*. I choose to write on film instead of photography for my PhD dissertation because I wanted to be a bit more diversified academically, though I never left photography entirely. I was always working on photographic projects on the side. During that period, I used photography to write about various topics such as exile, politics, and photography during the nineteenth century. I even wrote books on photography, including the Juan Crisóstomo Méndez archive and the Ava Vargas photographs that were still in Mexico. These are super interesting images that document women working in a brothel around the turn of the twentieth century. The best images from that collection had been acquired by a Mexican who was living in the Netherlands, but there were still many good images that remained in the Mexican archive. The book published from that project is called *Juan C. Méndez: La curiosidad en la mirada*.

Useful Methods for Studying Photography

I have had the good fortune of being taught many useful methods for studying photography. Many of them I learned directly from John Mraz. I remember that one of the first things he said was: "Forget about talking about the things around a photograph, or of writing history and then including a photograph as an illustration. You need to write directly about photography." What did he mean by that? He means that you must carefully consider the photographs on which you plan to write. That is the absolute first thing that you must do. You need to locate the right archive for your work and begin to review the material and its corresponding information. You must really look at the images and create an informational context. Who was the photographer? When did he live? When did he die? How did he learn to photograph? Who did he work with? Then you need to begin to look for the secondary information and question the photographic image itself. Is this image a staged photograph or is it spontaneous? You need to consider the individuals in the pictures in both the primary and secondary planes of view. What are they doing? Why are they doing it? Every photograph includes a large number of details that were not the expressed intention of the photographer. Often the researcher can learn a lot from studying those details.

In my book *Atila tinta y plata*, I dedicated a great deal of time to writing about a photograph of Emiliano Zapata and his brother Eufemio Zapata who are each with their respective wives in Hotel Moctezuma in Cuernavaca in 1911. I use this image to show how to study a photograph analytically. In the image you have two main characters and instead of writing about who Emiliano Zapata and his brother were, it is much more useful to discover other revealing details. To do so, you need to ask questions. Why are these gentlemen so stiff in the photograph? Why do they appear to be nervous? Why do the women look so relaxed? Why does Emiliano Zapata's wife have such an authoritative air about her in the photo? Then you should consider why there are so many people present. Who are these people? There is a woman who appears to be laughing hard. Then there is boy who is very well dressed. My methodological approach is to interrogate the photograph. I do not initially attempt to interrogate the people in the photograph nor the photograph's history. Then you try and answer all the questions that you formulated. After exploring all these points, you need to move on and draw on more information from more traditional methods for writing history: chronicles, memoirs, and written history to try and create the proper context and respond to the questions that you could not respond to directly with the photograph itself.

Though it might sound obvious, if you are going to write visual history, you need to focus on visual sources. In my case, that is photography. If you do not do that, then what you are doing is not visual history. If you are only using photographs as an illustration, then you will fall into the dangerous trap of just using photographs to illustrate your arguments. If you just write about the creator or the artist's private life, and you leave his or her images on the margin, then you are falling prey to one of the common temptations that exist in our line of research. Another temptation is to only focus on photography's technical aspects. If you only comment on the camera light or angle the photographer used, then you only have a technical reading. That type of information is great for creating context, but there is much more to explore, like the social perspective of the photograph.

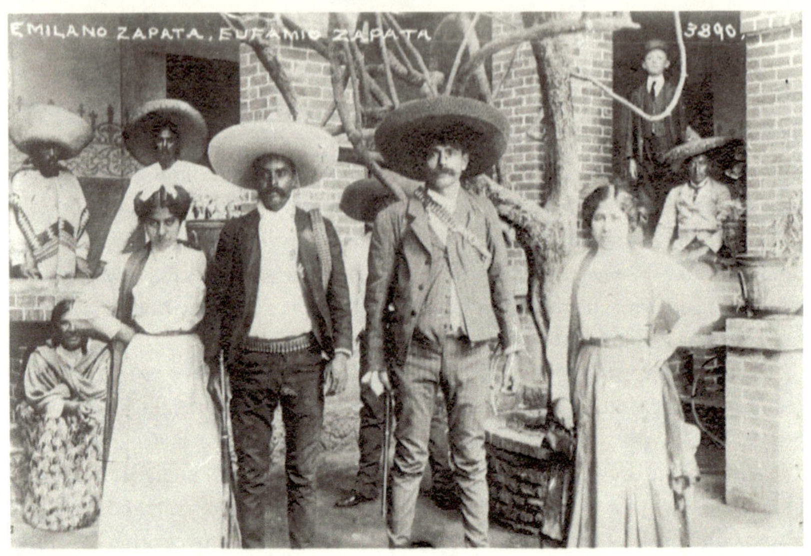

Figure 4.1. Josefa Espejo, Emiliano y Eufemio Zapata, Hotel Moctezuma, Cuernavaca, Mexico, May 26, 1911. Attributed to Hugo Breheme. Finah 5773 tif, Fondo Casasola.

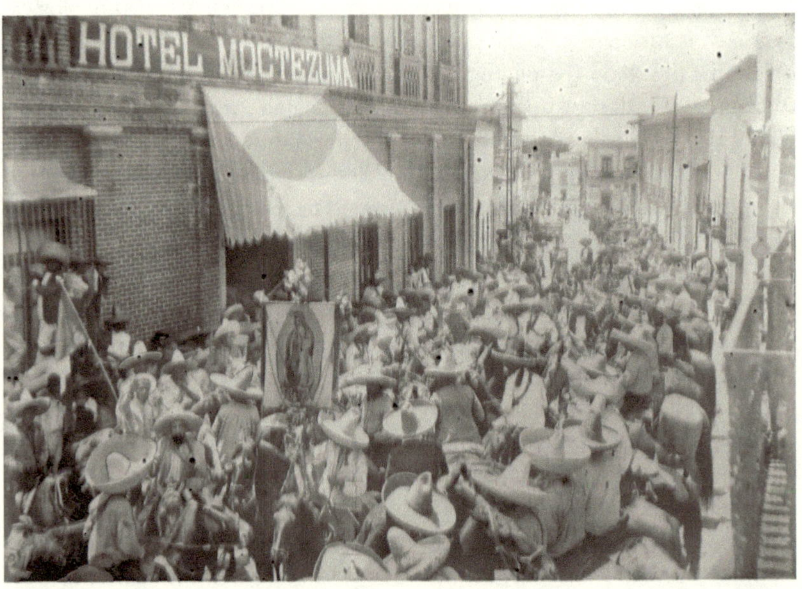

Figure 4.2. Entrada de Emiliano Zapata y su Estado Mayor al Hotel Moctezuma Cuernavaca (Emiliano Zapata and his staff at Hotel Moctezuma, Cuernavaca), Mexico, May 26, 1911. Hadsell y Cruz. Finah 597997 tif, Fondo Casasola.

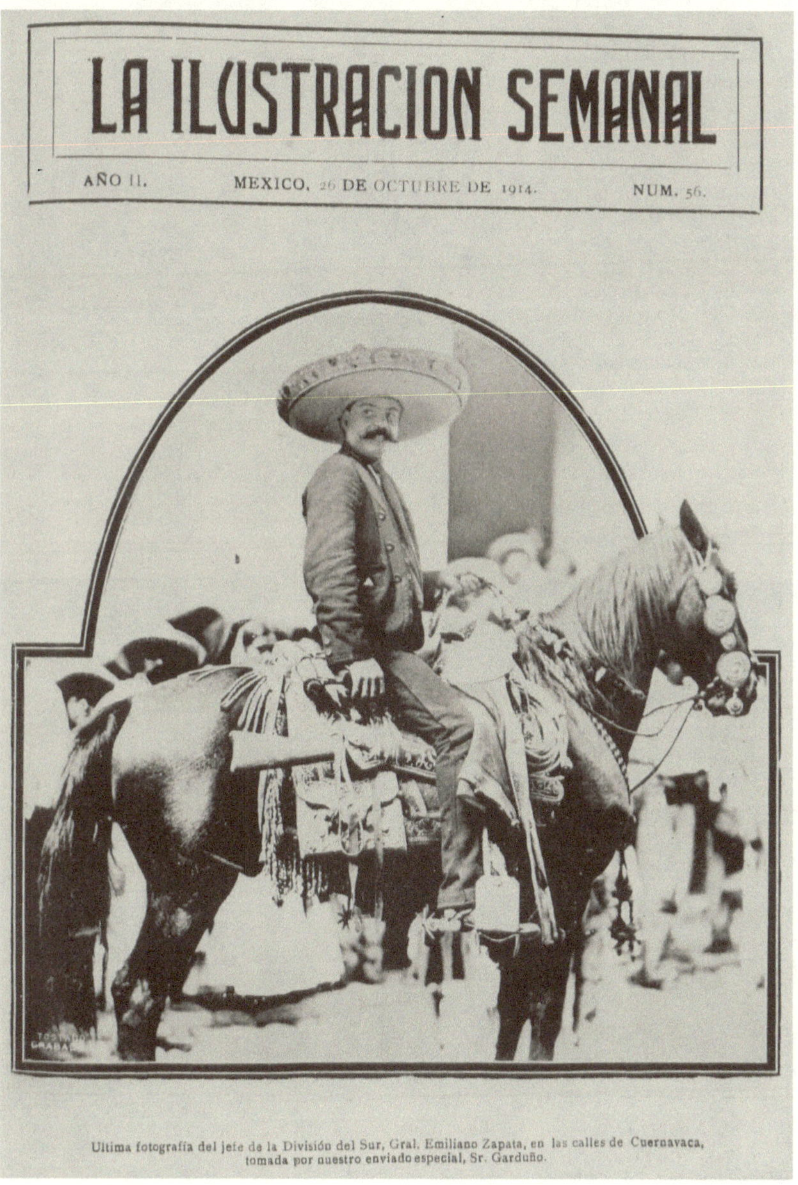

Figure 4.3. Emiliano Zapata y sus tropas en Cuernavaca (Emiliano Zapata and his troops in Cuernavaca), Mexico, c. Oct 20, 1914. Antonio Garduño. *La Ilustración Semanal*, October 26, 1914.

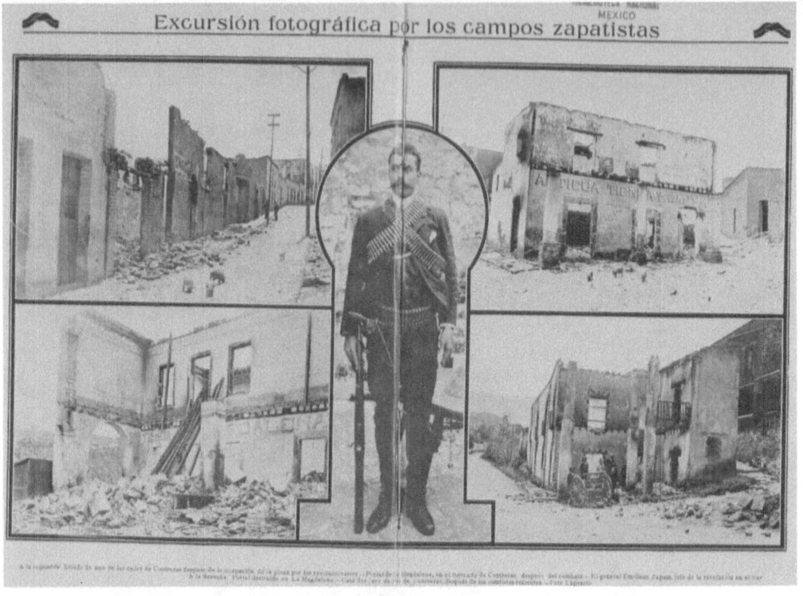

Figure 4.4. Magadalena Contreras, c. July 27, 1914. Abraham Lupercio. *La Ilustración Semanal*, August 3, 1914.

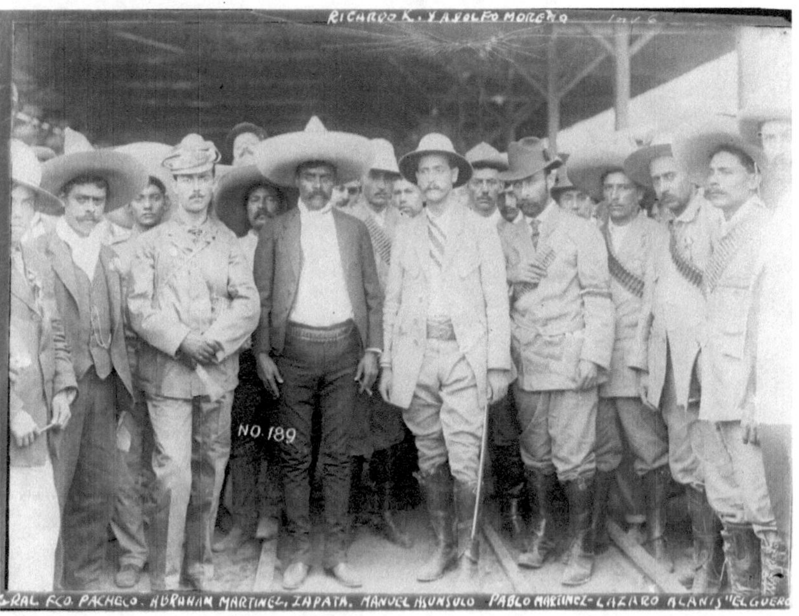

Figure 4.5. Emiliano Zapata y Manuel Asunsolo, entre otros (Emiliano Zapata and Manuel Asunsolo among others) Mexico, c. May 26, 1911. Agustin Victor Casasola. Finah 5868 tif, Fondo Casasola.

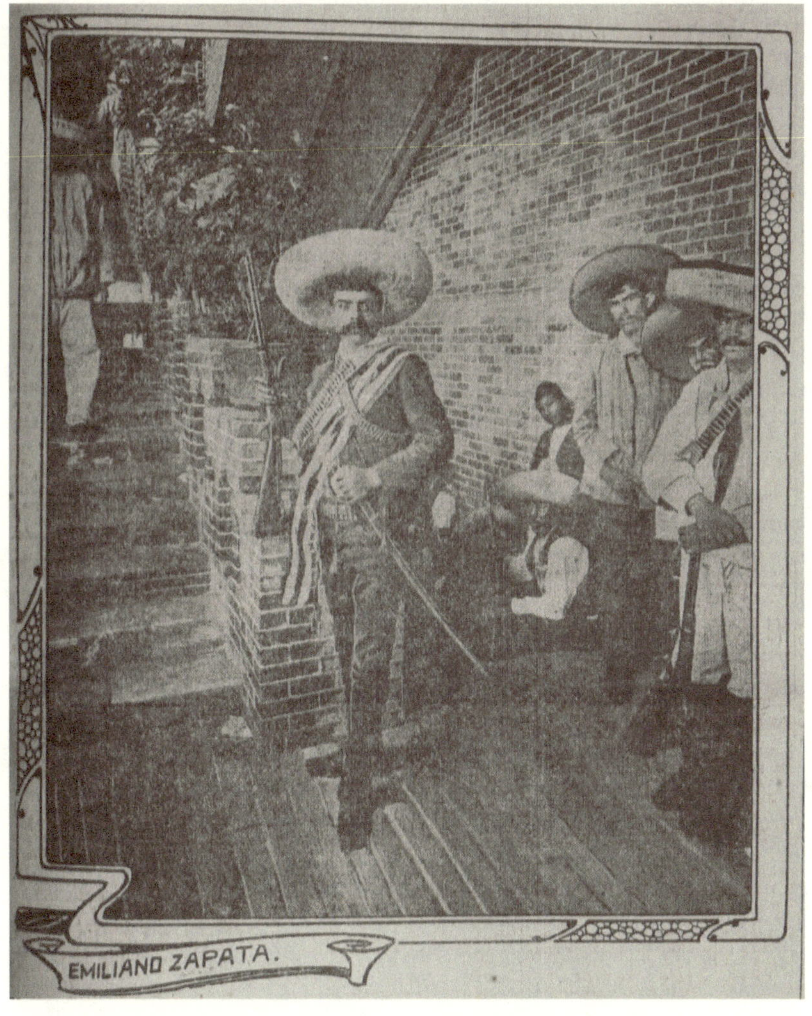

Figure 4.6. *El Imparcial*, April 16, 1913. Hugo Brehme.

Ideas That Lead to Analysis

When I first started researching photography, I worked a lot with photography theory. Then, back in the 1990s when there were just a few of us working on photography in Mexico, I realized that if I was going to be pioneering the field of visual history with my colleagues, I needed to do something different. I recognized that if we only focused on photography theory from abroad, we would only be creating a subfield that applied foreign ideas to the Latin American context. I have reflected on how we could avoid this. We needed to create a methodology to study photography in Latin America. I think that the solution is to work with the raw material that you have and begin to ask important critical questions that arise from it. After you have found the appropriate questions that correspond properly to your material, then some of your questions might be answerable through photography theory, or the history of photography, or social history, or with whatever else might be useful to work your analytical angle. Hence, in my quest to define our common field of the study of Latin American photography I have found myself leaving a lot of theory behind and advancing in my research thanks to other fields of knowledge. However, I never really left the photography theory classics, like Roland Barthes, behind. Working across certain disciplines has helped me to write as well. For example, literary theory has sometimes led me to a sociology-based analysis. Literary theory connected to poetry has helped me to work with photography also. This is because when we read an image, we are interpreting material and considering its symbols, and poetry is an interpretation of reality and imagery as well. When you write visual history, you must interpret and theorize around the images in your corpus. For that same reason many subdisciplines can help us find the tools that are useful to our work. The study of photography is so new that often we are faced with the need to create theory and methods to successfully interrogate our research questions. For example, I know a scholar, Arturo Guevara, who uses information from NASA's satellites and the shadows in the photographs to determine the time of day a certain photograph was taken, when that information is relevant to his analysis. I find myself benefitting from many different sources of information that one might not have thought would be used in the study of photography, but at the time, they gave me the tools that I needed to say something relevant. The important thing is not to fall victim to the siren's call of postmodernism: when you say a lot, but you have said nothing at all. You must be careful because it is very easy to say things that simply do not make sense. You must have scientific rigor when you write if you want to be taken seriously. I think that you need to avoid the idea that any interpretation is possible and is valid with photography. If everything is possible and everything is valid, then you have nothing at all, or you are simply writing fiction and not solid research with scientific rigor. If you do not have rigor when you write history using photography, then your work will not have any academic weight.

To acquire that weight, it is very important that you have enough sources and that you question those sources appropriately. In this sense, I think you want to use some nineteenth century positivism in that you need to have three independent sources verify your findings. If you have those three sources, then you have something noteworthy, and you should publish it. If you only have one or two sources, then it does not have the academic rigor to merit publishing without further work. The study of photography and history is no different. You must corroborate your sources and put them through rigorous academic tests. This is the key to penetrating the field of serious history writing and the intention of objectivity. It is true that the social sciences are not objective in the same way the hard sciences are, but our intentions should always be to work with objectivity. We can only achieve this by using traditional methodology that invites academic rigor.

I have met many foreigners who have come to research photography in Mexico with a strong grounding in academic theory, especially theory related to documentary photography. Other foreigners have brought more of an artist's perspective when it comes to the study of photography in Latin America. My suggestion to them is that they need to abandon their conception of Latin America and the tropics. The idea that you can apply magic realism to photography is a trap. Magic realism does not exist here in the same way that you might think that it does. For example, for years people have been describing Graciela Iturbide's photograph of the woman with the iguanas on her head, *Nuestra Señora de las Iguanas* in *Juchitán de las mujeres* as something that is magical. There is no magic realism in this image. It is based on simple buying and selling practices found in the local market (Iturbide *Eyes to Fly With*). When it comes to documentary photography, you need to approach it as you would with any other type of documentary photography you might find anywhere else. You cannot invent ideas based on preconceptions.

Right now, there is a problem when it comes to producing documentary images in Latin America. It is related to issues of safety (Kenny; Serrano; Sotomayor). The high levels of danger involved in taking photographs is affecting the production of photography here. People are simply taking less photographs due to a lack of public and private security. Conversely, photographs that have been having some of the largest impact in Europe at present have been those by Sinaloa's Fernando Brito who takes pictures of "narco-cadavers," or cadavers that are a byproduct of narco violence (Monroy Álvarez "La imagen del deshecho"). Brito is a self-taught photographer who knows his profession well and the dangers and risks it involves. The number of journalists who have been killed while doing their job here in Mexico is alarming. If you come here to study photography, you should listen to the people here and be patient. Our archives can often be like something you might expect from a teenager's bedroom. However, there are a few that are in really good shape. The Rodrigo

Moya archive is excellent. He and his English wife (Susan Flaherty) have spent a lot of time establishing it. Truthfully, she can take credit for the superb condition of the archive. It is as if it were a public archive that has been prepared by conservation and restoration experts. However, other archives require time to sit down and look at what is there. You need to take time and dedication to understand what is there and make sense of it so that you can study it properly.

Adopt New Models to Find New Insights

In recent years an increasing number of scholars from other fields are beginning to study photography. To them, I would reiterate my suggestions related to academic rigor that I set out earlier. Additionally, I recommend Allan Sekula's *Fish Story* as an example of interesting work that can be done. He uses photographs to help you think and write about relevant topics without being postmodernist. Here in Mexico we are beginning to develop this type of text on visual narratives. It takes a while to adopt new models and to leave behind old habits or approaches that we have learned elsewhere and might not be relevant to photography.

That is not to say that there are no important texts that lack the academic rigor I have been emphasizing. For example, the first book on the history of Mexican photography was Olivier Debroise's 1990 publication: *Fuga mexicana*. It was highly criticized with claims that it has very little academic rigor. Even though I agree with the critics, I defend the book because he was one of the pioneers who dared to do something different. He was willing to write a general history of Mexican photography when no one else was thinking about it and by doing so he marked an important pathway for us. I do think that we should rewrite the project and correct the book's errors. To do so, we would need help from a variety of experts in other fields. The critical viewpoints that foreign outsiders bring to the table can be very useful as well when it comes to doing an exercise such as this.

Rodrigo Moya

My University of Texas Press project on Rodrigo Moya offers the reader a general perspective on his work. Many researchers have written on the social movements that he covered with this photography: El Che, Cuba, las guerrillas, the 1968 Mexican student movement are the topics that are most covered by the scholars to date. When Moya decided to retire because he felt that he could no longer make a living as a photographer and that there wasn't enough freedom of speech, an important opportunity knocked on his door. Fernando Rafful, the general secretary for the fishing secretariat in Miguel de la Madrid's government, offered him the opportunity to create the magazine *Técnica pesquera*. At first, this publication was supported with funds by the fishing secretariat, but it later became a private, self-funded magazine. He was the director of that magazine for two decades until he retired from it in 2000. So, for twenty years Rodrigo Moya's photography was focused on topics related to the sea. About 25 percent of his entire archive is focused on fishermen and their way of life. It is a wonderful collection of images that asks important questions related to the sea. He worries about the fishermen and their way of life: Why do fishermen earn so little? How can they create more opportunities for themselves? How do the struggles between societies' social classes play out in the ocean? How are major industries and mammoth companies destroying the sea? For example, now we don't really see any sharks on the coast lines. In order to find them you must go out to sea. That is great news if you are going for a short swim on the beach, but truthfully it is not great news because it means that the sharks are disappearing. Rodrigo Moya's interest is focused on these concerns and how individuals involved in the fishing industry were living so precariously. His photographic work studies many contexts: commercialization, fishing politics, and the socio-historical conditions that the fishermen face. His documentary outlook is fantastic. As a photographer, he is in close connection with the human side of life. That is where he makes his mark as a photographer. It is what makes him "Rodrigo Moya." In every other way he is simply another photographer. At present, Rodrigo, his wife, and I are working with the photographs from his fishing period. Rodrigo Moya reflects a lot on his work just like Nacho López does (Consejo Nacional para la Cultura y las Artes *Nacho López*) but because he has been around much longer than Nacho López, he has had more time to reflect on his photography. Working with Moya has been fascinating and if there is one piece of advice I can give to others who study photography, it is to try and accept projects that really capture your attention. Because if they do not, then you aren't going to put your heart into them.

Mexican Research on Photography Varies Widely

It is important to pause and really reflect on the work that you are doing. In Mexico there are many examples of people who are doing good work. Just like there is a lot of variety in the different types of natural environments here in Mexico, you can also find a lot of different research topics related to photography here. The fact that there is so much work to do with the primary sources in Latin America is another one of the reasons that photography theory takes a back seat here. We tend to focus on researching material in archives and spend less time reflecting on theory. That is why our work tends toward the documentary and less toward the abstract. That said, Laura González has extended great effort to make photography theory more accessible to the general public and that type of work is very important here (*Fotografía y pintura*). She argues that in Mexico we need to write our own photography theory for Latin America, but to do so you do have to know what others say. This is true and I think that it is a very valuable initiative. The possibilities in Latin America are endless.

I think that it is important to mention that some of the outstanding names in photography (Manuel Álvarez Bravo and Graciela Iturbide for example) aren't really the object of study in Latin America because they are already so ubiquitous. Another point that I should mention is that Europe has been an important reference point for many of us who work on photography in Latin America. Gonzalo Leiva studied in Paris. I studied in Europe as well and I still have a very close relationship with Catalonia. However, many of the Latin American photographs that circulate in Europe are marked by tragedy or misery. The images from the 1985 Mexico City earthquake are a good example of this trend. When you have such an intense focus on human tragedy, it is difficult to have a clear understanding of daily life and reality, though some photographers have represented this aspect successfully. For example, in 1990 a Spanish photographer based in South America named Claudi Carreras Guillén produced some excellent images from Peru and Bolivia ("Claudi Carreras Guillén"). He also published a series of reports called "Autorretrato de América" in the Barcelona newspaper *La Vanguardia*. In them, he was able to capture a joie de vivre that provided a completely new outlook on the region. He told me that it was extremely difficult to get these images published and exhibited in Europe because they were so accustomed to associating Latin America with poverty and misery that those topics were what the public wanted from Latin American photography. That demand is one of the challenges our field faces. Hence, we need to be more emphatic when we are looking for new topics. We need to be open to daily life and what it might be able to offer us. It can be very revealing to study the daily lives and routines of normal citizens here in Latin America and see what photography can teach us about them. There is so much more to Latin America than poverty and violence.

Looking Back Will Help Us Move Forward

There is much more to come. We are long overdue for a retrospective analysis here in Mexico. During the last three decades we have been working with great rigor and produced key monographs on important photographers that has helped us to fill the voids of our visual history. We now need to go back and offer a more general panorama of photography in Mexico. We need to determine what the major and minor events in photography's history have been. The work is never-ending. The good news is that a new generation of researchers are taking root. They are the new students that have been graduating with their PhDs in the study of photography, and their work is noteworthy. Presently, there are between five to eight doctoral students and five master's students who successfully defend their theses on the study of photography in Latin America every semester at my university. The Mexico City seminar *La mirada inquieta*, run by Rebeca Monroy and Alberto del Castillo, has played an important role in their development.

Soon, we scholars will need to review the type of research that has been occurring here in Mexico and the rest of Latin America. There is much to be learned from academic exchanges. For example, Alberto del Castillo spent a sabbatical in Argentina, and he came back with many new ideas. He wrote a book on Eduardo Longoni, an important photographer and editor there (del Castillo *Fotografía y memoria*). Alberto del Castillo's book is a type of dialogue. In it, he interviews Longoni and then critically analyzes what Longoni says. This was very innovative because in Mexico we tend to only focus on our own history. However, this is a tendency that we need to change, and there are certain signs that we are. We have begun to study what has been occurring in our field in Brazil and Argentina. The work they are doing on documentary photography in Argentina is fabulous. Their work on the role of photography in history and anthropology in Brazil is groundbreaking. Both countries have methods to work with photography that are worth thoughtful consideration. In Peru there are people we do not yet know but who are doing great work. For example, the Peruvian journal *Kaypunku* publishes fantastic articles on photography theory and image analysis. I always wanted to create a journal like this, and then I found out that it already existed. This shows that we need to be in contact even more. New networking technologies help with this, but the conferences that were more frequent in the past and helped unite us are tending to disappear as funds become more limited. We need to stop constantly looking to the north for ideas and begin to explore new directions. We all need to share more and exchange more thoughts and ideas. I think that Latin America has a very bright future in the years to come with many good things that will come our way.

Selected Publications

Arnal, Ariel. *Atila de tinta y plata: Fotografía del zapatisimo en la prensa de la Ciudad de México. 1910–1915*. Instituto Nacional de Antropología e Historia (INAH), 2010.

———. "Certera voz de luz: Verdad y verdades en la fotografía documental latinoamericana" *América, lente solidaria*, edited by Ariel Arnal, Azucena Cháidez, and Edgar Valle. SIMO Cultura, 2016, pp. 10–17.

———. *Rodrigo Moya: Photography and Conscience/Fotografía y conciencia*. University of Texas Press, 2015.

Arnal, Ariel, and Juan Crisóstomo Méndez Avalos. *Juan C. Méndez: La curiosidad en la mirada*. Secretaría de Cultura de Puebla, 1999.

Anne Girard de Marroquín

Independent Scholar, Guatemala City

Switzerland to Guatemala

MY CONNECTIONS TO photography and Guatemala stem from my family and my studies in Switzerland. My uncle, Raphaël Girard, was an award-winning anthropologist who wrote many books on the Mayans, their history, and their culture. Among those publications are a translation of *El Popol Vuh*, *El calendario Maya Mexica*, and *Historia del origen y desarrollo de las civilizaciones*, just to mention a few of his more salient works. Thanks to my uncle and his research on Indigenous cultures in Central America, I have family all throughout Central America. Some of his children were born in Honduras and in El Salvador; however, I have always felt more drawn to Guatemala. Certain aspects of its multicultural culture captivate me. I first came to Guatemala on vacation in 1971 to spend some time with my uncle Raphaël. Then I came back again in 1972. In 1974 I returned to Guatemala with the firm determination to establish a photo studio that processed color film because by then I had already studied photography and knew all about its technical procedures. However, I lacked a clear understanding of the local environment and that led to my first business in Central America being a failure. So, I went back to Switzerland and started working there again to build capital and plan another attempt. I came back to Guatemala in 1976 and set up another photography studio. I was successful that time, and I have been here ever since.

I studied photography in Switzerland from 1964 to 1967. I did most of my studies in Martigny, my hometown, though I also took courses on the theory and practice of photography in Vevey during those years as well. I graduated with a diploma in photography. In Switzerland, I learned how to take architectural photos, perfecting my ability to capture both interiors and exteriors of the buildings I was shooting. I learned everything related to the art of developing color film in the Swiss photography lab Procolor de Sion. I have also taken many important figures to be my role models over the years. Among them are Henri Cartier Bresson, Robert Doisneau, Vivian Maier, and René Burri.

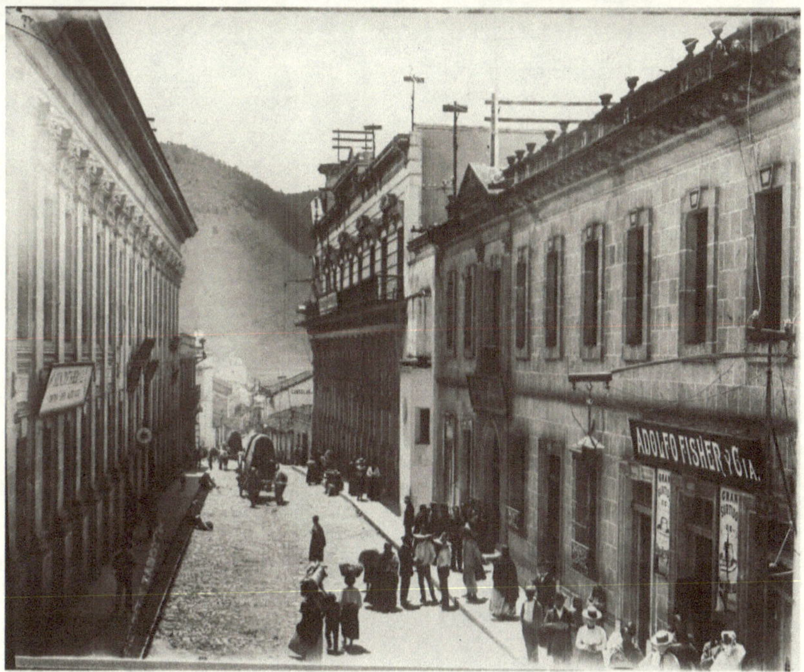

Figure 5.1. Calle de San Sebastián Quetzaltenango, Guatemala, c. 1900. Piggot and Zanotti. Anne Girard Collection.

Photographic Influences

Many ideas from photographic theory have influenced my work. I have read both Roland Barthes and Susan Sontag with great interest. I enjoy their writings and they have helped me to understand how a photograph can stand alone without a text and how images speak independently and maintain a presence through time. They have even helped me to change the way I take my pictures. Now, I always ask for permission before I take a picture of any person or place. Likewise, when I take pictures now, I always share my photographs with the people I photograph. Experience has taught me that while many of the older generations do not understand the technology behind photography, their grandchildren do. My habit of taking pictures and always sharing with the people in them has led to many of my subjects accepting me and my work.

I have taken many portraits, wedding pictures, and other types of commercial photography in order to make a living; however, I have always had a special interest in documentary photography. I have spent many years documenting native Guatemalan dress with my photography. One of the photo documentarians who has most inspired me is Manuel Álvarez Bravo, whom I met when he came here in 1980. Aside from Álvarez Bravo, Ricardo Mata (whose documentary work I find inspiring) and Diego Molina (whose work in the Lacandon Jungle is noteworthy) have been models whose work I have followed (Nelson *Un dedo en la llaga* 43).

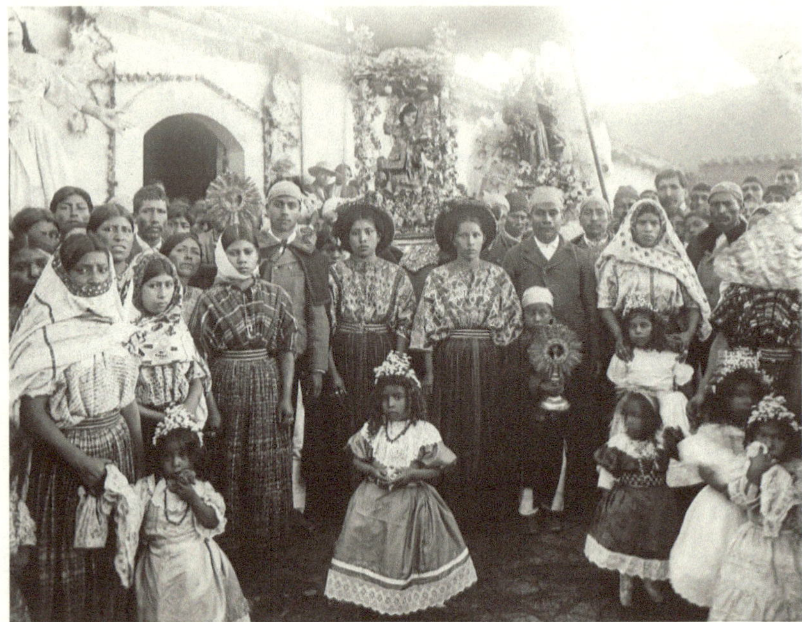

Figure 5.2. Cofradía de Quetzaltenango (Scene outside a church in Quetzaltenango) Quetzaltenango, Guatemala, c. 1900. Zanotti. Anne Girard Collection.

The study of photography in Mexico and Peru has really stood out for different reasons. For example, the academic work on Chambi is exemplary (see, for instance, *Martín Chambi, por sí mismo*). In comparison, in Guatemala, there has been very little academic work on photography. The very little that does exist tends to consist of short summaries. Guatemalan photography has a human warmth that you simply do not find in Switzerland, and it is this aspect of photography here that has fascinated me from the onset. Even so, as a woman, being accepted in Guatemala has not been easy. This was especially true in the beginning, because back then there were few women taking photographs. The technical processes of photography are the same in Europe and Latin America, but what they do with the final product can be different. In Switzerland they tend not to retouch photographs; here, they will even paint over them (*iluminarlas*).

In the 1980s I began collecting cameras and photographs from a variety of Guatemalan photographers as a means of learning about their history. I bought many antique photographs from local markets or directly from the photographers or their family. One type of antique photograph that is particularly

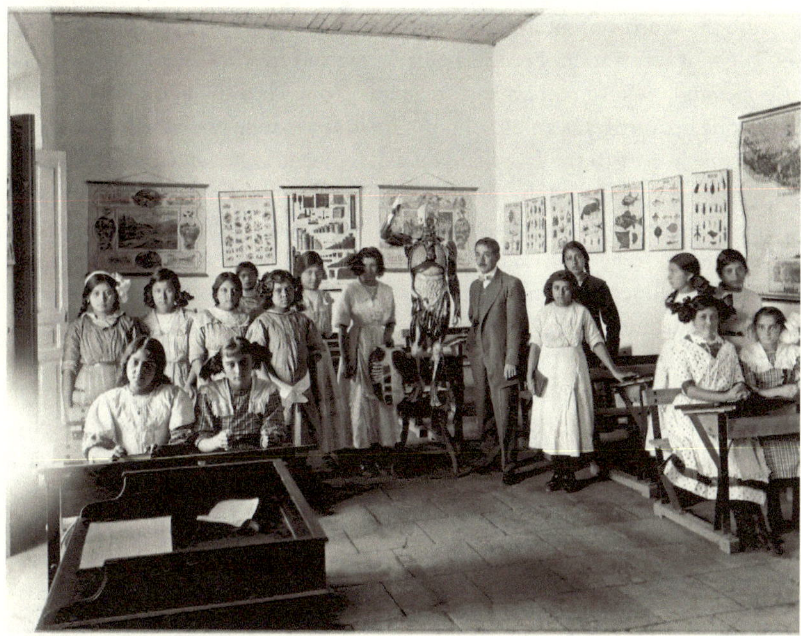

Figure 5.3. Escuela de Quetzaltenango (School in Quetzaltenango) Quetzaltenango, Guatemala, c. 1900. Zanotti. Anne Girard Collection.

difficult to acquire are those of Indians in Guatemala. Most of those images have left the country and are now in museums and private collections in the United States, Mexico, and Europe. In order to write my book *Visión etnográfica de la indumentaria maya de Guatemala*, I had to travel to many locations in Germany and the United States and purchase the photographs there. The rest of the images I used were from my own collection, photos my father had in Switzerland, and images that my friends here had in their private collections.

Documenting Photographic History

To be able to document each photograph's history, I had to acquire many books on the history of Guatemala and start researching. Some of the books that were especially useful are *Los Indígenas de Guatemala visto por el Fotógrafo Alberto Valdeavellano (1861–1928)* by Luis Luján, *Fotografías de Eduardo Santiago Muybridge en Guatemala (1875)* by Luis Luján, *La Antigua Guatemala de los Fotógrafos J. J. Yas, J. D. Noriega 1880–1960* by Juan José de Jesús Yas and José Domingo Noriega, and finally *Imágenes de Guatemala 1850–2005* by Arturo Taracena and Rosina Cazali. Researching in this country can be complicated because the sources of information you need are not very well signposted when you begin. It was not until people got to know and trust me that they started to help me, and my information base began to grow. Then the work became very interesting because I was able to obtain a lot of fascinating firsthand information. This is due in part to the fact that you can frequently encounter entire families working in the photography profession. For example, Emilio Herbruger and Emilio Herbruger Jr. were both photographers. The Ankerman family is another great example. Jorge Ankerman Canet Sr. was a man of German extraction from Palma de Mallorca. He immigrated to Quetzaltenango around 1905, and his sons and daughters Jorge, Jaime, Julio, Estela, and Alfredo have all kept the photography profession in the family. They were all portrait takers, and they all had studios in Guatemala City. Their archives are a gold mine of information for anyone who wants to learn about Guatemala's history through its photography.

Local newspaper archives and other local print media have greatly informed my research on photography and provided useful information. A few who have helped me advance my research are the newspaper *Là Gaceta de Guatemala* and early travel books and tourist guides such as *Directorio del viajero en la República de Guatemala* (1889), the *Guía Comercial y Turistíca de la ciudad de Guatemala* (1937), and *El Libro Azul.* As I go about my research, I strive to be thorough and work as a specialist in the field of photography. I have learned many research techniques from foreign researchers in the field of photography in Central America here like Iliana Seleján: a scholar at University College London. She has taught me how to incorporate academic rigor into my work. However, I do not belong to a research network. I am not aware of any research networks that focus on photography here in Guatemala. There is just a Club Fotográfico that I left decades ago to spend more time researching and documenting a variety of topics on photography and local dress in Guatemala. I am aware of a few other small research projects on photography in Guatemala, but at present they are still unpublished. I have another friend, Luis Escobar, who has spent a lot of time on photography in Guatemala, and we exchange a lot of information with each other as we find it. Our goal is to flesh out the history of photography here.

Writing the history of the photography here in Guatemala is one of my enduring passions. I have invested much effort into the writing of its history from 1843 to 1950. When my daughters were still young, my husband and I would interview old photographers while they were still alive. Many of them have passed away since our initial interviews. In those cases, we have continued collecting information on them thanks to their children or other relatives who share relevant information on their personal histories. Currently, I am writing two books: one on the photographer Tomás Zanotti with Iliana Selején and another on Mayan dress. I am always seeking opportunities to share my findings with other researchers and looking for someone with which to write a bilingual book on the history of Guatemalan photography.

As a part of my research skills, I have learned how to interview others and document the facts that I have taken from the interviews. I have also published an article on a Mexican photographer who worked in Guatemala for many years: Tomás Zanotti. That publication was part of a small exhibition on his work I curated in the 1980s. I will comment on his work a bit later when I explain how you can use archives as a valuable source of information here in Guatemala as you research photography. Experience has taught me that you need to be careful when you write because a lot of the information that you get from family members needs to be crosschecked for errors, but normally if you are a conscientious writer these small obstacles are easily overcome. It is all part of the research process.

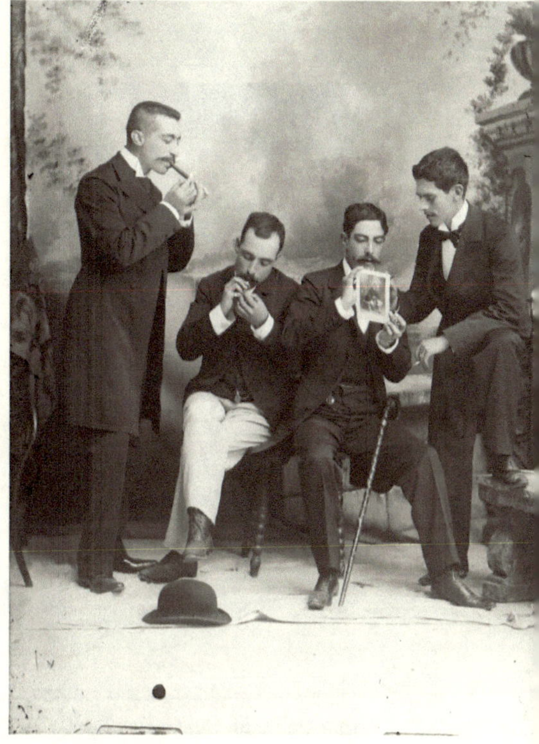

Figure 5.4. Jovenes posando (Young men posing for a photo) Quetzaltenango, Guatemala, c. 1900. Zanotti. Anne Girard Collection.

Aside from the firsthand information from interviews, I have been able to glean most of the rest of the information for my book on the history of photography from antique travel books, the aforementioned nineteenth-century newspaper *La Gaceta de Guatemala*, and other books from that period that make mention of photography. Much of what I want to know when I interview the photographers is how they learned the art of photography and other aspects of how they started out in this field. My most effective method for obtaining the information that I have needed is working with the local community. I simply talk to them about my projects and follow up on their leads. They have led me to many excellent sources of visual and written material. One thing that should be mentioned is the fact that many of the most famous photographers here are from other countries: Tomás Zanotti, Teódoro Miltz, Herbruger, Fitz Gibbon, Bourgois, Eichenberger, Yas, García Sanchez, Dionisio Remis, Pablo Sittler, and others like Someliani, Fuchs, and Donzel are just a few of them.

Presently, La Fototeca, a private photography school in Guatemala City, is

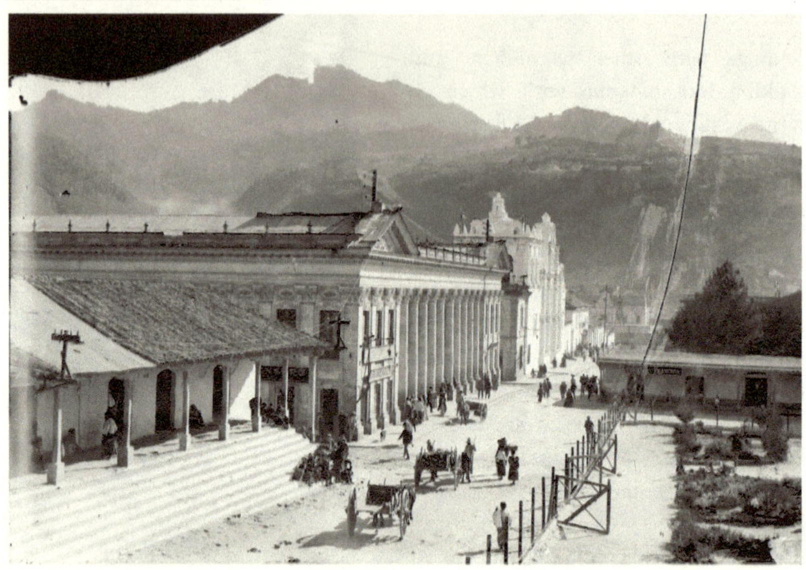

Figure 5.5. Municipalidad y plaza Quetzaltenango (City Hall and main plaza in Quetzaltenango), Guatemala, c. 1910. Zanotti. Anne Girard Collection.

writing a book on the history of modern photography in Guatemala. I have not worked on the project, but I think that it will really help the study of photography here to grow. I know that they have been focusing on the evolution and growth of the country's capital. We need to remember that visual history is also a part of our history, and there are many new projects that are possible. There are many archives to explore here and a lot of work for the next generation of researchers.

Building and Supporting Archives

One of the areas that can be developed further in Guatemala is archival work. I have been lucky enough to buy part of the Tomás Zanotti collection in Quetzaltenango. For months, I traveled back and forth to buy his negatives, his cameras, and other items from his studio while interviewing his daughters to learn more. That experience taught me many things. The Zanotti archive is one of the most valuable ones that I have. Tomás Zanotti Bosque (1867–1958) was a Mexican photographer who worked in Guatemala most of his life, creating a very valuable body of work to be studied. He was born in Minatitlán, Veracruz, to an Italian father (José María Zanotti) and a Mexican mother (Concepción Bosque). Tomás Zanotti came to Quetzaltenango around 1897 and learned how to be a photographer from a German by the name of Teodoro Miltz who was living in the city at that time. Zanotti married María Josefa López in 1901 and remained in Guatemala the rest of his life. As he aged, his daughter took over the business and kept up his extensive archive. Thanks to this archive we know that Zanotti collaborated with other foreign photographers such as Piggott and Lesher (whom we know very little about), that were operating in Guatemala at that time. The archive of Zanotti's studio work shows that he was interested in capturing the different layers of society through a wide range of classes: the elite, the workers, the Indigenous. He also took many pictures of the city, its architecture, and religious celebrations. His work is mostly very high-quality wet-plate collodion photographs: five-by-seven-inch or eight-by-ten-inch images. The material based on Quetzaltenango is the best preserved and most varied. They are a key part of that city's visual history and merit more study.

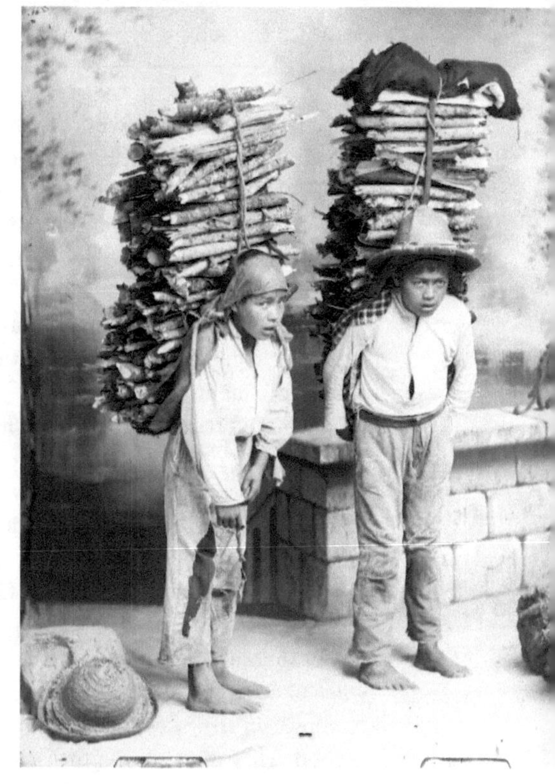

Figure 5.6. Niños cargando leña (Children carrying firewood) Quetzaltenango, Guatemala, c. 1910. Zanotti. Anne Girard Collection.

I am one of the authors of *Rostros de la Guatemala Indígena* (2012) and *Visión etnográfica de la indumentaria maya de Guatemala* (2017). The first book focuses on portraits of the Indigenous. I wrote the second book because I realized that no one had explored this topic. There have been many books on Mayan dress, but they focused solely on one region or one specific topic. No one had ever shown the evolution of Mayan dress over the years and included a variety of the regions where they live. My book studies photographs of Mayan dress from the nineteenth century to the twenty-first century and includes documents from sixty-five of the municipalities where the Mayans live in Guatemala. In addition to my written pieces on the photographs, it contains texts by the anthropologist Barbara Arathoon and the journalist Ingrid Roldán, and the book is bilingual (English-Spanish), so it is quite unique. My research is also noticeably different from other scholars' work in the field because I took many of the pictures that are included in my books. For example, I have carried out most of the work for the books published by the Museo Ixchel del Traje Indígena. In general, my photography is more documentary than artistic, though I believe that my images have an aesthetic impact. If I had to choose between studio photography and those taken in a natural environment, I would prefer the latter because they normally generate more natural reactions from your subjects.

I know I have emphasized this before, but I think I should do it again. There are many opportunities for the study of photography in Latin America, with many fantastic opportunities yet to be explored. There has been a lot of production in recent years as well. Many young people are experimenting with montages and other photographic techniques. At first, most photography here in Guatemala was studio photography or by people who went into the countryside to take interesting photographs. There were also many traveling photographers who had very modern backdrops (planes from the United States or Spain or depictions of large, foreign cities). Guatemala is a wonderful place to visit and research, but you must also be very cautious. Currently, it is very dangerous to go out shooting photographs in the countryside, and you need to be very careful when photographing children. The women who weave Native fabrics are trying to copyright their designs through local and international legislation, and this is good. They must protect their creative work as it is their livelihood and their culture. Their designs contain very important symbols for them and must be visually represented with special attention to that copyright. Notwithstanding these challenges, it is worth the trouble to document these subjects that are so precious. The tragedy here is the fact that priceless photos and documents are lost every day by the sons and daughters of photographers who cannot see the value of that work their mother or father did, and they simply throw them away. The guerrilla warfare that was occurring in Guatemala has died down since 1996, but even at that time, during the most intense periods of the conflict, we were able to continue our labors. Being careful was key (working only during daylight hours, for example). Now the social challenges that you face as a photographer are more connected to unemployment and urban violence.

I see many developments in the future for the study of photography in Guatemala. Digital photography is changing the panorama, but that will not change the fact that there will always be something important to study here. For example, Jorge Chavaría is experimenting with wet-plate collodion photography. It is a technique that came into practice thanks to Gustave le Gray and disappeared sometime between 1930 and 1940 in Guatemala. Chavaría is reproducing this type of photography so that today the public can better understand the photography of yesteryear. He is producing some excellent work. These images are made on glass-plate negatives with a layer of cellulose nitrate mixed with alcohol and a layer of silver nitrate. My research has shown that in

Guatemala many people replaced cellulose nitrate with egg whites, but many of the images made with cellulose nitrate detach from the glass plate negative with greater ease. To help Jorge Chavaría with those experiments, I gave him the silver nitrate from Zanotti's studio, and I loaned him Zanotti's old chemistry notebooks so that he could learn how to perfect his technique. With these and other developments in mind, you could say that in the present Guatemala is learning from the past, and it is producing some very interesting results.

Selected Publications

Girard de Marroquín, Anne. *Rostros de la Guatemala Indígena/ Images of Indigenous Guatemala*. Cifga, 2012.

———. *Visión etnográfica de la indumentaria maya de Guatemala/Ethnographic view of Maya dress in Guatemala*. Servi Prensa, 2017.

Pablo Hernández Hernández

Universidad de Costa Rica

Visual Culture and Academic Practice

IN 2005, AFTER having studied philosophy, philology, and art history at the University of Costa Rica, I moved to the Universidad de Potsdam (Germany) to undertake a PhD in aesthetics and cultural studies under Professor Ottmar Ette. Since then, I have been living and working in Berlin and San Jose, Costa Rica, where I research and am involved in projects on both continents. I study key thinkers within contemporary philosophy (such as Walter Benjamin), the analysis of the material manifestations of visual culture in Central America and how contemporary theory informs academic practice.

Professionally speaking, being in contact with both academic environments (in Europe and Latin America) has been very beneficial to me. It has helped me to develop my work by offering me a wide range of stimulating collaborations and scholarly dialogue in my areas of interest. This constant flow of information between my colleagues and I has allowed me to contemplate some of the differences between how Europe and the English-speaking world see and use photography versus its use and role in Latin America. I think that in Latin America, photographic images are viewed as a type of presence, a way in which the past influences the present. In other words, photography has more of a political role in the sense that these images are part of a constant meditation on dreams, hopes, and desires. However, they are also injustices and crimes yet to come, traces of the forgotten or the betrayed. Above all, photography is a reflection of how the social forces I just mentioned affect politics and community in the present. On the other hand, in Europe and the English-speaking world I think that there is a different emphasis. There, photographs are connected to the notion of facts: historical, scientific, legal, civil, or otherwise. Photographs are viewed as trustworthy evidence of an existence. Photographs are the starting point for a discussion on images. I think that both ways of using photographs—as a truthful document or as an element from the past that attempts to inform the present—can be complimentary. They both help us to stay on our toes and reflect on our current ethics and politics.

Philosophy and Image in the Contemporary Arts

Because I work in a philosophy department at the Universidad de Costa Rica, much of my work is focused on theory and concept-based philosophy. For that reason, I focus more on general trends (how we see and use things generally) than on specific cultural objects. At first, I mostly researched the relationship between literature and philosophy. I was more interested in how literature was produced—its meanings and how those meanings came to be. I was drawn to the philosophy of language, semiotics, post-structural philosophies, material aesthetics, and art philosophy. My doctoral research attempted to combine my interests in the study of images, literature, language, and philosophy. I studied the relationship between texts and images in the contemporary arts. I looked at the growing tendency of the presence of the written word within visual art, and I asked myself some important questions to begin the analysis. Are there models of the type of relationship between text and image in contemporary art? Do these models conflict with the dominant forms of communication media? To find the relevant answers, I began to analyze different cultural objects. I decided to work with the artistic production of Central American artists from the 1990s—the artists who were producing art just after the peace treaties in the zones of conflict in that region. As I studied this body of work, I noticed that artists were repeatedly using photographs to incorporate texts into their visual work. This increased my interest in photography. I was particularly fascinated by how photography kept appearing alongside written work, paintings, engravings, performances, and even art installations. Since then, I have come to see photography as something that is always in collaboration (Azoulay "Photography is collaboration"). When it comes to photography working in collaboration, I think that the mechanical apparatus of the camera makes photography different from the other arts, such as painting or engraving. This led me to be interested in photography as a technical object or an operating system as a first step in the production of images. I was interested in understanding the photographer's cultural position. I did not just want to study the camera as an object that produced images, but rather as an artifact that was programmed and the photographer as a cultural agent who must interface with technology, which has its technological limits (of course). There are certain things you simply can and cannot do with photography. I read a lot of Walter Benjamin, Vilèm Flusser, Jonathan Crary, W. J. T. Mitchell, and Allan Sekula's writings on photography, and I realized that all of them view photography as a form of technological production. They see photography as a system that can reproduce images with a precision previously unknown. These texts led me to another important point. The history of photography is also the history of a unique technology. Photography started in the realm of science and technology, and it has gradually entered the world of entertainment and the quotidian experience. The slow process of the normalization of photography struck me to the extent that now everyone has a camera, and all these questions on duplication, science, and entertainment are now a part of our daily existence.

As I discuss these ideas during my postgraduate research seminars on the philosophy of image and the philosophy of photography that I teach at the Universidad de Costa Rica, I have been able to deepen my ideas and study how writers have reacted to these philosophical theories. I have been able to study how their concepts on representation through photography have changed and how these modifications have affected the world of media and art.

Photography Questions What You Can See and Read

My doctoral thesis was also able to show how photography has been a key protagonist during moments of historic cultural change. I was able to study and use Central American artists to evidence that photography has become a key part of the conventions we use to question what we see, read, write, and do. Photography became one of the crucial elements that disputes what you can see and read. Its arrival coincides with a period that is marked by post-civil war conflicts and the reconstruction of democratic processes in Central America. In the 1990s, after decades of armed conflicts (some of them being the bloodiest in our contemporary history) Central America was entering a process of democracy and peace. It was a time when social and cultural elements needed reshaping and redefining, including what it meant to study text and image.

At that time, many visual artists in Central America were working with a diverse number of photographic productions from Central America's revolutionary past and reworking those images within the context of peace, democracy, cultural consequences, and social and cultural changes. They were turning photographs that were important cultural references into murals and illustrations. They were also using them in digital animations and putting them in comics. Photographs were no longer a "final point" of artistic representation and had become a starting frame of reference for new artistic representations (Ritchin *After Photography*). This change in the usage of photography became my focus. Many history-based narrations saw photography as a final step in a process in representing what is real. I wanted to understand how incorporating photography into other mediums pointed to the fact that photography is simply a way of representing and looking at the world.

If you think of photography as a starting point this can lead you to new insights. If you manipulate a photograph, if you change it, take it apart, and then reassemble it along different lines or series, then these procedures can be seen as part of the life and influence of a photograph. Hence, my research led me to think about photography in a different way. I began to think about how photography can be seen through the logic of guerrilla warfare, and Central America is an ideal location to carry out such an exercise.

One problem with that type of project is the archives. Their location and ownership can be problematic. Digitalization has made it easier to consult these images in some cases, but this also brings up new questions regarding the relationship between photographs and the context in which they are seen and shown. They can lose their sense of belonging to a specific cultural, historical, and social context. We are taught to research photography in relation to their archives: formal or informal, public or private. Every photograph belongs to an archive in some way in terms of space, time, and rhetoric. Those points can determine our research on photography and place the researcher in the position of actively trying to understand the image in the place where it was, where it is, and where it might go later.

My research has led me to archives such as the Instituto de Historia de Nicaragua y Centroamérica (IHNCA) and the Universidad Centroamericana de Managua (UCA) in Nicaragua. The UCA is still in the process of being cataloged and they are trying to determine the value and impact of each photograph. It is an immensely diverse archive that shows the literacy campaigns in Nicaragua during the Sandinista Revolution in the 1980s and the Somoza family's private photographic collection. I also work with the archive in the Museo de la Palabra y la Imagen in El Salvador. This archive is a community-based archive whose collection is made up of donated photographs that the directors try to exhibit. I also work with photographic material from the archive at the Centro de Investigaciones Regionales de Mesoamérica (CIRMA) in Guatemala. It is an important scientific, cultural, and scholarly institution. This specific archive is quite complicated to work with because it houses a wide variety of photographic material from a number of sources: ex-soldiers, members of international solidarity organizations, press and media, and journalistic images from local and global outlets.

I have observed that photographs from that period in Central America appear repeatedly in works of art, in new social movements, in education, in court trials, or even in civic ceremonies. These photographs form an archive that is very much alive, organic, and under constant reconstruction. Their influence must not be discounted because as recently as 2018 they were playing an active role in social movements in Nicaragua, Guatemala, and Honduras. The images are central to the revolutionary hopes of many individuals who strive for social and economic justice in Central America.

Revolution in Central America and Global Iconography

My research on the photography from this period also has another very relevant focus. I ask why many of the photographs from the Central American revolutions in the 1990s are part of the global iconography of popular revolution. This imagery has been so strong and so wide reaching that photographs of the revolution are what have become our strongest visual reference on Central America globally. Photographs made by documentary photographers such as Don McCullin, Susan Meiselas, James Nachtwey, Koen Wessing, and Jean-Marie Simon are some of the most well-known in this respect.

These photographs appear on their own, in history books, in illustrated magazines, and in books on the theory of photography. You only need to take into account Roland Barthes's usage of Koen Wessing's Nicaraguan photographs in *Camera Lucida* in order to explain *punctum* and *studium* to begin to visualize the impact of these Central American images. Year after year the global community uses Barthes to study photography and semiotics in photography by using Nicaraguan photographs that picture leftist revolutionary actions. In universities throughout the world, we analyze the ethics of photography with Susan Sontag's essays on photography and visual culture that draw directly on images of social conflict in Central America. The debate as to whether or not

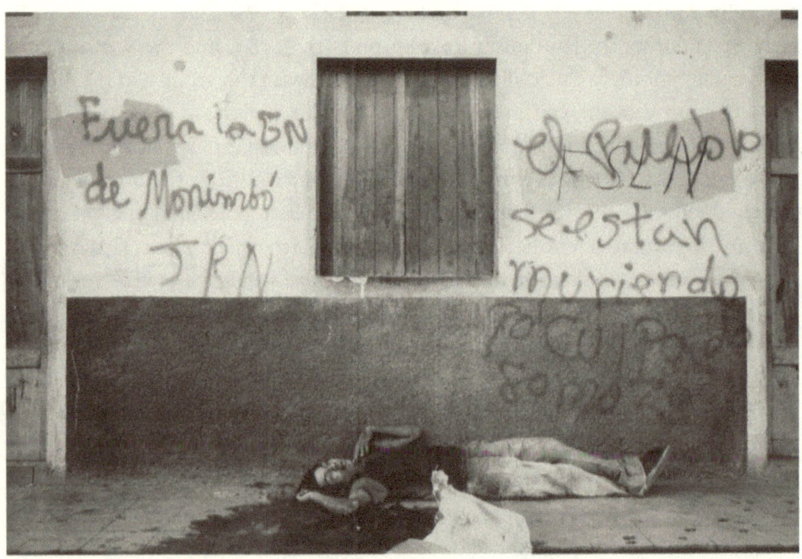

Figure 6.1. Assassination and warning. Nicaragua, c. 1978/79. Susan Meiselas, Magnum Photos.

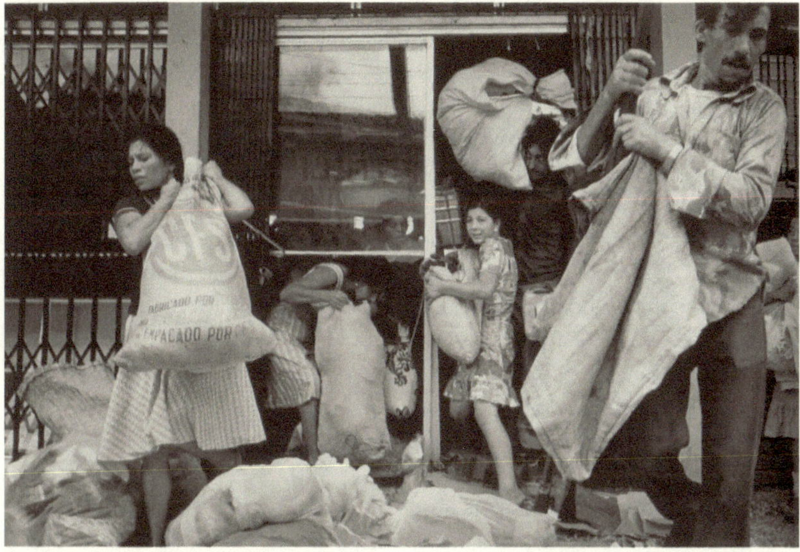

Figure 6.2. Citizens looting a store. Nicaragua. Susan Meiselas, Magnum Photos.

color photography was an appropriate medium to create documentary photography began thanks to Susan Meiselas's color photographs of Central American conflicts.

The cultural philosophers and theorists Hans Belting and Thomas Macho use photographs of violence in El Salvador, Nicaragua, and Guatemala to construct their theoretical arguments on the relationship between images and violence (Belting *Art History After Modernism* and *Face and Mask a Double History*; Macho "Zeit und Zahl"). These examples led me to conclude that this Central American visual archive is of great importance to the ways we understand photography globally. As a protagonist in the media, these Latin American photographs help us to see the state of contemporary visual culture with regard to image, media, and its globalization, as well as the delicate state of our critical knowledge of history.

I also collaborate with artists in Central America. Most of the work consists of research workshops and an opportunity to experiment with artistic processes that involve photographers and photographs in that region. These workshops are interdisciplinary and cross-disciplinary. They bring together social science, art, and literature to discuss the challenges that artistic cultural production faces in Central America. In every country in Central America, we can find cases of photographers whose work moves in many different circles: documentary photography, social criticism, cultural criticism, and other fields that enable us to see how photography spreads across different genres and is multifunctional. Today, there is a vast number of digital publications on the internet. Thanks to them and other areas that increase our visual exposure to Central American photography, I think it is possible to argue that Central American photography is coming to the forefront from among the imagery of the Global South and has become increasingly relevant in terms of social and cultural relevance. In the case of Central American photography from the 1990s, the photographs from this time period are highly relevant in terms of national and regional culture. And having shed associations with journalism or commercial photography, they are also seen as having considerable artistic, documentary, political, and critical presence.

Photography: Apparatus, Technology, Visual Subjectivity

My approach to photography as an object of study and as a research tool is based on the following steps: You must think about photography as an apparatus, a technology, and a visual subjectivity. You need to remember that photography is a process whose end game is to produce a photograph. However, this object can become independent of its production context more than other cultural objects. This is because it is easy to lift a photograph out of its first context and make it a part of a mural, a painting, an engraving, or some other art form. While you cannot disassociate it from the initial event of photography as Ariella Azoulay argues, you can lift the image out of its physical process. We open our history books today, and we are faced with photography. On those occasions, we do not ask how such images were produced, but rather, we contemplate them as mere illustrations. Those cultural and knowledge-focused books show us images as illustrations meant to represent something. They do not see them as objects that are the fruit of our modern culture. This is due in part to photography's natural qualities, which makes it very easy to decontextualize from its production process. I think that when you study Latin American photography from other contexts that are unrelated to the production of those images you tend to see them as coming forth from an invisible process. This elimination of the physical processes of the production of photography from the critical dialogue points to the mechanical nature of its production.

Constant Contact with Creators

I note this point because, like Walter Benjamin and John Berger have emphasized in their writings, the production process is important. In terms of ideology and rhetoric, this process is at least equally important or more important than the location of the photograph. It is so key that even some of the first critical writings on photography underscore the context of both its installation and its production ("The Work of Art" 110–11). Later, Berger reminds us that these contexts are immersed in fields of rhetoric and ideology that must be considered as we study photography (*Ways of Seeing* 19–21). Therefore, I think that it is very important to be in constant contact with photographers. We must understand and analyze their contexts of creation because they remind those of us that work in other fields (literature, philosophy, social sciences, and so forth) that photographs are images that form a part of a larger process that must be studied and understood. As a photography scholar, you must find the connections between the images and the rest of the reality to which they are connected. They are documents that are in constant motion because they are constantly being reinterpreted by new spectators and in the light of new knowledge and social contexts, as Azoulay explains in *The Civil Contract of Photography* (93–97).

Images must take a more active role in our lives and how we see the world. We must become aware of our own visual literacy and know how to use those skills in everything we do. One of the unavoidable experiences that you encounter if you study photography is the need to produce new ideas and new ways of looking at the world. Many of the critical tools we have and use to analyze photography come from painting, our own visual culture, and an abstract blend of what we think are texts and what we think are images. All these conceptual apparatuses are imprecise when we try to apply them directly to the study of photography. Hence, those that study photography find that they must create new concepts and language to be able to speak about images. As a researcher and a philosopher, I personally think that the opportunity to make these contributions to the ongoing critical discussions is energizing.

Selected Publications

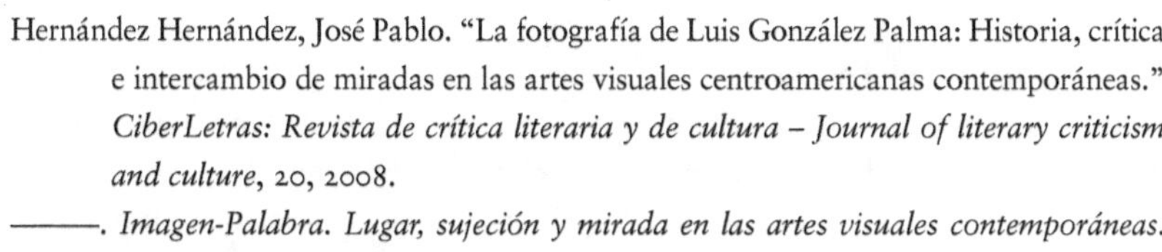

Hernández Hernández, José Pablo. "La fotografía de Luis González Palma: Historia, crítica e intercambio de miradas en las artes visuales centroamericanas contemporáneas." *CiberLetras: Revista de crítica literaria y de cultura – Journal of literary criticism and culture*, 20, 2008.

———. *Imagen-Palabra. Lugar, sujeción y mirada en las artes visuales contemporáneas.* Iberoamericana/Vervuert Verlag, 2012.

———. "Justice and Testimony between Image and Word. Foundations for a Photographic Study of Guerrilla Movements in Central America." *Nuevo mundo, mundos nuevos*, 2014, https://journals.openedition.org/nuevomundo/66886.

———. "Testimonio und Bildakt: Der Einsatz von Photographien als Dokumentation in den Guerrillas Lateinamerikas." *Möglichkeiten und Grenzen von Zeugenschaft in den romanischen Literaturen*, edited by C. Nickel and A. Ortiz-Wallner, Winter-Verlag, 2015.

Sussy Vargas Alvarado

Universidad Veritas

Photography and Fine Arts

I GRADUATED WITH a degree in fine arts from the Universidad de Costa Rica. While I was studying painting at that university, I met Giorgio Timms who taught photography as part of the advertising and design degree within the Faculty of Fine Arts. Because I was in the Fine Arts program, we were not allowed to take photography courses as part of our degree, but professor Timms let us audit the courses, and two of my classmates and I took all of the photography classes that they offered. I learned just about everything they would allow. It changed my life. At that time in Costa Rica a university degree in the field of photography did not exist. The only degree you could get in photography was a technical certificate offered in the Alajuela Province, and that was a long way from my home. Most photographers in Costa Rica at that time were simply amateurs. In 2000, Giorgio Timms established the school of photography at the Universidad Veritas, and he invited me to teach there as well.

While I was studying in high school and for my bachelor's degree, I took courses on ceramic art, painting, engraving, sculpture, drawing, design, and art history. Photography helped me to fill in the gaps I had in my artistic knowledge and allowed me to communicate in ways that other artistic expressions did not permit. That is why I fell so deeply in love with photography. It was during this time that I began to work as Robert Cabrera Padilla's assistant.[1] He was an extraordinary scholar and artist from Guatemala with a fantastic reputation. He had arrived in Costa Rica many years earlier, fleeing military conflict, and he stayed in our country where he enjoyed a fulfilling career in both academia and art. He gave me a research methodology and taught me how to understand vernacular culture and how to work with primary sources.

I began to combine painting and photography. At first, the aspect I liked the most about photography was the chemical process of analog photography, but over time, researching the history of photography became my passion. Now I teach the laboratory skills you need to develop photos with chemicals while I research in archives and write Costa Rica's history of photography. However, I do not limit myself to research on photography in Costa Rica. I also study other areas of art according to my interests.

Roberto Cabrera taught me many things about fieldwork in relation to research. As a teacher, artist, and scholar he is very methodical and teaches you to base your scholarly efforts on primary sources. I learned to work with primary material with him: original documents and individuals who were still alive and could give me direct information, materials, and objects. You could call that approach a kind of visual archaeology. He would work with ethnography, anthropology, art theory, and other sources as he wrote. When I studied art at university, most of what I learned was purely descriptive. He taught me how to be analytical. Cabrera taught me how to explore the context, to question, to delve deeper into the data. I was able to apply these lessons to my knowledge of the chemical processes of photography and expand the historical context as I studied and wrote about photography in Costa Rica.

When I began to research on the history of photography in Costa Rica, there was almost nothing on that topic here. There was only a three-page article Carlos Meléndez published in 1968: "Notas acerca de la historia de la fotografía en Costa Rica." He was a Central American historian, and he wrote an anecdotal history that considered some of the information on early photographers in Costa Rica during the nineteenth century. While I was Cabrera's assistant, I began researching newspapers and old magazines, and I started to copy many of the articles and advertisements on photography. Gradually, I accumulated a large archive on this topic that allowed me to build on what was known about photography here.

I started sharing my findings in different conferences and other presentations on Latin American photography. Because at that time the internet did still not exist, the process was much slower and had more obstacles. You needed to travel to different libraries and archives. You used interviews and other sources to gather information. In 1998 Ileana Alvarado, who was the curator for the Banco Central de Costa Rica, invited me to create an exhibition on the history of family portraits in Costa Rica. We named it *Retratos de familia*, and the project allowed me to reflect on and write about the subject as well as opened the possibility of creating an exhibition and catalog that focused on the history of photography here. Then we embarked on that project and focused on the history of photography in Costa Rica from a very wide and revisionist perspective. Our published project (2004) included more than 365 images and photographers (the majority of which had never been seen before). The book-exhibition catalog allowed me to write the first ever history of Costa Rican photography that studied and contextualized photography here between 1848 and 1940. After I completed my half of the book, Ileana Alvarado and Efraím Hernández wrote the other half of photography's history here (1950–2003). We named the combined edition *La mirada del tiempo: Historia de la Fotografía en Costa Rica 1848–2003*.

The History of Photography in Costa Rica

La mirada del tiempo was an extremely new venture. No one had ever tried to write a history of photography in Costa Rica before, at least not like we did with a wealth of authors and images that had never been viewed before by the reading public. Our corresponding exhibition lasted more than three months and was seen by hundreds of visitors. We had public talks about our findings, and the visitors and local photographers loved it. We proved that the history of photography in Costa Rica was bigger that what most people had ever imagined and that much more needs to be studied and integrated into Costa Rica's art history narrative.

Public financing was important to both that book and my next one: *El Caribe limonense a través de la mirada y la obra de Hans Wimmer: 1903–1947*. This second project analyzes the life and work of Hans Wimmer, a German immigrant who came to Puerto Limon, Costa Rica, and set up a photography business. For both of my books, the Colegio de Costa Rica (a branch of the Ministerio de Cultura y Juventud de Costa Rica) provided me a scholarship to

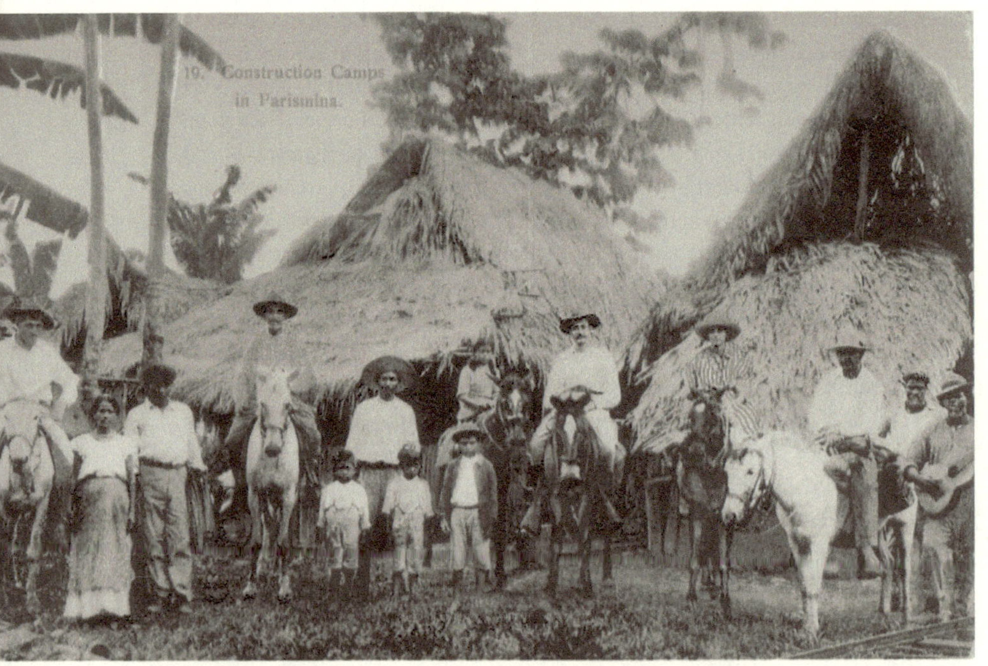

Figure 7.1. N. 19 Construction camps, Parismina, Limón, Costa Rica, 1906. Hans Wimmer. Image no. 31, Hans Wimmer Series, Sussy Vargas Private Archive. (Photograph was hand-colored by Hans Wimmer.)

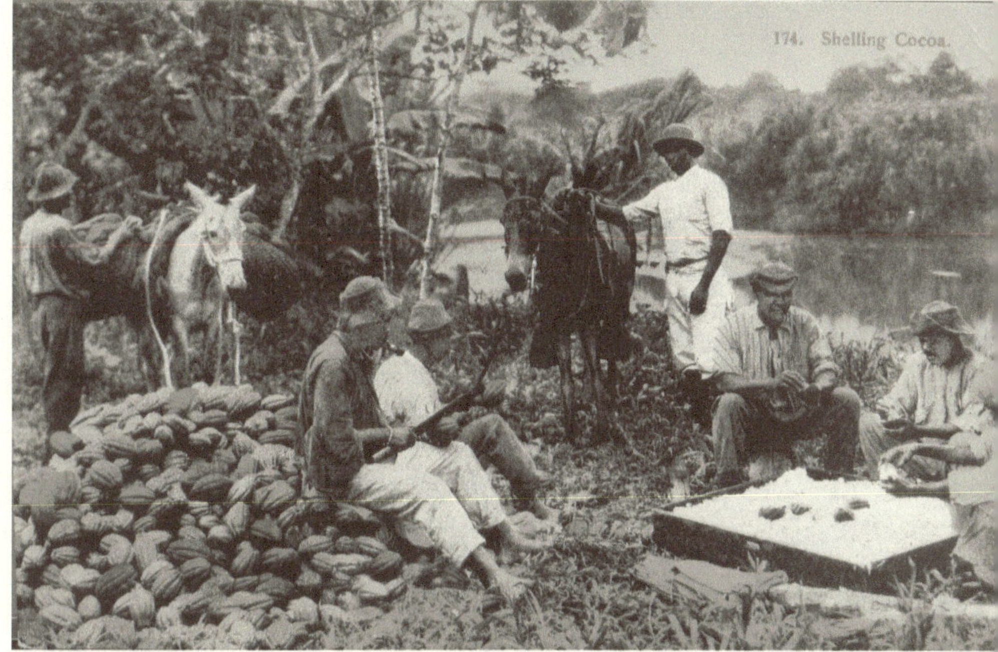

Figure 7.2. N. 174 Shelling cocoa, Costa Rica, c. 1906. Hans Wimmer. Image no. 79, Hans Wimmer Series, Sussy Vargas Private Archive. (Photograph was hand-colored by Hans Wimmer.)

conclude each of my research projects and publish them. Those scholarships did not fund the groundwork research process, which I had to finance myself. Here, unless you are a scholar for one of the state-run public universities, the onus is on you to finance that part of your work.

My book on Hans Wimmer involved several stages. First, I had to systematically search out different sources of information on the topic, such as newspapers from the first half of the twentieth century as well as guidebooks and other written material. I contacted Wimmer's descendants to try to consult what was left of his archive. Then I had to document, digitalize, study, and classify the material I encountered. Much of the photographic material in his archive needed cleaning and other elements of care. This took me months, but it enabled me to become acquainted with Wimmer's photographic production. The fact that I had studied the chemical processes of analog photography helped me immensely during these stages because I knew about its conservation and restoration. As an expert in this field, I am frequently called on to study collections of antique photographs and help preserve and conserve this type of photography by cleaning, restoring, and reproducing the images.

The Latin American Perspective

I would have to say that one of the books that has had the largest impact on me is *Image and Memory: Photography from Latin America, 1884–1994*. I was especially struck by Boris Kossoy's essay: "Photography in Nineteenth-Century Latin America." It was the first piece I had ever seen that engaged with photography from what I consider to be a Latin American perspective. Until that point in time, I had really only read about photography or Latin American photography in texts that came from abroad. Kossoy opened up a new world to me because he was writing about photography from an internal Latin American perspective and exploring ideas that I had not considered but I thought were extremely interesting and relevant. For example, he explored the impact of ideas related to exoticism and the Other and how these generate a reoccurring analytic discourse on Latin America. Likewise, the readings that my teacher Cabrera gave me had a lot of influence on the way I think about photography and art. He gave me many books to read, and they were extremely varied in their topics. Mircea Eliade's *The Sacred and the Profane* and James George Frazer's *The Golden Bough* both helped me to consider the role of magic and religion in Latin America. Lois Parkinson Zamora has enabled me to understand the *barroco novomundista* and Latin American literature, while Gilbert Durand's *The Anthropological Structures of the Imaginary* allowed me to comprehend how imagination within the field of anthropology functions.

There are many photography theorists whose writings are key to my work. Among others, Roland Barthes, Walter Benjamin, Susan Sontag, and Joan Fontcuberta have been very influential. However, I do not think of myself as anyone's disciple. I think that all of them tend to conceive images as material objects, whether they be political or social objects. I think that images are more than that. Images are texts that are connected to literature, semiotics, and hermeneutics. Just as Benjamin suggests, you can read images from the perspective of history, ethnography, and visual anthropology, or other fields like psychology, film studies, or science. Photography is more than a mere object that illustrates other ideas. The plurality and intertextuality of photography has kept me from following any one line of thought, discipline, theory, or analytical methodology, though when it comes to my methodology for studying photography, I am more qualitative than quantitative. I disagree with the idea of art as a simple statistic. I prefer to study art from other perspectives. I strive to understand vernacular art. I want to comprehend the role of kitsch photography, photographs that have been painted on (*iluminadas*), popular photography, and rural perspectives of art. Instead of forming part of one specific school of thought, I try to allow myself to be influenced by a wide variety of ideas. One of my work colleagues, Roberto Guerrero (a scholar and artist at the Universidad Veritas), helped me to create and curate the exhibition *Detrás del portón rojo, una vision de la erótica en el arte costarricense.* It was an exhibition on erotic art, the likes of which had never been seen in Costa Rica. We decided to organize it by topic, not chronology, so you would observe pre-Colombian art next to art from the 1980s, or even more recent pieces. The fact that we were able to place it in the Museo de Arte Costarricense was also key because that venue is canonical. This project continues to bear fruit. For example, right now I am writing an article on pre-Columbian erotic art in Costa Rica. This project grew out of another project on erotic art in Costa Rica in 2017. As I studied the topic, I had many questions and I realized that no one has written about it. The archaeologists here had not studied it, so I convinced two colleagues from that field to collaborate with me.

This project has involved art theory, too, such as the works by the Argentinean writer and anthropologist Adolfo Colombres. His book *Teoría transcultural del arte: Hacia un pensamiento visual independiente* (2005) has helped me to better understand the transcultural nature of art. Sandra Martínez Rossi's *La piel como superficie simbólica: Procesos de transculturación en el arte contemporáneo* (2014) has helped me to contextualize the notion of the body as seen by many different cultures. You need additional perspectives to help you speak more coherently about pre-Colombian erotic art.

Walter Benjamin's writings have left a deep impression on me. He was a pioneer, and his writings are extremely relevant even today. I love the way he writes about how images can be studied as layers and how images have an infinite number of possible interpretations. I try to show this as I write about photography. Likewise, his writings have helped me take a keen interest in context. When I approach a photograph, I now ask it questions: Who is in the photograph? What is the history behind this image? What chemical process made this photograph? I study the photograph as an object. I try to write the object's biography as Benjamin suggests. For example, the Hans Wimmer archive was an incredible discovery. That collection had survived the destruction of a government raid that President Rafael Calderón Guardia ordered in 1942. It also survived two fires and the fact that the family simply did not know what to do with those images. After so many years, so many problems, and so much neglect, the archive was in a poor state. Many of the negatives were broken, moldy, or had adhesions. The fact that Wimmer worked in the Caribbean meant that his body of work has faced an enormous amount of humidity and heat that is fatal to photographic material and makes the photographic process itself very challenging. Writing about these aspects of context is all a part of the research process and reveals important details that we must consider.

The research process has been never-ending. There is always more to do and find. After more than twenty years of searching I have been able to identify the first female photographer in Costa Rica. I have also been able to find

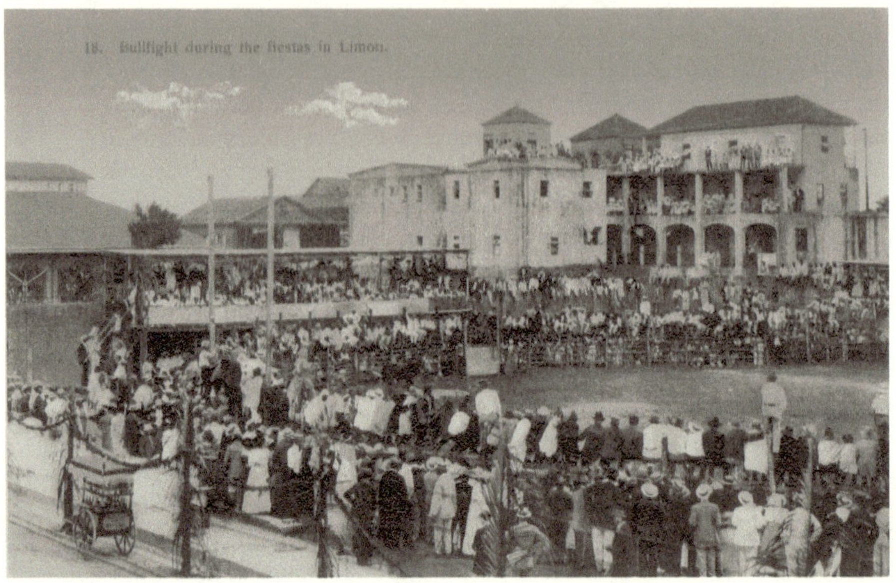

Figure 7.3. N.18 Bullfight during the fiestas in Puerto Limon, Costa Rica, c. 1906. Hans Wimmer. Image no. 22, Hans Wimmer Series, Sussy Vargas Private Archive. (Photograph was hand-colored by Hans Wimmer.)

the work of the very first Costa Rican photographer of African descent. Both individuals are key historical figures in our visual history, and I plan to reveal their identities in one of my future publications. These discoveries motivate me and lead me to others. I love to delve into the past and uncover the contexts, the artists, and the forces that produced the photographs I have been studying. Asking questions is part of that process. What is important here? Why is it important? Who was the artist? What did he or she do? These lines of inquiry allow me to discover the facts that enable my analysis. I often say that I do not study the history of photography; I study the forces that move the human mind.

Archives in Costa Rica

Costa Rica has been blessed to have avoided the civil wars and other long and destructive internal conflicts that have afflicted other parts of Latin America. Thanks to this, many of its archives have survived the test of time. The Biblioteca Nacional has wonderful collections of newspapers, magazines, books, photographs, and other images. The Archivo Nacional has a wide range of foundational documents that span from colonial times to our present day. The Museo Nacional de Costa Rica also has many wonderful documents and photographs in addition to other valuable objects. The Catholic Church in Costa Rica maintains the Archivo Arquidiocesano, which has an excellent collection of antique photographs and valuable objects.

It is not uncommon for me to find that the archivists are not totally aware of their photographic holdings. Indexes are incomplete. They give priority to the written word. I have helped many archivists structure their collections to try and remedy this. I have also helped to organize private photo collections. Frequently, my students lead me to these private collections. At the Universidad Veritas I teach the course "Latin American and Costa Rican Photography," and one of the exercises my students undertake is to research family archives. Those activities have led me to many different finds. One of the great tragedies our country suffers is when families, not able to recognize the extreme value of their family's photographs, simply throw them away. When that happens, you lose irreplaceable memories and historic material.

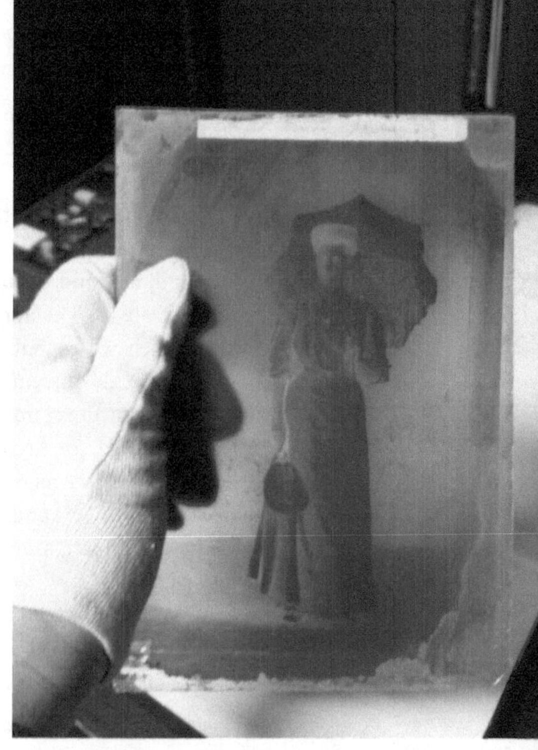

Figure 7.4. Untitled. Costa Rica, c. 1906. Hans Wimmer. Image no. 15, Hans Wimmer Series, Sussy Vargas Private Archive. (Black-and-white Hans Wimmer 1906 glass-plate negative in the process of being cleaned prior to developing a positive image from it.)

The Latin American Perspective

For many years we were guilty of a sin of omission. We focused so much on documentary photography in Latin America that we forgot about other types of photography. There is a huge focus on the documentary in Latin America, or occasionally, on portraiture. Recently, we have begun to see changes in these areas. We are beginning to see more interest in how we conceive the world: imagination from a Latin American perspective. This worldview comes from a wide range of influences. Because Latin America is a mixture of African, Indigenous, and European influences, hybridity is an important aspect of our culture and identity. It is our essence. As Latin American photographers begin to turn their gaze inward and ask what they are and what they see, we begin to observe that they stop replicating foreign models that do not represent our reality accurately. We are finally beginning to understand who we are and represent this with the work we do.

As a researcher, I have started to notice that we Latin Americans are finally beginning to get to know each other and understand the wide variety of ethnicities, music, food, art, and history that we have among us. These elements both unite and separate us. The internet has always supported the development of new ways in which we exchange information and see each other. We are brought together through our cinema that we watch over the internet or by participating in online forums (among other activities). For decades, I was only ever able to watch Mexican or Argentinean film. Now, I enjoy films from Brazil, Colombia, and other Latin American countries. These new connections allow us to create new joint projects and understand each other's work better. This is key because to be able create a more global perspective on photography here, we need to be in contact. If we are not, we will not be able to construct the needed context. We will not be able to identify what had united us and what has separated us historically.

Personal Context

I grew up in a lower-middle class family, and part of that experience meant that popular culture was part of my normal environment. Popular culture therefore influences the way I think, my thoughts themselves, and the topics that interest me as I research. I am drawn to aspects of culture that official culture has made "invisible," or that have only been studied under the guise of folklore, popular art, or popular culture. In recent years, the Museo de Arte y Diseño (MADC) in Costa Rica has made a space for this type of art, but aside from that, there have not been many more locations for this type of art to have an official impact. I try to underline the importance of seeing culture as something much broader than what we normally do in academia or other official channels. There is much fieldwork to do in these areas. We must comprehend what motivates and inspires these artists. I grew up listening to boleros and tangos while my grandfather watched boxing matches. I spent a lot of time attempting to understand the religious dynamics of the rosary and prayer. My first art school was what I saw in the market, the newspaper, and a small encyclopedia that my mother bought when she became a teacher. I did not enter any official art school until I was much older, when I started taking classes from Francisco Ulla, an important sculptor here. Hence, my work is related to understanding vernacular influences on art and how photography manifests them; how these images enrich our understanding of context, technology, chemistry, and memory; and how they all connect to imagery in one way or another.

New Research Possibilities in Costa Rica

Technological advances are allowing us to access new and different materials that help both artists and researchers in the study of photography in general. Now you can access archives and libraries throughout the whole world and have access to documents and Latin American photographs that we could only dream about in the past. You can consult collections in Europe and the United States without ever having to board a plane or boat. In Costa Rica you can now look at archives or consult old newspapers and photographic archives in the Biblioteca Nacional or the Archivo Nacional without ever having to leave the comfort of your home. Just a decade ago, this type of research would have hardly been possible.

Throughout all Latin America we are now beginning to see the appearance of previously undiscovered archives. This is true even of famous photographers such as the Colombian Benjamin de la Calle who everyone thought was simply a traditional portrait photographer (Poole *Vision, Race, and Modernity* 234). However, recently a collection of his self-portraits of him cross-dressing in the 1920s has converted him into a Latin American pioneer of queer aesthetic. We are also witnessing the appearance of archives such as that of Sara Castrejón (Villela and Castrejón Reza), one of the women who photographed the Mexican Revolution. Likewise, we are able to observe the importance of Mexican photographers such as Enrique Díaz or Agustín Jiménez (Monroy *Historias para ver*; Córdova and Jiménez *Agustín Jiménez y la vanguardia fotográfica mexicana*). When it comes to the study of Latin American photography, I have no doubt that Mexico is one of the countries at the forefront. However, now is a time of important discoveries. Hidden archives are surfacing. Memories are being resurrected thanks to individuals who share images online. Much of this new material is coming from smaller, more rural locations far from our capital and large cities. These new sources of information bring to light many new and important insights.

The ease of digital photography in our time helps us to value the work done in the 1970s and 1980s by Sara Facio and her publishing house La Azotea in Argentina. She was a true pioneer in the publication of Latin American photography. She produced a series of small books with a brief introduction and many photographs. Her series explored photographers such as Jesús Yas and José Noriega, Martín Chambi, Alejandro Witcomb, Grete Stern, Luis González Palma, Marcos López, Sandra Eleta, and others (Schwartz "Among Friends"). Online digital publications now let me research magazines on visual studies in Ecuador, Colombia, and Brazil, allowing me access to material that I would have struggled to reach or share in person. When you consider these developments, the future of the study of photography in Latin America seems very bright.

I have been teaching photography at the University of Veritas for the last eighteen years, and I have been able to start a course on Latin American and Costa Rican photography to teach the very basics of our history here. We have also begun to acquire many books and other material about Latin American photography for our library. Our goal is to have the best collection on this topic in the country. It is still in process, but we have made very important strides in the right direction.

One area of concern that impresses itself on my mind is the disappearance of archives within institutions. Costa Rica has some incredible archives, but we do not really have any measures in place to protect them. Unfortunately, sometimes we do not even know how to take care of our archives. We witness much effort and investment put into special archives and libraries for paintings, sculptures, and engravings, but we do not really have any photo libraries. This is one of our major challenges. I have seen some great work at the Centro de la Imagen in Mexico in this respect. We need this too. We must teach people about the historical value that photographic images have. The difficulty is that here people tend to only view photographs as illustrations or something to keep in the family archive.

The past two years I have been writing a book using the historical archive in the National Museum, and I hope to publish it soon. My work there has led me to want to underline the massive amount of effort needed to preserve the valuable material in its collection. We are making small improvements in this area. However, many of the negatives are falling apart because they are in the same archives as the paper documents, and those conditions are simply not appropriate for keeping photographic material. We need dedicated photographic libraries that can take care of, conserve, and protect material while enabling research and publication on their holdings. We need an increased understanding of the fundamental role that photography plays in the construction of our memory and our individual and collective identity.

Selected Publications

Vargas, Sussy. "Breve historia de la taxonomía del cuerpo y del pecado en el arte en Costa Rica." 2016. https://revistas.ucr.ac.cr/index.php/escena/article/view/25585.

———. *El caribe limonense a través de la mirada y la obra de Hans Wimmer, 1903–1947*. Universidad Veritas, 2017.

———, et al. *La mirada del tiempo: Historia de la fotografía en Costa Rica, 1843–2002*. Fotografía y memoria, Fundación Museos del Banco Central, 2006.

Vargas, Sussy, and Carolina Goodfellow. *Grafitica: Gráfica popular en Costa Rica*. Roger Union Printing, 2014.

Gisela Elvira Cánepa Koch

Pontificia Universidad Católica del Perú

Anthropology, Photography, and Andean Music

I AM AN anthropologist who works with photography. Aside from my PhD work at the University of Chicago, the Pontificia Universidad Católica del Perú (PUCP) has been my academic base for work and study. With regard to my beginnings in the study of photography, the university was instrumental in that as well. While I was studying anthropology as an undergraduate at the PUCP, I began to work as a research assistant on a project (sponsored by the Ford Foundation) that was documenting audiovisuals of Andean music and its corresponding rituals and festivals. At first, we designed the project with the aim of preserving Peruvian culture; however, as it grew, we decided to expand the research's impact and produce an archive that could be distributed physically. This led us to create items such as compact discs that contained the music, ethnographic documentaries, and photographic material of the events we covered. The project spanned six years in total. We established a vast archive called the "Archivo de Música Tradicional Andina."[1] It is one of the largest multimedia collections in Latin America of Peruvian music because it includes photography, video, and sound recordings.

The photographs in that archive allow you to observe the regional and ethnic differences in the expressive culture and the creation of social spheres via costumes, rituals, and different musical genres. To develop this project, we worked for one year in each region, covering each of its key festivals. What really motivated me to study photography from an anthropological perspective comes from two areas of concern within this project: First, the fact that, as technology has grown and become more accessible and popular, the dancers that we studied were tending to document their practices with photography. In fact, their photography has started to become an integral part of the choreographic discourse on these Peruvian dances because it enables individuals to reflect on

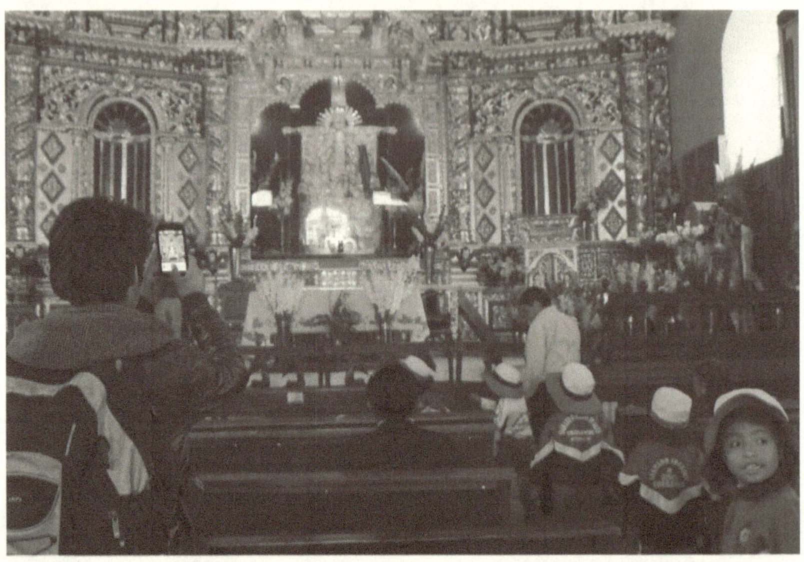

Figure 8.1. Religious follower captures the image of el Señor de Torrechayoc with his telephone in a church located just outside of the Urubamba district in Cusco, Peru, 2016. Pablo Espinoza.

their dance practice. And second, that, over time, the photographic records that we created for the Instituto de Etnomúsica began to acquire historic value, and they were beginning to appear widely throughout social media. Many individuals started to consult this material to help them recreate dances and music as well as reinforce claims of authenticity. Observing the value of these images, their permanence, and the new meaning they acquire thanks to social media helped to spark my interest in photography as an area of study.

I began to teach visual anthropology to undergraduate students in 1992 before traveling abroad for my PhD, and I have continued to do so since my return. I then established a master's program in visual anthropology in 2009. My academic base in Lima has been a wonderful place to work in the field of visual anthropology. Even so, only a few people research visual anthropology and photography here, but we are increasing in number. Since 2009, we have been witnessing some growth in this area in Lima and in the other regions in Peru. At our university, we have students from throughout the country (and other regions of Latin America such as Mexico, Colombia, and Chile) who are interested in the study of the visual and take our master's degree in visual anthropology at PUCP. There are three other Peruvian universities that study photography in relation to society and culture that are worth highlighting: the Universidad Nacional de San Antonio Abad del Cusco, the Universidad Nacional de San

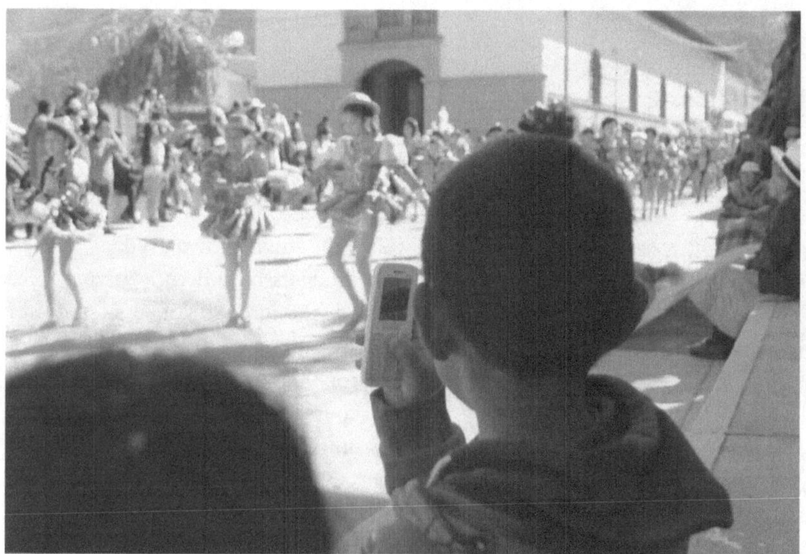

Figure 8.2. Young boy uses a phone to record dance steps just outside the local chapel dedicated to el Señor de Torrechayoc in Urubamba, Curso, Peru, c. 2016. Pablo Espinoza.

Agustín, and the Universidad de Piura. In the case of Universidad Nacional de San Agustín, they have made a strong effort to promote research in the area of visual anthropology and teach courses in this area. A group of our former students there are even working to create a visual anthropology program that focuses directly on photography as well as media and digital culture. Therefore, our master's program has been very influential with regard to the growth of the study of photography within the field of visual studies in Latin America. However, not everyone who studies visual anthropology specializes in photography. Our visual anthropology program has five different areas of focus from which to choose: documentary production; audiovisual methodology; photography and archives; anthropology and media; and material culture, art, and museums.

Photography, Identity, and Visual Representation

One of the reasons I felt inclined to study photography was because I have always been interested in representation. As an undergraduate, I studied the usage of masks in Peruvian festivals. My PhD thesis focused on Peruvian festivals and migration (with one chapter dedicated to filming and photographing the dancers at these festivals). The photographs allowed me to write about how

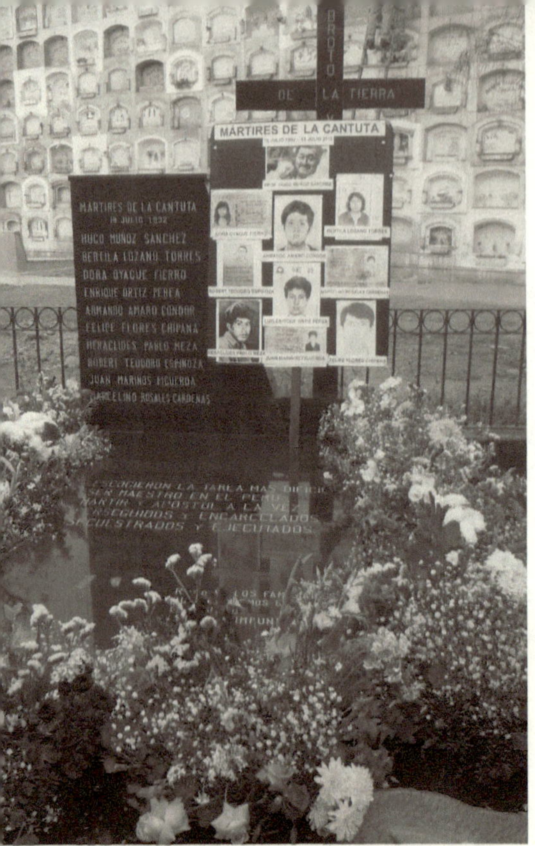

Figure 8.3. Romería en conmemoración por los 18 años de ocurridos los eventos de La Cantuta, Peru (Detail from pilgrimage commemorating the 18th anniversary of the events that happened in La Cantuta, Peru), July 18, 2010. Mercedes Figeroa.

individuals negotiated their identity through physical and visual representation. This focus on the visual came to the forefront through discussions on the authenticity of the cultural repertoires the subjects displayed.

Students have been a driving force behind the growth of the study of images and material culture in Peruvian anthropology. When we introduced the course on visual anthropology at my university, it was because the students were interested in the field and requested a course in this area. I was the fortunate individual who the director of the Faculty of Social Sciences invited to teach the class thanks to my work with the Archive of Traditional Music Project. That experience helped me to see photography as more than a just a vehicle that enabled me to visually document cultural expressions; it also contains a theoretical and thematic perspective. At that time (in the late 1980s and the early 1990s), it was very hard to get bibliographic sources. You depended on those who went abroad to bring you back recent publications, which I did. We started out slow and a bit behind in Peru, but eventually we caught up. After teaching on the subject of photography and anthropology for some time, I also began to publish in this area. My first publications helped me to understand the lay of the field of the study of photography in Peru. My first project was to edit a book on the topic of visual studies and anthropology in Peru: *Imaginación visual y cultura en el Perú* (2009). This publication was a summary of visual anthropology in Peru up to that point in time. I wrote a critical introduction and set the stage for the analytical essays to follow. The articles delved into topics such as photography as a cultural representation of the Amazon and the Andes and photography as memory during the recent years of violence in Peru. That book also included related visual topics such as material culture and visual arts (from painting to graffiti) and the anthropology of audiovisual mediums. My interest then was to

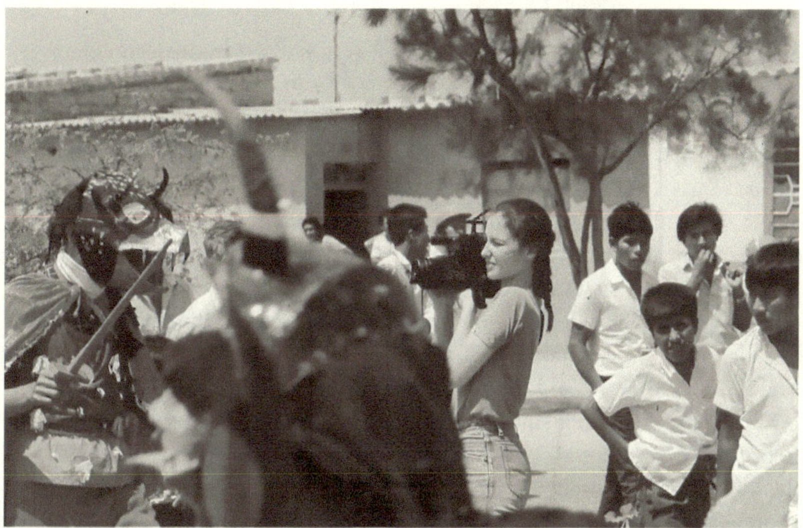

Figure 8.4. Gisela Canepa videoing the "danza de los diablitos" (dance of the devils) during La fiesta de la cruz de Pañala, a local celebration, Mórropa, Lambayaque, Peru, c. 1990. Raúl R. Romero.

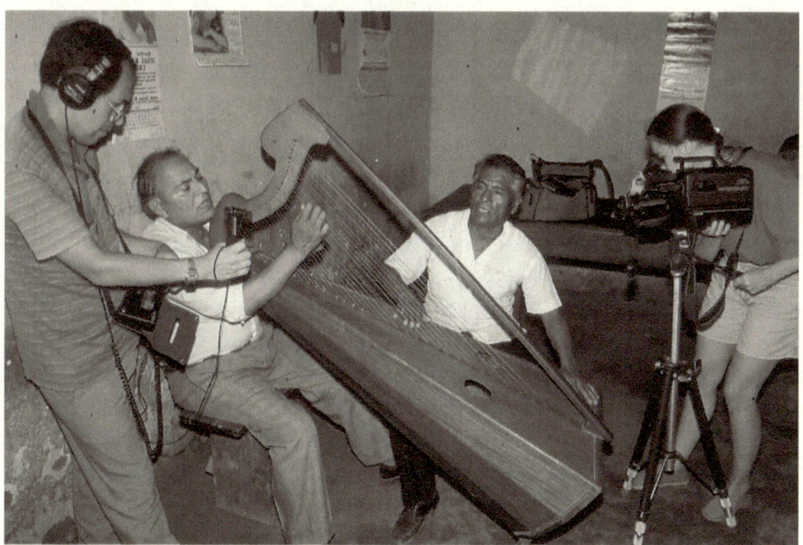

Figure 8.5. Gisela Canepa and Leo Casas making video and audio recordings of Don Andrés Mendoza's harp music in Monsefu, Chiclayo, Lambayaque, Peru, 1991. Raúl R. Romero.

understand the role of photography as well as film in the construction of an ethnographic imagination (as I did in my article "*La teta asustada*" which reviewed that film). I wanted to know the way Otherness is visually shaped in Peru.

Later, I was fortunate enough to receive the George Forster Scholarship for advanced researchers from the Alexander von Humboldt Foundation. These funds allowed me to travel to Germany and explore their ethnographic photography archives. I became acquainted with the photographic collections of German scientists that had visited Peru and Latin America during the final decades of the nineteenth century and the first decades of the twentieth. These included Max Uhle, Konrad Theodor Preuss, Robert Lehman Nitsche, Teobert Maler, Edward Seler, and Walter Lehmann, though I decided to concentrate my research efforts on Heinrich Brüning. Brüning's archives are part of the collections at the Ethnologisches Museum and Phonogram Archive in Berlin and the Völkerkunde Museum in Hamburgm, where I dedicated much of my work effort. The time I spent at the Freie Universität Berlin (the Free University of Berlin) was also productive because I was able to meet like-minded colleagues who also researched other ethnographic collections in Latin America or curated museum exhibitions on related topics. Thanks to the archives I mentioned and my newfound contacts, such as Professor Ingrid Kummels, I was able to identify very specific collections on photography and organize a book that Kummels and I have published together: *Photography in Latin America: Images and Identities Across Time and Space*. Hence, the Alexander von Humboldt Foundation funding for my research has been key to some of my recent outputs.

Photography, Ethnography, Peruvian Music, and Brüning

Hans Heinrich (Enrique) Brüning was a collector and a self-taught archaeologist, historian, and ethnographer who lived from 1875 to 1925 along the northern coast of Peru.[2] He is considered the father of ethnography in that region. I was aware of his photographs while I was carrying out fieldwork in the Lambayeque area in 1987 for our project on traditional Peruvian music that I described earlier. At that time, there were many intellectuals and activists who promoted the Mochica regional identity and would discuss the existence of a photographic collection, but no one was certain of its exact location. A year later, a North American scholar named Richard Schaedel at the University of Texas, Austin published a book called *La etnografía muchik en las fotografías de H. Brüning, 1886–1925* that contained a large number of Brüning's photographs. Schaedel (who had also spent a period of study at the Völkerkunde Museum in Hamburg) had located the photographic collections in the mid-1980s in the same German museums that I mentioned earlier (Dillehay "Richard Paul Schaedel"). The photographs he published contained images of architecture, technology, festivals, and rituals, and individuals wearing typical clothing from the period. I too was able to see the original photographs in those German archives, and I discovered that many of the images from Schaedel's book had been scanned and were circulating throughout social media sites in Peru.

There was a paradoxical element in all this that intrigued me. As a scholar, I had to travel to Germany to see the original archive. However, local promoters of the Mochica identity in Lambayeque, Peru, considered them one of their cultural treasures and promoted them online as part of their political identity. I began to ask myself questions regarding the mobility of these photographic objects. I also began to think about the accessibility of archival materials, their social uses, and the possibilities that digital technologies offer to make material accessible to new audiences. This led to my project focusing on the history of Brüning's photographic collection, its production, the circulation of its images, and their scientific, social, and economic value. I also brought into consideration the use of photographs on social media and the museums' politics and policies regarding the digitalization of that material.

What I have learned is that, though Brüning's original photographs are in still in Germany, thanks to social media they have acquired an unprecedented visibility and mobility. This movement has allowed certain activists and intellectuals to use the photographs to revitalize a regional Mochica identity by focusing on the ethnographic content of the photographs. However, the usage of these photographs on social media tends to favor detaching the images from their original contexts, challenging the authority of the archives that contain them, and creating what we could describe as "new originals."

Ideas That Have Influenced My Research

Elizabeth Edward's work, such as her article "The Colonial Archival Imaginaire at Home," has had a huge influence on my research, particularly in relation to the history of photographic ethnography. Gillian Rose's book *Visual Methodologies* on methodologies for interpreting photographs has been very useful, as has Sara Pink's edited volume *Visual Interventions* that studies methods for using audiovisual materials. I am very familiar with the classic texts of photographic analysis such as *Camera Lucida* by Roland Barthes, "The Work of Art in the Age of Mechanical Reproduction" by Walter Benjamin, and *On Photography* by Susan Sontag, for example. My students and I study them as part of my courses because they form our theoretical bases on photography. When I teach, I tend to use Barthes's terminology such as *studium* and *punctum* as they can reveal new ways to understand photography. I use them as a platform to be able to speak about objects, agents, and the fibers of social fabric as well as cultural values and effects.

Benjamin has helped me to historicize photography in terms of its technological conditions and the aesthetic mandates that define it. Replicability is central to that notion and is useful to our discussions on how to understand photography in our digital era. His work allows me to think about social uses of photography and how its performative mandates are linked to digital technology. Sontag's writings are useful in that they help us to discuss the existing relationships between consumerism, photographic appropriation, and capitalism. All three are important authors who engage with topics and have approaches that are useful to visual anthropology. I use theory from anthropology and ethnographic research to understand the material nature of photography and its role as an object and an agent in relation to social fabric. Theory allows me to underline photography's value and its place within culture. My research on photography requires me to think about concepts that can directly engage with multiple voices and gazes, agency, and the production of knowledge through committed means.

For me, one very influential book has been Deborah Poole's *Vision, Race, and Modernity: A Visual Economy of the Andean World* (1997). The Spanish translation of the book came out in 2000, when there was still very little in this area. This led to it becoming a key theoretical reference on how to study photography in Peru. Her work was particularly helpful with regard to understanding visual economy, as was her call to work more directly with the material dimension of photography. Poole's proposal to see photography as a transcontinental phenomenon was a theoretical aspect that I was able to use with my work on the Brüning material. Her study gave me an academic explanation that enabled me to describe what was occurring with Brüning's work and its impact on Peruvian society. I could perceive the material nature of photography and its relationship with technology, economy, and identity politics. Poole's arguments on the transcontinental production of photography are important and merit comment. Her ideas help us realize that we cannot think of the production of photography in Peru or anywhere in Latin America as something completely local. Other writers have also influenced the way I have approached my study of photography in Peru. Arjun Appadurai's ideas on the social lives of objects in the introduction of his edited volume *The Social Life of Things* has influenced my work greatly, as has George Marcus's ideas regarding the ethnography of the multi-local as he described them in "Ethnography in/of the World System: The Emergence of Multi-Sited Ethnography." Ann Laura Stoler's chapter "Colonial Archives and the Arts of Governance" in *Refiguring the Archive* has been very useful in helping me understand how we treat archival material when we study photography.

My research on Brüning has allowed me to follow the production of photography between Europe and Latin America and their interconnectedness during the moment the photographs were taken and the present. Now I look

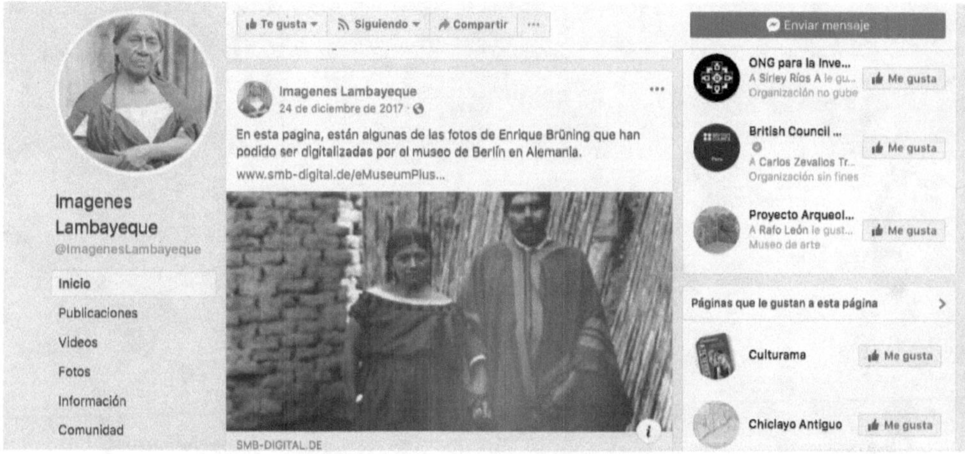

Figure 8.6. Social media usage of Bruning photograph by local Peruvian cultural society, screenshot, 2019. Nathanial Gardner.

at the role of digital technology, which allows image travel to be much more fluid and changes what people think about photography and what they want from it. Consider the following example in that regard. When I was working in northern Peru in the 1990s there was a strong interest in physically recovering Brüning's photograph archives held in Germany. At that time, the locals felt that the images were part of the regional patrimony and they wanted them returned to Peru. Now, however, with the advances in technology and the possibility to access these images from anywhere, there is not such a strong focus on the physical location of the archive if the images continue to circulate. The usage of the digital material has helped these local users to recalculate the meaning of the role of photographic patrimony.

The Multidisciplinary Nature of Photography

Students are now beginning to branch out and focus on photography from the vantage point of various fields. The study of ethnographic photography and the formation of photographic collections is one area. The analysis of photographic representations of the Indigenous communities in the Andes and in the Amazon regions of Peru has also been another important area of research. We are also beginning to explore the relationship between photography and art, and photography and the city. For example, in anthropological studies on photography collectives, groups of professional and self-taught photography experts unite to create cultural projects connected to multi-author photographic collections. These photography collectives are dedicated to a certain type of photography (i.e., journalistic, artistic, or documentary photography).

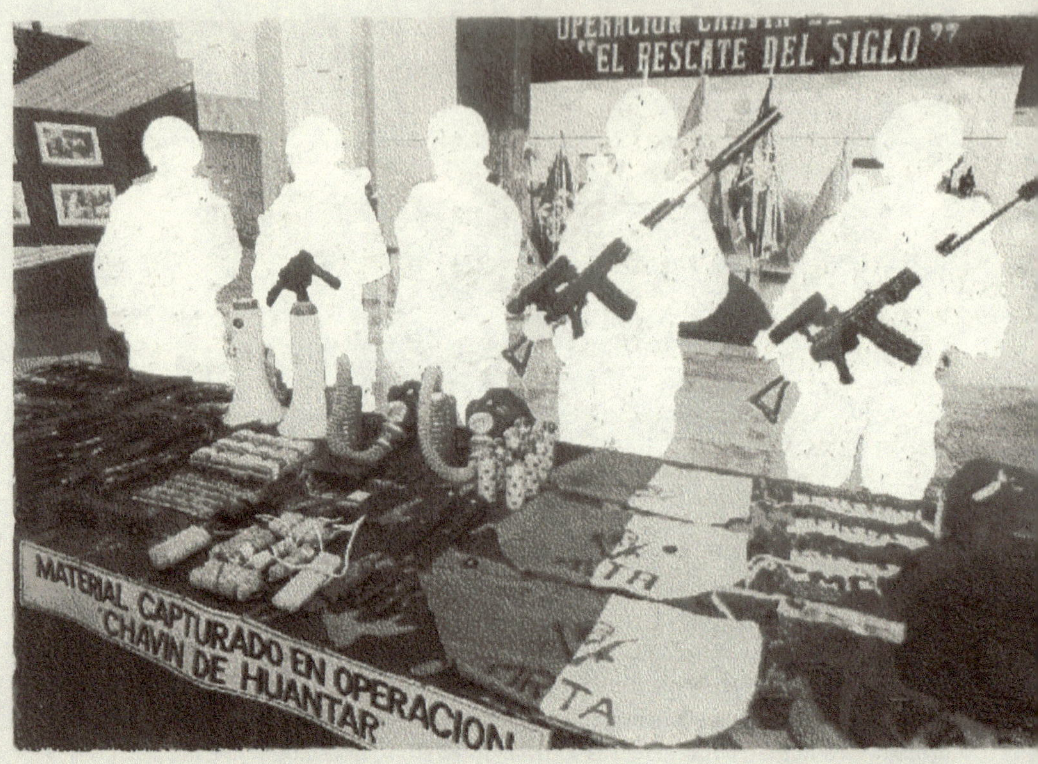

Figure 8.7. Sin título (Untitled), undated. Santigo Quintanilla. From the series *Objetos y cuerpos* (Objects and bodies).

The analysis of the relationship between photography and memory has been especially important as we study the memory of the internal conflicts in Peru that occurred between 1989 and 2000. The issue of violence in Latin America and the role of new photographic production and the establishment of photographic archives in the creation of new contemporary knowledge and history is connected to this and should be emphasized. There is a noteworthy line of research linked to memory and violence. In it, photography plays an important part and connects directly to Latin America. In Chile and Argentina, we have seen how photographs from identity documents are employed to symbolize the struggles of the family members of the *desaparecidos* in these regions or by human-rights defenders to refer to individuals whose rights were violated by military governments. In Peru's case, I am referring to the memory of the violence that occurred here between 1980 and 2000, violence perpetuated by the state and by other armed groups. In 2001, the Comisión de la Verdad y

Reconciliación (CVR) (The Truth and Reconciliation Commission) issued its official report. This document contained the results of a study based on official documents, oral testimonies, and photographic material. Therefore, they incorporated photographs into the research along with testimonies and official documents. These visual documents (photographs) linked to case studies of the massacres helped to fill in the gaps in the written documents. When the commission presented their report, they also created an exhibition with the material they used in the research and edited a book based on that exhibition. The project's corresponding archive was placed in the Centro de Documentación de la Defensoría del Pueblo and a digital copy was also placed in the Centro de Documentación del Lugar de la Memoria y la Inclusión Social (LUM). The archive, the exhibition, and the book are named *Yuyanapaq* (a Quechua word that means *para recordar*, or "so as to remember"). Hence, in recent years we are seeing how photography is becoming central to memory politics and the writing of our history.

This specific project's findings and its use of photography are important and unique for truth commissions and can be considered a pattern for these types of exercises elsewhere. Its materials have attracted significant academic attention, as scholars are interested in what has been collected and utilized. Additionally, this project demonstrates that the use of photography as a methodological tool for anthropological research has become more systematic and enjoys a wider dissemination. It elicits information, incorporates sensory aspects of social practice, and can create collaborative visual narratives with those studied and facilitate scholarly driven activism.

Photography, History, and Memory

This process also underlines what photographs have become emblematic. Some images have been repurposed to communicate messages that concern memory and violence. Artists have changed or modified them artistically or used them as a source of inspiration. They are crucial to how we understand recent history and interpret it as a society. These developments have led to photography being considered a legitimate medium for creating memory and enabling society to understand and interpret recent history.

However, this does not mean that everyone in Peru accepts all the findings referred to here with blind faith. For example, the truth commission's findings with photography are vital because they have created different reactions that merit discussion from alternate vantage points. In Ayacucho, for example (which was an area that was highly affected by the recent civil war), different groups remember the events differently and believe that *Yuyanapaq* does not represent them accurately. These associations that support relatives of the victims and their human rights have created their own archives and exhibitions in order to represent themselves, in their eyes, with greater accuracy. A key point to underline is that they too are using photographs and other bespoke visual expressions such as *tablas de Sarhua*, *retablos ayacuchanos*, and additional drawings as a means of creating these new representations.

Guiding Principles

For me, Latin America's colonial history is important to remember when you look at Latin American photographs. Photography has been fundamental in how we construct an image of the Other and how we compose racial classifications. This has also been a disputed topic connected to identity politics in Peru. These politics have arisen around the mechanisms we use to represent others and the postcolonial context. These conditions are the reason Mary Louis Pratt says that the production and consumption of cultural objects (such as photographs) occur within what she describes as a "contact zone" (*Imperial Eyes: Travel Writing and Transculturation*; "Arts of the Contact Zone"). Her term refers to the fact that intercultural exchanges occurred within the framework of the colonial project. This places it well within the power structures that set the terms for representations. These structures obliged the Indigenous to understand and master the colonial technologies, languages, and aesthetics to be able to represent themselves and make themselves understood by the conquistadores. This led to a process of reflection and negotiation between the colonized and the colonizers within the existing hierarchical framework. The visual repertoires of both created important instances of technological, material, aesthetic, expressive, and effective transformations within these contact zones.

This use of photography to represent the past consolidates many possible research avenues from the ethnographic material, the journalistic photography, and the artistic photography from which it draws. We benefit from photography to study the past, but photography also shows our aspirations for the future in Peru with great intensity. It underlines the value of cultural heritage as part of identity politics or tourism. In both instances, the goal is to make the country's ample cultural offerings visible. In the 1980s and 1990s when we were traveling around Peru creating recordings of these religious festivals as a part of our archival project for the Ford Foundation, we were the only people doing this. Now, if you go to these same events the local participants actively record these experiences. The organizers, the participants, and the spectator public all document them, including citizens who have migrated to other locations but who return home to gather with their families, worship their saints, and remember their traditions. They now proactively tap into these photographs in their efforts to create objects that possess cultural value. They believe that their documentary work helps to construct the *patrimonio de la nación* (national patrimony). New technology, like smartphones, plays an important role in this process. There are many photographers yet to be discovered and documented. There is still much work ahead in Peru.

Selected Publications

Cánepa Koch, Gisela. "Entre el museo e Internet: regímenes interpretativos y nuevos usos de la fotografía etnográfica de la costa norte peruana." *Transiciones Inciertas. Archivos, conocimientos y transformación digital en América Latina*, edited by Barbara Göbel and Gloria Beatriz Chicote, Universidad de la Plata/Ibero-Amerikanisches Institut, 2017, pp. 315–44.

———, editor. *Imaginación visual y cultura en el Perú*. PUCP, 2011.

Cánepa Koch, Gisela, and Ingrid Kummels, editors. *Fotografía en América Latina: Imágenes e identidades a través del tiempo y el espacio*. Instituto de Estudios Peruanos, 2018.

———, editors. *Photography in Latin America: Images and Identities Across Time and Space*. Verlag, 2016.

Pedro Querejazu Leyton

Academia Boliviana de la Historia

Family Roots in Photography

MY LOVE FOR photography came from my grandfather Fernando Leyton Hochkofler (1891–1974). Thanks to him, I was able to witness the entire photographic process because he was a photography enthusiast. His interest in photography instilled the same one in me from a young age. Recently, I discovered that he had his own darkroom in his home in Potosí, Bolivia, where he developed difficult photographs with excellent results. However, my pathway to becoming a photographer and a photography scholar emerged while I was a young adult. I began to work with photography somewhat indirectly while I was a fine arts student in Bolivia in the 1960s. Between 1962 and 1966 I studied fine arts at the Academia de Bellas Artes "Zacarías Benavides" which has been a part of the Universidad Mayor de San Francisco Xavier Chuquisaca in Sucre since 1949. After my graduation, I decided to study art restoration at the Instituto Central de Conservación y Restauración (ICCR) in Madrid (1967–1969). It was during that time that I began working more directly with photography. At that time, the art school I attended was based out of the Casón del Buen Retiro, which is behind the Museo del Prado. There I met a man who we called Don Justo, the institute's photographer. He taught several of us (students and my fellow classmates) photography: María Teresa Dávila and her sister Rocío Dávila, María Teresa Yravedra, Francisco Mohedano, Ángela Recio, Alberto Recciuto (Argentina), Graciela Barahona (Chile) and Regina da Costa Pinto (Brazil), just to name a few. After I returned to Bolivia in 1969, I continued learning photography on my own. I started using it to create visual documents that would help me with my art restoration projects. I also spent much time perfecting my photography processing technique and I practiced developing my negatives using chemicals such as Hypo Clearing Agent. Additionally, I worked on occasion with Doctor Celio Abela, a pediatrician and an important photography aficionado in Bolivia, a man of impeccable photography laboratory techniques. The studies I have just described have given me a profound sense of what a work of art is, its construction process, and how it behaves, be it a painting or a photograph. Therefore, I consider myself an art historian and an art restorer in the fields of painting and photography. I have written many books on art history and restored many paintings and sculptures from the viceregal period.

Over time, I began to write on photography as well. While writing many technical articles on sculpture and colonial painting in Bolivia and Andean art and further afield, I began to write in newspapers and magazines in La Paz. In 1990, to commemorate the 150 years since photography's arrival in Bolivia, I published a brief article on the growth of photography in Bolivia: "Ciento cincuenta años de fotografía. Los artistas de la luz." Given the unique nature of the article, it was republished and ultimately became a reference point. Thanks to it, people who were interested in the topic of the history of photography in Bolivia began to seek me out.

My first scholarly essay on photography would come in 1990 as well: *Una aproximación al arte fotográfico boliviano del siglo XIX*. Shortly after that publication, in January of 1991, I met an old friend (Plácido Molina Barbery), a photographer himself, who had built a collection of historic photographs from some of the longstanding Jesuit Missions in Santa Cruz, Bolivia:

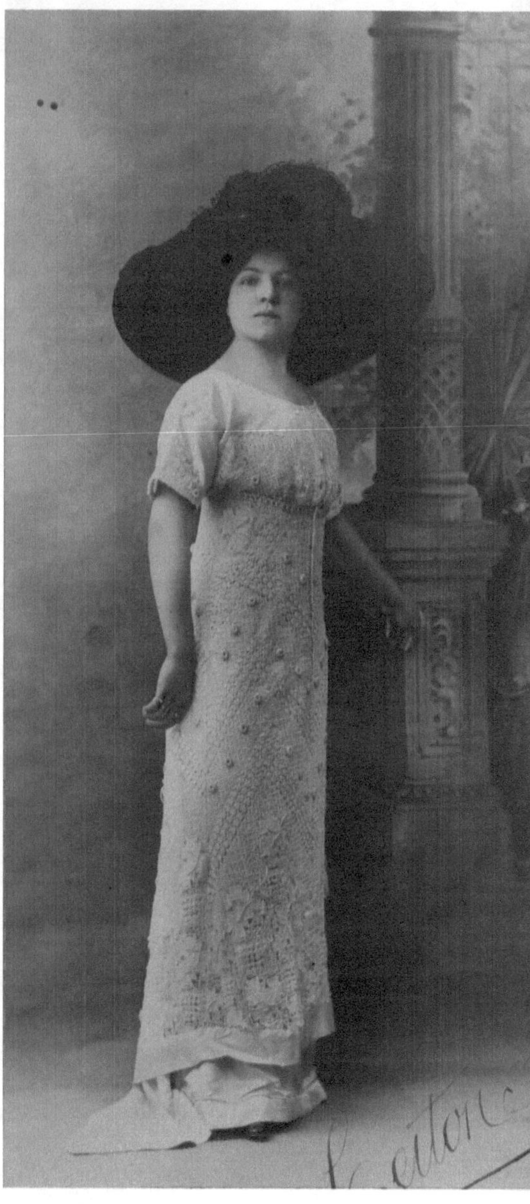

Figure 9.1. Señorita Eugenia Leyton Hochkofler, Sucre, Bolivia, 1912. Max. T. Vargas. Private Collection, La Paz, Bolivia.

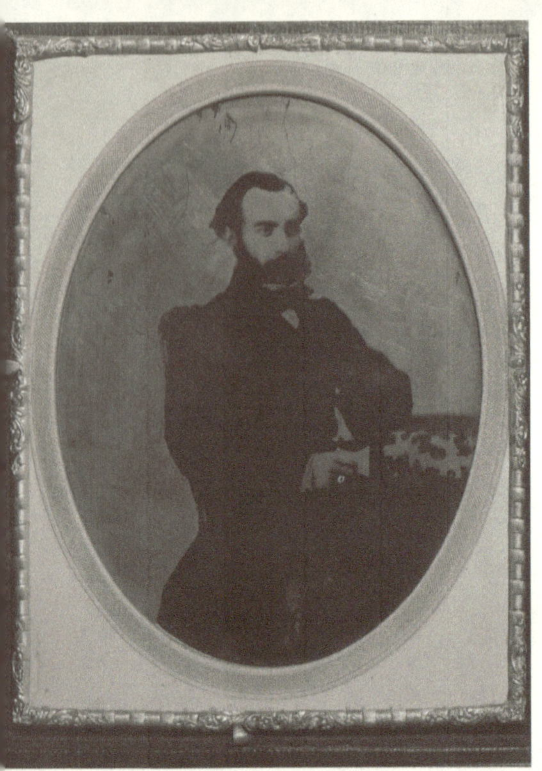

Figure 9.2. Víctor Arana Medeiros, Santa Cruz, Bolivia, c. 1855. Anonymous. Private Collection. (Possible daguerreotype.)

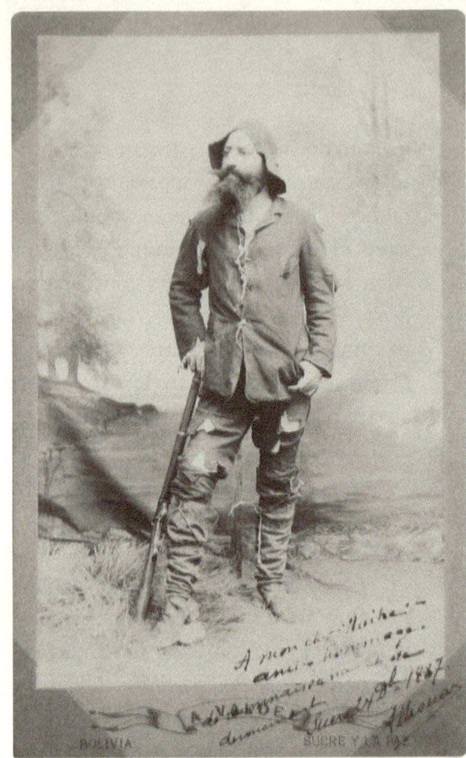

Figure 9.3. Retrato de Arthur Thouar (Arthur Thouar's self-portrait), Sucre, Bolivia, 1887. Aniceto Valdez. Private Collection, Sucre, Bolivia.

Chiquitos. This collection of photographs led to my first and perhaps best academic book on photography to date. My discovery of his collection coincided with the beginning of some activities sponsored by the Fundación BHN (Banco Hipotecario Nacional), a foundation dedicated to the promotion of art in Bolivia. Its president at that time, Fernando Romero Moreno, contacted me to encourage me to get in touch with Plácido Molina Barbery. I did, and Plácido showed me approximately twenty photographs from his collection. They were simply amazing! Plácido modestly commented that he had some more photographs and, bit by bit, he showed me his entire archive of photos on that subject. Unfortunately, the hot and humid weather in Santa Cruz had damaged many of the negatives, so I convinced him to allow me to take them to La Paz to try to restore them. That I did, and I also took them to Buenos Aires where a good friend of mine (and an expert in subject of photographic restoration), Diego Ortiz Múgica, was able to work on them. He produced new positives from the original negatives and did incredible work with them because many of the original images had faded. The book that I was able to produce from that project, *Las misiones Jesuíticas de Chiquitos*, took me five years to write and publish, and it has been one of my best works. It is 718 pages long and includes 919 photographs. The first half of the book contains 467 images Don Plácido gathered from the Archivo de Chiquitos. The project immersed me in the world of historic photography.

The book was a complete success and received praise from the Academia Boliviana de la Historia because it was the first book that had ever published an entire photographic archive in Bolivia. The Archivo Fotográfico de Chiquitos is important because it contains invaluable visual testimony of the people and the monuments from the ancient (though still continually inhabited) mission localities in the Chiquitos region. These photographs helped argue for change in cultural policy in Bolivia to protect, register, and conserve a physical monument and the intangible heritage of that Indigenous community (which was in danger of disappearing). Thanks in part to that photographic archive, the

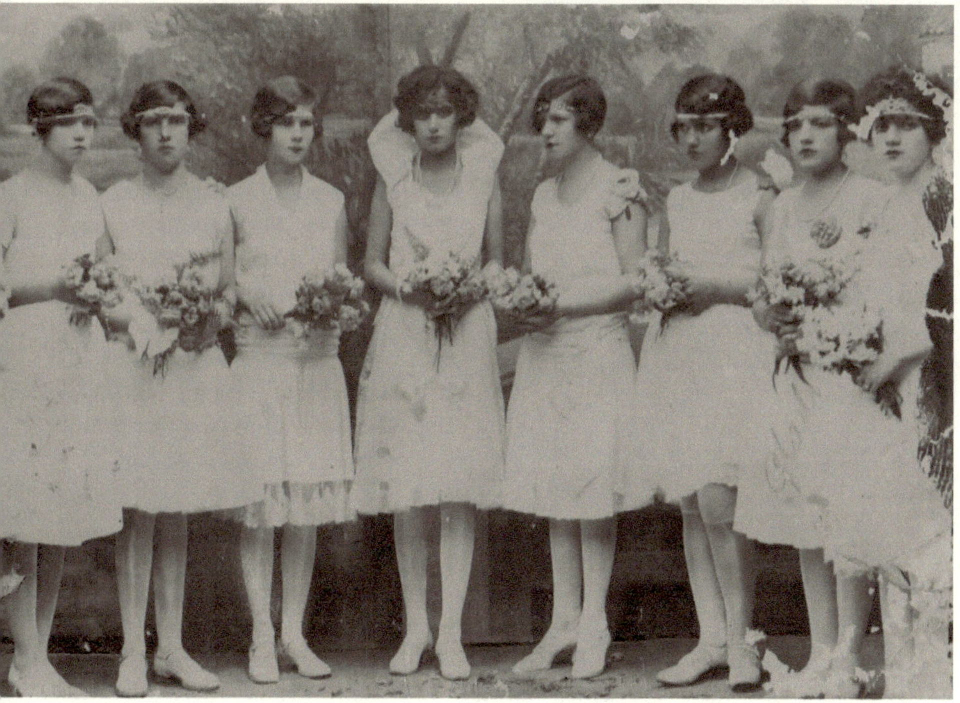

Figure 9.4. Despedida de solterío (Bridal shower), Santa Cruz, Bolivia, c. 1935. Casiano Vaca Pereira. Alberto Vásquez Machicado Archive, Alberto Vásquez Machicado Library. (Young women, from left to right: Elffy Albrecht, Lola Suárez, Dora Castedo, Carmen Foianini, Rosa Gutiérrez, Estela Astete, and Elvira Ferrante.)

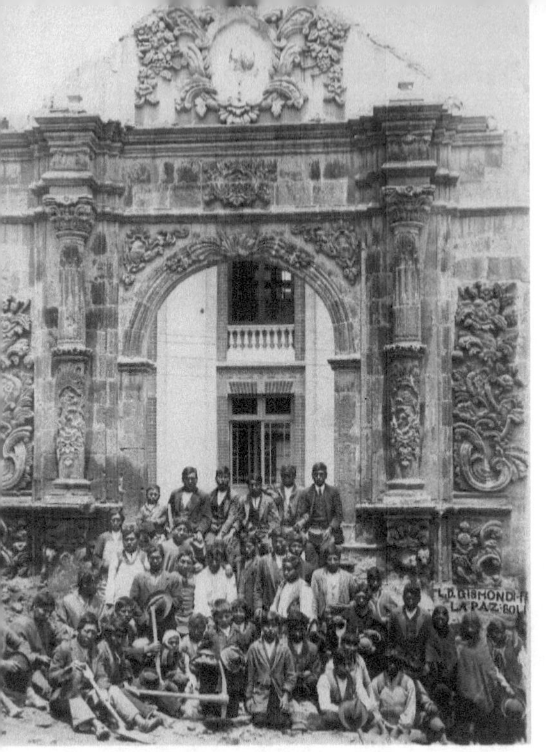

Figure 9.5. Obreros demoliendo el Seminario de La Paz (Workers demolishing a seminary building in La Paz), c. 1925. Luigi Doménico Gismondi. Mario Buschiazzo Collection, Centro de Documentación de Arquitectura Latinoamericana (CEDODAL), Buenos Aires, Argentina.

monuments and towns were declared World Heritage Sites by UNESCO. Additionally, the photographs and the original musical scores from different composers, including Chiquitano Indians, led to a series of music festivals called Festivales de Música Renacentista y Barroca Americana "Misiones de Chiquitos."

Another of my photography projects that I decided to undertake thanks to funding from the Biblioteca Nacional de Bolivia and the Central Bank was to scan two photograph albums that had been made between 1897 and 1898. This material became the base of my book, *Doroteo Gianecchini y Vincenzo Mascio: Álbum fotográfico de las misiones franciscanas de la República de Bolivia, 1898*. It contains a text written by Father Lorenzo Calzavarini and 103 photographs by Vincenzo de Mascio from that same period. This book contains some of the rare photographs of Indians from the Gran Chaco in the south of Bolivia and fills key voids within our visual history. These are just small samples of some of the value that books on photography can add to society.

The History of Photography in Bolivia

In 2000, a friend of mine who writes on the history of photography in Buenos Aires, Ramón Gutierrez da Costa, recommended that I study and write the history of photography in Bolivia. I thought about his advice and decided to follow his suggestions. Ramón Gutiérrez da Costa's assistance was not limited to good recommendations. He also put me in contact with many other South Americans who work on photography and told me about projects in which I could participate. I started researching photography in the Museo Nacional de Arte in Bolivia. There, I searched for photographs and information on photography studios in Bolivia. I found an important number of paintings and photographs that were able to help me construct the narrative. I also met many of the descendants of some of these earlier photographers. These contacts are the ones who have helped me to uncover the information on one of my most important projects: the work of Luigi Domenico Gismondi.

Gismondi Archive and Studio

Luigi Domenico Gismondi (1872–1946) was an Italian immigrant who worked in Bolivia (mostly in La Paz) between 1900 and 1946. His studio, which opened its doors in 1907, was first located along the Calle Yanacocha and then moved to the Calle Comercio just one block from the main plaza in the city center. Gismondi traveled up and down Bolivia taking pictures as a part of his activities, and he also kept a studio in Lima, Peru at that same time. Gismondi had eight children. Two of his sons, Luis Adolfo and Julio César, became photographers and took charge of their father's studios after his passing. Luis Adolfo managed the Bolivian studio in La Paz, and Julio César took charge of his father's studio in Lima, Peru. Luis Adolfo's daughter, Graciela Gismondi, and his granddaughter, Geraldine Gozálvez Gismondi, have maintained the Gismondi archive and the studio in Bolivia, which has now been at the same location for over seven decades.

In 2007, to celebrate the one-hundred-year anniversary of the opening of Estudio Fotográfico Gismondi, the studio and the Museo Nacional de Arte en Bolivia decided to have a photography exhibition of his work. I was able to curate the exhibition and select the material for the corresponding catalog. To that end, I worked closely with the present owners of the archive: Graciela Gismondi and Geraldine Gozálvez Gismondi. This exhibition led to the publication of my book *Luigi Domenico Gismondi: Un fotógrafo italiano en La Paz*, which was published thanks to the Fundación FAUTAPO and Dutch funds from Cooperación Internacional de Holanda. The Italian Embassy also sponsored the project. The book includes 205 photographs, most of which were from the Gismondi archive, though many also came from La Paz, Buenos Aires, and the Centro de Documentación de Arte y Arquitectura Latinoamericana (CEDODAL) in Argentina. In the end, I decided to research more on a period of photography (1840–1940) than on a specific area. This has led to me working on a large variety of projects, such as individual photographers and other general topics within that timeframe.

My work with the Gismondi archive also inspired me to write a history of photography in Bolivia from its beginnings to the middle of the twentieth century. That was why I applied for, and won, a John Simon Guggenheim Memorial Foundation grant. It has allowed me to gather a considerable amount of information and images from archives and collections all over the country and abroad and has given me a sense for the history of photography for that period in this country. I decided to use my material to write the different chapters of my book by organizing it chronologically into one final document. Meanwhile, I am continuing to write on Luigi Domenico Gismondi using the material I have found since the publication of my 2009 book.

At the same time, I am advancing other projects, and I have published an article on René Céspedes and Aída Troncoso's Studio René that existed in La Paz from 1954 to 2000. They were black-and-white specialists that would *iluminar* their photographs by painting them, a practice they carried into the twenty-first century in Latin America. I am also working on a project on the contemporary photographer Freddy Alborta Trigo (1937–2005). He was the photographer who became famous for having taken the 1967 photograph of Ernesto "Che" Guevara just after the revolutionary had been killed, which John Berger compared to the image of a Christ figure in *Understanding a Photograph*. I have used his work to write more microhistory.

Research Methodology

I learned much of my research methodology from Ramón Gutiérrez da Costa and my wife Laura Escobari Cardozo. Both taught me how to find, select, and document my research. They have taught me how to treat research material from different sources (oral, written, visual) and how to best use archives and libraries. Those are basic tools that I have been able to apply to any of my projects. Part of my research has been collecting visual material as well. I have approximately thirty-four thousand photographs in my digital archives that cover a wide range of topics from cartes de visite from the 1860s to recently produced digital material in Bolivia. In addition to the images, I have an extensive variety of articles that accompany the visual material: newspaper articles, critical commentary on the photographs, books, and other scholarly material. All of this is key to my academic study of photography.

As I compile the information, I tend to organize it chronologically. After that, I begin to study the symbols and codes that are part of the iconography of the photograph. I consider what might be the implicit and the explicit messages with the images. I then organize that information into subject matter to see where the data leads me in terms of the types of conclusions I can draw from it.

Comparing the data you encounter is essential for discovering new information and for being able to discern how social mentalities work in each period you study: how individuals engage with the photographic practice and in what conditions they allow themselves to be photographed. I also consider how technological advances have changed the field and what types of photographs are possible in every period that I study because every stage has different possibilities. My experience processing film and negatives in darkrooms has helped me

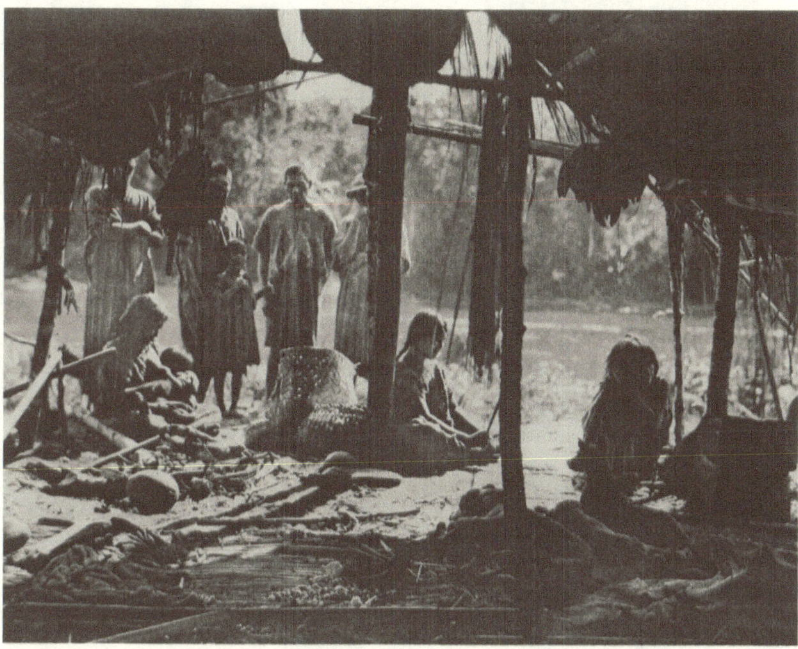

Figure 9.6. Indios Chimanes (Chiman Indians), Beni, Bolivia, 1928. Roberto Gerstmann. Vintage print in *Bolivia*, p. 35, Private Collection.

to develop this type of analysis. One of my final stages of analysis is to select the images I plan to use in my publications. I try to incorporate the images that best visually evidence the points I am attempting to make as I write.

Image Content Analysis

As I analyze, I look for information on the content of the images I am studying. I consider the type of photographic material used, the type of lighting they employed, accessories, and backgrounds in the picture as well. I also take into account any information that accompanies the photograph or that is on its reverse. I take note of the physical condition of the photograph. I reflect on what was possible in terms of resolution according to the period in which that photograph was taken. This, of course, is something that has varied widely and evolved significantly over time.

Biographical and historical information can also be very useful when writing about photography. Here is one example of how it has helped me. In the city of Oruro in 1890, an Italian photographer placed an advertisement in a newspaper to try and sell magnesium as material for photographic flashes to photographers who were taking pictures in the mines in that region.[1] By looking at the images themselves, you can determine if the photographer used tungsten, an electric lighting source, a flash bulb, or another type of material to create a flash (such as the magnesium the Italian photographer was offering). Hence, that advertisement gives us a notion of what was available and used at that time. Robert Gerstmann, a German who worked taking photographs in Bolivia a couple of decades after the publication of the advertisement I just mentioned, used another type of light source when he took his pictures in the mines. His photographs seem to indicate that he did not use a chemical flash, but rather a very powerful light source like a strong electric lamp that would have used a 500- to 1,000-watt bulb that had tungsten filaments in order to illuminate the tunnels of the mines he was photographing. I reached that conclusion because the material he was using to capture the images was very slow developing in comparison to current material. This meant that his images have very sharp contrasts between the dark and the light. The point of origin of the light is also very clear in this sort of image. In comparison, light from magnesium would have produced a more variable light and would have resulted in an image with shadows that evidence less definition. Knowing these differences in production and the resulting product they create helps us to form a context and understand the work of photographers such as Gismondi (who sometimes used magnesium and at other times used an electric reflector) and Robert Gerstmann (who mostly used a halogen reflector for his work). These finer details offer a better understanding of the context, but these readings are only possible when you know the technical processes involved in photography. Yet if you know them, they can be a part of your analytical approach and help you to reach important conclusions.

Unique Traits in Latin American Photography

As I compare Latin American photographs, I have noticed some important variations when it comes to photographs taken by locals and foreigners. A good example of those differences becomes evident when you compare the photography of Rodolfo Torrico Zamudio and Julio Cordero (locals) to Luigi Gismondi and Robert Gerstmann (foreigners). Those who came to Bolivia from abroad see things with another gaze, though they also have their own styles. Gerstmann was a bit of a philosopher, while Gismondi had a very sharp eye and paid attention to detail. I think that foreigners in Bolivia tend to see things differently because they have a curiosity for the quotidian elements of Bolivia that the national photographers simply do not have. The outsiders are amazed by the landscapes, the people, the customs, and other aspects that the locals simply take as a given because they have always been part of their daily reality.

As I have studied many photographs from this genre, I can assure you that this visual outlook is common among many of the foreign photographers who have worked in Bolivia. They underline the peculiar with their photographs. The diligence and interest that they take in our country is evident in their pictures and offer interesting visual readings. On the other hand, you should never forget that every photographer lives within social and cultural realities when they photograph, and these create very specific demands on them. I have found that studying postcards from different times and locations is one of the sources that can tell us much about these social pressures. The more you study them, the more you can see some of the unique and important photographic focuses within Latin America.

Experience Is an Excellent Teacher

My work has taught me many valuable lessons. My greatest challenge as I study photography has been when I have been denied access to material. When I ask to make copies of photographs in order to make a coffee table book of photographs, everyone seems to be happy to give me their permission. Sometimes they ask me to list the name of the person who owns the photograph. However, if I ask for permission to include their photographs in a scholarly study, often the owners of the images will strongly object to their usage and deny access to them. However, the paradox is that frequently these same people would simply throw those same images out or burn them because they have no personal connection to the ancestors in the photographs or because they have lost or are unfamiliar with their genealogical ties. They do not appreciate the historical or aesthetic value of the images, but if I want to use them for scholarly purposes, they have all kinds of questions and concerns. "Why you do care about these photographs?" "These people aren't related to you." "These are private photographs." They raise these concerns, and then they shut you out. Some of the owners are simply suspicious about what you might say about the photographs. Nonetheless, I have often been able to overcome these initial challenges and obstacles, see what they have, and even scan the material. In those cases, experience has taught me that having patience and speaking with different people can be help you gain access to material here in Bolivia. Diplomacy is key in those circumstances.

I have had some very ironic experiences here, too, as I have studied. Once, I helped a private foundation to organize and digitalize their photographic material (something I have done more than once when the occasion required), only for them to turn around and want to charge me exorbitant sums for permission to use their images. Their prices were so high that I had to abandon my project, though I hope that someday they might change their mind. The sad thing is that the owners do not recognize the true value of their material, which is not commercial, but rather documentary, historical, and cultural. My observations have led me to believe that the attempts to generate money from a collection of visual material will normally lead to the research in that area slowly stopping or stagnating because most people do not seem to understand how cultural documents work, the role of research on them, or the context in which scholars work.

The Dangers of Hyperfocus

One of the great traps that researchers can fall into when they study Latin American photography is to have an excessive focus on one topic. I have seen this happen with the study of Martín Chambi's photographs. When Chambi was taking the photographs that have made him famous then and now, I am confident that he did so without thinking that he was creating masterpieces. He was taking photographs because he was a professional photographer, and he wanted to do his best work in terms of product quality and content. His photography was of a high standard, and his name became his brand. His visual outlook does make him a photographer that is worthy of study. In 1974 when I was working in Cuzco, his daughter Julia had his photographic archive stored away, and no one was really doing anything with it or thinking about his work. In fact, his daughter would show me Chambi's old studio and let me use Chambi's old darkroom to develop my photographs because there were not any photography laboratories in Cuzco at that time. Just a few decades later after a few researchers from abroad published on Chambi's work, suddenly he had acquired a huge name for himself—a name I think that he and his work merit. However, Chambi was only one of several artists who were creating extremely valuable work at that time: the Hermanos Vargas in Arequipa, Miguel Chani and José Figueroa Aznar in Cuzco, and others (Bauer, Pinney, Peterson, and Thomas). All the people I just mentioned have done similar work in similar locations. However, the excessive focus on Chambi has eclipsed the others. This narrow focus has its roots in commercial objectives to a certain degree. Now, if you want to get in touch with the copyright owners to Chambi's work, it is next to impossible.

Nonetheless, this change in circumstances has led me to other interesting finds. For example, I discovered that a painter in La Paz, Arturo Borda, used at least one of Martín Chambi's photographs of Machu Picchu to do his work. Borda even wrote to Chambi asking for permission to use the image as a base image for one of his paintings. That information itself is a bit incredible. However, when I wanted to publish a case study on this topic, I could not, because a book was being written on Chambi and certain images were already promised to others as part of that project. Fame creates curious circumstances. While Chambi is placed on a pedestal, others are left behind. Chambi was one photographer among many, and the others should not be forgotten, even if they might not have performed at the same level that he did.

The Importance of Mutual Friendship and the Exchange of Material

Another important lesson to bear in mind if you work with photography in Latin America relates to determining the true author of an image. I learned this experience while working with Gismondi's material. I realized that there was a lot of mutual friendship and the exchange of material between photographers during the 1900s and the 1930s in this region. For example, I know that Gismondi was in Cuzco in 1935 because he took pictures of the area, and he processed and developed those negatives in Martín Chambi's studio. Gismondi had Chambi's photographs from that period in his archive as well. Other connections were also evident. When I was making blow-ups of some of the images in Gismondi's archive, I found dates that helped me to place the different photographs into their proper contexts. While I was studying a triplicate of Gismondi self-portraits, I discovered an embossed seal that was only just visible on the photograph. The seal indicated that the man who had taken the triplicate photographs was Lucien Gaulard, a French photographer who specialized in taking two or three portraits of the same person in different positions. Gaulard operated out of a studio in Marseille during the 1920s and 1930s, and he would have taken Gismondi's portrait while the South American photographer was on a trip to France and Italy. I mention this discovery for two specific reasons: One, to show the usefulness of technical knowledge, because it was that knowledge which allowed me to discover that information I just described. Two, in order to underline the fact that photography archives often contain photographs that were not made by the photographer, but rather the products of swaps with or presents from other photographers. Once discovered, these connections are extremely useful because they offer you new connections to explore and help to create a clearer context for photography in Latin America.

Everyone who studies photography sees it from a specific point of view that is based on their past. My connections with art history and fine arts mean that I see photography from those perspectives. Those that come to photography from other fields, such as literature, will have different approaches. Another important aspect is to engage with the images at hand and not to write around them. One of the problems that we have here is the fact that students are not taught visual literacy. We tend to prioritize written texts. For example, I recently encountered a bachelor's history thesis written here. It focused on the importation of photographic material to Bolivia. It is a very interesting thesis; however, no one considered the images that document this process, because those images do exist. It was a missed opportunity to interrogate the visual witness of that process.

While it might seem completely obvious, I think it is important to say that you need to look at images and speak about their content from a critical perspective. Another common occurrence is for writers to manipulate photographs so that they can say whatever might suit them. Often, they connect two photographs that do not really belong together, label them, or include cut lines that simply do not correspond to their circumstances and do nothing to respect their testimonial, documentary, or aesthetic value. Frequently, they create relationships that are unrealistic, inappropriate, or even false.

Theory

Much of the theory I use when I work with photography comes from art history. I have read and studied many texts from this field. Some of these that have informed my work include *Camera Lucida* and *Image, Music, Text* by Roland Barthes; *Historical Photo Analysis: A Research Method* by James Borchert; *Eyewitnessing: The Uses of Images as Historical Evidence* by Peter Burke; *La fotografía como documento social* by Giséle Freund; *Los usos de las imágenes: Estudios sobre la función social del arte y la comunicación visual* by Ernst Gombrich; *Images at War: Mexico From Columbus to Blade Runner (1492–2019)* by Serge Gruzinski; and Susan Sontag's *On Photography*. Local texts also play an important role in my work. I often read books on art and photography from Colombia, Peru, Chile, and Argentina, among other Latin American countries.

I have never tried to be a great theorist, write on theory, or adopt any of these models completely. I prefer to focus on the material at hand. I analyze it and publish it. I try to give the material the value it merits as objects of art or as historical testimony. I focus on social reality and how real historical characters connect to the visual document. I do not try to develop photography theory or attempt to test it using Bolivian photography.

When I won my Guggenheim grant, it included a year's worth of financing to undertake the research I proposed. I used my time to research the archives and libraries in Cochabamba, Santa Cruz, Sucre, and Tarija. I also researched in Argentina because there are important documents on the history of Bolivian photography there as well. I did not have enough time to study the archives in Potosi and Oruro, and I had already studied all the archives in La Paz. Hence, the grant enabled me to gather the bibliographical material that I needed to carry out my present writing project on the history of photography in Bolivia.

There are certain aspects of European art and photography that have simply continued along their same path here. Photography's invention benefitted painting and other visual arts the most during its early years and have been engaged in a long dialogue with this technical medium ever since. Europe offers you many examples of this. For example, Édgar Degás took pictures of dancers and then used them to paint his portraits. Eugene Delacroix also took photographs and used them as visual bases for his paintings. In this respect, Bolivia has Arturo Borda. I discovered that he systematically used photographs when painting. Sometimes he would buy postcards or take original photographs and use them as the basis of his paintings, like the case of Martín Chambi's photograph of Machu Picchu I mentioned earlier. This practice was not just limited to landscapes. He also took pictures of individuals and groups of individuals in order to create a painting of them. Another Bolivian painter, José García Mesa, also used photographs to inform his painting. Looking in the other direction, in Latin America there is a long history of photographers who paint or illuminate (*iluminar*) their photographs,[2] and they would also paint the backdrops for their photographs as well. Over time, many photographers became adept portrait and landscape painters. This tandem relationship between photography and painting is one that requires further exploration. Since the 1970s, you cannot really think about contemporary art without some type of connection to photography. Creating context as you write about photography is also very important. When I wrote about Robert Gerstmann, I went to great lengths to create context for his work. He was one of the few photographers operating in Bolivia during that time to theorize on his work.[3] That commentary adds an important testimony that deepens his work and gives it a personal touch.

History and Photography in Latin America

We are at an important stage regarding history and photography in Latin America. Several countries here have been working on their history of photography for decades, though we have yet to see some of those results. In certain areas, we have seen important advances in the conservation of their photographic history. They have created specialized archives and have preserved important photographic collections. There has been pioneering research on the history of photography carried out by important scholars in Latin America. Much work has been done to advance the study of photography in Mexico, Argentina, Brazil, and Chile, but the vast and growing body of material yet to be documented is growing even faster. We need to write the history of photography from the Latin American perspective with all the virtues and limits that might entail. I am confident that we will fill these gaps over time. We will soon see more histories and microhistories of photography in Latin America. In an ideal world, we would have more access to different archives, libraries, and digital material. Bolivia is making important strides in this direction. The Archivo y Biblioteca Nacionales de Bolivia in Sucre and the Archivo de La Paz have both worked hard to create important photographic archives, and the Alcaldía de La Paz has bought some collections from important Bolivian photographers with the intention of creating a museum of photographic history here.

One of the huge challenges that we face is isolation. Our national borders, which are often portrayed to symbolize strength, create a break in communication and a corresponding lack of understanding about what is happening in our field in neighboring countries. High postal and customs costs also add to the difficulties of obtaining books and other published material from other Latin American countries. An enormous boon to the interconnectedness of our research would come from those costs disappearing. It would really assist the flow of information here and foment international and multidisciplinary research projects.

That is not to say that this type of project does not occur. For example, I worked on the photographic work of Max T. Vargas at the Universidad de Piura with Andrés Garay Albújar, who was active in Arequipa and La Paz for the project *Fotografía Max T. Vargas, Arequipa y La Paz.* Several Latin American scholars worked on that project, which was extremely transdisciplinary. Pascale Absi from the Institut pour le Recherche et Development in Bolivia and Jorge Pávez from the Universidad Católica del Norte in the Chilean capital organized the 2016 book to which I am referring: *Imágenes de la revolución industrial. Robert Gerstmann en las minas de Bolivia (1925–1936).* The book was a collaborative effort that studied Robert Gerstmann's work on Colombia, Bolivia, and Chile held in Gerstmann's archives in Antofagasta, Chile.

Though the body of researchers on photography in Latin America is still small, the interest in this field has been growing exponentially over the last two decades. I have described research in this field as a solitary task, but I personally correspond with academics in Argentina, Chile, Peru, Holland, and the United States, and the volume of material exchanged is always on the rise. I think that is a very good sign indeed.

Selected Publications

Querejazu, Pedro. *Borda: 1883–1953*. Fundación SolyDes, 2017.

———. "Ciento cincuenta años de fotografía: Los artistas de la Luz." *Diario Presencia*, June 3, 1990, pp. 4–5.

———. *Luigi Domencio Gismondi: Un fotógrafo italiano en La Paz*. Fundación FAUTAPO, 2009.

———, editor. *Las misiones jesuíticas de Chiquitos*. Fundación BHN, 1995.

Gonzalo Leiva Quijada

Universidad Adolfo Ibáñez

My Unforeseen Entry into Photography

I STARTED WORKING with photography thanks to an unexpected series of circumstances related to my profession at that time. It was 1983, and I was in my fourth year of philosophy at the Universidad de Chile while working as a teacher at the Instituto Profesional Alpes. The institute offered to let me design a course on the history of photography. The motivation for the course was for it to help train photographers for employment in the fields of photojournalism and advertising.

At that time, the photo reporters were the best photographers in Chile because of an important association that had been growing substantially, AFI, Asociación de Fotógrafos Independientes (The Association of Independent Photographers). While describing the course's design to me, my bosses made it clear that they wanted documentary photography to be an important part of it. I agreed, in part because I was already a huge admirer of the documentary work done by the Farm Security Administration (FSA) photographs. Dorothea Lange's work fascinated me. However, I began to teach this course with a great deal of hesitation at first because I had never worked with photography before, and there was not that much material available on the subject then. Previously, I focused on the philosophy of aesthetics and had been an assistant to one of my university professors. However, I was interested in photography because of how it can uniquely represent life and beauty. The topic soon fascinated me, and I began to research it earnestly, reading and taking notes on anything and everything related to it. I was surprised by just how little had been written on photography in Chile and Latin America. Back then, most of what existed were texts on how to be a photo reporter. Over the next few years, I finished my thesis on philosophy pedagogy at the Universidad de Chile. In it, I wrote about how surrealist imagery focused on the interactions between our sense of image and our consciousness.

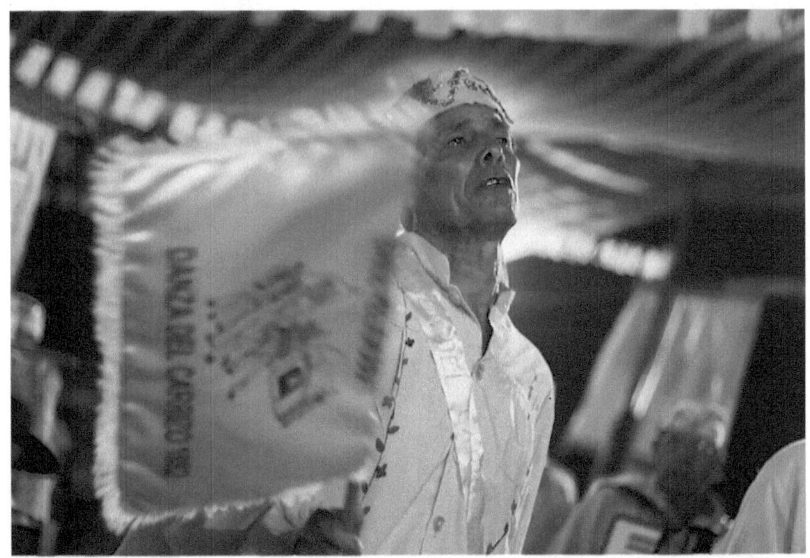

Figure 10.1. Gabino Miranda Capitán del baile de Carrizal (Gabino Miranda Captain of the Carrizal Dance), Chile, 2014. Gabino Miranda. Alexis Rodríguez. Private Collection.

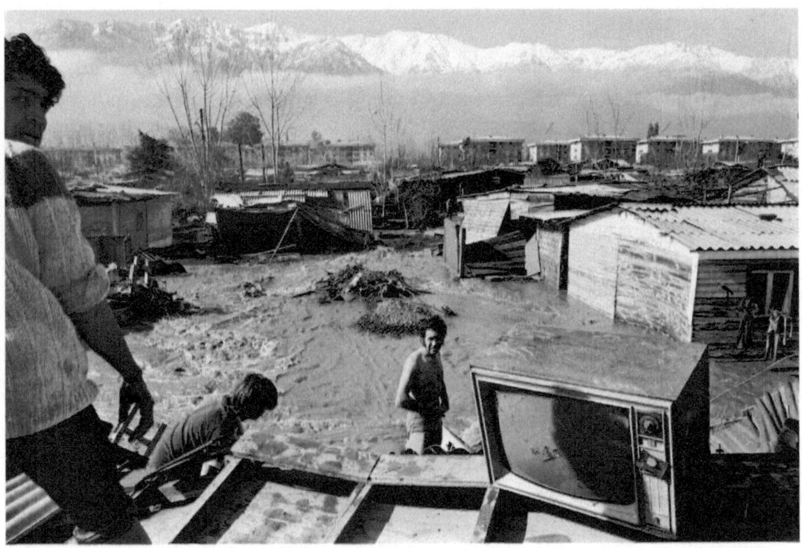

Figure 10.2. AFI (La Asociación de Fotógrafos Independientes), undated, Marco Ugarte. Private Collection.

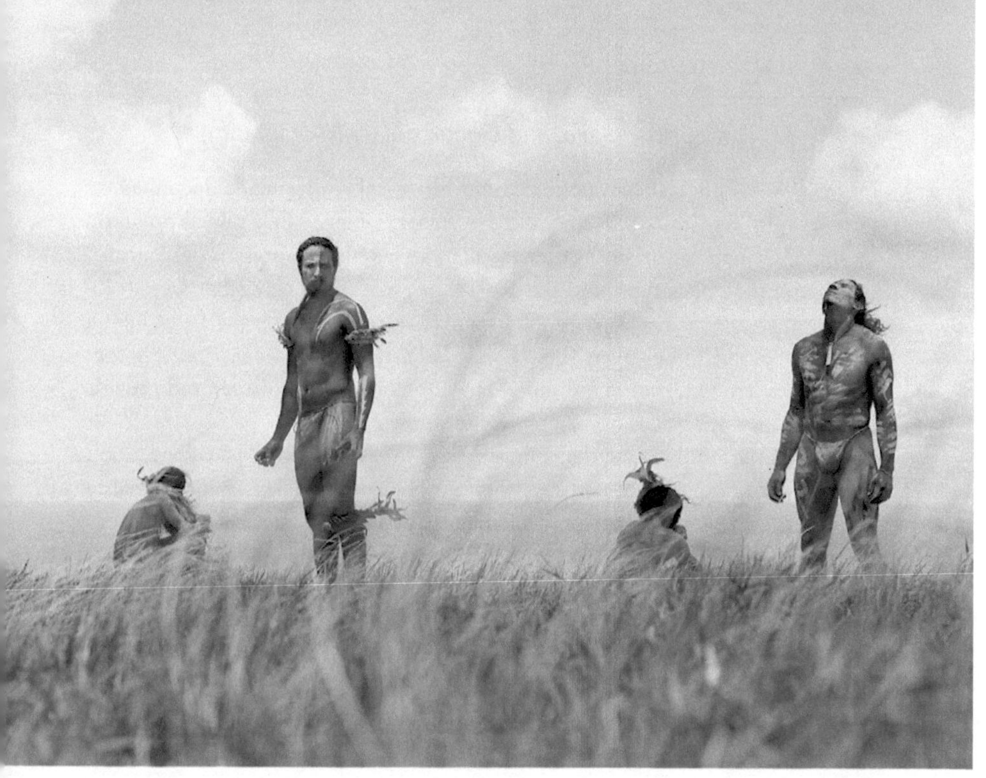

Figure 10.3. Tapati, Rapa Nui, Chile, 1998–2010 series. Francisco Bermejo. Private Collection.

After that, I began to work as an assistant to a professor of pre-Colombian history at the Universidad Metropolitana. While I was there, I began to develop a research project that envisioned how to teach history. In it, I wanted to combine my recent interests in photography and pre-Colombian history. I thought of a brilliant way of doing so. I traveled to southern Chile and the Tierra del Fuego where I encountered groups of hunters and gatherers. Their situation was very moving. Luckily, there were museums in Punta Arenas, Porvenir, and the Isla Navarino that contained a large amount of photography on these Indigenous communities: the Selknam and the Aoniquen. I traveled to the Ukika community to meet the last people who spoke the Yamana language. No one had done any type of ethnographical or ethnological work with these people. So, moved by their communities and daily reality, I decided to organize the material that was there. This work led to me use photography as a way of constructing a visual testimony of these people. Hence, you could say that using photography to create an anthropological document was my first major research project with photography.

The 1980s, Chile, and Documentary Photography

In the 1980s Chile's social, political, and historical reality made documentary photography especially relevant. The systematic violence that rained down on the political opposition and other dissidents was always present. The armed forces and the police repressed the general population in ways that were traumatizing. During that period, photographers were always on the front line in the struggles in Chile's streets (Pere *La ciudad de los fotógrafos*). Their photography bore strong testimony of those dark moments in our history and provide us with important pieces of memory to be studied.

It was during this time that I finished my thesis on history pedagogy, and I wanted to study another degree in aesthetics at the Pontificia Universidad Católica de Chile (PUC) because that would allow me to explore my interests on the theory of image, photography, and location. I thought this would enable me to create a critical dialogue between my own ideas and what I was witnessing in Latin America. However, my biggest problem was finding someone to direct a thesis on this specific topic. Finally, Milan Ivelic, the director of the Museo de Bellas Artes and a professor of aesthetics, agreed to help me. He suggested that I write a thesis on photography and identity in Latin America. We agreed on that topic and started to map out the theoretical framework I needed to consolidate this new information into the proper categories. As I did this, I was able to organize my knowledge on philosophy and history in such a way as to connect it to my interests in photography, connecting the three fields in a manner that allowed me to study them with the proper structure. I used material from photographic archives to debate concepts on the manifestation of identity on the American continent. That project was the beginning of my serious research on photography.

This period of research coincided with a very busy time for me because I was a student in one of the "contentious" degrees within a university controlled by the state. The state intervention at my university simply added more pressure to the environment, as there were already forces at play that controlled what happened there: the United Nations, the Catholic Church, and numerous popular uprisings and protests that coincided with the slow decay and death of the Pinochet regime. During that time, I simply dialogued with visual material on the dictatorship that would percolate to the surface and travel the world thanks to a number of news agencies. These images were often censored because they were critical of the regime. Sometimes the media censured them directly; on other occasions, they would simply throw the heads of the different publications in jail. Nonetheless, these images became an important cultural reservoir. Both the presence and the absence of images from this period spoke volumes on the way Chile saw itself at that time and became a unique testimony of identity.

In 1990, I decided to present a research project on the photographer Álvaro Hoppe. His influence is key, and his work is admirable. After many conversations with him, I was able to start a research project on the Asociación de Fotógrafos

Independientes (AFI) I mentioned earlier. Thanks to my teaching days at the Instituto Alpes, I knew them well. The FONDART government funding I won in 1992 meant I had the finances I needed to publish a book on Hoppe's work. It is called *Álvaro Hoppe: El ojo en la historia*, and it studies how news photography and civil society worked together to support democracy. It was one of many efforts to reestablish democracy in Chilean society at that time. The book received the Altazor prize in 2004, a testimony to the project's merit.

My book on Álvaro Hoppe became so well known that it enabled me to meet many other news reporters who I hadn't met previously. These contacts led to many research projects that transformed into new books and articles. I began a master's in history at the Universidad de Santiago de Chile, and I was preparing to write my thesis when I received the opportunity to write on history and identity in Chile during the nineteenth century. It involved writing on the Guerra del Pacífico (a war between Chile, Bolivia, and Peru over the control of nitrate reserves). In terms of Chilean history, this conflict is very important because it enabled Chile to take the Antofagasta region from Bolivia and the Arica region from Peru. Chilean armed forces went as far as Lima, Peru, during those invasions. I know this because I have seen pictures of the Chilean flag flown in Lima during that invasion. Photography offers you details omitted from the written narratives such as that one. During that period, a series of photography studios were able to collect images from war correspondents and create a series of albums on the war that favored the elite. All of this made for extremely useful material related to my topic of photography and identity during the nineteenth century.

While I was in the midst of this project on photography, identity, and conflict, I won a scholarship to pursue a PhD in Europe. After a small amount of deliberation, I decided to leave my Chilean project on standby and study in Paris. The EHESS, École des hautes études en sciences sociales (School for Advanced Studies in the Social Sciences) had accepted me. My doctoral thesis director was Jean François Revel, and he was an expert on the French Revolution. So, I began working with a topic that was related to cultural history as seen through visual images. However, not long after my arrival in France, Revel was elected director of the EHESS, and this meant that I needed to change to M. Duverger as my PhD dissertation advisor. Duverger had strong links to Latin America, having been a student of the great French Mexicanist Jacques Soustelle and having been France's cultural ambassador in Mexico for several years. Working with him allowed me to change my topic and focus on Chilean photography and modernity. In that research, I explain how photography is one of the technological vehicles that ushers in modernity to Chile and the Southern Cone. I drew on images such as the postcard, newspaper photographs, family photograph albums, and images from the Guerrra del Pacífico to build my argument. It also allowed me to form a methodology using a visual corpus that could be applied in Chile, France, or other locations as well.

While I was in the final year of my PhD, the director of the Museo Histórico Nacional in Chile called me. He offered me the job of curator for the most important photographic archive in Chile. I took it as a good sign to conclude my PhD in France and return to South America. I wrote and defended my dissertation in French, and the evaluating committee unanimously agreed to award it the highest distinction possible.

Museo Histórico Nacional in Santiago

On my arrival at the Museo Histórico Nacional (MHN) located in the Plaza de Armas in Santiago, I immediately began the work of cataloging, modernizing, and expanding the archive. I worked there for seven years, and we published books such as *Pinturas con historia* (and my project on the Guerra del Pacífico). I also started researching the ambrotypes and daguerreotypes that the museum had in its collection. Working in the MHN was a dream come true because it had all the original prints of the pictures I had been researching. It also afforded me the opportunity to bring together many of the people who were working on photography, and I met many photographers and other leaders in the field. We organized an institution called the Sociedad Chilena de Fotografía whose aim was to unify the field of photography in Chile. We would meet in the MHN and organize talks, seminars, and exhibitions. In 2000, we successfully organized the first conference, the Congreso de Fotografía Patrimonial Latinoamericana, with the help of the PUC in Chile. Boris Kossoy, Pablo Ortiz Monasterio, Rosa Casanova, and Graciela Iturbide came and delivered keynote lectures. We also awarded prizes to three photographers who have been key to Chile's photographic history: Sergio Larraín, Gustavo Pueller, and Luis Navarro.

Tools to Study Photography

I use two sets of tools to study photography. On the one hand, I work very hard to develop methodological devices to engage directly with photography. I have innovated a lot in this area. I formed an approach that created a structural vision of photography that enabled me to analyze symbols. To study those diverse signs and symbols I used semiotics. For example, I would consider the usage of light and shadows, hierarchy, structure, universal formats, and representations. These would enable me to establish the syntagmas within a photographic corpus. After using semiotics to study the images, I would incorporate study methods that came from art history and cultural anthropology. Now many new methodologies use anthropology to analyze photography, and this has expanded the way we understand images, what they represent, and their contexts.

On the other hand, I also work with all the classic texts that are linked to photography. Many of these authors have even been my teachers during

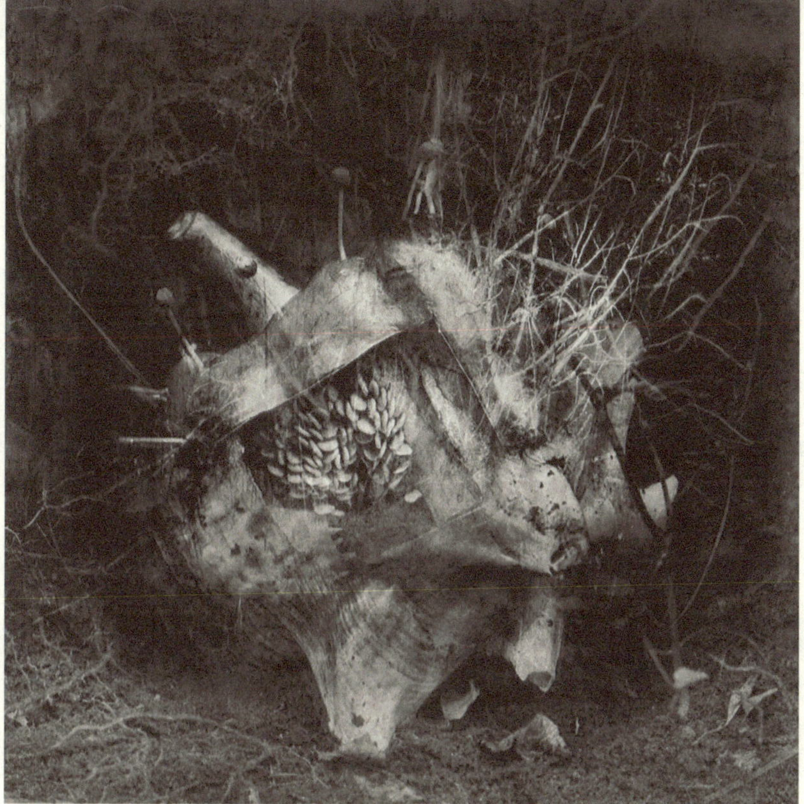

Figure 10.4. Serie de "Lo Primigenio" (From the series "Firstborn"), 2013. Francisco Donoso. Private Collection.

my master's and PhD studies. Umberto Eco, Pierre Bourdieu, Jacques Le Goff, Georges Vigarello, Marc Augé, Georges Didi-Hubermas, Hubert Damisch are just a few of the great minds under which I studied. Damisch taught me how to apply history of art methodology to the study of photography. He introduced me to the Vienna School of thought and the English cultural studies writings on photography. I took classes from Rosalynd Krauss. The Frankfurt School also influenced my way of thinking about photography as I considered what Walter Benjamin and Theodor Adorno wrote about photographs and how their ideologies grow and expand. Roland Barthes's work on photography and his theory on signs is always present in my work. His books *Camera Lucida* and *El grano de la voz* are foundational texts to the study of photography. John Murra's and Cifford Geertz's texts on anthropology and ethnological history have also influenced the way I see their work. After having read the authors that I just mentioned, I began to develop some of my own ideas regarding the study of photography. At first, I mixed theory to create new approaches. I began by using Geertz's way of understanding symbols with Bourdieu's analytical approaches. This allowed me to create a cultural fabric that enabled me to

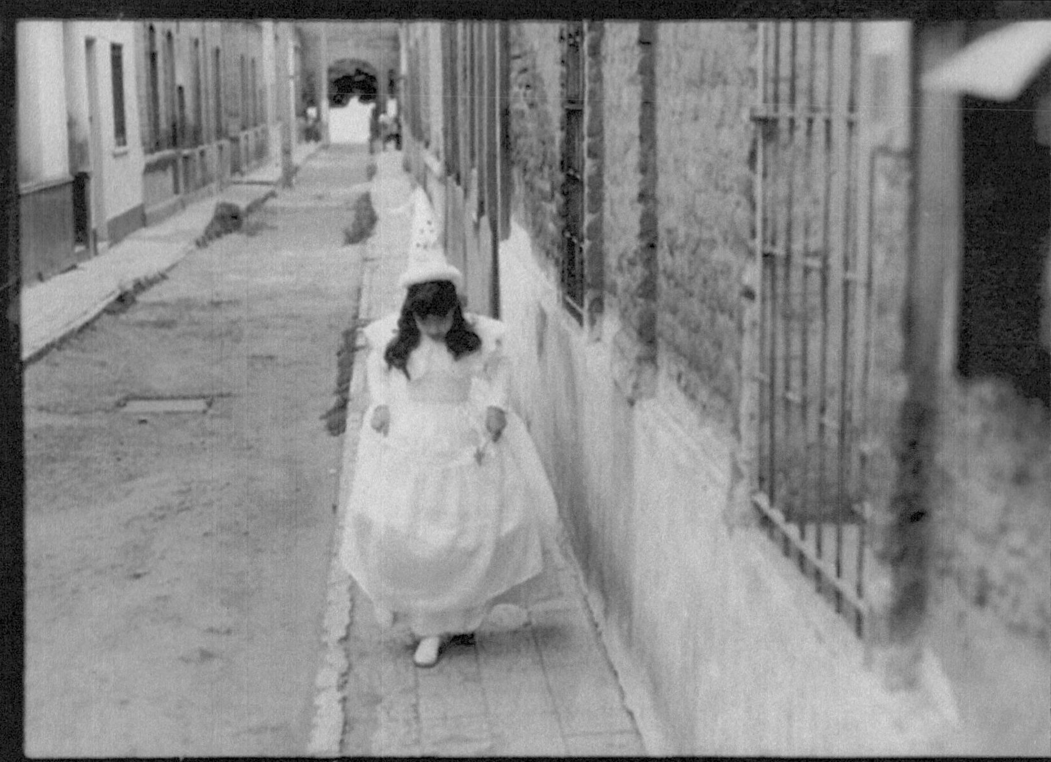

Figure 10.5. El hada (The fairy), 1980. Luis Prieto. La Asociación de Fotógrafos Independientes. Private Collection.

review images and understand photographs as cultural and aesthetic objects. Over time my methodology grew. Boris Kossoy's writings on the genealogy of photography in Latin America helped me to anchor my analysis in the evolution and movement of photography here in our local environment.

One of my greatest intellectual endeavors relates to my work with AFI, which I mentioned earlier. This project (which involved work from over 250 photographers) helped us discern the role photography played in society during the Pinochet dictatorship. It took me a long time to develop that project. I had to interview over one hundred people, select images, gather a bibliography, map how the photographic institution worked, and determine if the institution worked in one direction or if there were other diverse ones within it. Not only did I have to create a system to organize all the historical information; I had to study the photographer's visual portfolios and work documents, and I needed to analyze the minutes of their meetings. To be concise, I had to understand and organize a decade's worth of work of hundreds of artists. This was not easy because, as their name "Multitudes en sombras" (Multitudes in the Shadows) might suggest, many of them worked with alternate and secret identities. I was able to secure another FONDART scholarship that allowed me to garner financial support for this project. This time, the funds supported the time I needed to spend organizing and understanding all this information on the formation of what we could call a cultural resistance front.

Presently, I am focusing on a project that deals with microhistory. I am working on Lucho Prieto's body of work very closely, a corpus that is relatively unknown to many. He was a member of AFI who lived in fear for many years after the violence he witnessed during the Pinochet dictatorship. This made him extremely sensitive to violence. His work is very intimate, and he is extremely interested in the plight of the vulnerable. He uses photography and poetry to express his ideas. His oeuvre centers on capturing and underlining brief moments and the hidden side of life—those elements of life that became invisible during the Pinochet years. I published a book on his work called *Luciérnagas*. I decided on that name because it reflects a transient and delicate light that shares a type of visual poetry with his photography. I should also mention the 2013 Thames & Hudson book that I helped to edit: *Sergio Larraín: Vagabond Photographer*. This was not simply Sergio Larraín's biography. It peered into his private universe, one that tended to combine family decisions, photographs, and destiny with anonymity. Larraín was not just an important photographer. He used his camera to create visual poetry. He was a master of silence that observed Valparaíso through the creative lens of his camera.

Latin American Photography Has Unique Characteristics

Experience has taught me that Latin American photography has certain unique characteristics. One of those is the importance of documentary photography in Latin America. This is due to a tradition of registering mestiza cultures visually in Latin America because the truth is that these cultures never came to be what the colonizers wanted them to be. This has led to local cultures creatively reformulating and continually reinterpreting our visual reality. This is not only the idea of accepting our present reality offered by the photographic evidence. It is connected to visualizing how to negotiate our own identity through visual resistance. Photography is a cultural catalyst that contains our historical memory. Photographs allow oblique images, personal tragedy, and physical evidence of the past to reveal uncovered pieces of our history. Images are an integral part of the historical narrative of our everyday culture that is in constant transformation. That alone is highly valuable because it offers us further evidence that supports our written documents. Images also write our history directly because now there are many illiterate sectors of our society that produce photography. Their images help to define their place in history. In this sense, photography is key because every culture in Latin America has links to visual culture. The

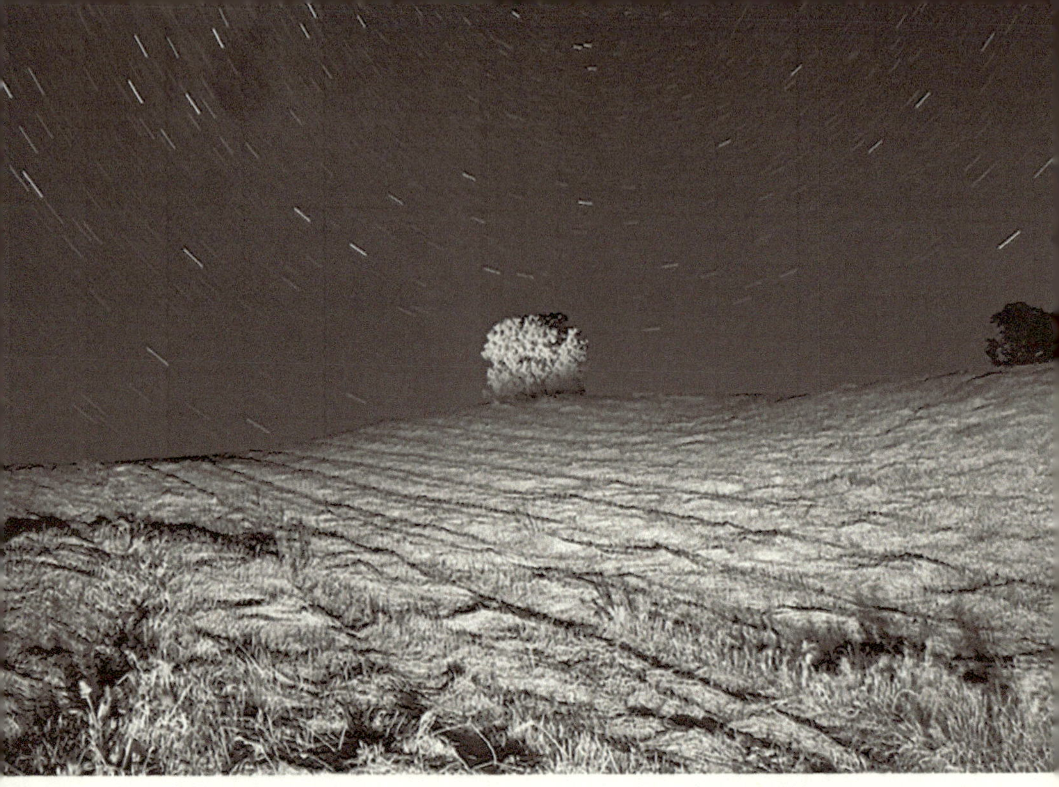

Figure 10.6. Loma intervenida. "Iluminación nocturna larga exposición" (Intervention on the hillside, "Long exposure of scene at night"), 2004. Rodrigo Casanova. AFI. Private Collection.

same cannot be said of written culture here. That is why visual mediums such as the news, magazines, television, and other information-sharing platforms on the internet are so important to our understanding of Latin American history. Hence, visual representation in all its aspects in Latin America gives our understanding of our culture a key vitality. It is an essential component of the visual hermeneutics that touches our communities, lives, and destinies in this region of the Global South.

My Research Focuses Have Evolved with Time

Thankfully, my research focuses have changed over the years. At first, I worked under a guise of history writing, using methodologies that came from the nineteenth century. Fernando Braudel's influence still affected the research methodology at the university where I studied in Paris. Braudel's influence was not only in history but in the social sciences too. More recently, I have left macrohistory to submerge myself in the world of microhistory. I think that microhistory can foreground and interrogate important moments in history in addition to

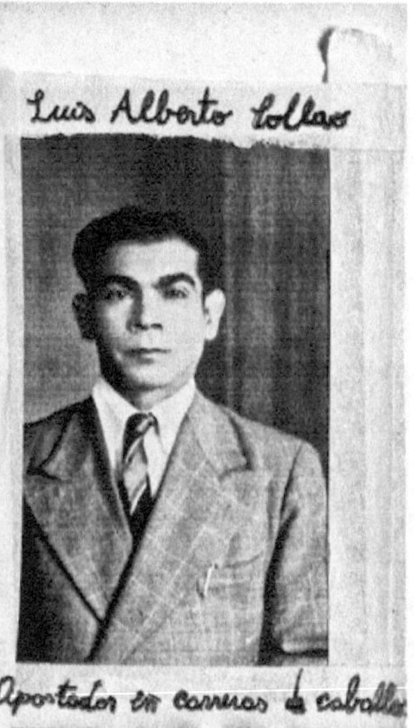

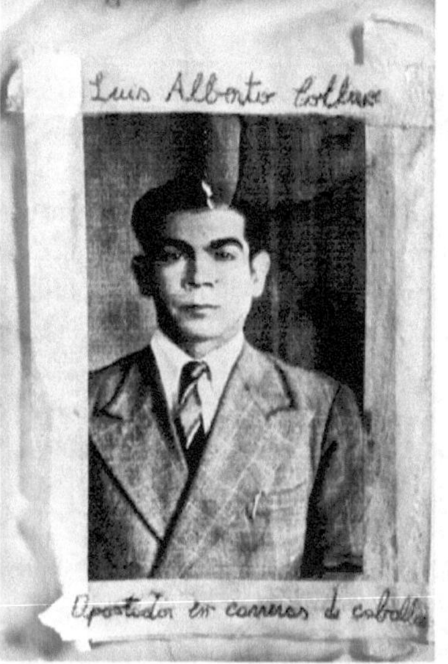

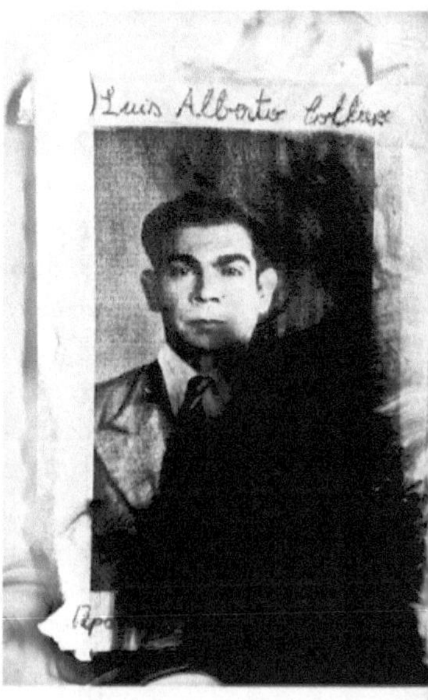

Figure 10.7. Barbara Ortiz, serie "La memoria líquida" (Barbara Ortiz, from the series "Liquid memory"), 2012. Barbara Ortiz. Private Collection.

suggesting the role of the individual in them. In that respect, I have been able to write about individuals and structures. It allows us to observe with greater clarity how the Latin American photographic narrative has evolved over time.

I think that in the future many important aspects of research methodology from history and cultural critiques will find their application to photography. Topics such as gender, ethnicity, social enclave, and local identities will become increasingly relevant. I think that we will begin to see thoughts and ideas forged from a type of epistemological dispersion. We will look less at the broad view of history and more at the meanings and aspects related to local communities and how photography can validate their identities. These cultural crossings and new combinations will bear important fruit.

Another topic that will come to the forefront in Latin America as we continue to build the study of photography will be some of the invisible communities that exist in our times—homosexuals, sex workers, and others who have been marginalized. These communities will begin to be studied and will have a new place in our cultural discourse thanks to new outlooks on integration and a desire to eliminate discrimination. To this end, photography and visual studies have already taken steps in the right direction.

One area in Chile that merits much more consideration is family photography. These images make up our historical memories of cities, families, neighborhoods, and countries. We already recognize their innate value, but in Latin America we need to do more to create networks and archives dedicated to preserving these important cultural artifacts because they authenticate who we are and our history. We have much more work to do in the Southern Cone regarding the formation of our own aesthetic theory on photography that can be applied directly to our work here. This theory will need to come from the research we do in archives that we have here in Latin America. Thankfully, to that end, there are many young people studying here in South America who are doing this type of scholarship. They no longer need to go abroad to study these topics like we did because there were no teachers to guide us down the path of our chosen fields or methodologies to apply to the new information we found. We now fill that gap for the coming generations. When I began to study cultural history in the 1990s, it had much less value than it does today. Now Santiago is a capital city with its own visual corpus that awaits researchers and requires analysis.

There is much work to do in the study of photography in Latin America. There are many photographers and image creators to be discovered and explored. Old analog ways of image creation will surely be absorbed by new digital technologies and new and hybrid forms of media. However, photography's core identity will remain. We will continue to research the new images that appear over time because their study helps us liberate our own identities.

Finally, I must mention that much of the value of photographic history today relates to visual ethics, as noted by Ariella Azoulay. I have reflected deeply on this topic in recent years. We live in a world in which we must not be indifferent as we witness some of today's atrocities, no matter where they might arise. We must learn to be more visually literate. We must train our gaze. As standard-bearers of visual studies in Latin America, we must help our students to learn how to look at the world they see. Some people believe that when they see something, to say that they like it (or not) is all they need to do. This is incorrect. We must learn how to formulate an aesthetic reaction to what we see. Why? Because behind every photograph there is a set of ethics and morality. We must learn to react to what we see because, as a society, we share a common destiny. That is why we cannot afford to be unmoved by what we see. We must exercise clean and clear critical judgement when we look at images.

Selected Publications

Leiva Quijada, Gonzalo. *Álvaro Hoppe: El Ojo En La Historia*. Gobierno De Chile Fondart, 2003.

———. *Luciérnagas Luis Prieto*. LOM Ediciones, 2013

———. *Multitudes en sombras: AFI Asociación de Fotógrafos Independientes*. Ocho libris editores, 2008.

———. *Sergio Larraín: Biografía, estética, obra*. Editorial Metales Pesados, 2012.

Cora Gamarnik

Universidad de Buenos Aires

Communication Studies, History, and Photography

I STUDIED COMMUNICATIONS at the Universidad de Buenos Aires (UBA), graduating in 1996. I later taught a class named "A History of Western Media" within the same degree program. In it, we studied the history of cinema, newspaper, television, photography, and other communication mediums. The course also focused on media in Argentina. While searching for bibliographical material for the course, I realized that there was absolutely no material on the history of photojournalism in Argentina, and there was only a small amount of information on the history of photography in Argentina. There was a lot of information on the history of photography in Argentina in the nineteenth century and a minimal amount on the beginnings of the twentieth century, but that was all. There was barely anything else. I was looking at an empty slate. The lack of information I am describing does not just include photojournalism; there was pretty much nothing written about the history of images in Argentina. After evaluating this situation, I began to contemplate the idea of creating a research project to fill the void. That project led to me to research photography in Latin America with keen interest.

I knew that I wanted to study media from the 1960s and the 1970s because the photography in that period was important in Argentina, but my challenge then was that there were no research models to follow. Notwithstanding, I assembled a project as best I could, and I applied for a PhD scholarship to develop my project at the Universidad de Buenos Aires (UBA), and I was accepted.[1] I decided to study the history of photojournalism in Argentina from 1960 to 1980. Those were very active years with many important political events here. You can also observe an increase in the creation of new illustrated magazines like the publication *LIFE* in the United States. Thanks to my scholarship, I was able to start studying Argentinian photography within that timeframe. In

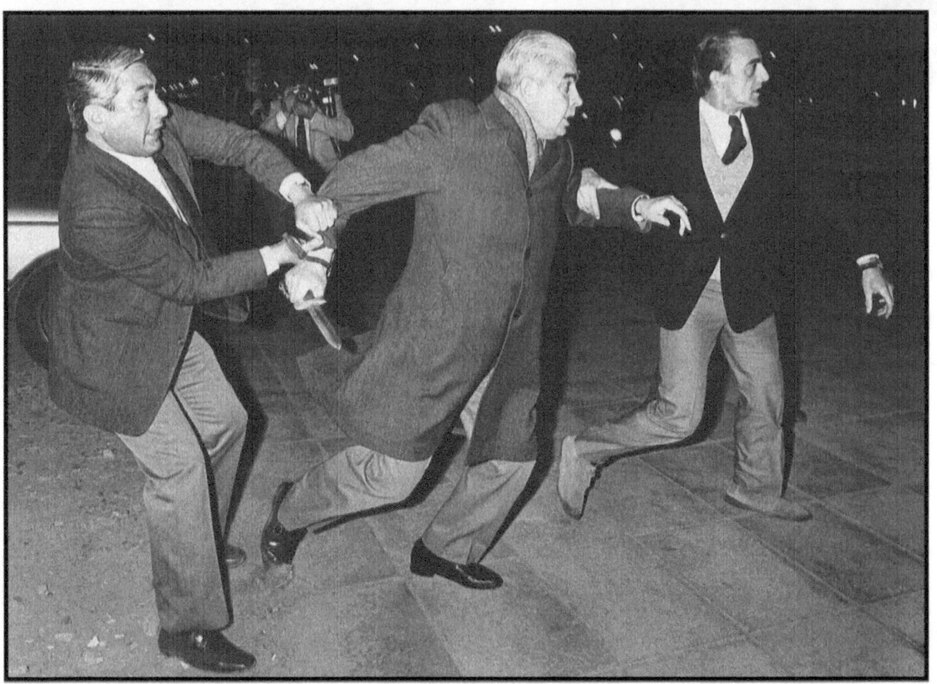

Figure 11.1. Hombre detenido (Detained man), Argentina, undated. Enrique Rosito. Personal Collection.

reality, researching in Argentina under those conditions (being paid to study) was a luxury afforded to very few individuals.

I started with the 1960s and moved forward. I began to study the first magazines in Argentina that copied *LIFE*'s format. This was a period of intense modernization in the country, but at the same time, in 1966, we were suffering a huge coup d'état: the Onganía. I studied the events as they were portrayed in Editorial Abril's *7 Días Ilustrados* and Atlántida's magazine *Gente y la actualidad*. I wanted to see if there were any connections between the modernization of the press and the new technologies for printing photographs and the increase in younger photographers with university degrees who were replacing (or sometimes working alongside) the older generation of self-taught photographers. These important changes in photography were occurring while there was a coup d'état, repression, and censorship.

The change in government generated certain special characteristics in those magazines: a generation of dedicated photographers. They would go out into the street to photograph the protests and social conflicts. They introduced many visual innovations and showed us the key role that an image can play in the presentation of history. I gathered much of my information through interviews at that time. Many of the important figures were quite old when I interviewed

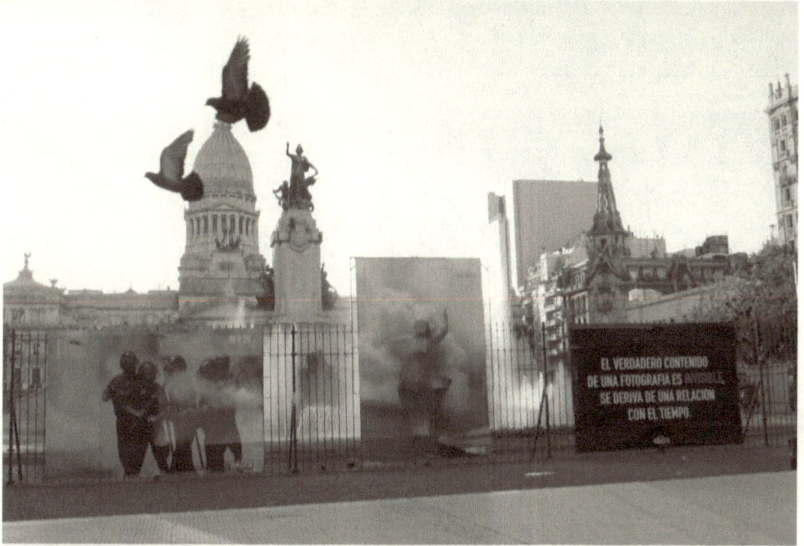

Figure 11.2. Intervención callejera en la Plaza del Congreso al cumplirse diez años de las protestas populares y la represión policial (Street protest in the Plaza del Congreso conmemorating ten years of police repression and popular protests), Buenos Aires, Argentina, December 12–19, 2011. Victoria Gesualdi.

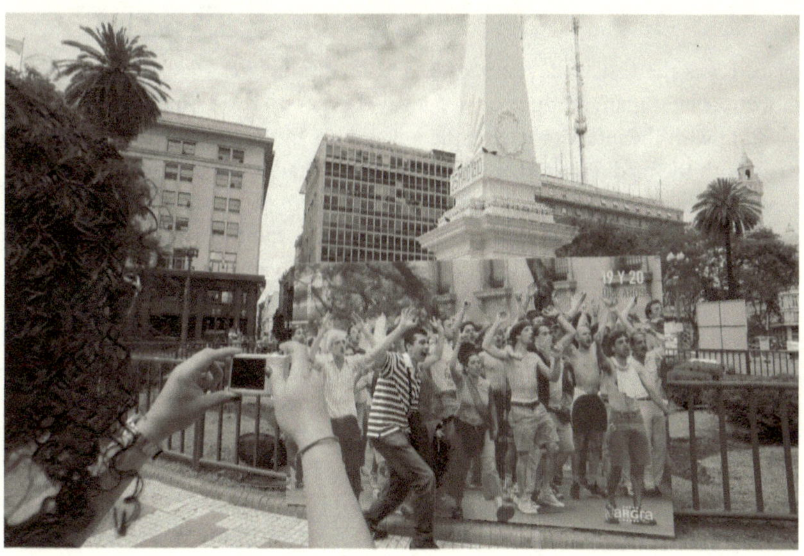

Figure 11.3. El frente de la Casa de Gobierno intervenida con gigantografías al cumplirse diez años de las protestas populares y la represión policial del 19 y 20 de diciembre de 2001. (Giant protest photographs in front of the Casa de Gobierno to commemorate the tenth anniversary of the 2001 political repression in Argentina), Buenos Aires, Argentina, December 12–19, 2011. Damián Dopacio.

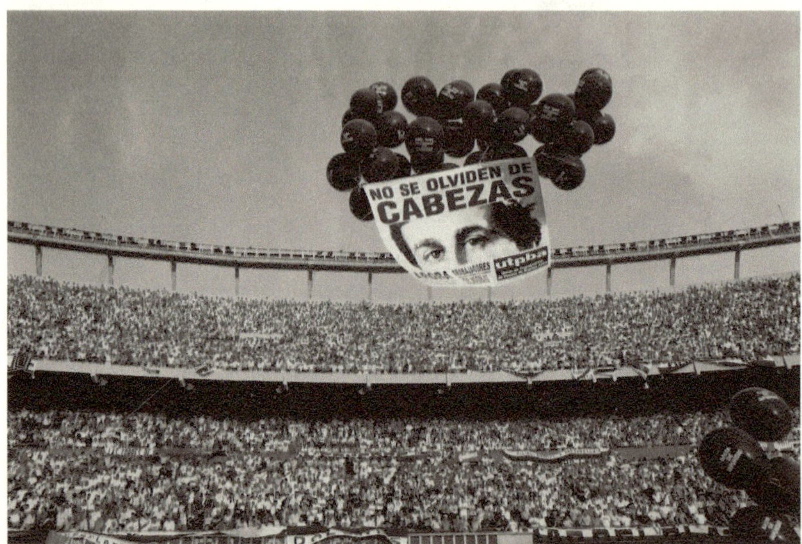

Figure 11.4. Homenaje a Cabezas (Homage to Cabezas). Eduardo Longoni. Personal Collection.

them. I was the first to have done so, and my timing was right because only a short time later many of them passed away. I began to realize that in addition to working with the interviews from the key players in the events, I also needed to work with the media from that period because it had much information to offer as well. Using these sources, I was able to recapture their vision as witnesses of history and observe how they used their work. Importantly, we were also able to detect the distortion of their work over time as well. Comparing the information gleaned from the interviews was very important when it came to overcoming pitfalls in the field of oral history: the lack of memory, self-aggrandizement, and gaps in the narrative. Bearing these issues in mind, I was able to create a study that I think was quite significant because it presented something entirely new to the field.

Models and Methodology

I worked alone for a long time at first. Because there were not really any models to draw on when I started, it took me a while to get a feel for how I would do the work. I did know some things at the beginning. I knew the topic and what I wanted to study. I was familiar with the historical period, so I started going to

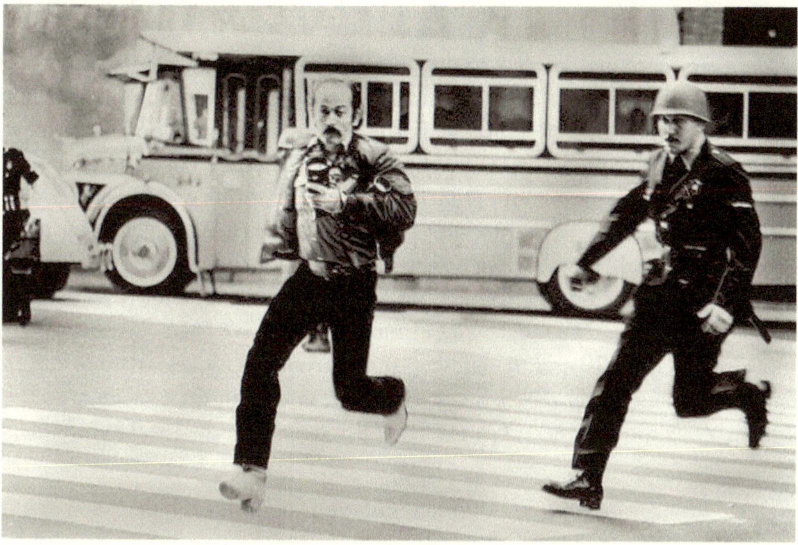

Figure 11.5. Sin título. (Untitled–Photographer running), undated. Mario Manusia. Personal Collection.

periodical libraries to read the newspapers and magazines. I did this because I wanted to determine the key issues and identify the images that portrayed them. At first, I learned by simple trial and error. I think I would have advanced much more quickly if I had been able to share my doubts and problems with others.[2] However, that simply was not possible. I gradually began to find the work of other researchers in Latin America who faced similar problems. Reading their work helped me to organize mine and know how to face my challenges. Nonetheless, I worked alone and was mostly self-taught for quite some time.

The contact I began to have with other researchers who helped me to tackle my challenges as I studied photography in Latin America became key. This was mostly because I began to see that I was not alone in the many research challenges that I faced. I also came to understand that there were certain tasks that all of us faced because we used oral and visual sources. In my case, I often needed to work with and combine knowledge from oral and visual sources because each field on its own was not enough to get the information that I needed to create the context and to write the corresponding historical narrative. Learning how to analyze photographic images, understanding their production, meanings, circulation, and how they narrated events, was needed in order to map out and understand the events I was studying.

Growth in the Field

In the years since my doctoral studies, many others have begun to research the topic of photography in Argentina and the field continues to grow.[3] It is not a fully developed field here per se, but there are many people who are now involved in the study of photography in Latin America. For example, I am teaching a class in a master's program in contemporary history at the Universidad Nacional de General Sarmiento with Natalia Fortuny called "Images, History, and Audio-Visual Sources." We had to create the course from scratch, but we are now at a point where there is a lot of potential. That is not to say we do not face challenges. We are lacking in funds. There have been cuts to scholarships, research funds, and the number of opportunities for research professors has been decreasing in recent times. However, even with these changes to the scholarly environment here, I can say that this area of study is still expanding.

Exchanging Ideas, Gaining Influences

I owe much of what I know regarding the study photography to many different authors. Didi Huberman and Peter Burke (especially his book *Eyewitnessing*) have been key intellectuals to read. I studied Sylvan Mareska and her work. I have worked directly with John Mraz, Ana Mauad, and Alberto del Castillo. Their work has been vital to my understanding of how to study photography in Latin America. I met them at a conference organized by the Centro de Fotografía (CdF) de Montevideo in 2012. The work they do at that center is marvelous in terms of their publication agenda and the research support they offer the field. Every year they have an annual contest for books and articles published on Latin American photography, and I was able to publish my first books with them.[4] Though the print edition is relatively small and the distribution is limited to Uruguay, their outstanding online platform allows your work to be read globally. I applaud the Uruguayan government for supporting this initiative. The CdF has wonderful staff that does excellent work. They have organized several conferences where I have met various researchers with whom I am still in contact in what I could describe as an informal network. Thanks to CdF I met Ana Mauad who has come on exchange to the Universidad Nacional de General Sarmiento and, thanks to the CdF as well, I have gone to Mexico to work with Alberto del Castillo and John Mraz. I have found these exchanges to be vital because they allow me to teach in other environments and to acquire valuable bibliography from other experts.

The academic exchanges that I just mentioned have helped me to come in direct contact with the research on photography that is occurring in Mexico, Brazil, Chile, Uruguay, and Argentina. However, there is so much that I still do not know. I have no idea what is taking place in our field in Paraguay or Bolivia for example, though I am sure there must be some research happening there. In an ideal world, we would have the funds to travel to these places and

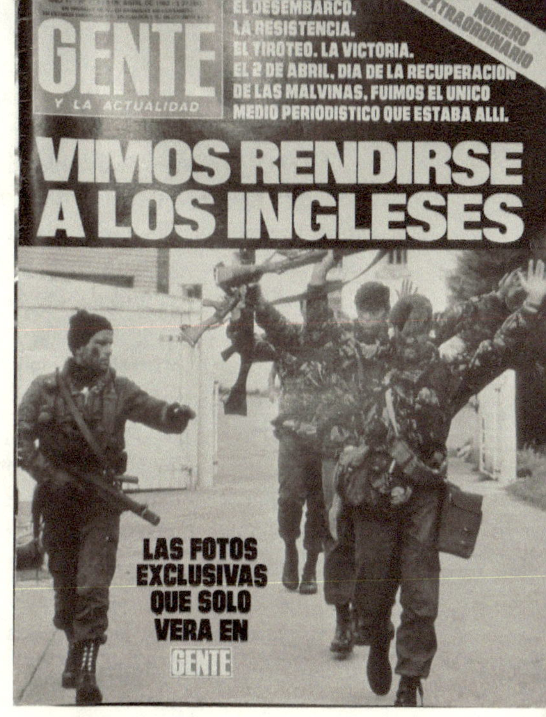

GENTE
Y LA ACTUALIDAD
EL DESEMBARCO.
LA RESISTENCIA.
EL TIROTEO. LA VICTORIA.
EL 2 DE ABRIL, DIA DE LA RECUPERACION
DE LAS MALVINAS, FUIMOS EL UNICO
MEDIO PERIODISTICO QUE ESTABA ALLI.
NUMERO EXTRAORDINARIO
VIMOS RENDIRSE A LOS INGLESES
LAS FOTOS EXCLUSIVAS QUE SOLO VERA EN GENTE

Figure 11.6. Vimos rendirse a los ingleses (We saw the English surrender), Argentina, April 1982. *Gente* magazine cover.

have meetings or seminars where we could have some knowledge exchange sessions and plan joint publications, but that is not our reality. Even so, good things are on the horizon. Now no one doubts the importance of our field. They have come to accept that we do work that is both qualitative and quantitative. Our work reaches into the social sciences, daily life, and history. We are now beginning to form knowledge networks that help us share and supply information that improves research in many fields. We still need to establish contact with other fields of knowledge and consider how we can develop our areas jointly. I am very interested in how photography changes the way we narrate and understand historical events and can function as a protagonist in the creation and writing of our history. There are moments in history where photography has made all the difference in our understanding of an event and has literally changed the course of history. I will tell you about one of those events that I have discovered as a part of my research.

Photographs That Create Watersheds

This particular event took place during the Guerra de las Malvinas (Falkland Islands War) between Argentina and the United Kingdom. The military dictatorship in Argentina sent troops to the las Malvinas/Falkland Islands with the idea of taking them from the United Kingdom, so they planned a surprise invasion, and they succeeded in maintaining their invasion a secret. Along with the invading Argentinian troops, they sent a photographer from an ultra-right newspaper to document that invasion visually. However, his photographs were essentially useless and even his own newspaper refused to publish them. He took what we would now describe as selfies as the troops disembarked. Nonetheless, a professional photographer by the name of Rafael Wollmann was also taking photographs on the island at the time of the landing. Wollmann was there taking pictures of the flora and fauna and daily life as part of another project that had been commissioned by the French photo agency Gamma.

Rafael Wollmann was able to take pictures of the British troops surrendering to the Argentinian soldiers. He hid those photographs and secretly sent them to Gamma. They were able to get them published in major world news outlets, and the photographs that the military dictatorship had commissioned simply did not exist. Instead, the world saw British soldiers lying on the ground with their hands in the air while the Argentinian soldiers pointed their guns at them. My research on this topic evidences how Wollmann's images helped to inform the decisions taken by the British and Argentinian governments. The photographs showed that the troops from Argentina had not acted according to plans, and the images also meant that the British troops were seen in a way that their government would have preferred to avoid, and this caused both governments to act in ways they had not previously contemplated. I have been able to publish my findings in Spanish as an article called "El fotoperiodismo y la guerra de Malvinas: Una batalla simbólica," and I continue to seek a publisher for the English version of this research.

Another article of mine: "El rol del fotoperiodismo en la construcción de la democracia en Argentina (1983–2002)" shows another instance when photography has played a major role in how historical events have developed. In 2002, the police in Argentina shot and killed two men who were participating in a march that was protesting unemployment. They first shot one of the protestors, and then they shot his friend who had stopped to help him. When this happened, the police and some major news outlets reported that the two protesters had shot and killed each other. However, there were four photographers who had pictures of what really happened, and, thanks to those images, they were able to tell a more accurate version of the events. The cover of the newspaper *Página 12* published one of the damning photographs with the testimony of the photographer. Thanks to photographs from all four of the different photographers, the true version of events unfolded, and it became very clear what had happened: the police shot the second protester in the back, murdering him.

After the photographs of the killing of the second protester were revealed, the whole discourse on the events changed radically. It even set into motion a chain of events that led to early national elections being called. The other photographs and the other testimonies proved who the killers were, and they are now in jail. After having lived a history of violence from a previous coup, the public was no longer willing to tolerate any more government officials committing murderous acts. The public's reaction to the murder is key, as is their reaction to the initial lies and manipulation of the media. In the end, the photographs and the photographers' testimonies set the record straight and changed the consequences for the perpetrators. This is why I argue that images used in a news article are so important: they have the power to change the entire discourse and discussions.

Photography has the marvelous capacity to bridge disciplines and enrich

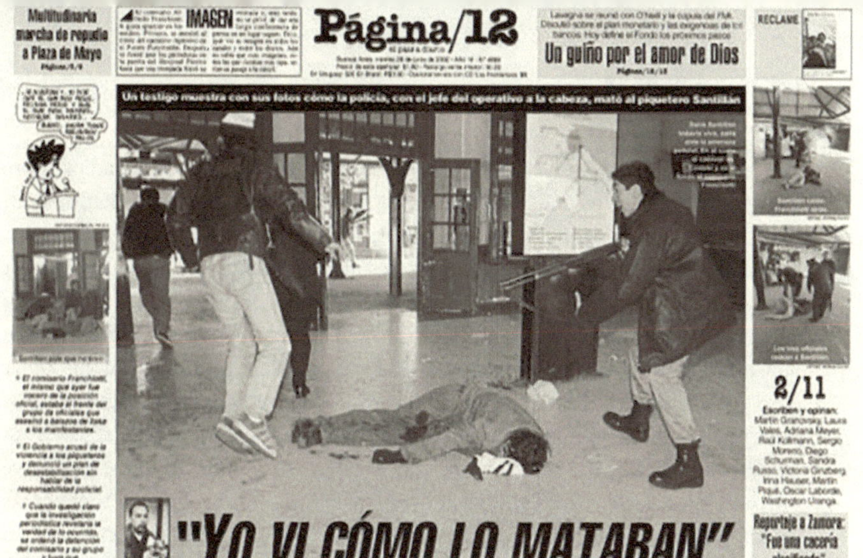

Multitudinaria marcha de repudio a Plaza de Mayo

IMAGEN

Página/12

Un guiño por el amor de Dios

RECLAME

Un testigo muestra con sus fotos cómo la policía, con el jefe del operativo a la cabeza, mató al piquetero Santillán

"YO VI CÓMO LO MATABAN"

2/11

Escriben y opinan: Martín Granovsky, Laura Vales, Adriana Meyer, Raúl Kollmann, Sergio Moreno, Diego Schurman, Sandra Russo, Victoria Ginzberg, Irina Hauser, Martín Piqué, Oscar Laborde, Washington Uranga

Reportaje a Zamora: "Fue una cacería planificada"

Figure 11.7. Cover page of *Página 12* newspaper, Argentina, 2002.

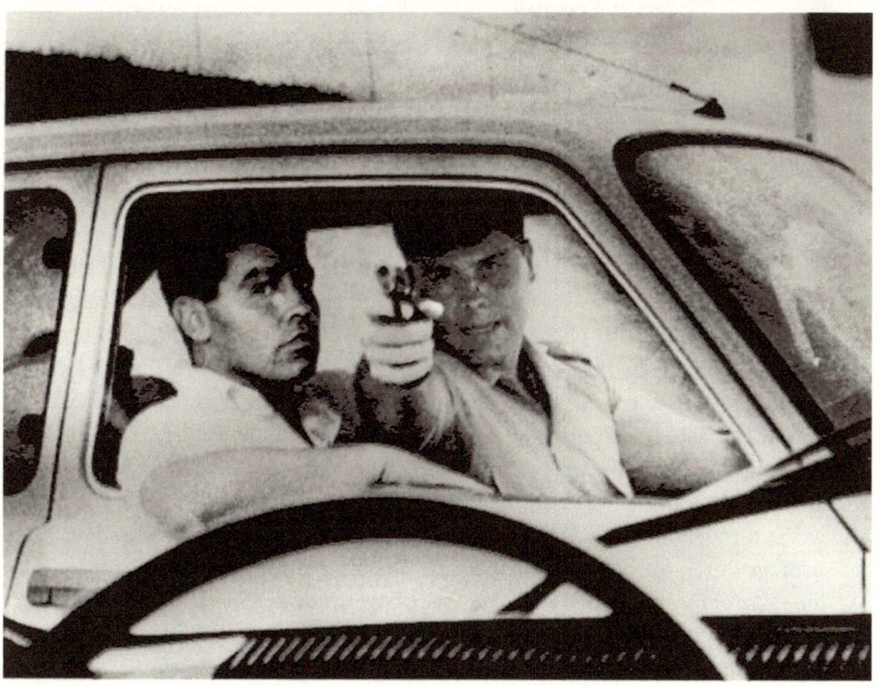

Figure 11.8. Amenza con pistola (Pistol-backed threat), Argentina, undated. Rafael Calviño. Personal Collection.

the fields where it is applied. We have a group called the Área de Estudios sobre Fotografía at the Universidad de Buenos Aires that brings together academics from the fields of sociology, anthropology, political science, literature, art, art history, and communications. We have very interesting discussions about our work that really expand our field. The interdisciplinary nature of our work is completely natural and enriching. As you work in the field of the study of photography, you must outline what you want to study and how you want to frame it within other fields of knowledge. I have seen excellent work on photography from the fields of semiotics, history, and sociology. I tell my students that they must select an area from which they plan to work and decide their approach. Once they have that established, they can then reach over into other fields to see how those areas of knowledge can help them too, because if they do not, then they can tend to lose their way. I think it is crucial to establish the correct contexts as well for the photographs that we study. Those who do not struggle to read the images in ways that are transcendent. Personally, I am interested in readings that establish the historical contexts and ask questions regarding how the images were produced, who distributed them, and how they were seen and understood. Finding the answers to research questions like those tend to be what makes the research interdisciplinary as I was mentioning earlier. We need more semiotic readings that speak on the form and the content of the photographic images as well.

As I research on photography in Latin America, I ask myself: Why are so few of the great Latin American photographers part of the canon of world photography? I think that it is linked to the poor dissemination of their work and the relatively small body of research on it. We need more scholars who write about Latin American photography in general. I also find myself wondering why bookstores in Argentina do not stock more books on Latin American photography, or why the publishing houses here are not willing to publish books with photos that include critical commentary or research on photography. Those would be helpful to the field of the study of photography here, and they represent some of the challenges that we face.

Even so, I see a very promising future for the study of photography in general. It is a field that is growing all throughout Latin America. There might be temporary setbacks due to budget cuts or other factors, but these will subside, and we will continue to grow. As we researchers go forth and expand our networks throughout Latin America, we will refine our scholarly projects and methodologies even further. Our numbers are already growing. I say this because of the effect of the intellectual exchanges we have already experienced. We have had very fruitful dialogues at different conferences and other professional meetings. For example, I know that my work on photojournalism in Argentina is being used by academics who study photojournalism in Brazil and allows for comparisons and contrasts within a Latin American context. The work the young photographers are currently developing in Latin America is very powerful and will provide a wealth of new material for researchers. This is only the beginning.

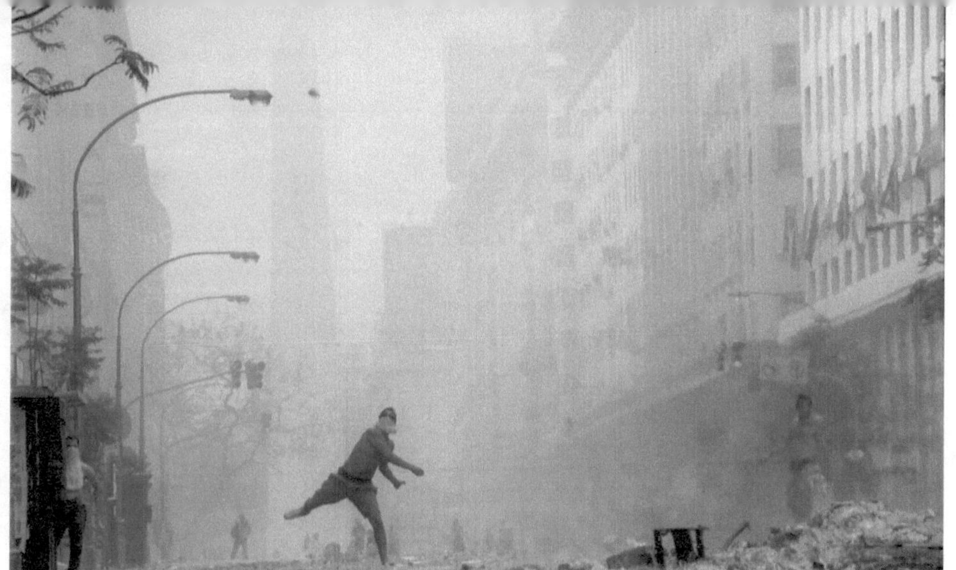

Figure 11.9. El obelisco, piedrazo (The obelisk, rock thrown during protest), Buenos Aires, Argentina, December 20, 2001. Enrique García Medina. Personal Collection.

I look forward to more intellectual exchanges further afield in the future because I am a firm believer that these experiences strengthen the field and enrich our labors. I also think that in Latin America we need to do more to see our field from within our own context. If you only work with tools made for other contexts, or ones based on superficial observations that have grown out of brief contact, this can bring difficulties. Research written here over the course of several years will be different from what is done quickly and from afar. Superficial glances frequently lend themselves to emphasize the exotic or the anecdotal, or they can generate narratives that focus on curiosities, outliers, or the eccentric. Overcoming these misconceptions makes the need for effective dialogue between us all even more imperative.

Selected Publications

Gamarnik, Cora. "La fotografía de prensa en Argentina durante la década del 60: modernización e internacionalización del periodismo gráfico." *Photo & Documento*, 2, 2016. http://gpaf.info/photoarch/index.php?journal=phd&page=article&op=view&path%5B%5D=68.

———. "La fotografía de prensa durante la guerra de Malvinas: la batalla por lo (in)visible." *Páginas: Revista digital de la Escuela de Historia*, 7.13, 2015, pp. 79–117.

———. "Imágenes de la post-dictadura en Argentina." *Photographie contemporaine en Amérique Latine*, 7, 2015.

———. "El rol del fotoperiodismo en la construcción de la democracia en Argentina (1983–2002)." *revistaRevue L´ordinaire des Ameriques, Instituto de Estudios sobre America* 219, 2015. http://orda.revues.org/.

Magdalena Broquetas

Universidad de la República, Uruguay

Photography and Archive

I HAVE A BA and a PhD in history, and I began to work with photography thanks to my archival research. In the early 2000s, toward the end of my bachelor's degree, I saw a scholarship to work in the archive of the Municipalidad, the Archivo de la Intendencia. One of my classmates and I decided to apply, and we both won a scholarship. We were tasked with documenting the Archivo Histórico Fotográfico de Montevideo. At that time, the archive was composed of approximately thirty thousand glass-plate negatives made between 1920 and 1970, although, in reality, the photo archive was much larger than that because it contained a vast collection of photographic prints from the second half of the nineteenth century up to the present day. Our job was to identify and date that material. However, when we started, we knew next to nothing about photography. We had to teach ourselves everything because up to that point everything that we had learned about writing history related to written documents. The only book we read on photography during our degree was *Eyewitnessing* by Peter Burke. He claims that very few historians are accustomed to working with images. I would also add that the number of historians who are used to working with photographs is even smaller still.

My experience at the Centro de Fotografía de Montevideo was much richer and more varied than if I had only engaged with written documents. Working in the archive, I began to understand the characteristics of visual documents and their possible uses. I started to bring out the full potential of the photography archive to write history, something that not all of my colleagues fully understand. During my time there I worked closely with photography conservation and photographic material. I faced many problems regarding the digitalization of photographs and their documentation. Many historians often overlook these questions, yet they are issues that you encounter if you are involved directly with photography archives.

When I started my employment at the Centro de Fotografía de Montevideo in 2002 (which at that time was called the Archivo Fotográfico de Montevideo) there were only six of us (including my university classmate, Isabel Wschebor, who also won the scholarship). Over time, the center grew to become a four-story building and supported around fifty employees. Though it was hard for me to leave it, in 2016 I left the Centro de Fotografía de Montevideo to focus on my tenured post at the university where I work. Even so, I will always consider it a privilege and an honor to have formed part of the foundational process of the center. It was a very interdisciplinary environment. We were in contact with many different specialists from Latin America. Aside from learning about photography conservation, I learned how to curate and how to do all the archival work necessary to keep photographs in order. There was a lot of variety in this rich milieu. We learned how to do everything thanks to our own efforts and the courses and workshops we took. We created a library on photography in Latin America as part of the process of setting up the center too. Many different colleagues from Chile, Argentina, Brazil, and Mexico helped us to know what to do and how to do it. Mexico was key, and not just due to its high-quality researchers but also because they continue to create a visual record of their cities. Mexico manifests a keen interest in documenting their cities photographically. In this effort, they are not only concerned about registering what is ideal or pretty. They also strive to document social dimensions and demographics. Mexico motivated the Centro de Fotografía de Montevideo (CdF) to study and promote photography in Uruguay. In that regard, CdF was the first place in the country to have an exhibition space entirely dedicated to photography. Now that space has grown to several rooms and galleries that are open to the public. It also has a publishing house that accepts peer-reviewed academic projects. I think it is the best place to study photography in Uruguay. The classes they hold to promote photography cover various areas. They have courses on how to take care of photographic material, how to publish on the web, and how to describe new discoveries and research outputs.

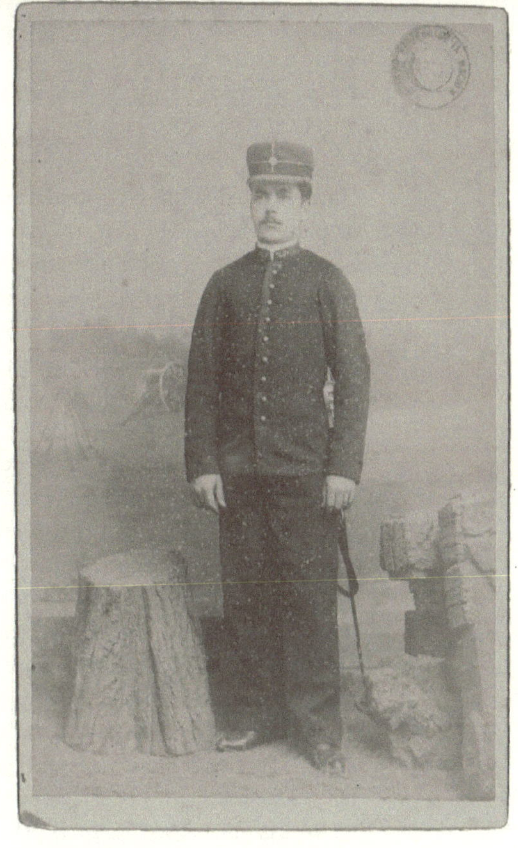

Figure 12.1. Portrait of Juan Carlos Fernández, June 19, 1895. Uruguay, Brunel. Colección fotográfica, Museo Histórico Nacional, Uruguay.

Photographs Narrate History

I always say that I have written history using photography as well as the history of photography. My first projects made use of documentary photographs to narrate the history of a place or event. I always tried to go beyond the image. I wanted to be sure that I was not just using the photographs as illustrations. After that, I started to work in photographic conservation, even though I never trained to be a conservationist. I integrated images into my research on photography and answered different questions such as "What can photographs tell me about certain social groups?" I worked with this specific focus while I was writing on the 1960s and the 1970s in Uruguay. That period spans the dictatorship in Uruguay to the restoration of democracy, and it has many holes in its visual history. As we began to work on it in 2003 (because it was the fortieth anniversary of the coup d'état) we wanted to recover that period's visual past. To do so, we went in search of the images.

Up to then, we only possessed the official images: those that were in the official archives such as the inauguration ceremonies. I wanted to obtain more material—images of the marches and the protests, but the archives did not have any of these. We could not locate any pictures of the opposition to the government. There were no images of repression, so we had to go in search of them. Once I found them, I began to publish on this topic. My chapter in *Fotografía e Historia en América Latina*, "De íconos a documentos: Las fotografías de la huelga general de Uruguay en 1973," is an example of that research focus. In that piece, I focus on the Communist Party newspaper that operated in Uruguay from 1957 to 1973. It has amazing photography. I worked with the photographs that had not disappeared—images of the coup and of the general strike that began with the coup and ended on the 27th of June 1973.

Once I finished that project, I began to explore an idea that would allow contemporary photography to represent the same period (the 1960s and the 1970s). We went to locations such as the prisons as well as other localities that had been prisons. These places had not kept any photographic records. We discovered that there were approximately forty "detention centers" (as they were called), in Montevideo alone, and none of them had been visually recorded. Therefore, we went to these places and took pictures. Some were unchanged. Others had acquired new functions. Even others had disappeared altogether. We researched who had been there and what had happened to its occupants. Then we enlarged these images to exhibit them better. It was fantastic.

My original idea for this project was a street exhibition. However, because many of these prisons are still owned and operated by the military, we could not do that there for security reasons. However, we were still able to have an open-air exhibition that people could visit while they were outside. It was a way of speaking about the past through contemporary images.

Even so, I think that my most important and ambitious project has been to

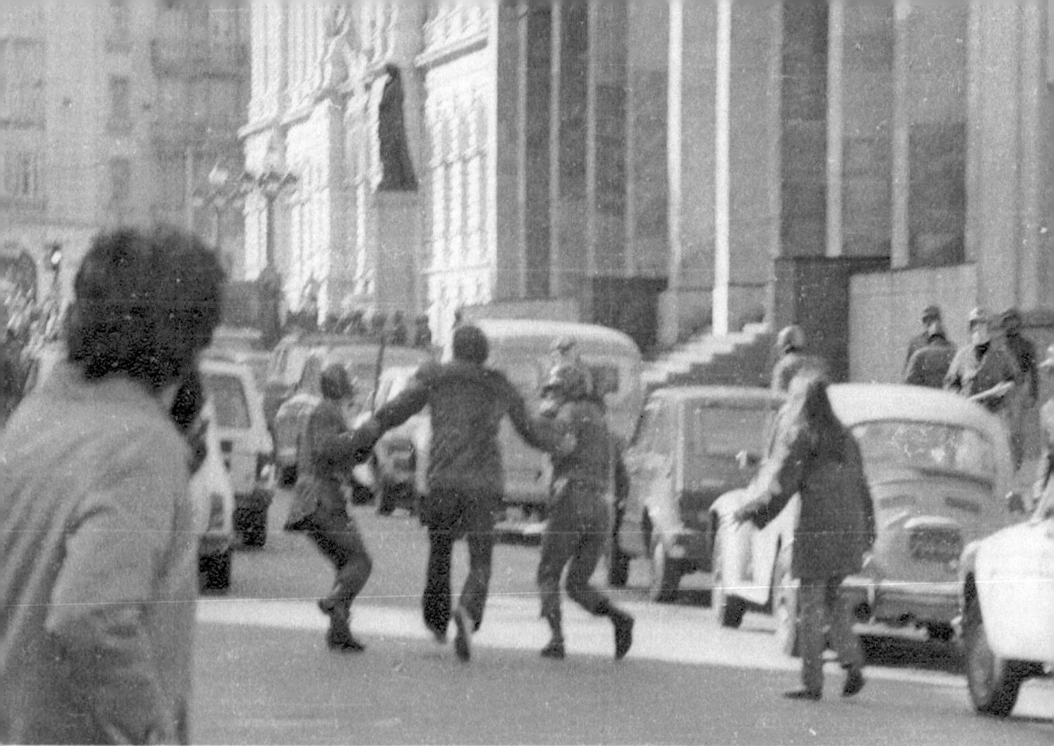

Figure 12.2. Las de Camaratres (Soldiers), Uraguay, Undated. Anonymous. Centro de Fotografía de Montevideo.

write a cultural history of photography in Uruguay. In 2011, we published the first volume, *Fotografía en Uruguay: Historia y usos sociales 1840–1930*, and in 2018, we published the second volume of the series, *Fotografía en Uruguay: Historia y usos sociales 1930–1990*. This project has been endearing and difficult. Several authors collaborated in the writing of it. It was a complicated task because of what we could not find in the archives. We would find photographs without any supporting material or information. We had to search the archives without knowing what we might find beforehand and decide what the subjects and the material would be and then make decisions regarding how to use the material and make it all work. We wrote a cultural and social history because we were not art historians, and this freed us of that hierarchy. We did not have to include certain authors because they had been in museums or markets. We followed Bourdieu's suggestion on the study of photography: to consider all kinds of photographs and understand photography through the spaces that human experience occupies (13–39). Hence, we discussed portraits, photo clubs, identification photography, and photography in the media, science, and many other areas. There were some conceptual models that were useful, so we did not really invent any conceptual models. We simply took those models and adapted them to Uruguay.

Many different books helped us to find inspiration. Marie-Loup Sougez's

Historia de la Fotografía and Bernardo Riego's *La construcción social de la realidad a través de la fotografía y el grabado informativo en la España del siglo XIX* were very useful and gave us many ideas. Lemagny's history of photography that goes beyond the Beaumont Newhall model for the history of photography provided important direction for the project too (Lemagny and Rouille *A History of Photography*). We found ourselves needing to create databases of both authors and dates. The university where I work gave us vital technical support to accomplish the task. That team and the team at the Centro de Fotografía de Montevideo were what made the project possible. The result was a beautiful and carefully crafted edition whose color photographs on high-quality paper are now a rarity for books on photography in Uruguay. Our book is more for reading and contemplation, not for marking up with a pen or pencil. Here, in recent years, the publishers have pushed for less images and smaller print to make cheaper books. Nonetheless, I think that even if you are not creating an art volume, you still want to have good quality images so that you can see them and understand their role in your narrative. Small and poor quality photographs will not be able to create that desired effect.

Photographs Preserve the Past and Need Contextualization

Our approach has been more of a documentary analysis of the photographs. We started from the base assumption that photographs have the intrinsic ability to preserve the past and its people and to carry that conserved information over the course of time. However, we do not think that photographs are able to speak for themselves. In my opinion, there is nothing more difficult to analyze than the arbitrary use of a photographic image. If you are in a psychology session, and you want to use an image as a detonator to spark poetic inspiration, that is fine. However, if you are using photography as a document, you must be very careful. The misuse of photography is dangerous in those circumstances. You must document everything with special care. On many occasions we are faced with an image that does not really have any secondary information. What would you do in those circumstances? You encounter an image that has two women walking down a main street, and on the back of the photograph it says, "women on a stroll," and an approximate date, "19th or 20th century." That information is essentially useless. They might as well have said nothing. You need to understand that photographs do not speak for themselves, and that when you find an image that has something written on it or a cutline that comes with it, you need to be careful with what you do with that information. You must use analytical questions to guide you to some of the important information that you can extract from the images. While some of the questions I list below might sound silly or obvious, answering them is important.

Who took the picture? (On many occasions the question "Who commissioned the picture?" is even more important.)
When was the picture taken?
Where was the picture taken?
Is the picture part of a documentary series? Was it originally intended to be part of sequence or another text?
What do we see? (Sometimes the question "Who is present?" is relevant.)
What do I know about the context? (Both in terms of what is in the photograph and what is not seen in the photograph.)

Those are initial questions for when you are writing history with photographs and are at the heart of any critical photographic analysis of any one image or series of images. After answering them, I ask even more questions to interrogate the information more fully and reach different levels of photographic analysis. The three levels that I am describing relate to historical research. Other fields of research, such as sociology, would require different questions.

These are those analytical levels:

> What the author wanted to show us, or what the person who ordered the creation of the image wanted to show us.
>
> The unique qualities the medium presents. Photography is a unique medium because it is a mechanically reproduced representation of reality. Photographs contain details that the photographer did not mean to capture that may or may not be relevant to the analysis. There are absences that need to be addressed in your study.
>
> What type of life does your photograph have? What kind of meaning has the photograph acquired over time as it is read in different contexts? How has our understanding of the photograph changed over time? These are questions that concern the context of the analysis. To be able to execute this style of analysis you need to know what you are looking at and the historical context surrounding the photograph in question.

If you work in archives, the technical processes of creating a photograph are also important to preserving it. In the case of a historian, the technical processes are going to help him understand the photo itself. You need to know the historical processes for creating photographic images that were possible in each different historical period. You must employ high-resolution scans when you digitize because these will enable you to preform detailed analysis of the photographs that standard observations will not allow. You must know how to use specialized tools to find all of the information you are searching out. Supplementary texts that accompany the images can also provide valuable information that can contribute to the analysis.

As a historian, I think about photography in terms of historical knowledge. I also consider photography research in terms of empirical methods of knowledge acquisition. The texts in the field of the study of photography that have most influenced me are connected to concepts and theory. I have not been strongly influenced by theory that is linked to philosophy, and I do not frequently draw on it as I write. I do admire the pioneering concepts in photography theory by scholars such as Gisele Freund or Walter Benjamin in which they develop theory and are writing about how society has changed thanks to the invention of photography. I have used their ideas as I have analyzed photography. Fred Ritchin's *After Photography* has helped me to face ideas connected to photography in our day. He has helped me to consider ideas related to the image itself, sequence, the narration of history via photography, and the question of truth and photography that have really been at the center of the notion of photography since its beginnings. He has also inspired me to consider the location of the photographic producers and the distribution chain when analyzing photographs.

Unique Topics in Latin American Photography

The story of photography as a technology is global and transnational; therefore, in the sense of processes and products, that would suggest that Latin American photography is not unique. However, Latin American photography can be unique in terms of its photographic topics. Subjects such as social practice, ethnicity, political conflicts, and the representation of life and reality that we will not find in other locations are what compose the distinctive body of work that Latin American photography offers us. I should also add here that not all Latin America is the same because Latin America is not homogenous. Hence, we should not expect that from its photography either.

Another aspect of Latin American photography to take into consideration is the fact that its archives have suffered a high level of abandonment. Many archives here look more like storage units than archives. Uruguay has four important public photography archives in the capital. The largest one is the Archivo Nacional de la Imagen. Then you have the Museo Histórico Nacional, the Biblioteca Nacional de Uruguay, and the Centro de la Fotografía de Montevideo.

Other useful archives exist, but they would benefit from additional work to make them more accessible. The photography archives at the Universidad de la República and the Universidad Católica are part of that group. There are also many archives in Uruguay's different departments, the occasional photo club, and other private archives. The newspaper *El País* has millions of photographs in its archive, making it one of the largest in the country. Until recently, its photographs were kept separately from the written documents, causing the images to lose all their written contexts. The data, the taxonomies, and the descriptions were all very vague or did not exist at all.

Presently in Uruguay, we do not have anyone who specializes in the description of audiovisual archives or in preventative conservation. It is important to remember that photographic material is very sensitive and fragile. In recent years, the institutions are beginning to become more aware of the necessary steps that you must take to control the storage environment: temperature, humidity, and other factors. We desperately need to leave associated written records with their corresponding photographs, and there must be more care in the environmental control of the archives. We are taking steps in the right direction. The CdF is starting a project to create a professional training center to teach people how to take care of photographs in Latin America. They will be bringing Latin American and other international experts to teach us how to handle our photographs here. Developments such as this will gradually change the panorama, but it will require much investment. However, if we do not invest in these areas, over time these cultural and historical reserves will simply disappear.

Evolution

We have rapidly evolved as a field when it comes to methodology and theoretical concepts. I have always been exploring the different types of potential that images have. I have worked hard to keep the photographs that I use from simply being illustrations and to employ them with the same rigor that other historical sources receive. (Though I am not against the use of photographs as mere illustrations.) My research flows against the normal currents. I think that I have been successful thus far because I engage with the photographs as documents. To be able to do that, you must have special skillsets and take the author into account as well as the context in which he or she was working. There are tools that guide us along this scholarly path.

It might sound painfully obvious, but in order to study photography successfully you must know about photography. You must understand what is technically possible and what is not in each stage of photography's history. If you do not, then you are running the risk of committing the very serious error of being anachronistic and judging the images from a perspective that is out of step with their place in history. For example, when you are looking at the photographs from the Crimean War in the nineteenth century you need to know that battle photographs were not technically possible. You need to know that they were using enormous cameras and glass plate negatives. The negatives were wet negatives that had to be developed in situ, after the photographs had been taken. It is also essential to know that this event was being censored. This means that you will not find any unfavorable photos, as is evident when you search for them in the Biblioteca Nacional de Uruguay. When Mauricio Bruno analyzes the Guerra de la Triple Alianza in Uruguay in *Fotografía en Uruguay: Historia y usos sociales 1840–1930* in the eastern front of the war with Paraguay (1865–1870) he shows that this event was subject to very similar circumstances. The Uruguayan government gave orders that its eastern front had to look good. That is why you cannot find any pictures of wounded troops on that side. They did not want any images that might lower anyone's morale.

One of photography's intrinsic characteristics is that we believe what we see. Even so, you must always remember that there is more than meets the eye. You must take into account the unseen factors. You have to remember that you can stage realistic-looking photographs. You must factor in the photographer's context or the objectives that were motivating the person who ordered the picture. To study photography properly is to have these elements in mind. You have to identify, recover, find the networks, and understand the techniques. You have to look at many photographs. When you do that, you begin to make important connections and bring together important ideas. This is the difference between good and poor research on photography. I think that one of the real dangers of this field is that many researchers move with a higher level of impunity than others.

Another danger is to write a piece of research using just one photograph. Occasionally, I have seen scholarly papers based on just one photograph. If you were working with written material, I think most researchers would not even consider working with just one source; but they think that it is possible to do this with photography. That is an error. You must create series that help you to stay close to the historical facts you are discussing. At the very least, you need to work with an entire archive or an entire collection.

Developments in the Study of Photography in Latin America

I feel very optimistic about the future of the study of photography in Latin America. With everything that is occurring at the CdF and other developments, it is a very dynamic field right now. Though presently in Uruguay there are no specific university degrees that focus on photography, there are many new schemes being developed in different institutions and universities. There are postgraduate degrees being created and professional development programs and other diplomas you can earn in this field that will come. Right now, you can find photography in arts degrees, communication degrees, or as a fundamental component of other given degrees. There are areas that will need more work. We have yet to create a specific university degree in photography, documentary photography, or museum/gallery curation. I think that we will see photography and its study play an increasing role in the academic world, and we will need individuals who know more about photography: how to approach it critically and how to curate it. Therefore, I emphasize the need to take care of our archives and why we require the resources to do so. Everything makes a difference, even small things. The undergraduate classes I teach at my university on photography's social uses and how to use photography to write about history make a difference. The CdF's courses and workshops have an important impact. When I look back and contemplate what we have done over the past fifteen years, I am optimistic about what will be able to happen in the future. There will be more scholarly material. There will be more jobs in academia, in archives, and in other academic activities. There will be more to talk about when we meet at academic encounters in other countries throughout the Americas.

The Digital Era and Society

Young people want to use more images in their theses and other projects because our digital era has given images a new and more important role in society. They work with photography in ways that we never did as students because now it is so easy to take pictures and use them. Photography is no longer considered something from the world of art. Not only is photography a more integrated part of our daily life but now it is cheaper to take and print pictures. Before it was difficult to include images in a dissertation, thesis, or a paper for the humanities or the social sciences. Those images might not always be the best in terms of quality, but you can now include them with relative ease. To be honest, who does not like the effect that an image has in a text? They are attractive. They draw us in, and they promote empathy.

However, these new uses of the image run the dangerous risk of having no correlation to what the author is writing. It is easy to include an image, but you need to create a direct correlation with what you are writing if you are going to generate the proper effect. Using photographs as mere illustrations can be good, and it can help you to illustrate and draw closer to a topic. You can have an image as a decoration, but the challenge is to use it to say something important. For example, I was analyzing some photographs from a strike in Uruguay, and to reach the level where I could say something significant about that strike with those photographs was difficult. In order to say more than "this is a picture of the protesters with their signs," I had to dig deep. I had to explore many questions. I needed to build the context. I had to study the newspaper and the photographers along with their working conditions. I had to find out how the

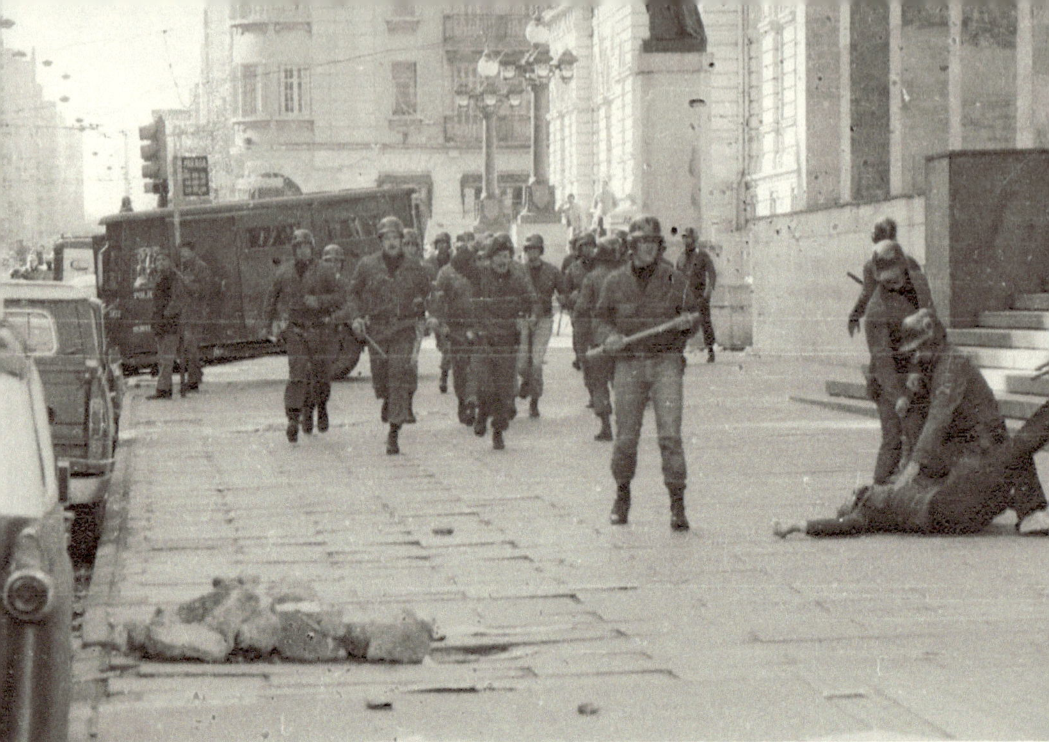

Figure 12.3. Repression of an anti-dictatorship protest, June 4, 1984. Camaratres. Centro de Fotografía de Montevideo.

photographers were able to get up close and how they were able to get permission to take the pictures they did. I needed to know what role the photographs played at that moment in history.

As I did this research, one thing that I discovered was that the photographer developed his photographs in one of the factories that the workers had occupied. He would take his pictures, develop them, and show them to others. Not only did this give them courage to keep striking but it also gave them a reason to do so. They did not have smartphones back then to be able to post or send pictures on social media and to say to the other workers on strike, "Hey, we too are occupying another building over here." The photographs played that role then. This type of research is not easy to do, but it is very invigorating. You have to use different methods. You must have interviews with the press, find the images they used and where they were published, and figure out how they were edited. You need to observe the context and see which works competed with others and what distribution circles existed then. This type of work requires more graft, but it does so much more than merely illustrate.

Studying photography means that you have to be in contact with many other fields of knowledge, and you cannot master all of them. I think that the key is working with all the different fields that enrich our research in dialogue and collaboration (Azoulay "Photography Consists of Collaboration"). You need to identify when you need other expertise and how to approach it. This careful dialogue will help you avoid careless mistakes or misreadings. For example, my book on the history of photography in Uruguay was possible thanks to many archivists, historians, anthropologists, photographers, and technical staff who helped me digitalize all the material. We even had biologists identify what type of fungi were growing on the negatives to determine if they were indigenous to Rio de la Plata or if they originated from somewhere else (and then determine what course of action would be best to combat it). That example offers you a tiny taste of just how interdisciplinary our research group was. Photographic conservation is not just a topic for those working in that field. It is intimately linked to the preservation of physical pieces of our history that could potentially be lost if we do not change our present course of action.

Selected Publications

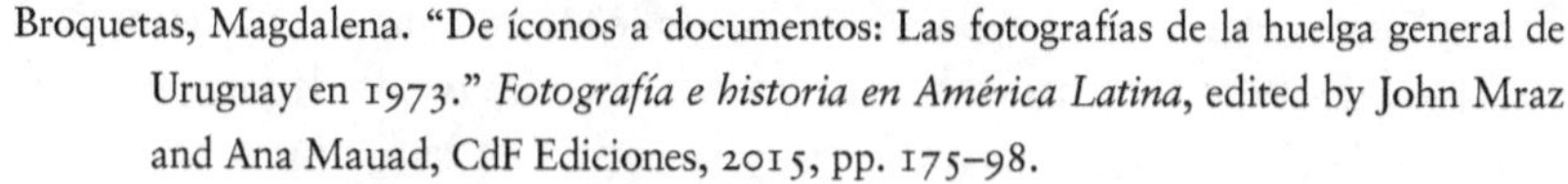
Broquetas, Magdalena. "De íconos a documentos: Las fotografías de la huelga general de Uruguay en 1973." *Fotografía e historia en América Latina*, edited by John Mraz and Ana Mauad, CdF Ediciones, 2015, pp. 175–98.

———, editor. *Fotografía en Uruguay: Historia y usos sociales (1840–1930)*. Vol. 1. Centro de Fotografía de Montevideo, 2011.

———, editor. *Fotografía en Uruguay: Historia y usos sociales (1930–1990)*. Vol. 2. Centro de Fotografía de Montevideo, 2018.

———, editor. "Las fotografías en la construcción de conocimiento histórico: usos, límites y potencialidades. Reflexiones teórico-metodológicas a partir de la presentación del trabajo del 'Núcleo interdisciplinario de investigación y preservación del patrimonio fotográfico uruguayo'" *Fuentes y Archivos*, 2, 2011, pp. 173–87.

Ana Mauad

Universidade Federal Fluminense

History and the Economically Disadvantaged Led Me to Photography

I GRADUATED WITH a degree in history in 1982 from the Fluminense Federal University in the city of Niterói in Brazil. Soon after that, I began teaching history classes at a primary school in Rio de Janeiro. I taught an afternoon shift at a public school that had students from economically disadvantaged communities. That teaching experience was very important in my formation as an intellectual because it foregrounded many questions regarding the teaching of history that led me to study photography.

A few years later, in 1985, I started a postgraduate program in history at the Fluminense Federal University in Niterói, with the intention of focusing on a project about teaching history to young people and adults. During that course I learned about a series of approaches associated with changes in historiography during the 1970s and 1980s that focused on cultural history, new approaches on microhistory, and challenges and methods for history writing with different kinds of documents, including visual sources. At the same time, I participated in debates on various topics, not only ones at the university, but also in intellectual gatherings off campus. In the 1980s, Brazilian society experienced the beginning of a military regime due to the mobilization of social movements. This led to a time of great political excitement in Brazil. Debates from that period focused on a wide variety of issues and were enriched by the participation of philosophers, writers, artists, and other professionals. However, none of these debates explored photography, even though at that moment photojournalism was playing an important political role. Hence, I decided that many of my research projects would study this phenomenon, and even in my recent research project, *Fotografia Pública: Usos, funções e circuitos sociais no Brasil, séculos XIX e XX*, I continue to use this focus.

Yet, for me, the idea to study photography did not simply come out of nowhere, because in addition to having several friends and family who were amateur photographers, photography was part of a deep-seated visual tradition in my family. I personally was not a photographer, but I liked to observe and collect photographs as a student, so I began to think: Why not be innovative in historical studies and use this medium? Hence, I prepared a research proposal focused on the idea of using photography to study history and submitted it to one of my thesis supervisors who welcomed the notion of working with photography and other visual sources and steered me to a semiotic approach as a methodology to work with photographs. My first line of inquiry toward photography used semiotics to analyze photographs as messages. Because I considered photography another medium of communication, I found it necessary to learn to decipher the systems of visual signs that composed this medium. During the 1980s, Marxist theory, specifically the Marxist British historians, had a strong influence in the way we shaped the questions we asked of the past in Brazil. This background, and the emergence of cultural history, has its influence on my work. Hence, I was challenged by all these new perspectives during my postgraduate studies. My doctoral dissertation responded to these critical approaches and questions.

I defended my PhD dissertation in December 1990: *Under the Sign of the Image: The Production of Photography and the Control of Codes of Social Representation by the Ruling Class in Rio de Janeiro During the First Half of the Twentieth Century (Sob o signo da imagen).* It was the first dissertation about photography within a history degree program in a graduate school in Brazil. It was based on the hypothesis that during the first half of the twentieth century the bourgeois way of life in Rio de Janeiro became a hegemonic pattern of conduct and social representation. My research aimed to link public representations of the bourgeoisie to their private representation. For this analysis, I identified the codes of behavior in Rio and commented on culture in the country and the city (urban and rural) of the public and the private spaces. To do so, I analyzed two series of photographs. The first was my own family photographs from 1900 to 1950: a family of Lebanese immigrants who arrived in Brazil in the early twentieth century and earned their fortune from the coffee trade. The second set of images were published in illustrated magazines from that same period, such as *O Cruzeiro*, *Careta*, *Fon-Fon*, *Revista da Semana*, and several others that showcased fashions and modes of urban culture in Brazil. So, crossing the private and public spaces of social representation enabled me to visually explain the building of a social class hegemony.

Unexpected Developments within Projects

After my dissertation defense, I continued to work with photography and history. This path has been full of all kinds of shortcuts and twists and turns that have appeared during my academic trajectory. At the Fluminense Federal

University, I work in the History Department in the areas of theory, methods, and historiography. In this case, my work with photography is not connected to a specific area but to photography as a historical experience. In my research, I try to show that taking photographs is part of society's social practice. For instance, in my chapter "Imagem e auto imagem do Império" in Alencastro's *História da Vida Privada no Brasil Imperial*, I evidenced how photography became one of the pivots of a society ruled by those of privilege. During the second half of the nineteenth century in Brazilian society, especially in Rio de Janeiro (the then capital of Brazil), a visual economy based on the production, distribution, and consumption of photographs—landscapes and portraits—created an image of the Brazilian Empire as an exotic land of abundance for international consumption. The carte-de-visite portraits formed an image of the upper class that suggested they were an aristocratic society of wealthy landowners. Their visual culture portrayed slaves as commodities that were simply a part of the exotic landscape while the image of Emperor Dom Pedro II became another important visual icon. This was due in part to his strong sponsorship of photographic practice in the Brazilian Empire during that time (Alencastro).

Photography as an attitude of recollection, documentation, and surveillance, and as a collection of material objects that can be changed, commercialized, and stored is what emerges from a study of photography at that time. Experiences from social life became historical not only because they were photographed but also because they took part in the social relations that produced them. Photographic images are sources to understand the past from a holistic perspective. This forces us to think of photography (both the material object and its production) as a historical experience that is closely connected to visual culture in each society. It is an experience that involves a social circuit of production, circulation, consumption, and agency, which is intimately linked to the uses and functions that different types of photographs have in social life.

A Plurality of Approaches

All my projects incorporate a more general and foundational perspective on photography that launches them directly into the world of social relations. In this sense, I am a historian who works with photography, not a photography historian. Because I use photography to consider the theory of history, photography has become a platform to understand cultural relationships, collective attitudes toward the past, and the role played by visuality in social relations. This is an interdisciplinary perspective, which is fundamental to establishing connections with different areas of knowledge that have been working with photographs. For me, these areas include anthropology, media, communication and cultural studies, and art history.

Thirty years ago, when I presented my PhD dissertation, the scholarly context was completely different than what we now have in terms of connections between social historians, cultural historians, and the field of visual studies. In Brazilian historiography, there have been important transformations in the field of history in relation to photography. I will mention three of them.

> The consolidation of research groups connected to new methodologies, such as oral history and visual history. Among them, the Laboratory of Oral History and Image (LABHOI-UFF), founded in 1982 at my university, which continually develops new projects, and connects oral and visual sources.
>
> The dissemination of new historical approaches in a great variety of national forums in which photographs became not only a source but also an object of history.
>
> An increase in dissertations based on the topic of visuality and visual culture using photographs. This has led to the 2004 formation of the Visual Culture Working Group in the Brazilian Historical Association (ANPUH), connecting academics and initiatives as well as promoting forums for debate around the historical uses of images, especially photography.

A new history of photography has arisen from those different epistemological appropriations of this medium. This approach to history makes more use of photography theory, art history, the social uses of photographs, and visual culture. This research seeks to comprehend how societies produce their images and the social circuits created for that purpose.

My methodological strategies vary significantly according to the questions that I strive to answer and the challenges that the images pose. In one of my more recent articles, "Imagens em fuga: Considerações sobre espaço público visual no tempo presente" (Images on the Road: Considerations about Visual Public Space at Present Time), I developed the idea of image flow to characterize the procedures for searching for photographs online through connections made by Google Images. This research question seeks to understand how images travel from their place of origin and take up residence in different environments, creating new meanings or recycling old ones. To understand this process of moving from one visual environment to another it is fundamental to recompose the biography of the images.

With the popularization of photography in almost all dimensions of social life, many avenues of inquiry exist. However, even when we do not have photographs, it is important to ask questions such as: Why they are absent? Or, what makes that experience unphotographical? The most important idea here is not to disconnect

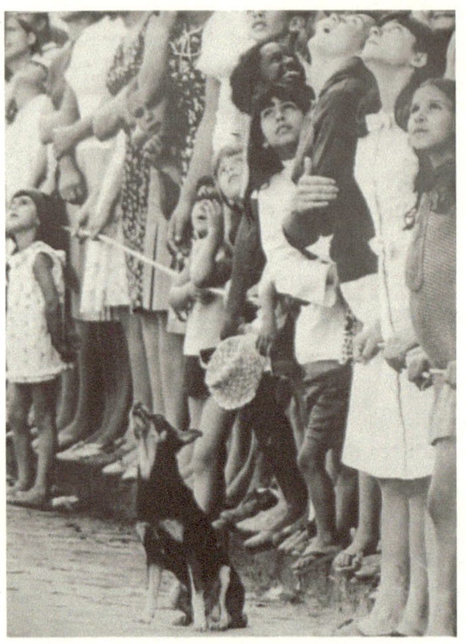

Figure 13.1. Inhabitants of the city of Joaçaba watching Brazilian Air Force, Joaçaba, Parana, Brazil, December 10, 1966. Erno Schneider. Private Collection. (Inhabitants stopped their routine to attend the aerial show of "Esquadrilha da Fumaça," or Smoke Squad, closing "anti-guerrilla" training, in the context of the Charrua operation.)

photos from photography and its practice from the historical and social experience because it is very connected to contemporary society. We must understand that contemporary subjectivity depends on photographic images and how they form the notion of self-image for individuals. Even today, the digital image has surpassed analog technology as we capture images with our phones and store them on our computers or social media sites. Yet, this process connects to a subjective and contemporary understanding of the use of images to represent our lives. For that reason, the system for studying images consists of a larger epistemological background, which informs my research on photography.

In another article, "How Are Images Born? A Study of Visual History," I deployed a strategy I outlined by following the trajectory of the French photographer Marc Riboud's 1967 photograph that shows a girl giving a flower to soldiers in Washington, DC. For this analysis I adopted a nonlinear perspective of historical time based on German art historian Hans Belting's *Anthropology of the Image* so as to understand how different visual cultures create similar images.

I mention these projects to underline that you must find the right tools for the projects on which you plan to work. For example, if I am working with an extensive and homogeneous photographic series, like I did during my PhD, semiotic analysis is useful. In this current research project I argue that photography is understood to be a message that conveys a certain meaning, and an analysis of the signs that compose it will help to decode that meaning. With that analysis, further conclusions can be inferred. In my dissertation this meant that the photographic messages conveyed by different series of family photographs and photographs from illustrated magazines communicate codes of behavior from Rio de Janeiro's upper class, urban bourgeois, and serve as an example of hegemonic cultural patterns for the whole country.

In my article "Por uma história fotográfica dos acontecimentos contemporâneos, Rio de Janeiro, 30 de junho de 1987" (For a Photographic History of Contemporary Events, Rio de Janeiro, June 30, 1987), I tried to go beyond semiotics by employing the notion of photographic history that photographs produce. This article analyzes a historical event (a "riot" in downtown Rio de Janeiro in June 1987) through photographs published in five newspapers from Rio de Janeiro and one from the city of Niterói on the day after the event (July 1, 1987). The reconstruction of the photographic history of the 1987 event is based on the notions of public photography and visual public space, to analyze the meanings of the event produced by the newspapers and evaluate the role played by photojournalism in the making of a historical event.

Hermeneutical analysis can also increase our understanding of the meanings that are attributed to the photographs in different environments. This occurs via the analysis of the forms of reception and the uses and functions that photography assumes in different contexts. We contemplate the roles that photography assumes as an object of material culture. The visual repertoires that give a photograph one specific sense or attribute, and not another, can also be operated by the hermeneutic approach. One of the consequences of this perspective is that photography becomes a material object with key roles in the writing of biographies and describing social life.

Photographs Are More Than Illustrations

We must avoid the illustrative use of photographs if we wish to use them to study history. We must understand photography as an image, as a document, and as a phenomenon that registers aspects of social life in a very specific way. It does so from a certain point of view based on learned cultural repertoires. What I mean is that when you learn to take photographs, you need to acknowledge culturally codified patterns of visual representations that vary through time and space. Photographs are the result of a social practice; therefore, one should not forego the analysis of the social contexts, functions, and the uses of photographic images.

All my projects share a complex conceptual framework that guides the understanding of photography as a historical experience based on photographic practice in which individuals are involved through the visual dimension of social experience. This framework is closely connected to W. J. T. Mitchell's notions on picture theory and the discussion of the agency of images in the historicity of visuality (*What do pictures want?*). His words best describe this: "In short, a dialectical concept of visual culture cannot rest content with a definition of its object as the 'social construction of the visual,' but must insist on exploring the chiastic reversal of this proposition, *the visual construction of the social field*. It is not just that we see the way we do because we are social animals, but also that our social arrangements take the forms they do because we are seeing animals" (*What do pictures want?* 345).

These ideas make it possible to propose different observation platforms for different types of photography. In this respect, my current project, "Public Photography: Uses, Functions, and Social Circuits in Brazil, 19th and 20th century," has a very ambitious perspective. In it, I try to develop the notion of public photography and how during the mid-nineteenth and twentieth century, photographic practice played an important role in the construction of the public visual space. I consider environments in which photographs began to circulate among a larger audience: newspapers, magazines, posters in the public space, governmental advertising, institutional reports, and so forth. I also created a common and shared meaning for photographs. Therefore, I am interested in photojournalism, documentary photography, government photography, independent photography, as well as photography exhibitions and how photography became part of the art world. This research is about tracing the social routes of photography, which I call public photography because, historically speaking, the definition of vernacular photography varies. This is closely related to the way the visual public or the audiences for photographs are created or how the public is called to participate, and the idea Ariella Azoulay refers to when she speaks of the civil contract of photography (*Civil Contract*).

Looking Ahead

In Brazil, the study of photography is now accepted, but it has evolved. I experienced much resistance at first. Though my advisor embraced my ideas, before I had finished my dissertation, I went to a conference to share some of my findings where I had an experience that demonstrates how this field has developed. In 1987 I went to the Brazilian Historians National Association Conference (ANPUH) in Brasília, and I presented a paper analyzing photographs published in newspapers about a riot in Rio de Janeiro that had just occurred the month before the conference. The audience at my presentation argued that I was doing journalism because I was using photos to write about a recent event. Hence, the topic's temporality and the fact that I studied photographs caused them to reject my paper as academic scholarship. Twenty years later, I turned this paper into the article I mentioned earlier, "Por uma história fotográfica dos acontecimentos contemporâneos," and published it in a special issue focusing on the history and the present. Now historical approaches that incorporate the visual and discuss problems regarding the visual are widely accepted. Another article of mine, "Fotograficamente Rio: A cidade e seus temas" (Rio through Photographs: The City and its Subjects), evidences this point even better. This article belongs to a book of compiled essays that focuses on a visual history of the city of Rio de Janeiro. Guided by photographic practice, it proposes a new approach to this history and its broad set of photographs to help create the

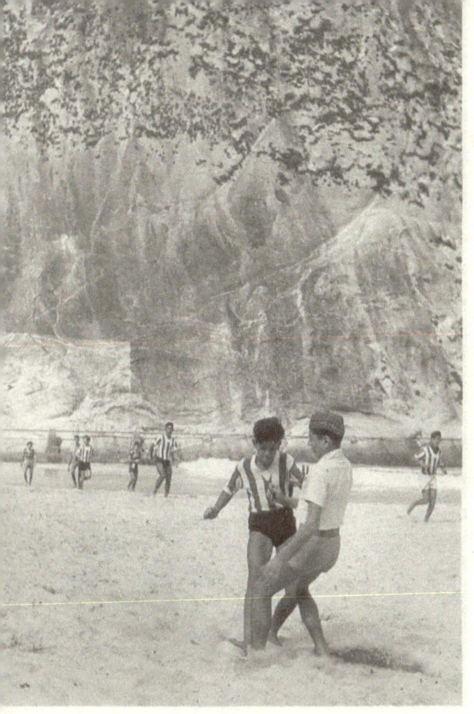

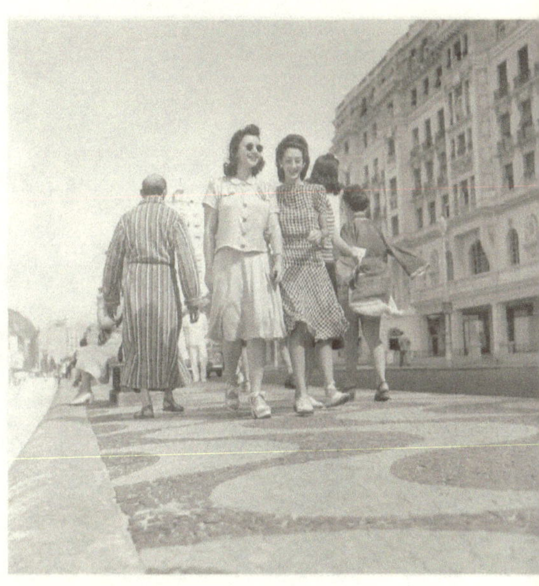

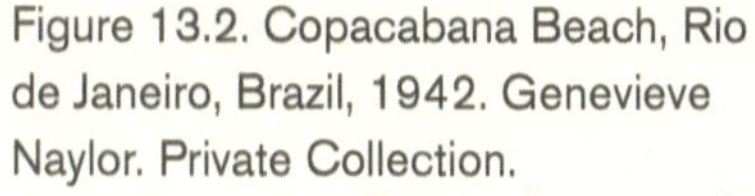

Figure 13.2. Copacabana Beach, Rio de Janeiro, Brazil, 1942. Genevieve Naylor. Private Collection.

Figure 13.3. Copacabana Beach, Rio de Janeiro, Brazil, 1942. Genevieve Naylor. Private Collection.

public memory of Rio de Janeiro as a part of commemorating its 450th anniversary. To compose the visual history of the city of Rio de Janeiro we considered two sides of photographic practice: one that reveals Rio in its relationship with the sea and another that linked characters to locations within the city.

Characteristics of the Study of Photography Here

I cannot be 100 percent certain if there is anything particularly unique about the study of photography in Latin America, but it is worth considering the decentralization of perspective and approaches that have been happening over the last twenty years. I vividly recall when I first met John Mraz, Ariel Arnal, and Eli Bartra during one of the sections of the 1998 LASA conference in Chicago. This was because at that moment we were all discussing images from a Latin American perspective. We all had the opportunity to identify our theoretical references and how they informed our work, and we were developing original methodologies in order to give a proper response to the historical challenges we face as Latin American scholars.

From the point of view of the practice of photography, the challenges that

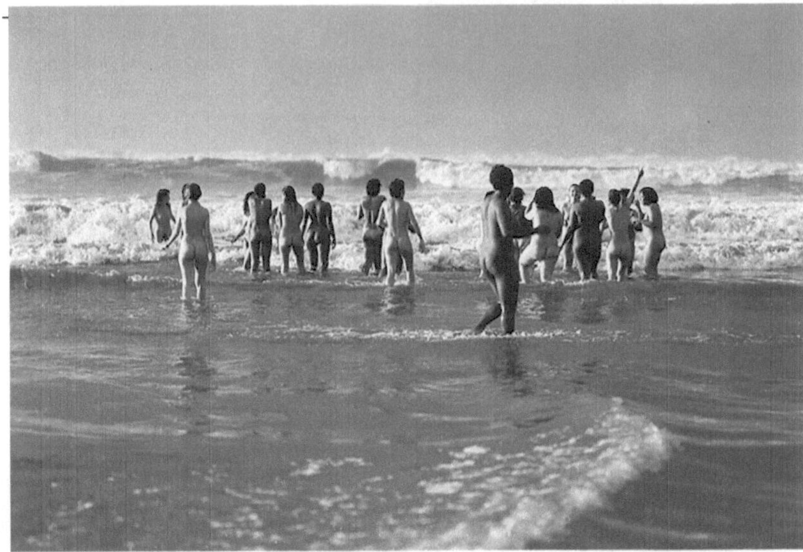

Figure 13.4. Margaridas Parade, Brasilia, Brazil, 2000. Claudia Ferreira. Personal Collection. (Margarida's movement is made up of women that belong to peasant movements, marching to the National Congress in Brasilia.)

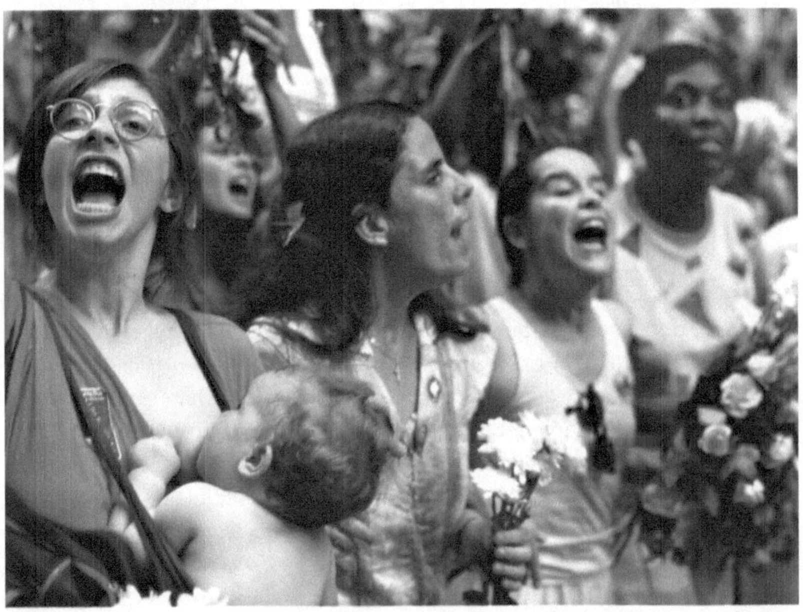

Figure 13.5. 10th Feminist Conference in the city of Bertioga, Brazil, 1989. Claudia Ferreira. Personal Collection.

photographers and those who study this field face are connected to political censorship and how this affects us. In countries such as Brazil and Mexico that have an authoritarian political tradition deeply embedded in its societal fabric, working with photography also involves the cultural and intellectual formation of those who interpret the world through the photographic image. In this sense, the Latin American condition poses challenges that, as they are overcome, often imply an incomparable originality.

In our capitalist world, everything has to do with the market, movement of goods, and value added. This is true regarding the information that images contain or the agency to which the photographer may or may not be connected. In developed countries, the advantage is that the motor runs at full throttle, assimilating young talent into the dynamics of the art, information, and communication markets. In Latin America, except for a few names that leave the periphery (as is the case of Sebastião Salgado), competition in that market is virtually impossible.

On the other hand, this situation creates a space where completely original experiences can be found in the photographic collectives in the urban peripheries. For example, visual inclusion movements and visual occupation, such as Mão na Lata, has young people working with pinhole cameras. Another example is Imagens do Povo project that was created in the Mare Favela. Both projects are located in the city of Rio de Janeiro and are helping to create a fascinating visual archive. These are the centripetal forces within the Latin American periphery that make a difference in other ways.

Collaboration Is Key

My thinking and approach are linked to a perspective that associates cultural history with social history and the history of the image. Today, the transdisciplinary approach has brought important challenges that have been faced with collaborative work in the field of photography. I have partnered with many different academics to advance research projects. For example, I have worked with Claudia Ferreira, Claudia Andujar, Milton Guran, Erno Schneider, Flavio Damm, Rogério Reis, and Pedro Vasquez. We organize our research on image and history and make it available via an online dictionary database that is updated regularly: the *Dicionário Histórico-Biográfico da Fotografia*.

In recent years, the discourse on the demise of narrative and the death of photography emerged. Neither of these predictions really became true. As I understand it, following Walter Benjamin's ideas, photography and history will intertwine as principles of understanding the social world. The vitality of both remains the basic condition of our existence as a community that creates meaning.

Sources Do Not Speak without Help

Experience has brought with it many insights that I share with my students. I tell my students who work with me in any research capacity that sources do not speak without help. You must ask them questions. Research with photographs obeys the same principle. We must regard photography as an object of material culture and a social representation. We must view photography as a historical experience that translates the past into a tangible element through chemical and social processes. Hence, their existence relies on social relations. As I mentioned with the W. J. T. Mitchell quote earlier, the visual dimension of the social and the social dimension of the visual must be considered.

When I was a historian in training, I learned that when I focused on photography as a source and as an object of study, I needed to learn aspects of the chemical process of making photographs to understand its mechanics. However, this was not the only new field I was required to navigate. I had to read current debates on photography, interview photographers, and learn about their creative motivations through their creative trajectories. You were required to create a base where one did not exist previously. Even so, growth in the field has borne excellent fruits here. There is a lot of original work occurring in Latin America in the study of photography. Two excellent examples come to mind that show the strength and growth of the field in recent years: *Caminar entre Fotones: Formas y estilos de la mirada documental* and *Investigación con imágenes: Usos y retos metodológicos* (Monroy and del Castillo; Roca). If you are interested in studying Brazilian historiography and photography there are now important subject specific texts such as Menezes's "Fontes visuais, cultura visual, história visual: Balanço provisório, propostas cautelares" and *Rumo a uma "história visual"*; Knauss's "*O desafio de fazer História com imagens: Arte e cultura visual*"; and Fabris's book *Fotografia: Usos e funções no século XIX*, as well as her article "Discutindo a imagem fotográfica."

I mentioned that I started to work with photography during a time full of challenges, but there have also been many opportunities and support. After several years of attempting, we were able to gather a group of historians in 2004 and created the Working Group of Visual Culture in the Brazilian Historical Association (ANPUH). We have been working together to form a critical perspective for the study of image in history. In 2016, in Rio de Janeiro, Maria Teresa Bandeira de Mello and I created an annual forum to discuss photography that we coordinate. We are trying to meet every year and raise questions regarding the study of photography, theory, and other topics. We are not limited to historians. We also invite creators, curators, collectors, and other scholars. Hence, we are trying to enlarge the debate and reach audiences outside academia. Brazil contains a wealth of resources for the study of photographs: The Sociedade Fluminense de Fotografia (Niterói); the Maria Thereza Christina Collection (National Library); the police archives in Rio's Public State Archive;

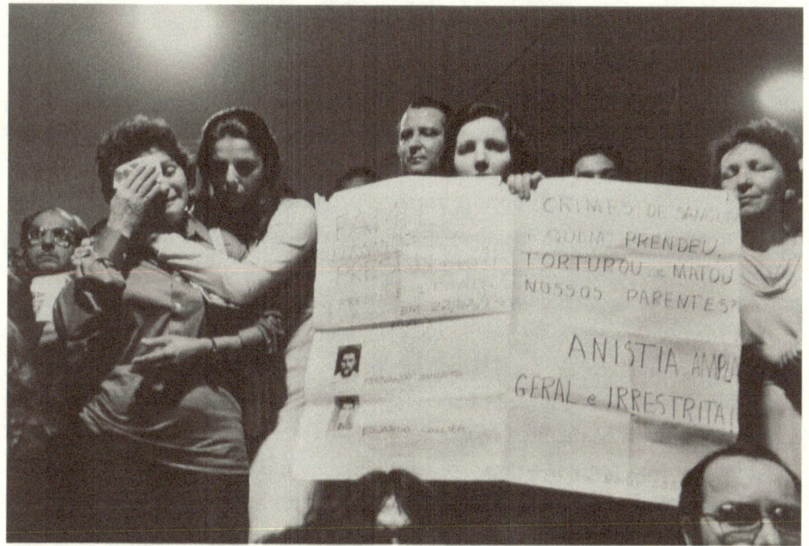

Figure 13.6. Missing activist's relatives demanding justice at the Brazilian National Congress, Brasilia, Brazil, 1979. Milton Guran. Personal Collection.

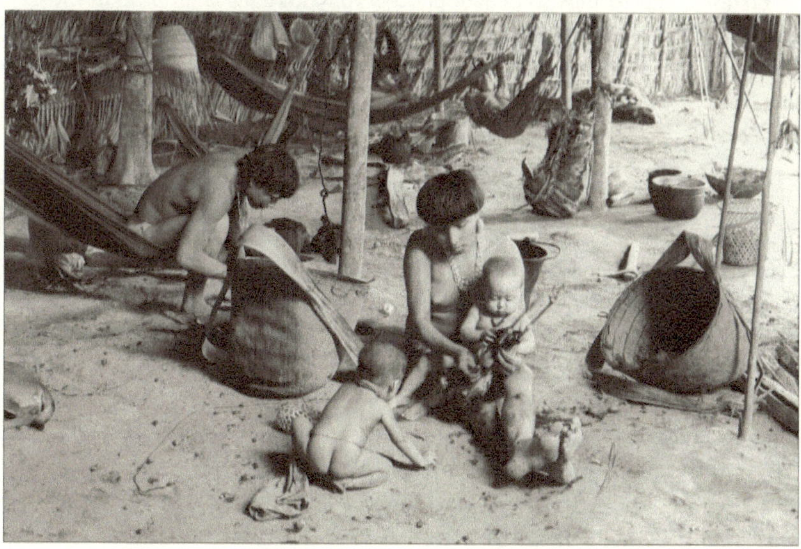

Figure 13.7. Yanomami domestic photograph, Rio de Janiero, Brazil, c. 1980. Milton Guran. Personal Collection. (Part of a Milton Guran documentary made for the "Indian Museum" in Rio de Janeiro during the 1980s.)

the Augusto Malta Collection (Museum of Image and Sound and General Archive of the City of Rio de Janeiro); and the Marc Ferrez Collection (Moreira Salles Institute). Each has a rich abundance of material to be studied. Brazil offers researchers financial support for their projects as well. Several of my projects connected to photojournalism have received funding from the Brazilian National Council of Research (CNPq) including *Fotografia Pública: Usos, funções e circuitos sociais no Brasil, séculos XIX e XX*; *O Olhar Engajado: Prática fotográfica e os sentidos da história*; and *Memórias do contemporâneo: Narrativas e imagens do fotojornalismo no Brasil do Século XX*, to mention just three. This funding is one of the ways that the local environment helps to enable the growth of the field in Brazil.

I believe that there is a network being created in Latin America that brings together researchers from different parts. This can be seen in our collective book *Fotografía e historia en América Latina* that the Centro de Fotografía de Montevideo published. It is also evident in the permanent discussion forums and the knowledge produced with photography that is not limited to academic production, such as FotoRio, a large photography event organized since 2002 by the photographer and anthropologist Milton Guran. This is a very important initiative because over the course of three months photography exhibitions, workshops, and forums to debate photography take place all around the city of Rio de Janeiro, all of which connect the academic and nonacademic spheres. It is important that our work acquires a broad audience and that our research involves critical analysis that probes deeply into the world around us.

Selected Publications

Mauad, Ana Maria. *Poses e Flagrantes: Ensaios sobre historia e fotografias*. EDUFF, 2008.

Mauad, Ana Maria, and Marcos Felipe de Brum Lopes, guest editors. "Imagen, História e ciencia." *Ciencias Humanas: Dossiê*, 9.2, 2014. pp. 283–86.

Mauad, Ana Maria, and Charles Monteiro, guest editors. *Estudos Ibero Americanos: Dossiê Fotografia. Cultura Visual e História: perspectivas teóricas e metodológicas*, 44.1, 2018.

Mraz, John, and Ana Maria Mauad, editors. *Fotografía e Historia en America Latina*. CdF, 2015.

Mauricio Lissovsky

Universidade Federal do Rio de Janeiro

History and Civil War Photographs

I STUDIED HISTORY at the Universidade Federal Fluminense in Niterói, near Rio de Janeiro. At that time (the 1980s), photography was not a topic of focus. There was no discussion on photography or other still images at that time. There was some debate on movies, but even those conversations were marginal then. They were never seen as a central issue or a relevant historical source. For that reason, in the 1980s Ana Mauad and I were the first generation in Rio de Janeiro to work on history and photography. As a student, I was an intern at a research center for Brazilian contemporary history at the Fundação Getúlio Vargas Centro: the CPDOC (Pesquisa e Documentação de Historia Contemporánea do Brasil, da Fundação Getúlio Vargas). When I finished my degree in history, the research group was starting its first project on photography and history. It was an exhibition on pictures related to São Paulo's 1932 civil war, approaching its fiftieth anniversary. We researched that event, which became my first large research project. I was the youngest member of the team then, and my main task was to write captions and collect quotes in newspapers and firsthand accounts of the civil war that could engage directly with the photographs. It was my first experience creating an exhibition in which texts and images directly interfaced with each other.

After that, I also researched modern architecture in Rio de Janeiro, but I was always interested in images; however, photography was not the only subject of focus. In the 1980s I wrote a book on the introduction of modern architecture in Rio de Janeiro called *Colunas da Educação: A construção do Ministério da Educação e Saúde* (though it was not published until 1996). Rio had the first public government building designed in Corbusian style in the world. It was the Ministry of Education building. This is important because

---

Mauricio Lissovsky passed away in August 2022.

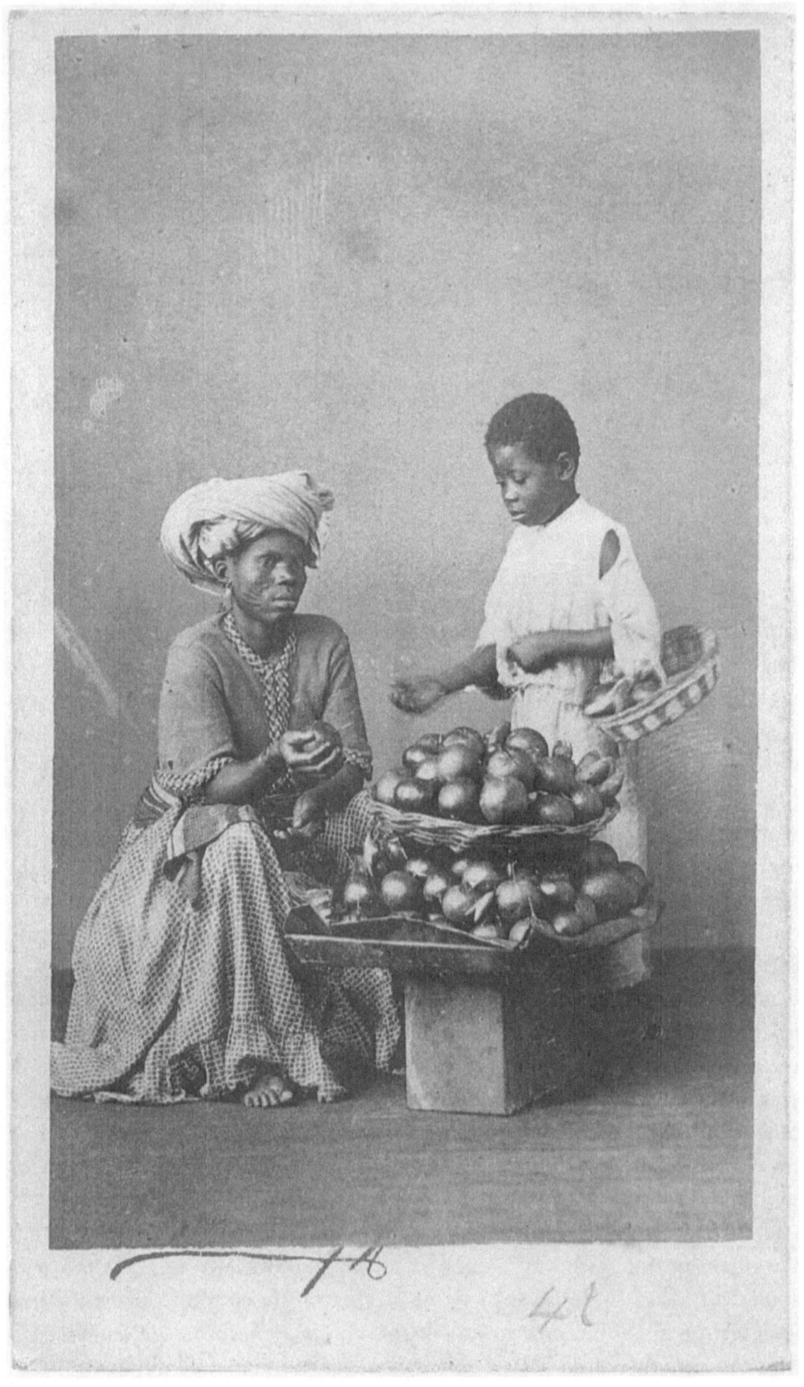

Figure 14.1 Street scene with slave woman and slave boy, Rio de Janeiro, Brazil, c. 1865. Cristiano Jr. Private Collection.

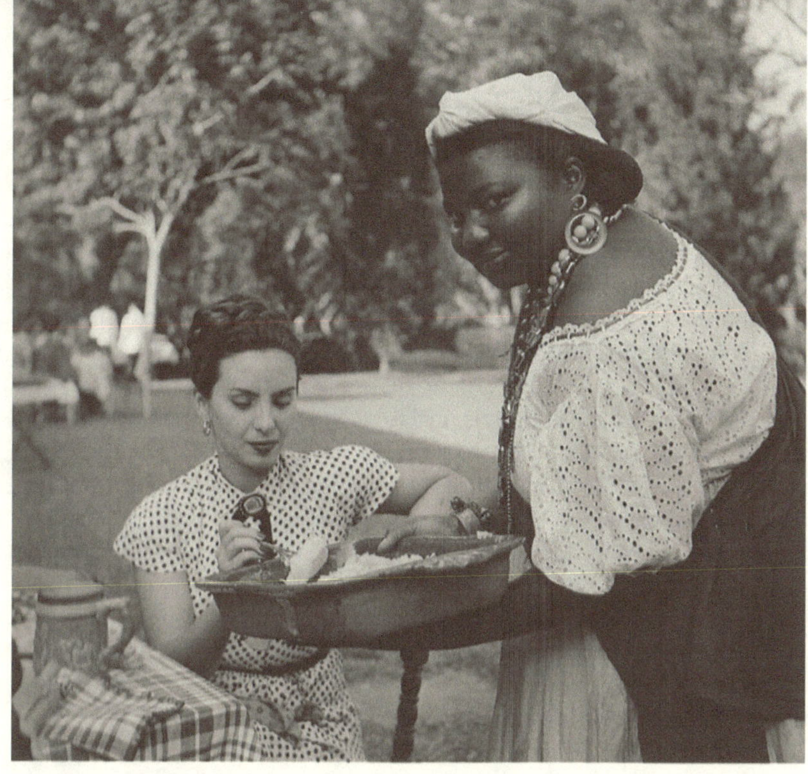

Figure 14.2. Party in a high society residence, Rio de Janeiro, 1946. Kurt Klagsbrunn. Private Collection.

in 1986, while I was developing that book using the Ministry of Education archives, a friend of mine found a set of fifty carte-de-visite photographs made by Christiano Junior in the IPHAN (the Institute of National Artistic and Historical Heritage) files. Christiano Junior was a Portuguese photographer who took pictures of slaves in 1865. This was an amazing discovery. They had been completely unknown, and they depict an aspect of Brazilian slavery in the nineteenth century, which at that time had received very little attention: urban slaves in Rio de Janeiro. Called *escravos de ganho*, these were the people whose job it was to go to the market or to some specific places in town every day and earn money for their masters working as vendors, artisans, movers, or transporters. We started to look for similar pictures in different institutions in Brazil, such as the National Library and the Imperial Museum, and we gathered more than seventy slave portraits made by this previously unknown photographer. We published *Escravos Brasieliros na Fotografia de Christiano Junior* in 1988 to document our study of the photographs. I believe that this is the largest set of pictures of nineteenth-century slaves in carte-de-visite format made by a single photographer in the entire world. This project made me a photo historian, but

I still think of myself more as a visual historian who focuses on photography. I have done some research on aesthetics and the theory of photography too. I am not a professor in a history department. I work in the communications department at the Federal University of Rio de Janeiro (because I am also a screenwriter, and I teach screenwriting to undergraduates). I had to move to the communications department because in the past there was almost no place for photography among historians.

Just to give you an idea of how the study of photography has evolved since the 1980s, back then I was invited to a conference in Minas Gerais. It was the Congress of the National Association of Historians (ANPUH). My roundtable was called "Non-Conventional Sources for History." There I presented a paper about photography. Another colleague presented a paper on film, and yet another on oral history interviews. At that time none of us were teaching or working in a history department at a university. Since we were from new fields and worked with new sources, back then everyone thought that we were kind of exotic and unconventional, but I remember the room was full of young students (so you could see that there was a growing interest). Ana Mauad was the very first academic to find a tenured post linked to photography in a history department in Rio de Janeiro. However, the true pioneer in the field of the study of photography in Brazil was Boris Kossoy, who published the first scholarly book on a history of photography in Brazil in the 1980s: *Fotografía e História.* He was also in the Communications Department within the University of São Paulo. With time, this has changed. Now you can find classes on photography and history all over Brazil. The last three decades have revolutionized the field.

Speaking about Photography Intellectually

When I began to study in the 1980s, the first references were Roland Barthes's *Camera Lucida* and Susan Sontag and her writings on photography. Sontag's *On Photography* was translated in the 1980s. The 1980s were very important. Photography was a growing field. Photographers were fighting for their rights in the newspapers. The first photography galleries were being inaugurated in Rio de Janeiro and São Paulo. There was a lot of photography-related activity occurring then. We used to have national meetings that brought together photographers, photojournalists, publishers, researchers, collectors, conservators, and others. One of the movement's participants, a collector named Joaquim Paiva, translated Susan Sontag's *On Photography* into *Ensaios sobre fotografia* in Portuguese. The book had a great impact, and it still does. People began to discover that it was possible to speak about photography intellectually. The history of thought on photographers that even practitioners of photography could read and understand was very important. Walter Benjamin was also a key

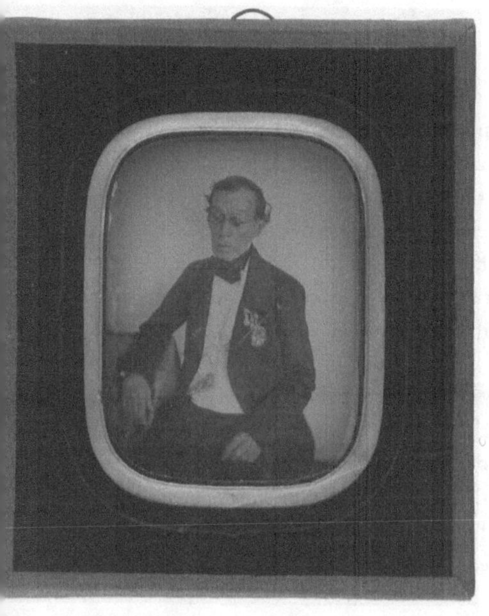

Figure 14.3. Manoel Joaquim de Meneses, Rio de Janeiro, Brazil, May 1855. Diogo Luís Cipriano, National Archive, Rio de Janeiro, Brazil. (Daguerreotype)

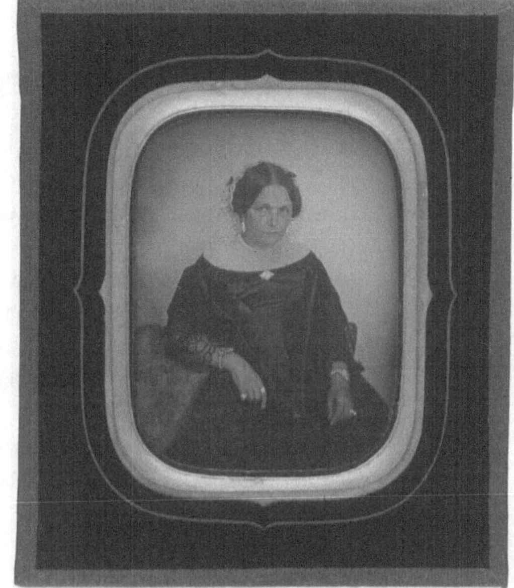

Figure 14.4. Euêmia Marciana Mendonça de Meneses, Rio de Janeiro, Brazil, May 1855. Diogo Luís Cipriano. National Archive, Rio de Janeiro, Brazil. (Daguerreotype)

academic reference for me. My master's degree was on the concept of history in Walter Benjamin and his relation to the idea of photography. Later, I discovered Eduardo Cadava's work at Princeton, whose approach to reading was quite like mine. Thanks to his book, *Words of Light: Theses on the Photography of History*, I discovered I was not alone in my academic pursuits.

My PhD dissertation on the aesthetics of modern photography was also strongly influenced by Benjamin. As part of my critical approach, I invented an abstract concept to describe the aesthetic experience of the modern photographer that I described as a "waiting machine." What I am referring to with this is the subjective apparatus of modern photography. The camera takes pictures. The waiting machine is the person who takes the picture, the person who waits for the image to appear and then captures it with technology. This waiting is the nonmechanical work the photographer must undertake as part of the technological process of photography; it is the human element that combines with the technology to create the image. I wrote an article, "The Photographic Device as a Waiting Machine," that explained this idea more fully after my PhD. After Walter Benjamin, reading Rosalind Krauss was very important to my theoretical background in photography. More recently, the anthropologist Christopher Pinney has been important to my theoretical background. With regards to methodology, I now think that I have an eclectic approach. If I had to map it out, it might take the form of this equation: Georges Didi-Huberman + Walter Benjamin + Aby Warburg + Gisèle Freund. My work is always looking at pictures as if they were symptom-like statements. I think of myself as a historian in the Walter Benjamin-centered field. Perhaps the best way to describe my work is to think of me as someone who has an eclectic approach toward photography with a very philosophical bent. In the communication faculty where I work, I am a part of a group that has a strong philosophical background. We all studied philosophy informally with a certain scholar there: Claudio Ulpiano. You could describe him as a Deleuzian ambassador in Rio de Janeiro. My PhD advisor, Márcio Tavares D'Amaral, was a Heidegger and Foucault specialist. So, there was a lot of that philosophical thought circulating while I studied my PhD that has influenced how I approach my research and my interests.

The Canon Is Not Yet Established

When it comes to speaking about that which is unique about the study of photography in Latin America, if you contrast Latin America and the United States or Europe, we do not have an established historical canon. In the United States, and for the world of photography in general in the West, the MoMA has established much of the canon. *A History of Photography* published by Cambridge University Press, *The History of Photography from the Earliest Use of the Camera Obscura in the Eleventh Century up to 1914* and *The Oxford Companion to the Photograph* published by Oxford University Press, and Beaumont Newhall's *The History of Photography* for the MoMA are all examples of this trend. They established the visual canon on photography in English-speaking North America and western Europe. We do not have canons in that same sense in Latin America. Therefore, for me, the difference is that we must invent the canon and destroy it at the same time. By this I mean that we must establish the criteria that helps identify what is relevant and deserves attention (and sometimes, for some in other circumstances, this means to establish what is good and what is not), and then soon criticize, or reevaluate, those choices (which is what I mean by destroying it). We do not have a canon to struggle against here when you consider the study of photography in Latin America. For example, you will not find a book titled *The History of Photography in Brazil.* It simply does not exist. It has not been written because there has not been an institution that could say: "This is the canon. These are the photographers who are canonical." Now the Instituto Moreira Salles in Brazil is amassing a very large archive, buying pictures from photographers, and maybe one day they will

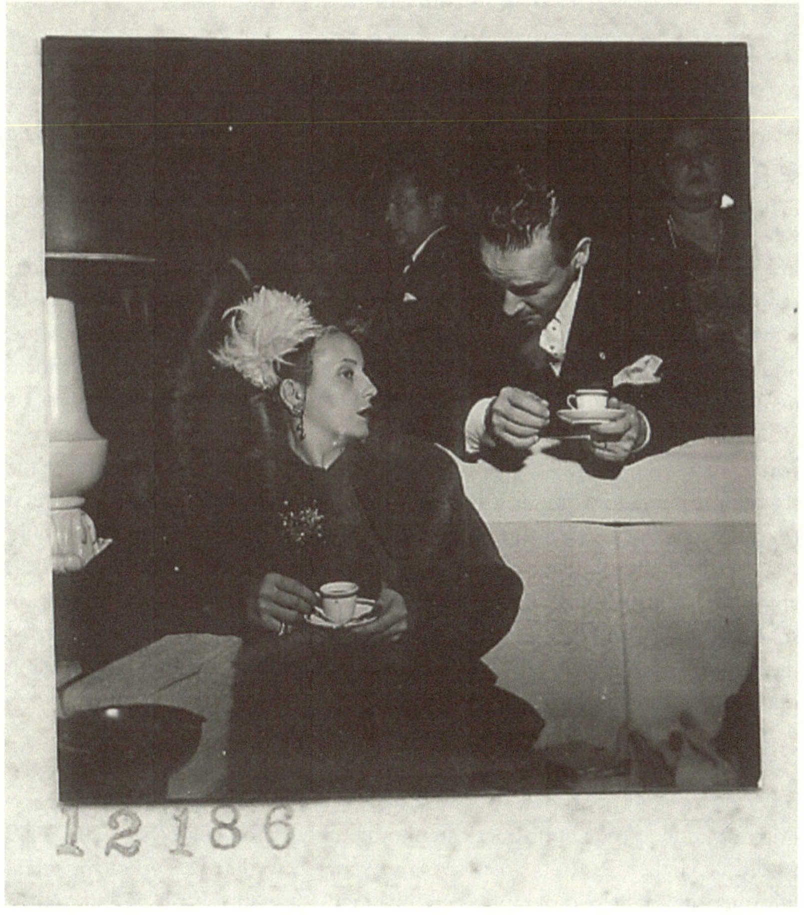

Figure 14.5. Evita Perón talking with the Argentinian Minister Juan Braguglia, Petrópolis, Brazil, 1947. Kurt Klagsbrunn. Personal Collection. (Contact print)

establish some type of canon of photography in Brazil. Since they own the pictures, they might establish the canon in favor of those images, and their photos might become the canon. I expect that they will draw on historians to build their case for this in the future. However, the point is that if you think about classical, postmodern, or revisionist essays in English like the MIT-published article by Christopher Philips in the journal *October*, "The Judgement Seat of Photography" (1982), which criticizes the MoMA version of the history of photography, there is no institution that we can fight against in Latin America. We must build this canon and be critical of it at the same time if we want the study of photography to grow in Latin America.

Specialist Guidance

When considering how to study photography in Latin America, I have some specialist guidance. First, never be satisfied with just one image. Learn to work with series of images and collections of photographs. You need to work with vast groups of photographs. Do not draw hasty conclusions from only one image. The size of the body of work you consider as you write about photography might make the difference between research that has a lasting and serious influence and a text that is here today and forgotten tomorrow. You can always find an image that you will use as the example or as the synthesis of your idea, or as the problematic image of the series. These are the dialectic images as Walter Benjamin would call them (Auerbach). These key images only emerge if you have a large set to work with. If you don't have one, you must create the set you are going to work with as part of your research. You must look for relationships, for the relatives of this picture (diachronic or synchronic: you should consider both areas). Almost everything that I write has this kind of analytical approach. When I work, I find two hundred photos related to the issue I am studying and then I begin to select. Finally, I settle on the three, four, or five of them that would allow me to say something important or reach a conclusion that has academic rigor.

Challenges Ahead

I do not know if the Latin American photography canon will be created. There would be challenges to its creation. For example, we have a gap of historical information about photography here in Brazil between the 1920s and 1950s. It is the gap of the avant-garde, a period that is quite an important milestone for European and American photo histories. So, our history does not fit the usual chronology. Many photographers and much photographic practice remains unseen or not yet understood. In a certain way, this also happens in

India, Africa, and many Latin American countries (Pinney *Photography's Other Histories*). I think the next generation (my students and their students) will understand and fill these gaps. They will have something we did not: advisors who study photography and understand it. My students who work on photography now have me as an expert advisor. This represents a big difference. Hence, they will probably be better professionals. This is good, but there are also some challenges to face. For example, in the 1980s there was a link between photographers, historians, and researchers. These groups were friends in my generation of researchers because we were building the *field* of photography in Brazil, in Pierre Bourdieu's sense of it (*Photography*). Now, I think that photographers, researchers, and historians no longer occupy the same territory. They are now no longer together in conferences and meetings that unite the different fields. Everyone works with colleagues in their own respective field. We almost never interact in the same space anymore like we did previously. This is regrettable, but it tends to happen all over academia, especially as the academic fields grow and then disconnect with the practice and the professionals who work in the practical areas of the field. Perhaps this is the price we must pay for the growth of photography as an academic subject in Latin America. Those links between scholars and photographers were important in the 1980s. Brazil was not the only place to have them. You can see them in Mexico as well, and in Uruguay. The process of growth has been the greatest in Mexico because they began before we did in Brazil.

Institutions, Archives, Photographers

There are many archives that merit further exploration in Brazil. Our main archive is the National Library's collections. It was originally the Emperor's Collection, and here in Brazil it was named the Teresa Cristina Collection. Emperor Dom Pedro II was a great lover of photography, and his collection is considerable. Most of it is in the National Library. Another part of it is in Petropolis (a city that is close to Rio de Janeiro). The National Library in Rio de Janeiro has the largest collection of nineteenth century photographs in Latin America (with more than twenty thousand pictures). The other important institution is the Instituto Moreira Salles (IMS), which is in Rio de Janeiro. To build their archives, they buy private collections of very distinguished photographers, anything from the 1900s, as well as photographs they deem to be of worth from any historical period. This institute now also works with contemporary photographers. The IMS also gives scholarships to contemporary photographers so they can create new work. Of course, some public archives like the National Archive, and public archives in the great metropolis in Brazil, also have vast and important collections. Some of them, like Instituto Moreira Salles, which has the largest public archive on photography in Brazil, contain more than two million pictures. However, the bulk of this collection at IMS is mainly composed of twentieth-century photos from newspapers archives.

Establishing Common Ground

The field of visual studies and photography is still not fully established in Brazil. What we do have is still very compartmentalized: very few historians will write an essay where you can see both a painting and a photograph as part of their analysis. Hence, the field of image studies in general has much left to be built. We need to construct more competence in visual culture in general. Another analysis you rarely see is one that combines popular (vernacular) photography and fine art photography. These two areas are treated as if they happened in different worlds, yet they are from the same visual culture and society. Even so, images are treated as though art photos are for art critics, curators, and art historians; vernacular photography for anthropologists; and photojournalism and advertisements for media researchers. We have yet to establish the common ground of visual culture as a field of research that would facilitate the studies that combine those images. My main concern and objective for my future projects is to contrast and combine materials, to think about the visual field and visual culture while considering photography and other methods of visual expression in addition to the materials that correspond to them. These considerations will broaden the way in which we study photography.

Selected Publications

Lissovsky, Mauricio. "The Photographic Device as a Waiting Machine." *Image & Narrative* 23, 2008. www.imageandnarrative.be/inarchive/Timeandphotography/lissovsky.html.

Lissovsky, Mauricio, and Paulo Cesar de Azevedo. *Escravos brasileiros do século XIX na fotografia de Cristiano Jr.* Ex Libris, 1988.

Lissovsky, Mauricio, and Paulo Sérgio Sá. *Colunas da Educação: A construção do Ministério da Educação e Saúde.* MINC/IPHAN/CPDOC, 1996.

Lissovsky, Mauricio, and Marcia Mello. *Refúgio do Olhar: A fotografia de Kurt Klagsbrunn no Brasil dos anos 1940.* Casa da Palavra, 2013.

Maria do Carmo Teixeira Rainho

Arquivo Nacional, Brazil

Clothing, Visual Culture, and Photography

I STUDIED HISTORY at the Universidade do Estado do Rio de Janeiro (UERJ) where I obtained a bachelor's degree in 1984, and I have a master's degree in the social history of culture from the Pontifícia Universidade Católica (PUC) of Rio de Janeiro, which I was awarded in 1992. My PhD is in social history from the Universidade Federal Fluminense (2012). During my doctorate, I focused on the dimensions of the clothing revolution of the 1960s in Rio de Janeiro, from the perspective of visual culture. The Brazilian newspaper *Correio da Manhã* provided the samples that enabled my photographic analysis. My doctoral dissertation addressed the possibility of describing the 1960s in Brazil as a period (that accompanied the vigorous upsurge of women in universities and in the labor market) of accelerated social change as evidenced through one's dress as an agent of that change. I researched on what clothing could teach us about sexuality, gender, and youth. I did not work from a historical perspective or try to use the photographs to confirm what common sense says about fashion in the sixties. I put the images into perspective and examined fashion photographs, photojournalism, and advertisements. I compiled and compared a body of *fashion fiction* created by photographers/editors and the clothing used in everyday life. This allowed me to reveal society's tensions and the contradictions within these two mediums. My research shows that the greater the political repression, the more clothing styles manifest disruption and change.

I have been employed at the Brazilian National Archives (BNA) since the mid-1980s. In the early 1990s I started working with photographs there. This was at the time when the Brazilian National Archives were starting to create exhibitions to showcase their collections. Their first exhibition on photography was *Cenas cariocas*, curated by the historian Luciano Figueiredo. The first photography exhibition I curated was *Pão, Terra e Liberdade: O levante comunista de 1935* that took place in 1995 in the Museu da República in Rio de Janeiro.

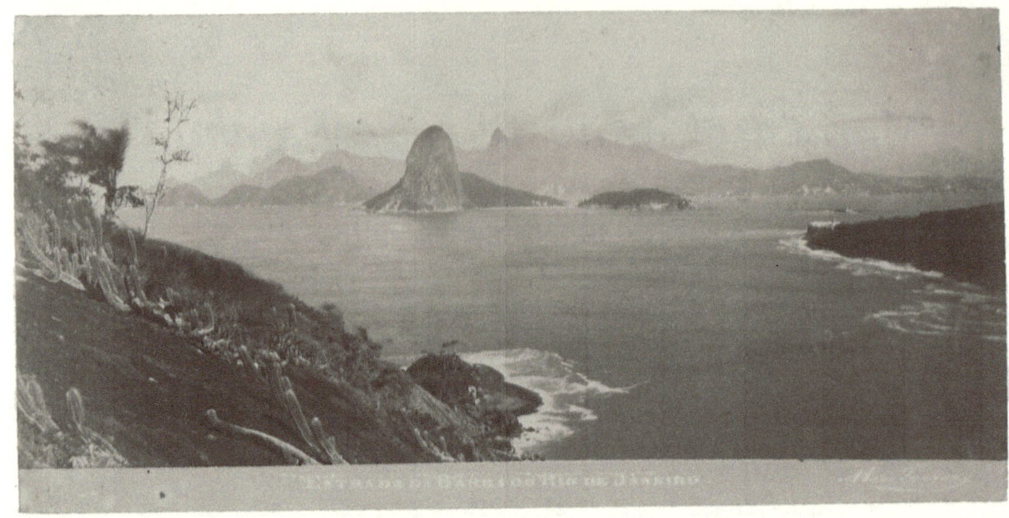

Figure 15.1. Entrada da barra do Rio de Janeiro. Álbum Festas Republicanas: ordem e progresso. (Rio de Janeiro Landscape. From the Republican Celebrations: Order and Progress series), Rio de Janeiro, Brazil, 1894. Marc Ferrez. Floriano Peixoto Collection, Arquivo Nacional.

It was about the armed movements of November 1935, which took place in the cities of Natal, Recife, and Rio de Janeiro, and which many Brazilians still refer to as a "communist uprising": a subject that still raises a lot of discussion and enjoys several critical interpretations. Although it represents Brazil's first and only concrete attempt to reproduce the Russian Revolution of 1917, the uprising is not only a landmark event for the history of the Brazilian Communist Party but also significant for expressing part of the dissatisfactions that affected several sectors of Brazilian society since the beginning of the twentieth century. For the exhibition, we studied photos and documents from the Brazilian newspaper *Correio da Manhã* and the criminal processes related to some of the men and women who took part in the movement. It was the first time the BNA used photographs belonging to historical processes in an exhibition, its pamphlets, textual documents, and other books.

Those were analogical times when studios produced the photographic enlargements for the exhibitions. The size of photo paper dictated the photographic enlargement possibilities. The formatting of images to correct imperfections that we do now was very difficult then. It is interesting to think about those times as I reflect on the evolution of my work in exhibitions using photography.

The National Archives had few research tools at that time. The internet did not exist, and it was not easy to find information about the production of the photographs (i.e., date, photographers' names, and so forth). In Brazil, the

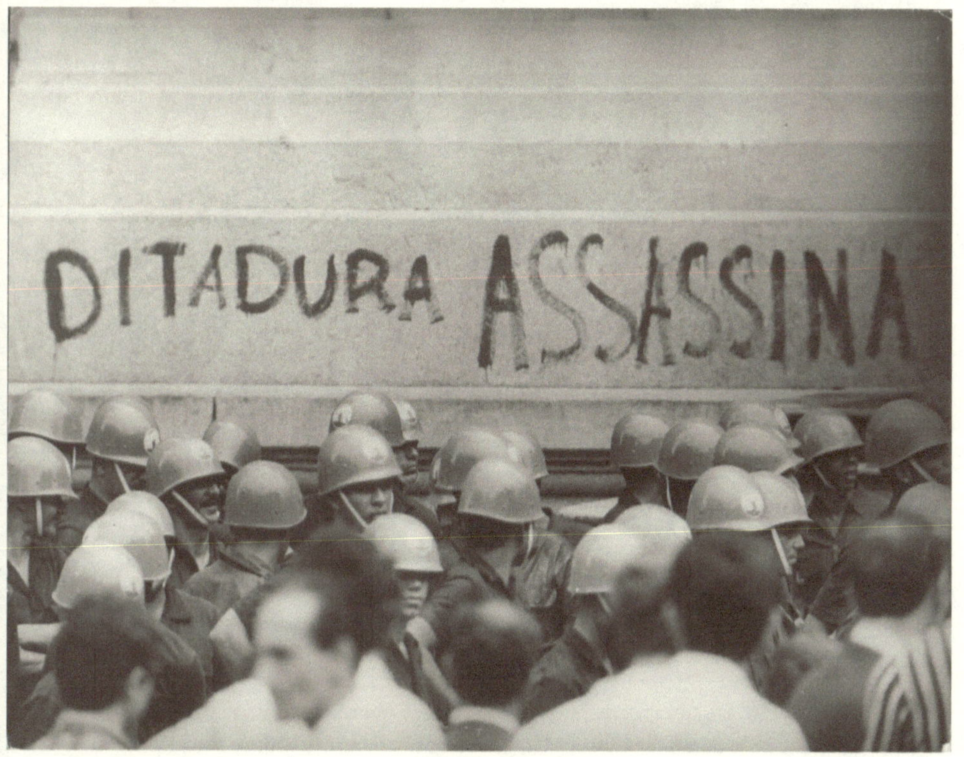

Figure 15.2. Manifestação em muro do centro do Rio de Janeiro contra a ditadura militar (Graffiti on a wall in downtown Rio de Janeiro protesting the military dictatorship), April 2, 1968. Correio da Manhã Collection, Arquivo Nacional.

bibliography about photography in general and about the history of photography was still in its infant stages. We were pioneers.

In the two and a half decades I have been working with the diffusion of the National Archives' photography collections, I have explored various topics. For example, in my time there I have worked on the struggles of Brazilian women, *Imagens da mulher brasileira* (1995), at the Espaço BNDES; Brazil during WWII, *Tempos de Guerra* (1995), at Centro Cultural da Light; and Brazil in the World Cups of 1950 to 1970, *Drama e euforia: O Brasil nas Copas de 50 a 70* (2006).

Much of my research over the past twenty years, like the project I just mentioned (*Drama e euforia*) has often been done in tandem with Cláudia Heynemann, another historian and National Archives researcher. Some of our projects related to the history of Rio de Janeiro, like the exhibition *Rio 1908: A cidade de portos abertos* (2007), have taken place at the National Archives. Others, such as *Estampas do Rio* (2001), have taken place in Espaço BNDES.

At the National Archives, our first aim is to disseminate our archive's

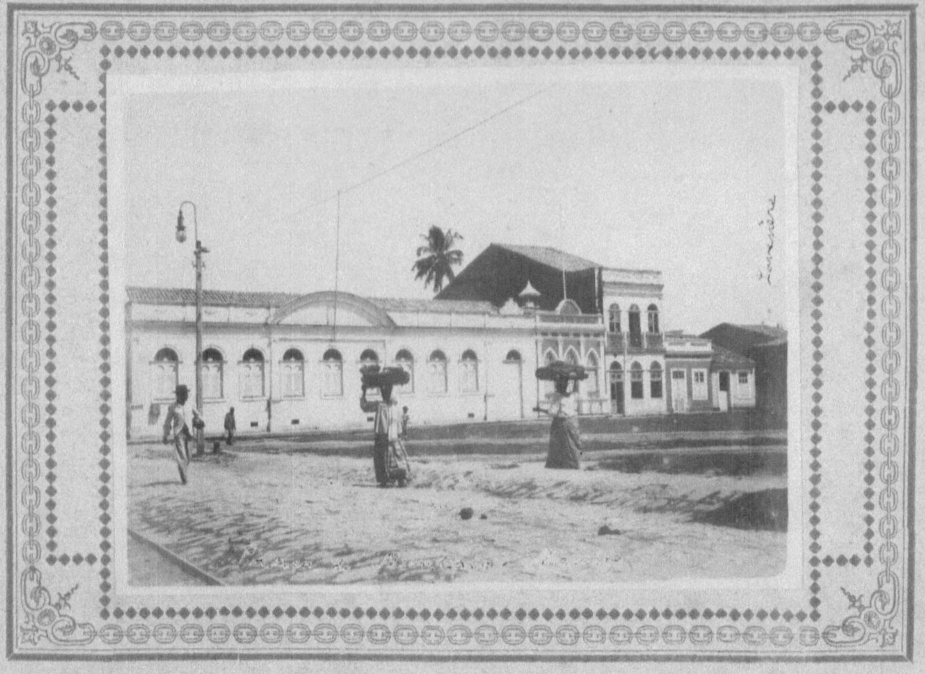

Figure 15.3. Quituteiras na praça do Montepio em Maceió Alagoas (Vegtable vendors on Montepio plaza in Maceió Alagoas), Brazil, 1906. Afonso Pena Collection, Arquivo Nacional.

holdings and collections. The topics we research are assigned to us, and we must disseminate all kinds of written and visual documents in our work. We are always receiving more material, more documents (including photos), so our work is always improving. We create new research tools, such as websites, and this increases access to the holdings. The fact that we receive new documents also forces us to establish new dialogues with the rest of the holdings and motivates us to study new subjects or to analyze past subjects from different perspectives. We must stay current with modern trends of study—Brazilian history, visual culture, history of photography—and take part in academic events where we speak and listen to our colleagues at universities.

Our access to these images and the methods we use to employ them are improving, and the way we look to the images and the production and research on photographs has been greatly enhanced over the past ten years. So has the cultural history of photography. My colleagues and I have really benefitted from such changes. Now we have more tools to work on our material and put it into an analytical perspective. We have much more information about the history of photography in Brazil and its pioneering photographers. We also have access to an extensive bibliography on visual culture, the study of images from the perspective of philosophy, sociology, art history and critical studies of the arts, the use of photographs as sources for the historians, and other academic material. New photographic documents are being incorporated into the National Archives and have begun to generate new books and exhibitions constantly. One example of this is *O Rio em movimento: Cidade natural, cidade construção*, curated by our colleague Renata William, with the photographs produced by an important family of photographers, the Ferrez family, that are available within our virtual gallery for *O Rio em movimento*.

Thanks to the exhibitions and the continuous research on the collection of the National Archives, we have been working on other projects in which the photographic images are the protagonists. For example, *Retratos Modernos* (Modern Portraits) is a case study Cláudia Heynemann designed. The project consisted of an exhibition, a book I coauthored, and a website. *Modern Portraits* is comprised of 120 images selected from the National Archives records in the "Fotografias Avulsas Collection" that consist of the main characteristic formats of photographs in the nineteenth century, such as carte de visite and carte cabinet from private files of well-known figures from Brazilian society. These images for the *Modern Portraits* project were selected from commissioned photographs that were produced at the request of the Brazilian government and related to public works and events; vistas from Rio de Janeiro and other cities like Salvador (Bahia), São Paulo, Florianópolis, Maceió; and portraits that were taken in studios. We intended to present the pioneering trajectory of national and international photographers who worked in Brazil between the middle of the nineteenth century and the first decades of the twentieth century. In my opinion, this project was a turning point in Brazil because for the first time, photography itself and its history were the principal focus of the study, which underlines the field's ability to stand alone.

With the project *Modern Portraits*, we worked with photographs produced by almost eighty photographers, including classics such as Marc Ferrez, one of the most important and successful photographers working in Rio de Janeiro in the second half of the nineteenth century whose work was in high demand by the imperial court. Likewise, the work of Juan Gutierrez, a Spanish photographer whose most important contribution was his documentation of the Revolt of the Navy, which took place in Guanabara Bay, Rio de Janeiro, between September 6, 1893, and March 13, 1894, is included in the exhibition book. Gutierrez's work is, from the technical point of view, the best record of an armed conflict in nineteenth-century Brazil, and it allows us to use images from the capital to evidence the transition from the imperial to the republican period.

Methodology Varies

The methodology that we follow on each project in the National Archives varies according to the needs of the product and our aims. Sometimes we work exclusively with photographs, but we use different sets of photographs from a variety

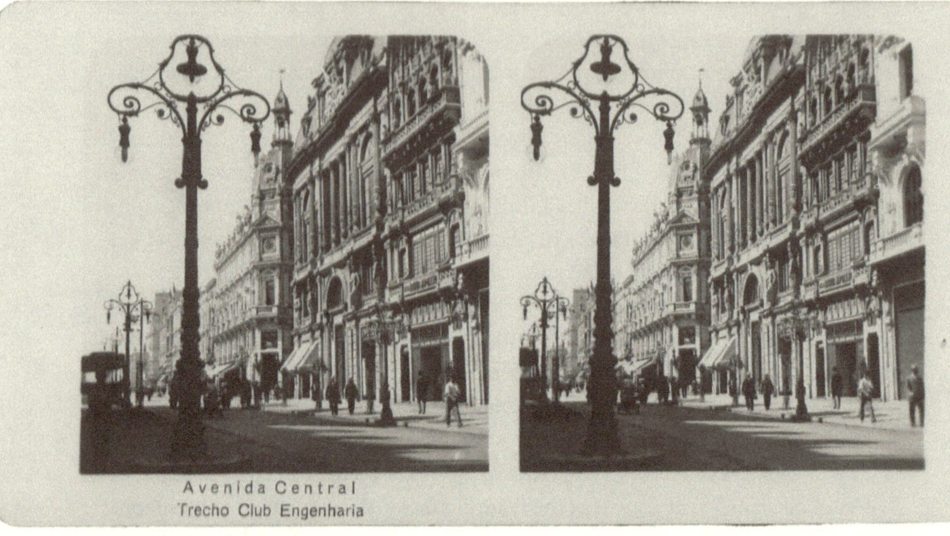

Figure 15.4. Avenida Central, atual Avenida Rio Branco, com destaque para os prédios do Jornal O País, do Clube de Engenharia e da Casa Artur Napoleão (Avenida Central, present-day Avenida Rio Branco, profiling the Jornal O País, the Engineering Club, and the Casa Artur Napoleão buildings), Rio de Janeiro, 1906. Fotografias Avulsas Collection, Arquivo Nacional.

---

of collections, combining, for example, photojournalism and official images (produced by government agencies) as we did with the exhibition *Estampas do Rio*. Sometimes, photographs are associated with different documents, such as texts and books, or other types of images, like drawings, engravings, or maps like we used in the exhibition *Brasil: O império nos trópicos*. In this example, our objective was to explore the notion of a Luso-Brazilian Empire during the second half of the nineteenth century.

Brasiliana Fotográfica, an online database, includes a digital repository that draws on different institutions to create visibility and promote debate and reflection on the photographic collections. In that instance, we worked exclusively with photographs from the nineteenth century to the 1930s. We wanted to disseminate different types of photographs from the National Archives (public and private ones) produced using a wide variety of techniques and referring to an ample range of themes.

At first, I learned how to study photography through my work in the National Archives. Then my PhD thesis, "Moda e revolução nos anos 1960" (Fashion and Revolution in the Sixties), taught me even more. My supervisor introduced me to authors and references, such as W. J. T. Mitchell, Ulpiano Bezerra de Meneses, Mauricio Lissovsky, John Pultz, André Rouillé, and many others. When I started writing my thesis, I knew that I wanted to cover more than the history of fashion

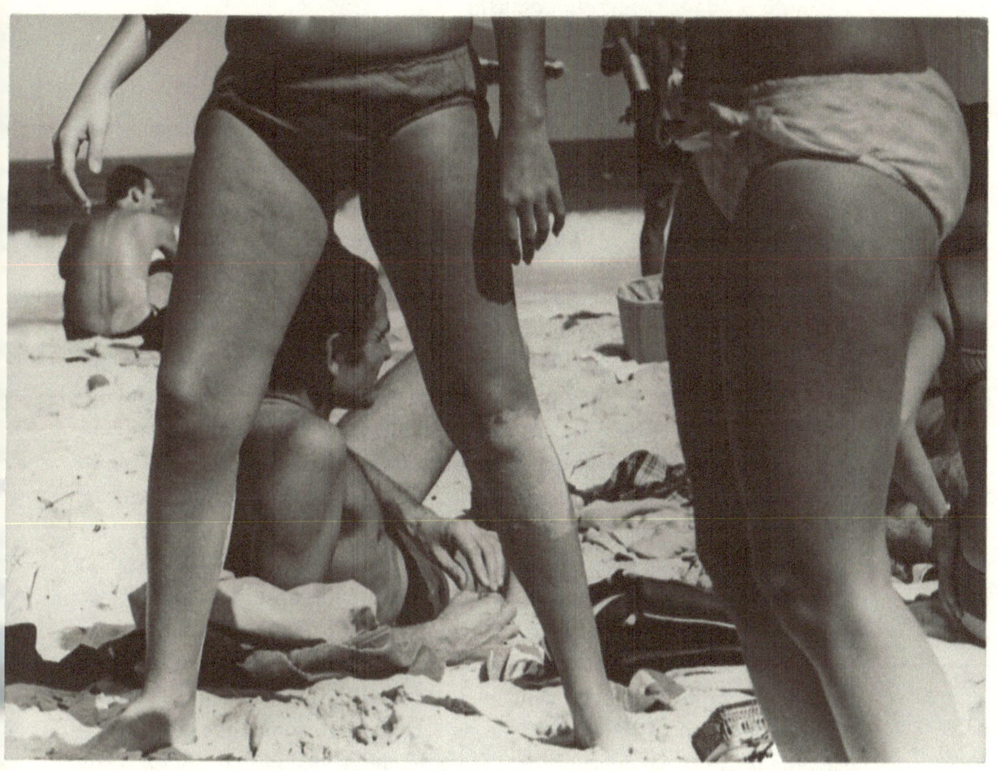

Figure 15.5. O costureiro francês Pierre Cardin e suas manequins na praia de Copacabana. Rio de Janeiro (The French designer Pierre Cardin and his mannequins on Copacabana beach), Rio de Janeiro, Brazil, August 26, 1967. Pimentel. Correio da Manhã Collection, Arquivo Nacional.

photography. Hence, I studied the literature related to visual culture and visuality. This was very important to me because my personal research is related to fashion and to the history of fashion and clothing. So, I always intend to relate fashion photos and their images from the world of fashion to clothing. I have been working with fashion history in general for a long time now; however, I have not always used photographs. At first, I did not even intend to use fashion photographs at all. My idea was to examine the way clothing was really used and study fashion from the perspective of photojournalism. Indeed, the photojournalists also create a certain reality when they choose a special person, theme, or perspective to represent their view. How can we say that there is real fashion in images? As Roland Barthes writes in *The Fashion System*, it is difficult to determine what people really wear. Barthes notes that, within fashion magazines, there is always an image accompanied by text: there is always "image-clothing," accompanied by the "written-garment." Each of these exists in relation to what he calls "real clothing." In the case of real clothing, it must be known not by sight, for its visual image does not reveal all its intricacies. For Barthes, it is possible to examine a fragment of what the real clothing fashion photos show the viewer and not its actual use in the quotidian experience (3–18).

Photographs: More Than Objective Observation

My postgraduate work changed the way I thought about photography. I learned to ask the images questions and not to accept them at face value. I began to think about photos in ways that are not empirical, as mere portraits of one time, person, or event. Photographs create time and events; they do not merely register them. To me, they are not a mimesis of a society or an illustration or appendices of texts. That was one of the great notions that I learned as I studied fashion and photography in general: the need to study photographs without seeing them as self-evident truths.

I think that some researchers still use photography as a type of proof, as something that will bring forth ideas or can be used as an illustration of fact. W. J. T. Mitchell, Didi-Huberman, and (in Brazil) Ulpiano Bezerra de Meneses help us reflect on the visual construction of the social. They help me to think about photography as a statement, as something that informs and conforms to a certain vision of the world, and as a mediation, something that is produced thanks to social relations between different agents. In that respect, Didi-Huberman's *Confronting Images* and *Ce que nous voyons, ce qui nous regarde* have helped me to engage more successfully with images. Ulpiano also examines photography as an artifact and calls our attention to the story of the trajectory of the images. We must remember that the photograph articulates with other images that can be contemporaneous and/or with those that have historically preceded it. Images always tell us something about the future, so as Ulpiano and Mitchell recommend, we must think about photography in terms of social constructs and other related perspectives (Menses "Fontes visuais, cultura visual" and Mitchell *What Do Pictures Want?*). When researching fashion photography, I also found studies on performance and performativity and fashion photography including the ones of Erving Goffman, such as *Gender Advertisements* and "La ritualisation de la feminité," to be relevant. Although Goffman uses advertisements in his research, he helped me to consider fashion photography and gender as well as how fashion and fashion photography construct them.

Paul Jobling's *Fashion Spreads: Word and Image in Fashion Photography since 1980* is key. Jobling examines the fashion spreads from *Vogue*, *The Face*, and *Arena*, and he uses them as starting points to analyze Barthes's axiom that the magazine is "a machine for making fashion" (*The Fashion System* 51). He explores how meaning is constructed in word and image, but he refutes Barthes's claim that the fashion system is a form of signification that lacks substance (*The Fashion System* 64). He also analyzes the paradox between sexual objectification

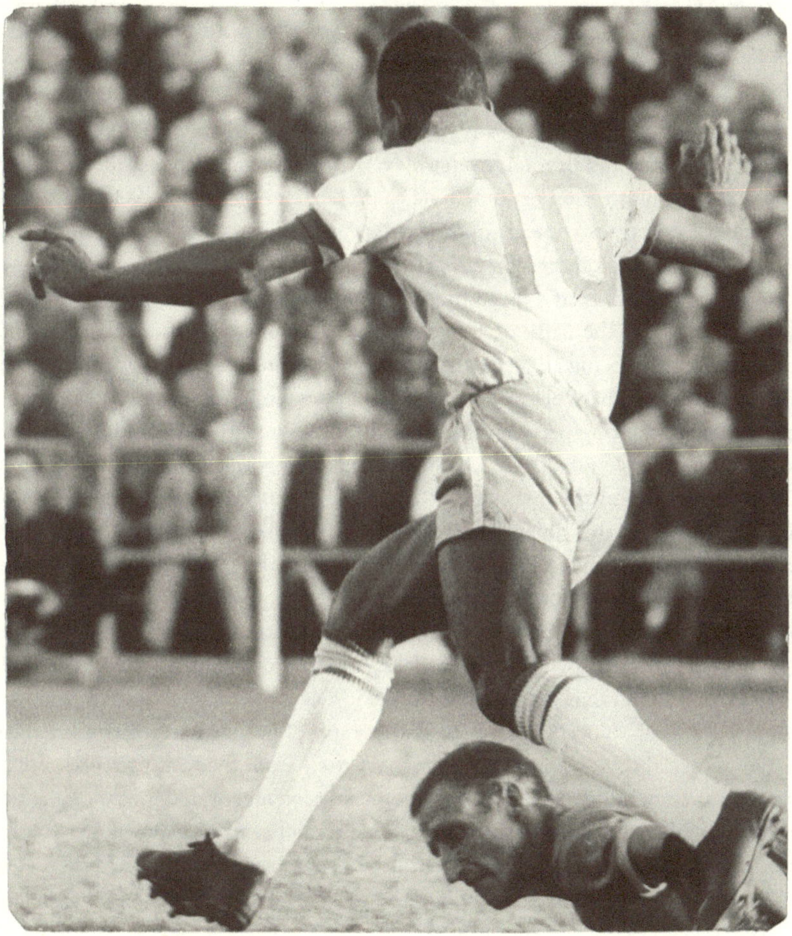

Figure 15.6. Pelé no amistoso Brasil X Suécia (Pelé during a friendly Brazil vs Sweden match), Gotemburg, Sweden, June 30, 1966. Erno Schneider. Correio da Manhã Collection, Arquivo Nacional.

and spectatorship and what the depiction of both male and female bodies in fashion images reveals about power, knowledge, and pleasure (Jobling 108–9).

Research on fashion photography is extremely engaging, but most approaches toward it in the past have been very uneven. Much has been written on the topic of fashion, dress, and photography. There are many books related to the history of fashion photography, but there are not many that really think about how potent fashion photography is when discussing gender, power, and politics or books in which photography itself is the protagonist. This is not only a problem with photography, but it is also a problem with images more generally. Images in many fashion books are only viewed as illustrations. The study of photography along those lines could really grow and improve how we use and think about photography. This is true not only in Brazil, but also in other areas of Latin America and beyond. Even today, the biggest trap is to consider photography a mere illustration or something to present or represent ideas that are discussed. That usage is endemic in the field of fashion and clothing. In some texts on the history of clothing, images generalize the styles or trends as if everyone dressed the same way at a given time. The writers use images to help shape and build the case for the work of a given couturier, designer, or style. Photographs are used without being contextualized, and those same photos reappear in other books and academic works. We forego the opportunity to penetrate and investigate the relationship between fashion and clothes and identity, and power and gender. One of the biggest problems with fashion and other fields that use photos as an illustration of the text is that they help to reinforce these notions. This is because using the same images, like leading brands do, are conducive to a loss of contextualization that can cause confusion. We use the same images that everybody all over the world uses: the same model, the same dress, and so forth. This is a big problem in fashion studies and in fashion photography studies.

In my article "Imagens encenadas? Atos performativos e construção de sujeitos nas fotografias de moda" / "Staged Images? Performative Acts and the Construction of Subjects in Fashion Photographs," I argue that fashion photography, especially after the 1960s, has freed itself from the task of representing fashion as commodity. It has become more experimental or unconventional, and thus strengthens its relationship with art. It also characterizes fashion photography and the fact that, today, in addition to its commercial purposes, it discusses issues that other types of images do not in terms of beauty, gender, and age.

Latin American Images

In Brazil and the rest of Latin America in general, we have been influenced by many photographers from all over the world. Since the nineteenth century we have had scores of foreign photographers from everywhere in Brazil. This is interesting, but it is also a problem because the image of Brazil, and especially that of Rio de Janeiro, has been forged by those photographs, influencing how we see ourselves and how we shape and showcase our visual history.

Consider the work of Marc Ferrez in this regard. He was a photographer that was born in Rio de Janeiro in 1843, son of Zépherin Ferrez, a French sculptor and engraver, who had arrived in Rio de Janeiro in 1817, joining the French Mission. After the death of his parents in 1851, Ferrez went to live in Paris with the medal engraver Joseph Eugène Dubois, and on returning to Brazil, he worked as a photographer almost until his death in 1923. Ferrez was Rio de Janeiro's most brilliant visual landscape chronicler in the second half of the nineteenth century and the beginning of the twentieth, influencing many photographers who copied his style.

For many years Brazilian photographers continued to replicate the same pictures and use the same photographic styles, angles, and viewpoints that foreign photographers did when they worked here. In illustrated magazines like *O Cruzeiro* (i.e., Jean Manzon), in government agencies (i.e., Marcel Gautherot), or in advertising and social columns (i.e., Kurt Klagsbrunn), foreign photographers continued to lead the photographic production in the country and created a notion of Brazil to which many artists would conform. This does not diminish the relevance of Brazilian photographers, but it obliges us to consider this perspective of the foreign gaze on photography here. I think that we have taken too long to abandon this gaze and produce images that were different than those that were so strongly forged in the nineteenth century and in the first years of the twentieth.

Thanks to digital cameras and smartphones, photography has become increasingly democratic, with practically everyone offering a greater number of photos that produce the images of ourselves and our society. For example, we now have photographers that live in the favelas and produce images of their communities for different social media outlets. Some of them are not professional photographers; however, these communities produce their images and disseminate them. We must bear this in mind when contemplating in Latin America. This is because more than ever we know we have the possibility of presenting a more varied image of ourselves to the world. We are now becoming free of the notion that we must reproduce those early images that have been shaping the understanding of our country; what appear are no longer the typical or folkloric images of Brazil. It is very interesting to see different people producing the images. I think that the history of photography will change in Brazil, thanks to the media. Hence, I think that the new technologies like smartphones help to promote a new image of Brazil's multiple cultural expressions.

The project Imagems do Povo is exemplary. It provides documentation, research, training, and a center for vernacular photographers to enter the job market. Created in 2004, the program combines photographic technique with social issues, recording the daily life of favelas through a critical perception that considers and respects human rights and local culture. We must also mention Luiz Baltar ("Luiz Baltar"), who believes in photography as a form of activism and critical expression; hence, his quest is to establish a dialogue between photography and social issues, especially regarding urban photography. In 2009, he began photographing daily life in Rio: the process of forced removals and military occupations in various communities and favelas in this city. His interests include social movements, urban mobility, and the right to housing. He participated in the Imagems do Povo program, and now is a member of Favela em Foco, a multimedia collective of photographers from the popular classes. I think that the low cost and easy accessibility of modern photography is facilitating the growth of such projects.

Research Tools

On the other hand, we are still lacking in research tools in our institutions. We need more databases and websites in our national and international institutions. At present, they are scarce and under-utilized. Occasionally, I use websites such as Europeana Photography and institutional databases as well as virtual exhibitions from around the world. I think that we have much to do to improve how we study and how we make photographs accessible in our Brazilian institutions.

In Brazil, we need courses where we can learn how to study images from the vantage point of the social sciences. We do not stimulate research that uses photography as a source or as an object of study enough. Even so, there are many Brazilian collections that are open to research. We have great collections in the National Archives, the National Library, the Historical and Geographical Institute, the National Historical Museum in Rio de Janeiro, the Joaquim Nabuco Foundation in Recife, and the Public Archive of the State of São Paulo, not to mention the Instituto Moreira Salles collection. These are collections on the history of photography and the work of contemporary photographers in Brazil that are simply waiting for researchers to utilize them. There are important documents that enable you to study photography from the very beginning of photography in Brazil, or from the beginning of photojournalism in this country in those archives I just mentioned. You can also study the professional trajectory of many photographers. Another place to highlight is the LABHOI, the Laboratory of Oral History and Image, created in the 1980s at the Fluminense Federal University. It is one of the first research institutions in the field of image history in Latin America.

We need more tools to make our work and resources visible, and we must engage more with different networks. I know that in the field of photography, many collections are scattered among a variety of locations, and our contact with those collections can be very fruitful. You can see this with one project we are currently undertaking that links the National Archives and the Instituto Moreira Salles. We are researching nine notebooks produced by Marc Ferrez (mentioned earlier) which we will soon publish online. They are the notebooks that Ferrez produced during the span of thirty years from the end of the nineteenth century into the twentieth century. He traveled a lot, especially to France, because he was from a French family and because he worked in the photographic and film industry as one of the pioneers of cinema in Brazil in the early twentieth century. Ferrez was the creator of panoramic photographs of Rio de Janeiro and produced numerous records of public works, especially the opening of the Avenida Central (now Rio Branco), in Rio de Janeiro in the beginning of the twentieth century. He photographed the railways of the nineteenth century. He had one of the largest photographic studios in Brazil and maintained diverse interests. He also expanded the possibilities of landscape photography by perfecting panoramic scan photography equipment, the Brandon camera, and he was the only photographer in Brazil during 1881 to perform this type of large-format recording. This line of photography later culminated with his architectural masterpieces made during the construction of Avenida Central. Additionally, Ferrez became involved in the introduction of stereoscopic color photography in Brazil in the early twentieth century.

Our research focuses on the notebooks he produced during those three decades. They contain his travel impressions, the photographic equipment and the photos he sold via his business, his experiences with formulas and techniques related to photography, and many other issues. The notebooks also discuss his business in the field of cinema, his reflections on French restaurants, people with whom he had contact (professional and personal), and the reviews he wrote. Each one of these points are aspects of his life and work that merit individual study. These nine notebooks (seven from the National Archives and two from the Instituto Moreira Salles) are now fully digitized and will be available online. Each one of the notebooks will be the subject of an article on research topics I just mentioned. It is a collaborative project involving several coauthors: myself and two additional historians from the National Archives, another from the Instituto Moreira Salles, and other specialists in the history of photography.

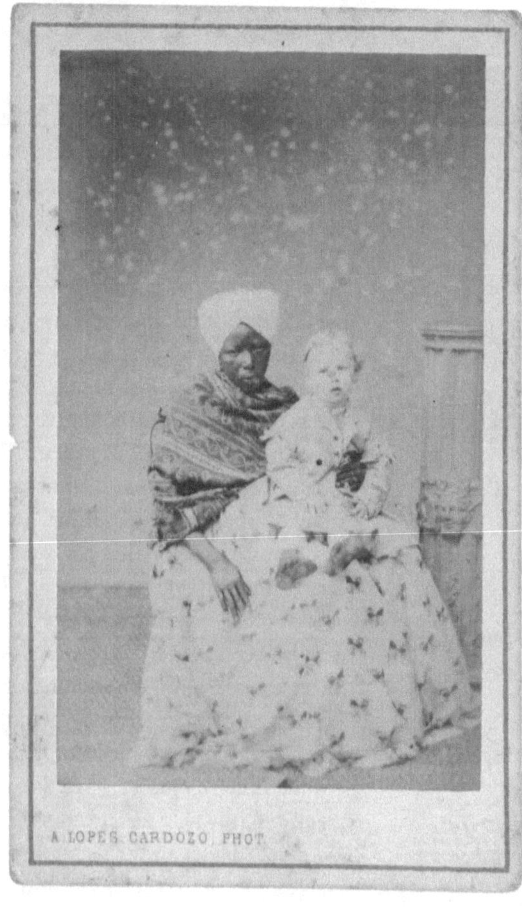

Figure 15.7. Antônio da Costa Pinto com sua ama de leite (Antônio da Costa Pinto with his wet nurse), Salvador, Bahia, 1868. Antônio Lopes Cardoso. Fotografias Avulsas Collection, Arquivo Nacional.

Another collaborative initiative worthy of mention is the website Brasiliana Fotográfica, created by the National Library of Brazil and the Instituto Moreira Salles. Its aim is to disseminate images of Brazil produced in the nineteenth century up to the 1920s. This digital resource unites many Brazilian institutions, museums, archives, and libraries. We have uploaded more than three hundred photographs to the site in the past two years, along with its metadata and articles written by myself and other researchers at my institution. Among the subjects that we uploaded were photographs of women's struggles in Brazil during the first decades of the twentieth century, including those for civil rights, and the first

Brazilian women to vote and to stand for election. Another topic we uploaded on the site is the Brazilian participation in the International Exhibitions that took place in locations such as Buenos Aires, Philadelphia, and Paris in the nineteenth century. An interesting collection is related to the Indigenous Brazilians of the Amazon during the first decades of the twentieth century and some landscape photography that includes several Brazilian cities, including Rio de Janeiro, during the last decades of the nineteenth century, as well as some cartes de visite of the Brazilian elite from that period. We will continue to expand our collaboration by providing more photos and articles onto this digital platform. I think that this is one of the great initiatives that disseminates photographs and research on photography in Brazil. Brasiliana Fotográfica and very soon the Cadernos Ferrez section of the National Archives website will uncover great possibilities for the study of photography in Brazil and generate new perspectives.

I am confident that the study of photography will grow exponentially in Latin America, not only because of the wealth of the collections, but because the access to the collections—despite all the difficulties that the institutions face—has greatly increased in recent years. Although we have much ahead, when I review my research from the beginning of the 1990s and what I do now, everything has vastly improved in terms of quantity, quality, and possibility. One difficulty we face is the fact that some institutions charge very high prices to use certain images. On the other hand, we have done an excellent job preserving images, digitizing them, and giving access to them. The production of books and exhibitions has increased significantly. Technology is continually expanding the visibility of the images. However, there is still much to be done in terms of how we teach photography at universities, and how we use the abundant material at our disposal.

We need to encourage researchers that are working in institutions that maintain photographic collections in Brazil and in other areas of Latin America to carry out more collaborative projects that integrate different collections on a specific subject, specific photographers, or a specific point in the history of photography. For example, my work colleague I mentioned earlier, Cláudia Heynemann, and I had an idea regarding the history of children in Brazil and want to produce an exhibition and (or) a book using images about children in the country from the middle of the nineteenth century to the 1960s. I soon discovered that a friend of mine, a researcher in the National Historical Museum in Chile, also had this same idea. Now we are considering the possibility of uniting our photographic collections because the one she has of children is excellent. This is one of the many projects that we can develop in Latin America through collaboration and networks.

The fact that we speak Portuguese leads to missed opportunities in Latin America because we tend to associate our studies to ideas that are coming out of the United States and Europe. This trend is not unique to the study of

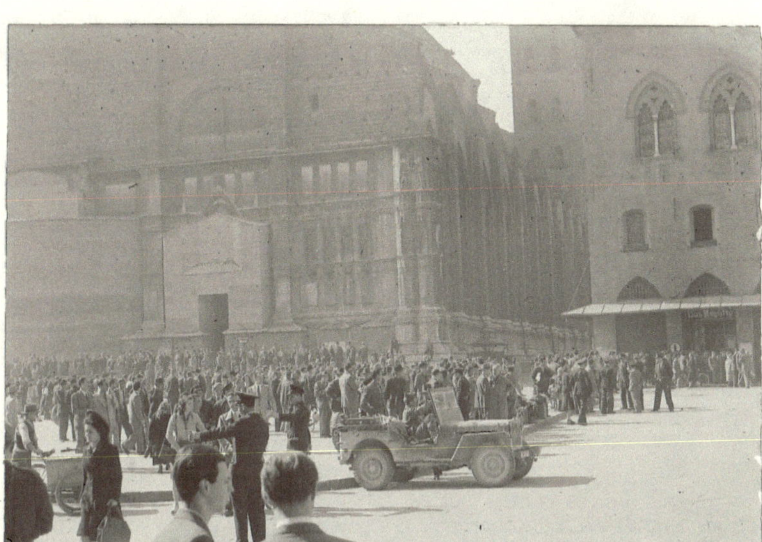

Figure 15.8. Aspecto de cidade italiana durante a II Guerra Mundial (Snapshot of an Italian city during WWII), Italy, May 16, 1945. Arquivo Nacional, Agência Nacional.

photography. It exists across many academic fields. This causes us to forego opportunities to integrate and create more collaborative projects with the other countries close to us. There are many research questions for us and other Latin American partners to consider. We must overcome the different barriers that separate us.

Selected Publications

Rainho, Maria do Carmo Teixeira. "La cittá e la moda nell'immagine di Rio de Janeiro degli anni sessanta." *Moda, Cittá e Immaginari*, edited by Alessandra Vaccari, Mimesis, 2016, pp. 218–27.

———. "Imagens encenadas? Atos performativos e construção de sujeitos nas fotografias de moda." *Estudos Ibero-americanos*, 44, 2018, pp. 28–40.

———. *Moda e Revolução nos anos 1960*. Contra Capa Editora, 2014.

Rainho, Maria do Carmo Teixeira, and Claudia Heynemann, editors. *Retratos Modernos*. Arquivo Nacional, 2005.

Boris Kossoy

Universidade de São Paulo

Early Influences

I BECAME INTERESTED in photography at a young age, but my research on photography began while I was studying to be an architect. It grew even further when I became an academic and began to analyze history, social science, museum sciences, and communication studies. Over the past five decades, my academic career, my work as a professional photographer, and my own personal photography have all contributed to my thoughts and ideas on photography.

As a photographer, literature and film were my first points of reference. German expressionism and Italian neorealism made a lasting impression on me. Many different directors such as Fritz Lang, Orson Welles, Michelangelo Antonioni, Ingmar Bergman, Luchino Visconti, Alfred Hitchcock, and Stanley Kubrick have been key to my visual outlook. Many literary authors have exerted an important influence on me as well: Edgar Allan Poe, Julio Cortázar, Gabriel García Márquez, Jorge Luis Borges, Adolfo Bioy Casares, Sir Arthur Conan Doyle, Franz Kafka, and Fyodor Dostoyevsky, among others. As that list suggests, magic realism and the poetics of fantasy have always influenced me and my photographic work. I have always produced photography and written work in tandem. In 1970, the Museum of Modern Art in New York acquired three of my photographs for their permanent collection, and the next year my first book, *Viagem pelo fantástico*, was published. I have published internationally, and my photographs are included in the permanent collections of important museums in Brazil, Mexico, the United States, and France.

I fell in love with photography's history while studying architecture. That love allowed me to cultivate a strong interest in urban iconography, the quotidian, and rituals in Indigenous communities. The topic of iconography in history captured my attention as I saw this as a starting point for researching fact and hidden narratives. I have a perennial interest in photography as artifacts because they can explain objectively. They focus on physical existence and content. The challenge of uncovering what images hide fascinates me as a researcher.

My interests centered on history and theory as I built my academic career. While I was undertaking my postgraduate degree in the 1970s, I became aware of the dire poverty the history of photography has suffered in Brazil. You could say the same of the bibliography on photography theory in general during that same period. I think that this situation was the same throughout all Latin America. However, when you consider photography theory, there was not much being produced internationally either. Beaumont Newhall, Helmut Gernsheim, and others had written the histories of photography that we had by that time, but they did not really include Latin America. Gisèle Freund's book *La fotografia como documento social* was a noteworthy exception to that trend and created an important counterpoint.

At that time, most of us in Latin America who have written about the history of photography were at the beginning of our research endeavors, and we felt the weight of the classic models I just mentioned. I think that you can question the validity of those models for writing history and the breadth of their cultural vision. I was struck by how their narrative focused on historic moments in photography. Positivism appeared to have a strong influence in it, and they seemed to take little care for any type of concepts. Nonetheless, their patterns for the narrating of history would have innumerable followers everywhere. I specifically wrote about this phenomenon in "Reflexiones sobre la história de la fotografía / Reflexions on the history of photography" for Joan Fontcuberta's *Photography: Crisis of History*. On the other hand, we need to clarify that the studies on the history of photography in Latin America are still in their infancy. It was not until the 1980s that the first publications on these topics began to appear.

Hercule Florence's Photography

As a graduate student in the 1970s, I discovered Hercule Florence's work. This corpus became an enormous project that I undertook in the years to follow. Florence was from Nice, France, and experimented with the use of a camera obscura to create original contact impressions on paper that had been sensitized by gold and silver salts. His experiments began in 1833 and took place in Campinas, Brazil. He is credited with independently discovering photography in Brazil. His pioneering work in the Americas was a contemporary of the work that was taking place in France by Niépce, Daguerre, and Bayard and in England by Fox Talbot. The history of Florence's work and proof that his methods bring real photographic results are part of my study *Hercule Florence: A descoberta isolada da fotografia no Brasil*. The road to recognition for this portion of history has been long. The first edition was published in 1977, the second in 1980. With time, it came to enjoy international recognition and has since been published twice in Spanish (first in Mexico and later in Spain) and in French, German, and more recently in English. My research on Hercule Florence

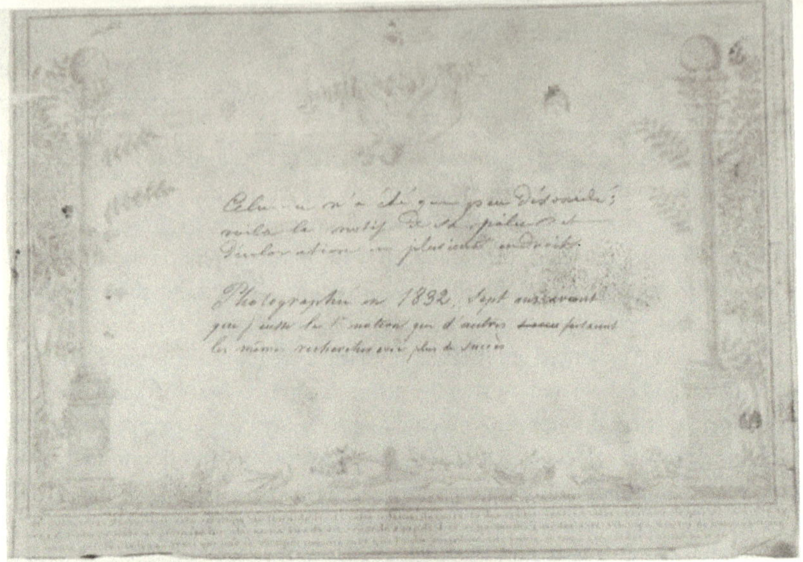

Figure 16.1. Masonic diploma, São Carlos, c. 1833. Antoine Hercule Romuald Florence. Arnaldo Machado Florence Collection, Instituto Hercule Florence, São Paulo. (A photographic copy of a Masonic diploma captured with photosensitive paper.)

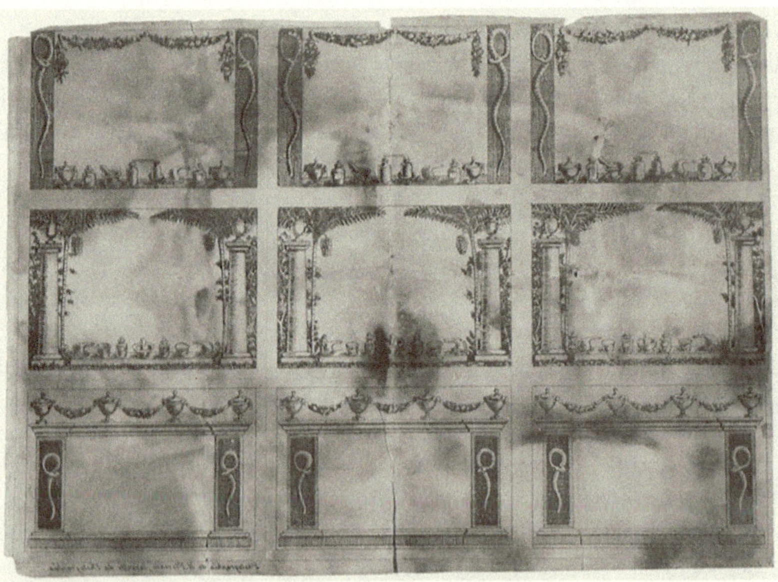

Figure 16.2. Pharmacy labels. São Carlos, c. 1833. Antoine Hercule Romuald Florence. Arnaldo Machado Florence Collection, Instituto Hercule Florence, São Paulo, Brazil. (A photographic copy of pharmacy labels, captured with photosensitive paper, possibly gold chloride.)

is my work with the greatest international impact. It is a groundbreaking topic with serious repercussions that could be discussed at length in another forum.

I defended my PhD dissertation, "Elementos para o estudo da fotografia nso Brasil; Século XIX," in 1979 while at the School of Sociology and Politics in São Paulo. That research outlines my methodological approach. It was an analysis and interpretation of photographic images that helped to inform another one of my books: *A fotografia como fonte histórica; introdução à pesquisa e interpretação das imagens do passado.* In those projects, I also attempted to demonstrate the need to link images to narratives as well as social, political, and cultural reality. This approach was not customary in the classic approaches to the writing of the history of photography, but you can get a sense for how I do this work in *Origens e expansão da fotografia no Brasil; Século XIX.*

Theory

The books I have just mentioned became the nucleus for several other books that I would write over the years. Among them are my books on photographic theory. The first two are named *Realidades e ficções na trama Fotográfica* and *Os tempos da fotografia.* The former is in its fifth edition and the latter in its third edition. Both of those books were combined to become a third one that was published in Spanish: *Lo efímero y lo perpetuo en la imagen fotográfica.* These books made a huge impact in academia in Latin America, which had been lacking in locally written critical theory.

My thoughts have not been limited to a theoretical proposition for the study of the history of photography. They expand into our understanding of how we use photography as a historical source in the humanities and the methods we employ to achieve this. This means that I have become concerned with the past and the knowledge of the past that different periods of photography offer us. Therein lies my challenge: to demonstrate the general need to use iconography and photography to acquire knowledge that is useful in the writing of history and creating methodologies that could be drawn on as we undertake our analysis and interpretation of that material.

I should clarify that history and other fields of knowledge were late to recognize the importance of photography as an effective knowledge-gathering instrument. This is due to an exclusivity of text; be it printed or handwritten. No matter what form it might take, we tend to privilege the imprisonment of verbal communication. Admitting that the image is an autonomous form of knowledge and a research instrument has been viewed as accepting an unreliable source. Traditionally, the image has generally been associated with the idea of adornment and art. When it is included in historical works, the written narrative traditionally relegates it to the appendix.

In the year 2000 I defended my Livre-Docência project at the Escola de

Comunicações e Artes da Universidade de São Paulo.[1] It was the *Dicionário histórico-fotográfico brasileiro* in which I mapped the work and identities of approximately nine hundred photographers from all over the country. Most of these photographers were completely unknown before and had never been mentioned in the history of Brazilian photography. My dictionary found a warm welcome in the context of the study of the history of photography and by archives, museums, and libraries all over the country that started to use it as a reference book for determining the dates, precise locations, and authorships of the photographs they had in their collections. In many cases those images had been previously labeled as anonymous. Hence, my book became a tool for the recovery of lost historical and technical information. The press was an important part of this research because the information for each entry came from newspapers from the period in question. The book created a methodology that allowed for the mapping of the photographers from within all of Brazil's provinces.

The Depth, Nature, and Essence of Photography

I think that writing history through photography or a history of photography are both activities at risk of becoming lost through the creation of superficial chronologies that are simply illustrated by photographs. Both types of histories are necessary, but both need to understand the world of images independently. What I mean by this is that we must understand the depth and nature and the essence of photography: its reach and its limits, its elements, its intentions, its ideologies, and its fictions. I am referring to a realm that has maintained its links to what we like to call the real world. That world, however, is an ambiguous world of constructed and elaborate appearances that must be unraveled. We must understand the messages that photographic images offer. We must understand their role as a form of communication and expression, their value as a vehicle of knowledge, their political content, their ideological power, their force as an instrument of propaganda, and their multiple faces. As we study images, it becomes obvious that we need to draw on many disciplines to analyze them properly. Scenarios and characters represented by photography cannot simply be understood by what we see. We need knowledge from other disciplines. Without knowingly applying the cultural and historical data that surrounds the photographic subject, the history of photography will be reduced to appearances and other information that is far from the essence of the facts in our world.

Analysis will become useless if it does not originate from the images themselves and their language of expression. A discussion on images needs words and language, but photographs do not need the rules of linguistics to be understood. Neither should they be considered illustrations that are always tied to written texts. This type of error should be locked in the past, associated with a time when only the written and spoken word was accepted as a historical source. Like language, the image has its own specific rules that govern its expression.

Methodology and Critical Approaches

Early on in my work, I searched for theoretical foundations that were inherent to visual expression to establish a methodological approach that could provide a consistent critical examination of photographic sources. I have always attempted to work with images as historical testimonies and expressive visual documents. I never thought of them as illustrative documents. We must consider photographic images as an autonomous field of knowledge and study them in that capacity.

When we understand that photography is not a harmless record that is purely mechanical in its production, but that it is a record obtained through a creative process, we will begin to comprehend the aesthetic power this form of communication and expression contains. Photography allows us to visualize and comprehend the proximity that exists between documents and propaganda, politics and poetry, and reality and fiction. Hence, photography is an expressive record that enables us to observe what we often call reality in a plural form: multiple masks for a single face.

In this sense, photography mirrors real life because it is a technical record, which is why we consider it a document that purports to represent reality on neutral terms. However, nothing is neutral, because everything is the product of a creation process. We create everything to suit specific purposes and intentions that are aimed at certain uses and applications by the camera operator or under the command of its commissioners.

Photographic Image as Representation

We speak of the photographic image as a representation. However, one cannot strictly understand the image as a document or as a representation alone, but rather as having an indivisible relationship between these two forms of perception of photography: a document and a representation. As representations, photographs are always products of a construction that has been used to compose realities (which is what I consider to be photography's true vocation). I am referring to processes of the construction of realities that occur both in the production and the reception of image: a planned and idealized trajectory that incorporates fictions by its very nature; a trajectory that is drawn with technique, aesthetics, culture, and ideology. All of this has its base in a wide and varied range of interests: prejudice, politics, ethnicity, race, religion, culture, and more.

Fiction has a privileged place in the universe of photographic images: documentary fictions are a seemingly ambiguous formulation, even a paradox if we consider that normally the notion of "documents" or "the documentary" imply in themselves the idea of "truth." We need to break this construct down into its codes and plots. We must observe its internal organization so that we can come as close as possible to the facts, circumstances, and contexts that existed during the making of the document. We need to identify the moment of its genesis so that we understand the meanings of the masks that disguise the visual information presented to us. This does not mean that we will discard the aesthetic values implicit in the images. On the contrary, it means that we will highlight these values even more.

My thoughts on photography focus on how we perceive images, ideologies, mentalities, signs, and clues. I constantly search for cultural history and visual culture's gaze. Key teachers such as Pierre Francastel, Michel Vovelle, Carlo Ginzburg, Erwin Panofsky, Ernst Gombrich, Tzvetan Todorov, and Eric Hobsbawm have inspired those thoughts along the way.

I wrote my three books on critical theory over the course of approximately twenty-five years, and they did not focus on discussing the fundamental philosophies of photography. The fundamental objective of my theoretical work has been to seek the applicability of my theoretical formulations and methodological propositions, using them to interpret and analyze photographs. I have strived to extend the borders of our knowledge insofar as I proposed bases that seemed to me to be consistent with the critical examination of photographic artifacts being read as historical sources. The goal was to formulate a way of thinking that could become an instrument that enabled us to understand photography with greater depth and precision.

Much time has passed since the 1970s when I began to attempt to understand how to study, use, and theorize about photography or to employ photography to carry out research on historical or social analysis or interpretation. Learning how to confirm the processes of creation of realities that are inherent to image production and reception mechanisms have guided my studies in photography. My goal has been to break those mechanisms down into understandable and applicable units. I strive to use my concepts and methodologies to reveal the apparent and the hidden elements within the images I study. Likewise, I seek to decipher their codes, to dismantle their technical, aesthetic, cultural, and ideological constructs. Finally, I strive to determine the reasons for their existences and their senses.

A Strong Grounding in Latin America Is Essential

You must have a good base in the different histories of Latin American countries, a knowledge of their culture and photography as well as the principles of photography to effectively research on Latin American photography. You must

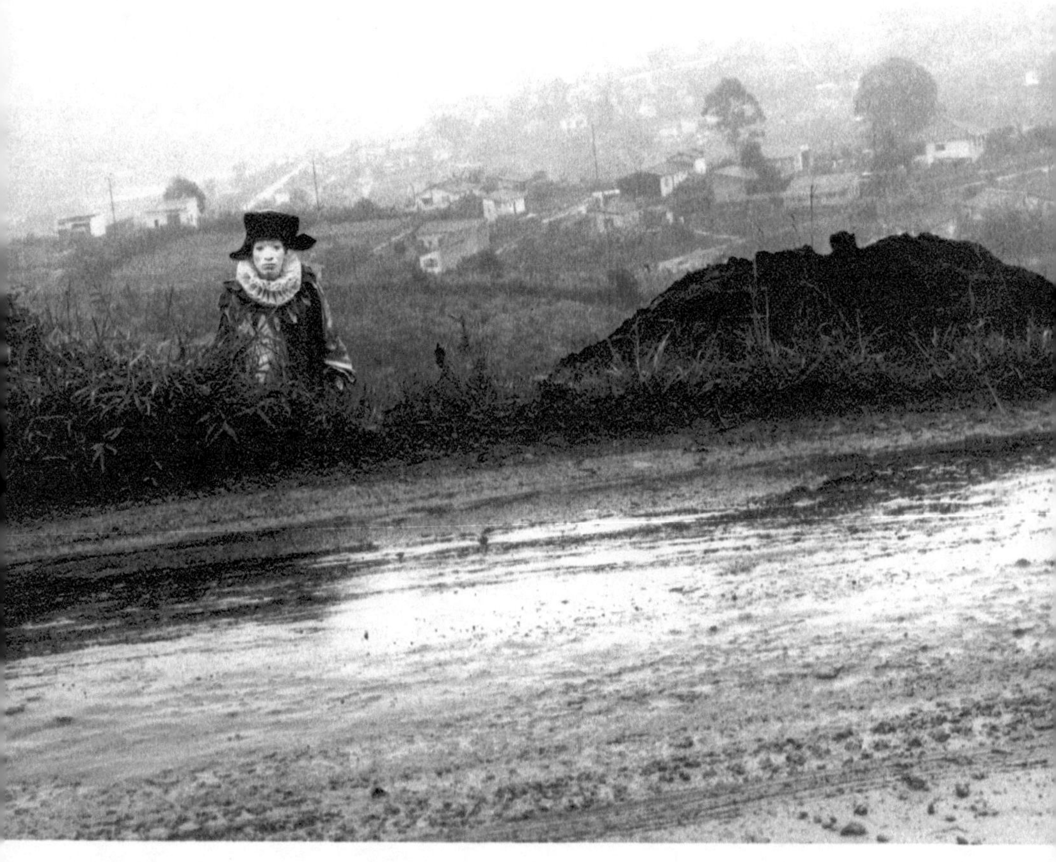

Figure 16.3 Surpresa na Estrada. Viagem pelo Fantástico serie. (Surprise along the road. Viagem pelo Fantástico series.), São Paulo, Brazil, 1970. Boris Kossoy. ©Boris Kossoy.

remember that many salient mental images on Latin America are filled with prejudices. They become manifest by maintaining a mentality of superiority in relation to the customs, culture, and the appearance of others: the inhabitants of the tropics. This reaction has undoubtedly led to a standard interpretation that has been perpetuated for centuries and continues to inform our present. Hence, you must have a clear awareness of this mentality and how it influences your outlook.

My research strives to demonstrate the extent to which photographic representation has contributed to the reinforcing of the ethnocentric posture of the European white man when faced with Latin American realities. For some authors, what happened, and what continues to happen in the third world is exotic because it is unashamedly generous and clearly different when compared to the ethnocentric patterns found in their own way of interpreting the world.

When non Latin America–based researchers use these photographs, they are

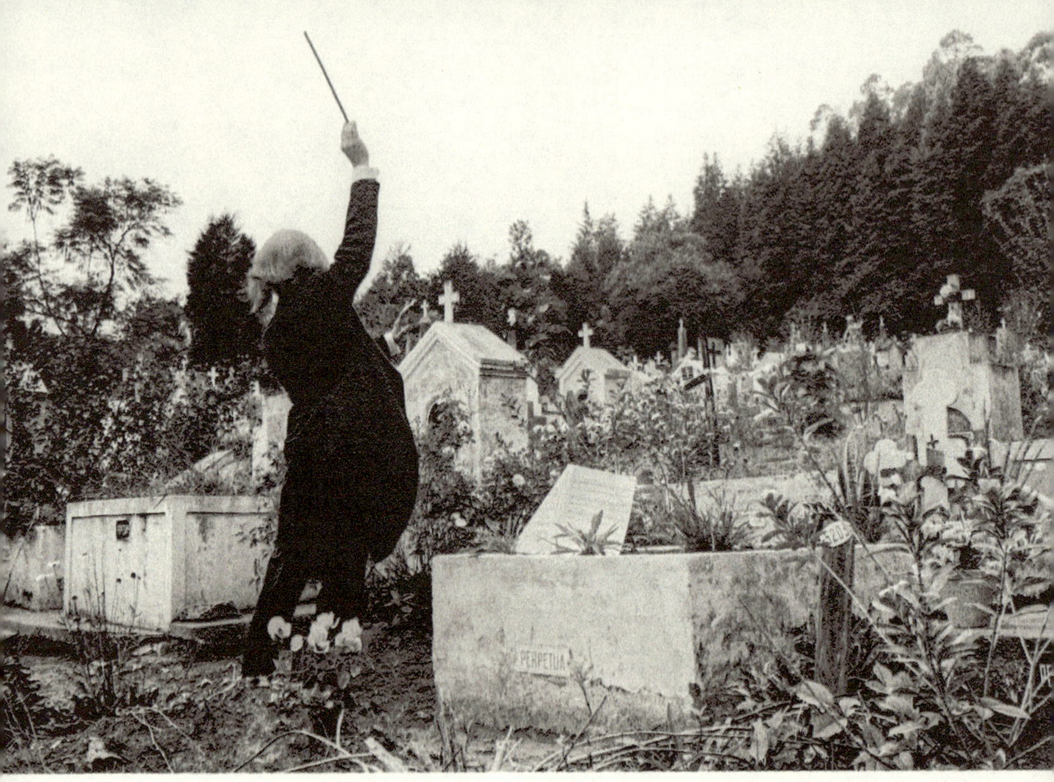

Figure 16.4. O Maestro. Viagem pelo Fantástico series. (The teacher. Viagem pelo Fantástico series.), São Paulo, Brazil, 1970. Boris Kossoy. ©Boris Kossoy.

often employed as proof of their preconceived stereotypes. The images appear to offer proof of common themes associated with the tropics: the underdeveloped, the backward, the inferior, and so on. Perhaps the best example of one of these stereotypical themes is the so-called ethnographic photography where, under the guise of thematic interest, such prejudices are broadly manifested. That mentality has been incorporated into the thought patterns of cultural producers in various ways and forms and was a theme that I specifically explored in my essay "Photography in Latin America in the Nineteenth Century: The European Experience and the Exotic Experience" in *Image and Memory: Photography from Latin America, 1866–1994*.

1978: A Decisive Year

In 1978 the study of photography in Latin America experienced a decisive event in its history. That event was the Primer Coloquio Latinoamericano de Fotografía that was organized by the Consejo Mexicano de Fotografía. We could say that 1978 was the year that the multiple presences and influences of Latin

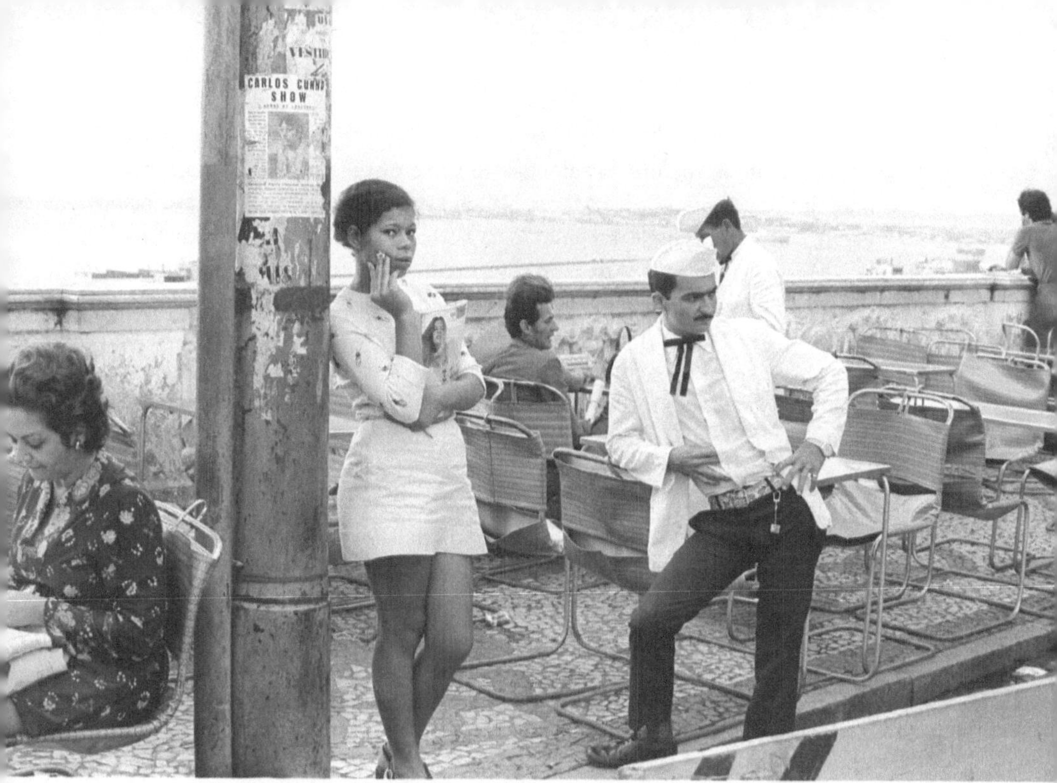

Figure 16.5. Sem título (Untitled), Bahia, Brazil, 1972. Boris Kossy. ©Boris Kossoy.

American photography began to be felt beyond each other's borders, spilling into the different Latin American regions and beyond. I am confident that the colloquium was the foundational event that sparked the international influence of Latin American photography around the world. While a discussion of the reasons why the colloquium took place go beyond the scope of our parameters here, I remember very clearly that in the midst of our conversations there, often rich and saturated with different ideologies, one of the most prominent issues was the urgent need to establish channels of information and dissemination. We desired to forge ways to exchange our knowledge, ideas, research, theory, and history on photography that we had developed in our own countries. We argued that it was absurd to try to apply knowledge sporadically produced in the United States and Europe to our local contexts. We learned from each other thanks to the formal presentations as well as through lectures and conversations with others who attended. Many of these conversations continued more informally in other spaces, allowing us to get to know our fellow participants even better and have a clearer idea of the similar challenges that they faced in their own countries. I was privileged to have been invited and to have been able to participate in the process along with some of the greats in Latin American photography such as Pedro Meyer, Nacho Lopez, Raquel Tibol, Lazaro Blanco, Paolo Gasparini, Gisèle Freund, Alan Porter, Cornell Capa, Lucien Clergue, and Mario Garcia Joya. After the 1978 event, the notion of working with Latin American photography from within Latin America began to gain ground internationally. In 1979 Latin American photography was visibly present in Venice thanks to exhibitions, conferences, and debates at the colloquium "Como nos vemos a nós mesmos e como nos vêm de fora os centros do poder" held there. Next, Latin American photography became the focus of the tenth Rencontres Internationales de la Photographie in Arles, France, and that momentum has continued forward.

Other colloquiums and various encounters would systematically follow those events during the 1980s and the 1990s all over Latin America. They occurred in Mexico, Cuba, Venezuela, Chile, and later in Brazil, Uruguay, and Argentina. Photography brought with it an approach to Latin America that has been cultural, historical, political, and artistic. It is important to emphasize that these events had repercussions in the Latin American countries themselves and encouraged the development of local and regional programs to support and foment photography.

I think that speculation on the future of the study of photography does very little, as we have witnessed it evolve so much in recent decades. Photography as a medium is different too. Its new reality is full of *selfies* and *fake news*, as well as surveillance cameras that examine public and private spaces. All of these are new forces that control where we go and how we act. Where will all of this take us? In the future, history will tell us.

Selected Publications

Kossoy, Boris. *Dicionário Histórico-Fotográfico Brasileiro*. Instituto Moreira Salles, 2002.

———. *Fotografia e História*. Ateliê Editorial, 1989. Also published in Spanish.

———. *The Pioneering Photographic Work of Hercule Florence*. Routledge, 2017. First edition published in Portuguese in 1977.

———. *Realidades e Ficções na Trama Fotográfica*. Ateliê Editorial, 1999. Also published in Spanish.

Closing Thoughts

THE GOAL OF this book has been to create a bridge between the study of photography in Latin America and the English-speaking world. It has identified connections between European and United States theorists and the research trends and movements taking place in Latin America. The book has also underscored the diverse areas in which these photography scholars in Latin America work and how this informs their academic projects.

Aside from sketching a panorama of this field and suggesting its future directions based on a collection of specialists, this book contains an implicit invitation: to deepen our knowledge about this subject and to enable new connections. One form of collaboration will be purely intellectual as readers gain inspiration from the ideas and suggestions provided in the book that may offer a positive impulse for their own research projects. Other collaborations might be more direct in nature. My work here attempts to fill a void that has existed around the knowledge of what is occurring in the study of photography in Latin America. This book is simply a beginning. Scholars can expand on this base in numerous ways. One of the first elements that academics could cultivate with great success regards the number of scholars studied. While this work has been wide-ranging, an in-depth analysis of the study of photography in Argentina, Brazil, Central America, Chile, Mexico, Peru, Uruguay, and other areas of Latin America would greatly expand this field and help map out the detailed nuances that each national and regional context offers. This study has shown differences between fields and areas, but studies with a narrower scope could successfully delineate more ways that could move scholarship further forward.

This book has evidenced how Latin American scholars do not demonstrate strong connections with postmodern theory in its critical approach to photography. Instead, the scholars there cultivate rich photographic analysis that focuses on the images rather than how they relate to literature and other areas of cultural studies. This approach offers useful springboards that launch future work into other areas where the discipline develops in diversified manners. Likewise, given the wide variety of fields from which the scholars studied in this book proceed, and considering that a large proportion of those who study photography in the English-speaking world research in fields of literature and cultural studies, this study invites the forging of new connections and cross-disciplinary initiatives that can further enliven this field of scholarship. Additionally, it is important that those who study photography in Latin America reflect deeply on what this medium can uniquely teach us about that region. Addressing that question opens many potential studies.

Another of the important thrusts of this book was to introduce readers to new practitioners of photography, archives, and centers of photography research. This study shows that the Instituto de Moriera Salles in Brazil, the Centro de la Imagen in Mexico, and the Centro de Fotografía de Montevideo in Uruguay do much to advance the study of photography in Latin America and that these centers would greatly benefit from further research on their efforts and current holdings. Another important direction along these lines would be to analyze events in the study of photography that have proven to be key impulses for the production and expansion of the study of photography, as the *Hecho en Latinoamerica* conference series has been. This would allow us to draw new connections between existing collections of work. These focuses would help scholars to engage more directly with the centers for research on photography in Latin America and identify areas where further study would be advantageous; an academic study of these institutions and events (such as *La mirada inquieta* research series in Mexico City Rebeca Monroy mentions) also becomes an additional invitation to engage with photographers and photographic works that currently lie outside the established photographic canon. Such studies will allow for comparative studies between visual movements and enable us to identify their strongest examples. In turn, the work of their creators can be analyzed with greater depth. These academic ventures would benefit from joint collaborations between Latin American scholars and other international scholars whose work in tandem could greatly expand our knowledge of this area through events and publications whose impact reaches across and beyond Latin America. Such studies will also enable us to engage with new ideas and visual perspectives, all with the intention of revealing new aspects of the study of Latin American photography. As future studies move away from the well-known photographers and engage with high quality, though presently understudied material, new avenues of research will also sprout and blossom.

Studies of lesser-known photographers will open the door to fruitful regional studies. As I mentioned previously, the number of photography scholars whose work I could cover in depth has been limited. Many factors influenced this, including availability, visibility, knowability, the impact of their influence, and their willingness to enable primary research. Further studies will be able to widen the scope and expand on the legacy of this project by including more scholars as new experts emerge and the geographic scope segments further to allow for the individual coverage of different countries and regions. This activity could be undertaken from within Latin America or by regional or national specialists in those areas, or as a joint initiative. Such studies will allow the study of photography to rise beyond archival work in Latin American capitals and other major centers and find new homes in regional and private archives that will bring with it a wealth of information that only regional research can provide. Such interest may well bring further investment in these archives that could contribute to better archival conditions and an improved conservation of the information and memory they contain. I am confident that those activities will create a fuller, crisper image of photography and its ability to offer unique knowledge on the region that could radically change how we study Latin American photography and even Latin America itself.

Along with the expansion of the study of regional and national photography, the study of areas of society that are traditionally invisible or silent is another one of the new directions in which this study can grow. The study of women, children, migrants, and other sectors of society whose voices and experiences are often invisible in the hegemonic national narratives can become visible when seen through the lens of photography. One example of how photography allows migrants to self-represent is shown by the efforts of the Secretaría del Zacatecano Migrante (SEZAMI) in northern Mexico. This Mexican government institution lends support to migrants and regularly holds photography competitions that enable migrants to express their experiences and show how migration has affected their lives and outlooks. Their 2019–2020 photography competition allowed migrants to use photography to speak about migration in ways that hegemonic discourse has not yet included, underlining new narratives for future scholars to explore and study. The SEZAMI archive presents another vision on the migratory experience. The archive speaks of love, success, tradition, and the side of the encounter between the migrant and the national that is usually hidden behind language, power, and culture barriers—elements that photography can overcome with its easy technological access and multiple interface platforms. In sum, that initiative enables us to see migration from the inside and reveal new faces just as Claudia Andújar uncovers in *Amazônia* with her vision of the Amazon and its inhabitants and Maya Goded explores with Mexicans of African extraction in *Tierra negra*. Additionally, photography made by the Indigenous, women, youth, and others who are less represented in Latin America provides a wealth of material that can be studied to reveal the aesthetic, the social, and other aspects of Latin America. This goes in hand with the important study of vernacular photography in Latin America. With the growing number of photographs that are used in the media and other areas of society that are made by nonprofessionals, we are beginning to observe the importance of vernacular photography and the role that it plays in how we interpret and engage with our surrounding world. While it is excellent to study photographers who have revealed Latin American life and society like the Hermanos Mayo and Martín Chambi, it is equally important in our times to be able to recognize the work of worthy vernacular photography and photographers so we can analyze and demonstrate the key information that they offer those who engage with their work.

The establishment of the Latin American photography canon is possibly the future project that could most influence the study of photography in Latin America. An idea underlined by Mauricio Lissovsky in our critical conversations, the lack of a recognized Latin American photography canon may be one of the reasons why it plays a lesser role in the world canon of photography. An established Latin American photography canon would be a base text to be studied and an archive that can be used to promote Latin American photography and a body around which to create and base future studies. It is possible to speculate as to how this might happen. (For example, it could be formed in terms of regions or countries and from there begin to shape a Latin American canon. Another possibility is that a major institution could undertake the task to embark on a Beaumont Newhall-like venture and map out the Latin American canon with the strength and support needed to gain acceptance.) What is certain though is that in order to be a credible and lasting canon, Latin America would be its ideal creator.

This book has also made evident the need for new encounters on Latin American photography within Latin America. If the 1978 conference was groundbreaking for the field of the study of photography in Latin America, it is also clear that greater interaction between the Latin American scholars will also be fruitful. Over the course of this project, it became manifest that a number of the scholars covered in this book did not know the work of the other scholars that well. Hence, for this reason the translation of texts such as this and others that study Latin American photography will help connect these scholars and others who read them. It is true that I wrote this book to connect Latin American photography with the English-speaking world with greater depth, but versions in other languages will also bring different scholars together. Future studies would do well to take this initiative even further.

Finally, new studies on photography in Latin America would benefit by identifying (and/or creating in tandem) more tools that are uniquely suited to study Latin American photography. Finding the connections between art and cultural movements from the Global North and demonstrating how they might apply to the Global South is useful in that we can envision how it is possible to relate one context to another. Yet to identify tools from the Global South that explain how we can understand it on its own terms will allow for Latin America to be studied from a unique perspective that underlines its exclusive abilities and autochthonous influences. This would do much to help us to comprehend Latin America in ways that are more relevant and acquire a depth of analysis that might not be possible any other way. Likewise, it would also enable this field of study to advance from being seen as a subset of other areas of the study of photography and be viewed as one with greater autonomy. I am confident that such a venture would enhance the consideration and the study of Latin American photography at every level.

As I undertook this project, I began to expand my vision of the vastness of the study of photography in Latin America. I was impressed by how photography unified a diverse field of interests and research. While a great number of scholars in the Global North who study Latin American photography are based in the humanities, our counterparts in the Spanish- and Portuguese-speaking Global South are spread out across a much wider base (history, anthropology, fine arts, media studies, and other areas) and collaborate with great success, evidencing how naturally interdisciplinary this field is. Their research on photography reveals unique areas of study that uncover new insights into Latin America and shows how this medium expands our knowledge of this region in ways that other sources do not. Through this study I have become more convinced than ever that photography is an exceptionally democratic technology that has the power to represent the hidden, to narrate key events with efficacy, to create a more dynamic and egalitarian vision of what it portrays, and to give a clear and understandable voice to those who seek to be heard. As we delve deeper into the research and find natural points of contact, I am confident that the potential for uncovering new and compelling insights will be significant. I am eager to witness these developments in my own work and that of my fellow scholars.

Notes

Introduction

1. Newhall "lavished attention on Weston's work" (Mora 15).

2. The exhibition catalog lists Manuel Álvarez Bravo's wife Lola Álvarez Bravo as the photographer of a Mexican funeral procession (140), yet the official MoMA checklist only lists Manuel as the photographer. It is unclear which source is mistaken. The sole recurring image in *Family of Man* is a Peruvian flute player, which becomes a leitmotiv in the exhibition and its catalog. Taken by US photographer Eugene Harris, it was meant to add a sense of musicality to the visual narrative as well as pay tribute to Werner Bischoff, Harris's friend and photographer who had recently died in an automobile accident while on assignment in Peru (Sandeen *Picturing an Exhibition* 45, 75).

3. For example, Flor Garduño is listed as a male photographer (Herschdorfer 174–75).

4. The poverty featured in *Timeless Mexico* is mostly of children whose clothing suggests economic deficiency because they are pictured in beautiful environments.

5. Centro de la Imagen, "Archivo 1978," http://cdf.montevideo.gub.uy/exposicion/archivo-1978-revisiones-al-fondo-del-consejo-mexicano-de-fotografia.

6. I am considering the Peruvian piper leitmotiv that is repeated several times over the course of the book.

7. Throlichen was a German citizen who lived for many years in Argentina while working as one of Perón's official photographers before returning to Europe to live in Spain. Marcos Chamudes was born in Chile but immigrated to the United States and was a US citizen when he submitted his work under his anglicized name.

8. A brief history of the Centro de la Imagen is found in Claudi Carreras's *Tercer Coloquio Latinoamericano de Fotografía* (209–11).

9. For a current list of the CdF open-access publications, please see https://issuu.com/cmdf/docs.

10. The copy I sourced and read in researching Gerstmann's Colombian project had been given by an ex-Colombian president (Eduardo Santos) as a gift to a visitor by the name of Harold W. Sands, providing anecdotal evidence of this book's importance.

11. Pedro Meyer is an important Latin American photographer who also breaks this trend and incorporates elements of fantasy or the bizarre in his photographs (Foster).

12. Pablo Gasparini's *Para verte mejor, América Latina* was also included in this series.

13. One possible exception is the occasional visual monographs of the ornate Día de los Muertos altars (Programa de Arte Popular).

John Mraz

1. Hayden White, *Metahistory*.

2. Mraz, "'En calidad de esclavas': Obreras en los molinos de nixtamal, México, diciembre, 1919."

3. The Hermanos Mayo was a collective of Spanish photojournalists made up of two sets of brothers. Paco, Cándido, and Julio Souza Fernández were brothers, as were Faustino and Pablo del Castillo Cubillo. Together they formed a photo agency in Spain, Hermanos Mayo, which later transferred its activities to Mexico where its members sought refuge after the Spanish Civil War. Their archive in the Archivo General de la Nación contains five million negatives.

4. Fototeca Nacional is short for Fototeca Nacional del Instituto Nacional de Antropología e Historia, the National archive of photographs in Mexico.

5. This dissertation has been published as a book: *Winfield Scott: Retrato de un fotógrafo norteamericano en el Porfiriato*.

6. Sekula, *Mining Photographs and Other Pictures, 1948–1968*; Pinney, *Camera Indica: The Social Life of Indian Photographs*; Poole, *Vision, Race, and Modernity: A Visual Economy of the Andean World*; Faris, James C., *Navajo and Photography*; Sandweiss, *Print the Legend: Photography and the American West*.

7. Monroy Nasr, *Historias para ver: Enrique Díaz, fotorreportero*; Massé Zendejas; del Castillo Troncoso, *Ensayo sobre el movimiento estudiantil de 1968*; Aguayo, Fernando; Casanova; Sampaio Barbosa; Escorza Rodríguez; Arnal, *Atila de tinta y plata*; Berumen, Miguel Ángel. *1911: La batalla de Ciudad Juárez*; Broquetas, Magdalena. *Fotografía en Uruguay: Historia y usos sociales, 1840–1930;* Rodríguez, *Fotógrafas en México, 1872–1960*.

8. Kossoy, *Fotografía e historia*; Levine, *Images of History*; Mauad, *Poses e flagrantes: Ensaios sobre história e fotografias*; Burke, *Eyewitnessing*.

9. See Berger's *Ways of Seeing* and writings on photography in *Understanding a Photograph*. See also Benjamin, *On Photography*, and Freund's *Photography & Society*.

10. See Kracauer's *Theory of Film: The Redemption of Physical Reality*.

11. "The photograph, however, introduces something new and strange: in every fishwife from Newhaven who gazes at the ground with such nonchalant, beguiling modesty, there remains something that is not completely absorbed by the artistry of the photographer Hill, something that cannot be silenced, obstreperously demanding the name of she who has lived, who even now is still real here and will never entirely perish into 'art'" (Benjamin, *On Photography*, 66). The translation by Leslie has been slightly altered.

12. Sekula says in *Photography Against the Grain*: "The photograph, as it stands alone, presents merely the *possibility* of meaning. Only by its embeddedness in a concrete discourse situation can the photograph yield a clear semantic outcome" (7).

13. Barthes, *Camera Lucida*; Sontag, *On Photography*; Flusser, *Toward A Philosophy of Photography*; Flusser, *Writings*; Flusser, *Into the Universe of Technical Images*.

14. See Ritchin, *In Our Own Image: The Coming Revolution in Photography* and Ritchin, *After Photography*.

15. See Azoulay, *Civil Imagination.*

16. This image is taken from the photo essay "Cuando una mujer guapa parte plaza por Madero," first published in 1953. Mraz's discussion of this image can be found in *Nacho López: Mexican Photographer* 117–21.

17. This photograph by Ruth Orkin is commonly titled *American Girl in Italy.*

18. On directed photojournalism, see Mraz's "What's Documentary about Photography?"

19. "Being profound and seeming profound: those who know that they are profound strive for clarity. Those who would like to seem profound to the crowd strive for obscurity" (Nietzsche 201–2).

20. See Mraz's "Mexican History in Photographs." The photograph referred to here is located on page 304 of that essay.

21. Segments of this chapter were published as part of my article "'We Have Entered a Third [Visual] Period of History': Thoughts on the Study of Photography by John Mraz." *The Americas*, 73.4, 2016, pp. 459–75. Reprinted with permission.

Ariel Arnal

1. Walter Reuter (1906–2005) was a Mexican photojournalist of German origin. Fleeing the rise of the Nazis in Germany and the defeat of the Republicans in Spain, Walter Reuter sought refuge in Mexico. Already an established photojournalist in Spain, Reuter introduced many modern techniques in Mexico. He acquired a strong reputation for documenting Mexico's Indigenous people and their culture.

Sussy Vargas Alvarado

1. Roberto Cabrera Padilla (1939–2014) was a Guatemalan artist who also wrote about art, geography, popular culture, and expressions of popular religious art. Two of his important books are *Tierra y ganadería en Guanacaste* and *El cristo de Esquipulas.*

Gisela Elvira Cánepa Koch

1. This growing archive is accessible today via the Instituto de Etnomusicologa at the PUCP, online at http://ide.pucp.edu.pe.

2. Hans Heinrich (Enrique) Brüning (1848–1928) was a German-born ethnologist and collector of antiquities. Educated as an engineer in Germany, he immigrated to Peru in his late twenties. Though he quickly found work as a mechanic on a sugar plantation in the Chiclayo province, his photographs of ancient buildings, local inhabitants, and his extensive collection of Peruvian artifacts made him a local expert on culture. His early work that had an ethnography focus was encouraged by Adolph Bandelier, a specialist in pre-Hispanic buildings. Brüning's photographic collection of over two thousand glass negatives provides an extensive visual archive of Peruvian history and culture during the late nineteenth and early twentieth century.

Pedro Querejazu Leyton

1. The advertisement was in a newspaper in Oruro. This information might seem irrelevant at first, but it offers an important perspective on the writing of history and image analysis.

2. The practice of creating *fotografías iluminadas* in the Andes consisted of painting photographs with oil paints in order to create idealized features and to add color to the image (Poole "Figueroa Aznar" 177).

3. See Gerstmann's notes in the section "Mis cuadros" in his book *Chile* (63–66).

Cora Gamarnik

1. I had a Universidad Buenos Aires Ciencia y Técnica (UBACYT) scholarship between 2008 and 2013. The Universidad de Buenos Aires awards these scholarships. Mine enabled me to write my PhD dissertation, "El fotoperiodismo en Argentina: De *Siete Días Ilustrados* a la *Agencia Sigla* (1965–1975)," which I successfully defended in 2015.

2. I had many different questions. Shall I write the history of a magazine, a photographer, or a publishing house? Shall I focus on photographic technique? Shall I do a combination of these approaches?

3. At present, there are many different dissertations in progress on several different topics, such as the photographs of the Guerra del Paraguay and the photography of the Falkland Islands/Malvinas.

4. Cora Gamarnik. "El fotoperiodismo y la guerra de Malvinas: Una batalla simbólica." *Fotografía e Historia en América Latina*, ed. John Mraz and Ana Maria Mauad, Ediciones CdF, 2015, pp. 225–56; Silvia Pérez Fernández and Cora Gamarnik. *Artículos de Investigación sobre Fotografía*. Centro Municipal de Fotografía de Montevideo, 2011, http://cdf.montevideo.gub.uy/fotografia/convocatorias/edicionescmdf/libros/investigacion_2011.html.

Boris Kossoy

1. This is a Brazilian academic title available to PhD holders. It denotes superior quality in teaching and research and is acquired through the development of a significant postdoctoral research-led monograph and passing a written and teaching exam.

Bibliography

Abbot, Brett, and Edward Weston. *Edward Weston: Photographs from the J. Paul Getty Museum*. Getty Publications, 2005.

Aguayo, Fernando. *Estampas ferrocarrileras: Fotografía y grabado 1860–1890*. Instituto Mora, 2003.

Alencastro, Luiz Felipe de, editor. *História da Vida Privada no Brasil*, vol. 2: *Império, a corte e a modernidade nacional*. Companhia das Letras, 1997.

Alexander, Abel. *Historia de la Fotografía: Memoria del 90 Congreso de Historia de la Fotografía, Rosario, agosto de 2006*. Sociedad Iberoamericana de Historia de la Fotografía, 2007.

Alonso, Idurre, and Judith Keller, editors. *Photography in Argentina: Contradiction and Continuity*. Getty Publications, 2017.

Andújar, Claudia, and George Love. *Amazônia*. Editorial Praxis, 1978.

Appadurai, Arjun, editor. *The Social Life of Things: Commodities in Cultural Perspective*. Cambridge University Press, 2014.

Argenteri, Letizia. *Tina Modotti: Between Art and Revolution*. Yale University Press, 2003.

Arnal, Ariel. *Atila de tinta y plata: Fotografía del zapatisimo en la prensa de la Ciudad de México 1910–1915*. INAH, 2010.

———. "Certera voz de luz: Verdad y verdades en la fotografía documental latinoamericana." *América, lente solidaria*, edited by Ariel Arnal, Azucena Cháidez, and Edgar Valle, SIMO Cultura, 2016, pp. 10–17.

———. *Rodrigo Moya: Photography and Conscience/Fotografía y conciencia*. University of Texas Press, 2015.

Arnal, Ariel, and Juan Crisóstomo Méndez Avalos. *Juan C. Méndez: La curiosidad en la mirada*. Secretaría de Cultura de Puebla, 1999.

Auerbach, Anthony. "Imagine no Metaphors: The Dialectical Image of Walter Benjamin." *Image & Narrative*, 18, 2007, http://www.imageandnarrative.be/inarchive/thinking_pictures/auerbach.html.

Azoulay, Ariella. *The Civil Contract of Photography*. Zone Books, 2008.

———. *Civil Imagination: A Political Ontology of Photography*. Verso Books, 2015.

———. *Historia potencial: Y otros ensayos*. Conaculta, 2014.

———. "The Lethal Art of Portraiture." *Photography and Culture*, 8.2, 2016, pp. 213–26.

———. "Photography Consists of Collaboration: Susan Meiselas, Wendy Ewald, and Ariella Azoulay." *Camera Obscura*, 31.1, 2016, pp. 186–201.

Bacon Hales, Peter. *Silver Cities: The Photography of American Urbanization, 1839–1915*. Temple University Press, 1984.

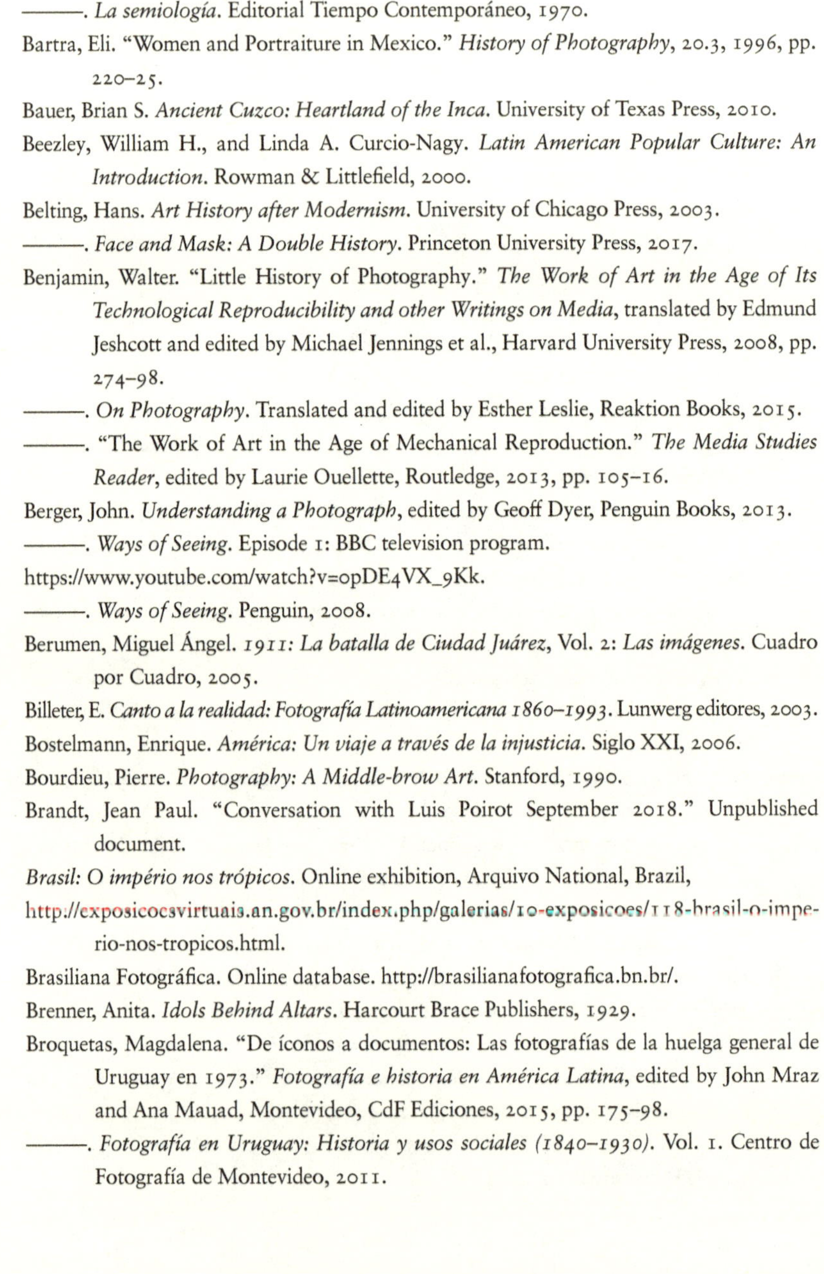

Barthes, Roland. *Camera Lucida: Reflections on Photography*. Farrar, Straus and Giroux, 1981.

———. *The Fashion System*. Translated by Matthew Ward and Richard Howard, University of California Press, 1990.

———. *El Grano de la voz: Entrevistas 1962–1980*. Siglo XXI, 2005.

———. *Image-Music-Text*. Farrar, Straus and Giroux, 1978.

———. *La semiología*. Editorial Tiempo Contemporáneo, 1970.

Bartra, Eli. "Women and Portraiture in Mexico." *History of Photography*, 20.3, 1996, pp. 220–25.

Bauer, Brian S. *Ancient Cuzco: Heartland of the Inca*. University of Texas Press, 2010.

Beezley, William H., and Linda A. Curcio-Nagy. *Latin American Popular Culture: An Introduction*. Rowman & Littlefield, 2000.

Belting, Hans. *Art History after Modernism*. University of Chicago Press, 2003.

———. *Face and Mask: A Double History*. Princeton University Press, 2017.

Benjamin, Walter. "Little History of Photography." *The Work of Art in the Age of Its Technological Reproducibility and other Writings on Media*, translated by Edmund Jeshcott and edited by Michael Jennings et al., Harvard University Press, 2008, pp. 274–98.

———. *On Photography*. Translated and edited by Esther Leslie, Reaktion Books, 2015.

———. "The Work of Art in the Age of Mechanical Reproduction." *The Media Studies Reader*, edited by Laurie Ouellette, Routledge, 2013, pp. 105–16.

Berger, John. *Understanding a Photograph*, edited by Geoff Dyer, Penguin Books, 2013.

———. *Ways of Seeing*. Episode 1: BBC television program.
https://www.youtube.com/watch?v=opDE4VX_9Kk.

———. *Ways of Seeing*. Penguin, 2008.

Berumen, Miguel Ángel. *1911: La batalla de Ciudad Juárez*, Vol. 2: *Las imágenes*. Cuadro por Cuadro, 2005.

Billeter, E. *Canto a la realidad: Fotografía Latinoamericana 1860–1993*. Lunwerg editores, 2003.

Bostelmann, Enrique. *América: Un viaje a través de la injusticia*. Siglo XXI, 2006.

Bourdieu, Pierre. *Photography: A Middle-brow Art*. Stanford, 1990.

Brandt, Jean Paul. "Conversation with Luis Poirot September 2018." Unpublished document.

Brasil: O império nos trópicos. Online exhibition, Arquivo National, Brazil,
http://exposicoesvirtuais.an.gov.br/index.php/galerias/10-exposicoes/118-brasil-o-imperio-nos-tropicos.html.

Brasiliana Fotográfica. Online database. http://brasilianafotografica.bn.br/.

Brenner, Anita. *Idols Behind Altars*. Harcourt Brace Publishers, 1929.

Broquetas, Magdalena. "De íconos a documentos: Las fotografías de la huelga general de Uruguay en 1973." *Fotografía e historia en América Latina*, edited by John Mraz and Ana Mauad, Montevideo, CdF Ediciones, 2015, pp. 175–98.

———. *Fotografía en Uruguay: Historia y usos sociales (1840–1930)*. Vol. 1. Centro de Fotografía de Montevideo, 2011.

———. *Fotografía en Uruguay: Historia y usos sociales (1930–1990)*. Vol. 2. Centro de Fotografía de Montevideo, 2018.

———. "Las fotografías en la construcción de conocimiento histórico: Usos, límites y potencialidades. Reflexiones teórico-metodológicas a partir de la presentación del trabajo del "Núcleo interdisciplinario de investigación y preservación del patrimonio fotográfico uruguayo." *Fuentes y Archivos* 2, 2011, pp. 173–87.

Brunet, Francois. "Redefining Visual Studies." *inMedia: The French Journal of Media Studies* 3, 2013, pp. 1–4.

Burgi, Sergio, and Mariana Newlands. *Marc Ferrez/Robert Polidori: Rio*. The Metropolitan Museum of Art, 2015.

Burke, Peter. *Eyewitnessing: The Uses of Images as Historical Evidence*. Cornell University Press, 2001.

Cabrera Padilla, Roberto. *El cristo de Esquipulas*. Editorial Tecnológica de CR, 1996.

———. *Tierra y ganadería en Guanacaste*. Editorial Tecnológica de CR, 2007.

Cadava, Eduardo. *Words of Light: Theses on the Photography of History*. Princeton University Press, 1997.

Calzavarini, Lorenzo. *Doroteo Gianecchini y Vincenzo Mascio: Álbum fotográfico de las misiones franciscanas de la República de Bolivia a cargo de los Colegios Apostólicos de Tarija y Potosí. 1898*. Banco Central de Bolivia/Archivo y Biblioteca Nacionales de Bolivia, 1995.

Canales, Claudia. *México: Fotografía y revolución*. Lunwerg Editores, 2009.

Cánepa Koch, Gisela. "Entre el museo e Internet: Regímenes interpretativos y nuevos usos de la fotografía etnográfica de la costa norte peruana." *Transiciones Inciertas: Archivos, conocimientos y transformación digital en América Latina*, edited by Barbara Göbel and Gloria Beatriz Chicote, Universidad de la Plata/Ibero-Amerikanisches Institut, 2017, pp. 315–44.

———, editor. *Imaginación visual y cultura en el Perú*. PUCP, 2011.

———. "La teta asustada de Claudia Llosa." http://blog.pucp.edu.pe/blog/latravesiadelfantasma/2011/01/19/la-teta-asustada-de-claudia-llosa-gisela-canepa-koch/.

Cánepa Koch, Gisela, and Ingrid Kummels, editors. *Fotografía en América Latina: Imágenes e identidades a través del tiempo y el espacio*. Instituto de Estudios Peruanos, 2018.

Carreras, Claudi, editor. *Tercer coloquio latinoamericano de fotografía: La Habana Cuba, 1984*. Centro de Fotografía de Montevideo, 2018.

Casanova, Rosa. *Guillermo Kahlo: Luz, piedra y rostro*. Fondo Editorial Estado de México, 2013.

Centro de Fotografía de Montevideo. "Archivo 1978: Revisiones al Fondo del Consejo Mexicano de Fotografía." https://cdf.montevideo.gub.uy/exposicion/archivo-1978-revisiones-al-fondo-del-consejo-mexicano-de-fotografia.

Cestelli Guidi, Benedetta, and Nicholas Mann. *Photographs at the Frontier: Aby Warburg in America 1895–1896*. Warburg Institute, 1998.

Chartier, Roger. *On the Edge of the Cliff: History, Language and Practices*. Johns Hopkins University Press, 1997.

Choi, Jong-chul. "Photo-Graphy, 'The Shadow in the Cave,' Its Pain and Love: The Ethics of Photography." *photographies*, 11.1, 2018, pp. 95–111.

"Claudi Carreras Guillén." World Press Photo. https://www.worldpressphoto.org/people/claudi-carreras-guill%C3%A9n.

Coleman, Kevin. *A Camera in the Garden of Eden: The Self-forging of a Banana Republic.* University of Texas Press, 2016.

Colombres, Adolfo. *Teoría transcultural del arte: Hacia un pensamiento visual independiente*. Ediciones Del Sol, 2004.

Conger, Amy. *Edward Weston in Mexico 1923–1926*. University of New Mexico Press, 1983.

———. *Edward Weston: The Form of Nude*. Phaidon Press, 2006.

Conrad Murray, Derek, and Soraya Murray. "Uneasy Bedfellows: Canonical Art Theory and the Politics of Identity." *Art Journal* 65.1, 2014, pp. 22–39.

Consejo Mexicano de Fotografía. *Hecho en Latinoamérica: Primera muestra de la fotografía latinoamericana contemporánea*. Museo Nacional de Arte Moderno, 1978.

———. *Hecho en Latinoamérica: Segundo coloquio latinoamericano de fotografía.* Instituto Nacional de Bellas Artes, 1982.

Consejo Nacional para la Cultura y las Artes, Centro Nacional de las Artes, and Centro de la Imagen, editors. *Nacho López*. Editorial RM, 2007.

Constantine, Mildred. *Tina Modotti: A Fragile Life*. Chronicle Books, 1993.

Coppola, Horacio. *Buenos Aires: Visión fotográfica*. Municipalidad, 1937.

Córdova, Carlos A. and Agustín Jiménez. *Agustín Jiménez y la vanguardia fotográfica mexicana*. Editorial RM, 2005.

Cotton, Charlotte. *The Photograph as Contemporary Art*. Thames & Hudson, 2014.

Cronin, Paul. *A Time to Stir: Colombia '68*. Columbia University Press, 2018.

Cruz, Marco Antonio. *Contra la pared*. Grupo Desea, 1993.

———. *Nicaragua: Testimonio de fotógrafos mexicanos*. Museo de Arte Moderno, 1985.

Currie, Gregory. "Visible Traces: Documentary and the Contents of Photographs." *The Journal of Aesthetics and Art Criticism*, 57.3, 1999, pp. 285–97.

D'Amico, Alicia, Sara Facio, and María Elena Walsh. *Fotografía Argentina: 1960–1985*. La Azotea Editorial Fotográfica, 1985.

Damisch, Hubert. *Semiotics and Iconography*. BRILL, 1975.

Debroise, Olivier. *Age of Discrepancies*. UNAM, 2006.

———. *Fuga mexicana: Un recorrido por la fotografía en México*. Consejo Nacional para la Cultura y las Artes, 1998.

———. *Mexican Suite: A History of Photography in Mexico*. University of Texas Press, 2001.

del Castillo Troncoso, Alberto. *Conceptos, imágenes y representaciones de la niñez en México, 1880–1920*. Instituto Mora/COLMEX, 2006.

———. *Ensayo sobre el movimiento estudiantil: La fotografía y la construcción de un imaginario*. Instituto Mora. 2012.

———. *Fotografía y memoria: Conversaciones con Eduardo Longoni/Alberto del Castillo Troncoso*. Fondo de la Cultura Económica, 2017.

———. *Las mujeres de X´oyep: La historia detrás de la fotografía.* Conaculta, México, 2014.

———. *Rodrigo Moya: Una visión crítica de la modernidad.* CONACULTA, 2006.

De Los Reyes, Aurelio. *Historia De La Vida Cotidiana En México: Siglo XX: La Imagen, ¿Espejo de la Vida?* El Colegio de México, 2006.

Dicionário Histórico-Biográfico da Fotografia. Online database. http://www.labhoi.uff.br/verbetesfotografia/.

Didi-Huberman, Georges. *Ante la imagen: Pregunta formulada a los fines de una historia del arte.* Cendeac, 2010.

———. *Ce que nous voyons, ce qui nous regarde.* Les Éditions de Minuit, 1999.

———. *Confronting Images: Questioning the Ends of a Certain History of Art.* Penn State Press, 2005.

———. *Devant l'image: Questions posées aux fins d'une histoire de l'art.* Minuit, 1990.

———. *Invention de l'hystérie: Charcot et l'Iconographie photographique de la Salpêtrière.* Macula, 1982.

———. *L'image survivante: Histoire de l'art et temps des fantômes selon Aby Warburg.* Les Éditions de Minuit, 2002.

———. *La invención de la histeria: Charcot y la iconografía fotográfica de la Salpêtrière,* Cátedra, 2007.

Dillehay, Tom D. "Richard Paul Schaedel (1920–2005)." *Andean Past,* 8, 2007, pp. 45–54.

Dubois, Philippe. *El acto fotográfico: De la Representación a la Recepción.* Ediciones Paidos, 1994.

Durand, Gilbert. *The Anthropological Structures of the Imaginary.* Boombana Publications, 1999.

Eco, Umberto. "A Photograph." *The Photography Reader,* edited by Liz Wells, Routledge, 2003, pp. 126–29.

———. "Critique of the Image." *Thinking Photography,* edited by Victor Burgin, Macmillan, 1982, pp. 32–38.

Eder, Rita, and Eugenia Meyer. *Imagen histórica de la fotografía en México.* SEP, 1978.

Edwards, Elizabeth. "The colonial archival imaginaire at home." *Social Anthropology/Anthropologie Sociale,* 24.1, 2016, 52–66.

Eliade, Mircea. *The Sacred and the Profane: The Nature of Religion.* Houghton Mifflin Harcourt, 1959.

Escorza Rodríguez, Daniel. *Agustín Víctor Casasola: El fotógrafo y su agencia.* INAH, 2014.

Fabris, Annateresa. "Discutindo a imagem fotográfica." *Domínios da Imagem,* 1.1, 2007.

———, editor. *Fotografia: Usos e funções no século XIX.* Edusp, 1991.

Facio, Sara. *La fotografía en la Argentina: Desde 1840 a nuestros días.* La Azotea Editorial Fotográfica, 2008.

Faris, James C. *Navajo and Photography: A Critical History of the Representation of an American People.* University of New Mexico Press, 1996.

"Frenando Brito." World Press Photo, https://www.worldpressphoto.org/people/fernando-brito.

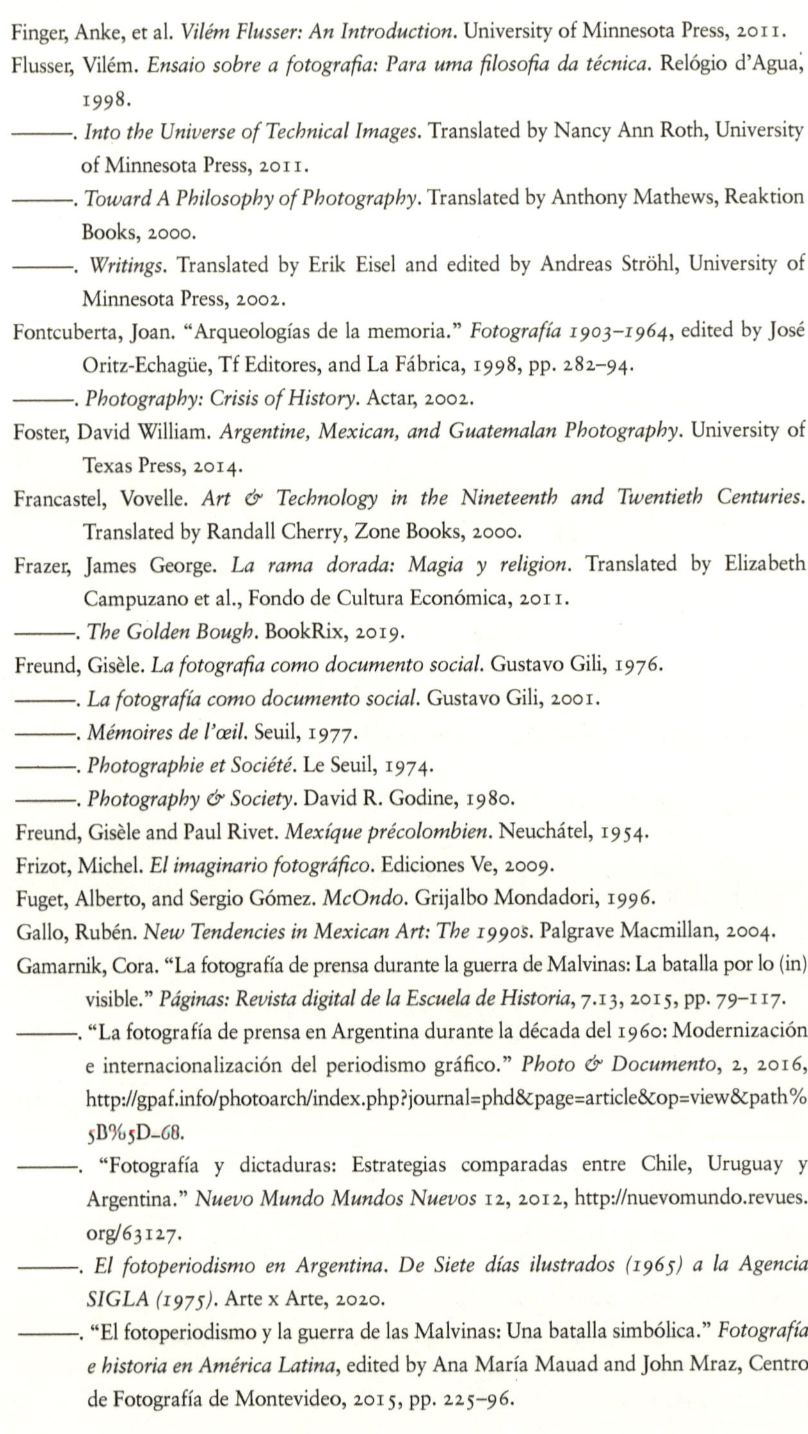

Finger, Anke, et al. *Vilém Flusser: An Introduction*. University of Minnesota Press, 2011.

Flusser, Vilém. *Ensaio sobre a fotografia: Para uma filosofia da técnica*. Relógio d'Agua, 1998.

———. *Into the Universe of Technical Images*. Translated by Nancy Ann Roth, University of Minnesota Press, 2011.

———. *Toward A Philosophy of Photography*. Translated by Anthony Mathews, Reaktion Books, 2000.

———. *Writings*. Translated by Erik Eisel and edited by Andreas Ströhl, University of Minnesota Press, 2002.

Fontcuberta, Joan. "Arqueologías de la memoria." *Fotografía 1903–1964*, edited by José Oritz-Echagüe, Tf Editores, and La Fábrica, 1998, pp. 282–94.

———. *Photography: Crisis of History*. Actar, 2002.

Foster, David William. *Argentine, Mexican, and Guatemalan Photography*. University of Texas Press, 2014.

Francastel, Vovelle. *Art & Technology in the Nineteenth and Twentieth Centuries*. Translated by Randall Cherry, Zone Books, 2000.

Frazer, James George. *La rama dorada: Magia y religion*. Translated by Elizabeth Campuzano et al., Fondo de Cultura Económica, 2011.

———. *The Golden Bough*. BookRix, 2019.

Freund, Gisèle. *La fotografia como documento social*. Gustavo Gili, 1976.

———. *La fotografía como documento social*. Gustavo Gili, 2001.

———. *Mémoires de l'œil*. Seuil, 1977.

———. *Photographie et Société*. Le Seuil, 1974.

———. *Photography & Society*. David R. Godine, 1980.

Freund, Gisèle and Paul Rivet. *Mexíque précolombien*. Neuchâtel, 1954.

Frizot, Michel. *El imaginario fotográfico*. Ediciones Ve, 2009.

Fuget, Alberto, and Sergio Gómez. *McOndo*. Grijalbo Mondadori, 1996.

Gallo, Rubén. *New Tendencies in Mexican Art: The 1990s*. Palgrave Macmillan, 2004.

Gamarnik, Cora. "La fotografía de prensa durante la guerra de Malvinas: La batalla por lo (in) visible." *Páginas: Revista digital de la Escuela de Historia*, 7.13, 2015, pp. 79–117.

———. "La fotografía de prensa en Argentina durante la década del 1960: Modernización e internacionalización del periodismo gráfico." *Photo & Documento*, 2, 2016, http://gpaf.info/photoarch/index.php?journal=phd&page=article&op=view&path%5B%5D–68.

———. "Fotografía y dictaduras: Estrategias comparadas entre Chile, Uruguay y Argentina." *Nuevo Mundo Mundos Nuevos* 12, 2012, http://nuevomundo.revues.org/63127.

———. *El fotoperiodismo en Argentina. De Siete días ilustrados (1965) a la Agencia SIGLA (1975)*. Arte x Arte, 2020.

———. "El fotoperiodismo y la guerra de las Malvinas: Una batalla simbólica." *Fotografía e historia en América Latina*, edited by Ana María Mauad and John Mraz, Centro de Fotografía de Montevideo, 2015, pp. 225–96.

———. "Imágenes de la post-dictadura en Argentina." *Photographie contemporaine en Amérique Latine* 7, 2015.

———. "El rol del fotoperiodismo en la construcción de la democracia en Argentina (1983–2002)." *L'Ordinaire des Amériques*, 219, 2015, http://journals.openedition.org/orda/2179.

Garay Albújar, Andrés. *Martín Chambi, por sí mismo*. Universidad de Piura, 2006.

———, editor. *Fotografía Max T. Vargas, Arequipa y La Paz*. Universidad de Piura, 2015.

García Canclini, Néstor. *Transforming Modernity: Popular Culture in Mexico*. University of Texas Press, 1993.

———. *Hybrid Cultures: Strategies for Entering and Leaving Modernity*. University of Minnesota Press, 1995.

Gardner, Nathanial. "'We have entered a Third [Visual] Period of History': Thoughts on the Study of Photography by John Mraz." *Americas*, 73.4, 2016, 459–73.

Garduño, Flor. *Witnesses of Time*. Aperture, 2000.

Gasiorowiski, Dominika. *Photographing the Unseen Mexico: Maya Goded's Socially Engaged Documentaries*. Legenda, 2019.

Gasparini, Pablo. *Para verte mejor, América Latina*. Siglo XXI, 1972.

Gates Warren, Beth. *Artful Lives: Edward Weston, Margrethe Mather, and the Bohemians of Los Angeles*. Getty Publications, 2011.

Geertz, Clifford. *The Interpretation of Cultures*. Hachette, 2017.

Gernsheim, Alison, and Helmut Gernsheim. *The History of Photography from the Earliest Use of the Camera Obscura in the Eleventh Century up to 1914*. Oxford University Press, 1955.

Gerstmann, Roberto. *Bolivia: 150 grabados en cobre*. Paris: Braun & Cie Editeurs, 1928.

———. *Chile: 280 grabados en cobre*. Paris: Braun & Cie Editeurs, 1932.

———. *Colombia: 200 grabados en cobre*. Paris: Braun & Cie Editeurs, 1951.

———. "Mis cuadros." *Chile: 280 grabados en cobre*. Paris: Braun & Cie Editeurs, 1932, pp. 63–66.

Gesualdo, Vicente. *Historia de la Fotografía en América: Desde Alaska a Tierra del Fuego en el siglo XIX*. Editorial Sui Generis, 1990.

Ginzburg, Carlo. *History, Rhetoric, and Proof*. UPNE, 1999.

Girard, Rafael. *El calendario maya-méxica: Origen, función, desarrollo y lugar de procedencia*. Editorial Stylo, 1948.

———. *Historia del origen y desarrollo de las civilizaciones indo-americanas*. Imprenta Universitaria, 1951.

———. *El Popol-vuh: Fuente histórica*. Vol. 1. Editorial del Ministerio de Educación Pública, 1952.

Girard de Marroquín, Anne. *Rostros de la Guatemala Indígena/Images of Indigenous Guatemala*. Cifga, 2012.

———. *Visión etnográfica de la indumentaria maya de Guatemala/Ethnographic view of Maya dress in Guatemala*. Servi Prensa, 2017.

Goded, Maya. *Tierra negra: Fotografías de la costa chica en Guerrero y Oaxaca, Mexico*. Conaculta, 1994.

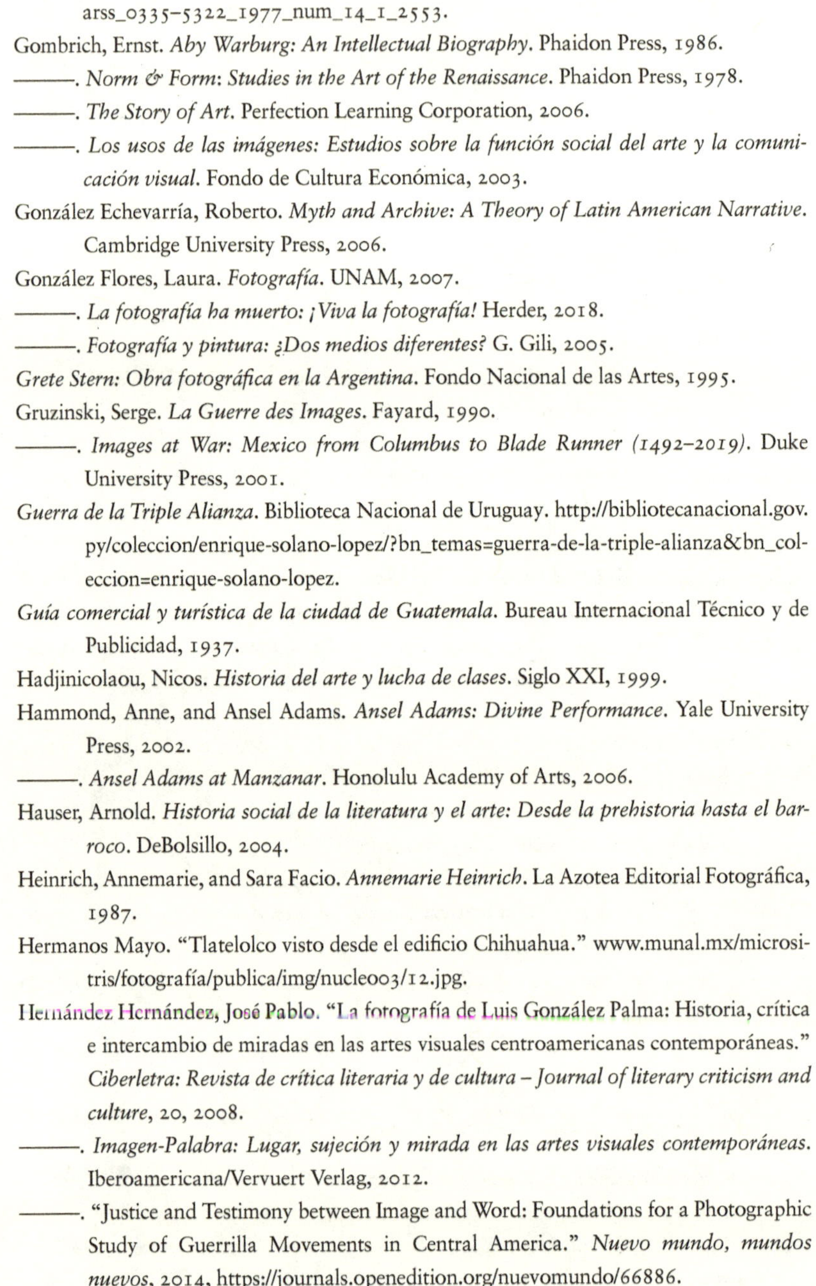

Goffman, Erving. *Gender Advertisements*. Harper & Row, 1976.

———. "La ritualisation de la feminité." *Actes de la recherche en sciences sociales*, 14, 1977, pp. 34–50, http://www.persee.fr/web/revues/home/prescript/article/arss_0335-5322_1977_num_14_1_2553.

Gombrich, Ernst. *Aby Warburg: An Intellectual Biography*. Phaidon Press, 1986.

———. *Norm & Form: Studies in the Art of the Renaissance*. Phaidon Press, 1978.

———. *The Story of Art*. Perfection Learning Corporation, 2006.

———. *Los usos de las imágenes: Estudios sobre la función social del arte y la comunicación visual*. Fondo de Cultura Económica, 2003.

González Echevarría, Roberto. *Myth and Archive: A Theory of Latin American Narrative*. Cambridge University Press, 2006.

González Flores, Laura. *Fotografía*. UNAM, 2007.

———. *La fotografía ha muerto: ¡Viva la fotografía!* Herder, 2018.

———. *Fotografía y pintura: ¿Dos medios diferentes?* G. Gili, 2005.

Grete Stern: Obra fotográfica en la Argentina. Fondo Nacional de las Artes, 1995.

Gruzinski, Serge. *La Guerre des Images*. Fayard, 1990.

———. *Images at War: Mexico from Columbus to Blade Runner (1492–2019)*. Duke University Press, 2001.

Guerra de la Triple Alianza. Biblioteca Nacional de Uruguay. http://bibliotecanacional.gov.py/coleccion/enrique-solano-lopez/?bn_temas=guerra-de-la-triple-alianza&bn_coleccion=enrique-solano-lopez.

Guía comercial y turística de la ciudad de Guatemala. Bureau Internacional Técnico y de Publicidad, 1937.

Hadjinicolaou, Nicos. *Historia del arte y lucha de clases*. Siglo XXI, 1999.

Hammond, Anne, and Ansel Adams. *Ansel Adams: Divine Performance*. Yale University Press, 2002.

———. *Ansel Adams at Manzanar*. Honolulu Academy of Arts, 2006.

Hauser, Arnold. *Historia social de la literatura y el arte: Desde la prehistoria hasta el barroco*. DeBolsillo, 2004.

Heinrich, Annemarie, and Sara Facio. *Annemarie Heinrich*. La Azotea Editorial Fotográfica, 1987.

Hermanos Mayo. "Tlatelolco visto desde el edificio Chihuahua." www.munal.mx/micrositris/fotografía/publica/img/nucleo03/12.jpg.

Hernández Hernández, José Pablo. "La fotografía de Luis González Palma: Historia, crítica e intercambio de miradas en las artes visuales centroamericanas contemporáneas." *Ciberletra: Revista de crítica literaria y de cultura – Journal of literary criticism and culture*, 20, 2008.

———. *Imagen-Palabra: Lugar, sujeción y mirada en las artes visuales contemporáneas*. Iberoamericana/Vervuert Verlag, 2012.

———. "Justice and Testimony between Image and Word: Foundations for a Photographic Study of Guerrilla Movements in Central America." *Nuevo mundo, mundos nuevos*, 2014, https://journals.openedition.org/nuevomundo/66886.

———. "Testimonio und Bildakt: Der Einsatz von Photographien als Dokumentation in den Guerrillas Lateinamerikas." *Möglichkeiten und Grenzen von Zeugenschaft in den romanischen Literaturen*, edited by Nickel and A. Ortiz-Wallner, Winter-Verlag, 2015.

Hernández-Salazar, David. *So that all Shall Know/Para que todos sepan.* University of Texas Press, 2007.

Herschdorfer, Nathalie, editor. *Dictionary of Photography.* Thames & Hudson, 2015.

Heynemann, Cláudia, and Maria do Carmo Teixeira Rainho. "Imagens do consumo: Rótulos e marcas no acervo do Arquivo Nacional." *Marcas do Progresso: Consumo e design no Brasil no século XIX*, Mauad X/Arquivo Nacional, 2009, pp. 208–19.

———. "*Uma história das imagens*: O acervo iconográfico do Arquivo Nacional." *Estudos Históricos* 38, 2006, http://bibliotecadigital.fgv.br/ojs/index.php/reh/article/view/2269/1408.

———, editors. *Retratos Modernos.* Arquivo Nacional, 2005.

———, et al., editors. *Festas Chilenas no Rio de Janeiro: Sociabilidade e política no ocaso do Império.* EDIPUCRS, 2014.

Hobsbawm, Eric. *Viva la Revolución: Hobsbawm on Latin America.* Hachette, 2016.

———, et al. *1968 Magnum Throughout the World.* Hazan, 1998.

Hoelscher, Steve, and Harry Ransom Center. *Reading Magnum: A Visual Archive of the Modern World.* University of Texas Press, 2013.

Hopkinson, Amanda. *Manuel Alvarez Bravo.* Phaidon Press, 2002.

Hubert, Damisch. *A Theory of Cloud: Toward a History of Painting.* Stanford University Press, 2002.

Hurm, Gero, et al. *The Family of Man: Photography in a Global Age.* I.B. Tauris, 2017.

Instituto Moreira Salles. "Acervos." https://ims.com.br/acervos/fotografia/.

Instituto Nacional de Antropología e Historia. *Imagen histórica de la fotografía en México: Museo Nacional de Historia, Museo Nacional de Antropología, mayo/agosto de 1978.* SEP, 1978.

Iturbide, Graciela. *Eyes to Fly With: Portraits, Self-Portraits, and Other Photographs.* University of Texas Press, 2006.

Iturbide, Graciela, and Elena Ponitatowska. *Juchitán de las mujeres.* Ediciones Toledo, 1989.

Jeffrey, Ian. *How to Read a Photograph: Understanding, Interpreting and Enjoying the Great Photographers.* Thames & Hudson, 2008.

Jobling, Paul. *Fashion Spreads: Word and Image in Fashion Photography since 1980.* Berg, 2006.

Jones, J. Bascome, et al. *El "Libro azul" de Guatemala, 1915: Relato e historia sobre la vida de las personas más prominentes; historia condensada de la república; artículos especiales sobre el comercio, agricultura y riqueza mineral, basado sobre las estadísticas oficiales.* Searcy & Pfaff, 2015.

Jurado, Carlos. *El arte de la aprehensión de las imágenes y el unicornio: Dos pequeñas historias acerca de la cámara fotográfica.* Universidad de Ciencias y Artes de Chiapas, 2009.

Kenny, Paul, et al. *Mexico's Security Failure: Collapse into Criminal Violence*. Routledge, 2013.

Kismaric, Susan. *Manuel Alvarez Bravo*. Museum of Modern Art, 1997.

Klich, Kent, and Elena Poniatowska. *El niño: niños de la calle, Ciudad de Mexico*. Syracuse University Press, 1999.

Knauss, Paulo. "O desafio de fazer História com imagens: Arte e cultura visual." *ArtCultura: Uberlândia*, 8.12, 2006, pp. 97–115.

Kossoy, Boris. *Lo efímero y lo perpetuo en la imagen fotográfica*. Cátedra, 2014.

———. *A fotografia como fonte histórica; introdução à pesquisa e interpretação das imagens do pasado*. Museu da Indústria, Comércio e Tecnologia de São Paulo, 1980.

———. *Fotografía & historia*. Atica, 1989.

———. *Fotografia e história*. Ateliê, 1988.

———. *Fotografía e historia*. Translated by Paula Sibilia. Biblioteca de la Mirada, 2001.

———. *Hercule Florence a descoberta isolada da fotografia no Brasil*. Edusp-Editora da Universidade de São Paulo, 2006.

———. *Hercule Florence: La découverte isolée de la photographie au Brésil*. L'Harmattan, 2016.

———. *Hercule Florence: El descubrimiento aislado de la fotografía*. Cátedra, 2017.

———. *Hercule Florence: El descubrimiento aislado de la fotografía*. Instituto Nacional de Antropología e Historia (INAH), 2004.

———. *Hercule Florence: Die entdeckung der fotografie in Brasilien*. LIT Verlag, 2015.

———. "Hercule Florence: Pioneer of Photography." *Image*, 20.1, 1976, pp. 1–11.

———. *Origens e expansão da fotografia no Brasil; Século XIX*. Funarte, 1980.

———. *Os tempos da fotografía*. Ateliê, 2007.

———. "Photography in Nineteenth-Century Latin America: The European Experience and the Exotic Experience." *Image and Memory*, edited by Wendy Watriss and Lois Parkinson Zamora, University of Texas Press, 1998, pp. 19–54.

———. *The Pioneering Photographic Work of Hercule Florence*. Routledge, 2017.

———. *Realidades e ficções na trama Fotográfica*. Ateliê, 1999.

———. *Viagem pelo fantástico*. Kosmos, 1971.

Kracauer, Siegfried. *Theory of Film: The Redemption of Physical Reality*. Oxford University Press, 1960.

Krauss, Rosalind. *Le Photographique: Pour une théorie des écarts*. Translated by Marc Bloch and Jean Kempf, Macula, 1990.

Krippner, James. *Paul Strand in Mexico*. Aperture, 2010.

Kummels, Ingrid. *Transborder Media Spaces: Ayuujk Videomaking between Mexico and the USA*. Berghahn, 2016.

Le Goff, Jacques, and Steven Rendall. *History and Memory*. Columbia University Press, 1996.

Lear, John. "*Looking for Mexico* Review." *Americas*, 67.2, 2010, pp. 286–88.

Leiva Quijada, Gonzalo. *Álvaro Hoppe: El Ojo En La Historia*. Gobierno De Chile Fondart, 2003.

———. *Luciérnagas Luis Prieto*. LOM Ediciones, 2013.

———. *Pintura con historia*. Editorial Trineo, 1998.

———. *Multitudes en sombras, AFI Asociación de Fotógrafos Independientes*. Ocho libris editores, 2008.

———. *Sergio Larraín: Biografía, estética, obra*. Editorial Metales Pesados, 2012.

Lemagny, Jean-Claude, and Andre Rouille. *A History of Photography*. Cambridge University Press, 1987.

Lenman, Robin. *The Oxford Companion to the Photograph*. Oxford University Press, 2005.

Levine, Robert. "*Image and Memory* Review." *Hispanic American Historical Review*, 79.3, 1999, pp. 536–38.

———. *Images of History: Nineteenth and Early Twentieth Century Latin American Photographs as Documents*. Duke University Press, 1989.

———, editor. *Windows on Latin America: Understanding Society through Photographs*. South Eastern Council on Latin American Studies, 1987.

Lissovsky, Mauricio. *A Máquina de Esperar: Origem e estética da fotografia moderna*. Mauad X, 2008.

———. *Pausas do Destino: Teoria, Arte e História da Fotografia*. Mauad X, 2014.

———. "The Photographic Device as a Waiting Machine." *Image & Narrative* 23, 2008, www.imageandnarrative.be/inarchive/Timeandphotography/lissovsky.html.

Lissovsky, Mauricio, and Marcia Mello. *Refúgio do Olhar: A fotografia de Kurt Klagsbrunn no Brasil dos anos 1940*. Casa da Palavra, 2013.

Lissovsky, Mauricio, and Paulo Cesar de Azevedo. *Escravos brasileiros do século XIX na fotografia de Cristiano Jr.* Ex Libris, 1988.

Lissovsky, Mauricio, and Paulo Sérgio Sá. *Colunas da Educação; A construção do Ministério da Educação e Saúde*. MINC/IPHAN/CPDOC, 1996.

Lowe, Paul. *1001 Photographs You Must See Before You Die*. Murdock Books Pty Limited, 2017.

"Luiz Baltar." Flickr. https://www.flickr.com/photos/luizbaltar/.

Luján Muñoz, Luis, and Edward Muybridge. *Fotografías de Eduardo Santiago Muybridge en Guatemala, 1875*. CENALTEX/Ministerio de Educación, 1984.

Lumnitz, Claudio. *Death and the Idea of Mexico*. Zone Books, 2005.

Lunghi, Enrico. *The 90s: A Family of Man? Images of Mankind in Contemporary Art*. Art Data Interactive Inc., 1997.

Macho, Thomas. "Zeit und Zahl – *Kalender – und Zeitrechnung als Kulturtechniken*." *Bild – Schrift – Zahl*, edited by Krämer S. and Bredekamp H., Wilhelm Fink, 2003, pp. 179–92.

MacNaughton, et al. *Revolution and Ritual: The Photographs of Sara Castrejón, Graciela Iturbide and Tatiana Parcero*. Getty Publications, 2017.

Majluf, Natalia, and Luis Eduardo Wuffarden, editors. *La recuperación de la memoria: El primer siglo de la fotografía. Perú 1842–1942*. Museo de Arte de Lima, 2001.

Malagón Girón, Beatriz. *Winfield Scott: Retrato de un fotógrafo norteamericano en el Porfiriato*. Universidad Autónoma Metropolitana, 2012.

Marbot, Bernard. "Toward the Discovery: (before 1839)." *A History of Photography: Social and Cultural Perspectives*, edited by Jean-Claude Lemagny and André Rouillé, translated by Janet Lloyd, Cambridge University Press, 1987, pp. 11–18.

"Marc Ferrez." Getty Museum Collection, https://www.getty.edu/art/collection/person/103KDG.

"Marc Ferrez." Instituto Moreira Salles, https://ims.com.br/titular-colecao/marc-ferrez/.

Marcus George E. "Ethnography in/of the World System: The Emergence of Multi-Sited Ethnography." *Annual Review of Anthropology*, 24.1, pp. 95–117.

Markarian, Vania, et al. *Uruguay 1968: Student Activism from Global Counterculture to Molotov Cocktails*. University of California Press, 2016.

Martínez Rossi, Sandra. *La piel como superficie simbólica: procesos de transculturación en el arte contemporáneo*. Fondo de Cultura Económica, 2011.

Mason, Jerry. *The Family of Woman*. Putnam, 1979.

Massé, Patricia. "Photographs of Mexican Prostitutes in 1865." *History of Photography*, 20.3, 1996, pp. 231–34.

Massé Zendejas, Patricia. *Simulacro y elegancia en tarjetas de visita: Fotografías de Cruces y Campa*. INAH, 1998.

Mauad, Ana Maria. "Como nascem as imagens? Um estudo de história visual." *História: Questões & Debates*, 61, 2014, pp. 105–32, https://revistas.ufpr.br/historia/article/viewFile/39008/23769.

———. "Concerned America - photographs of Genevieve Naylor (1941–1942) and Sebastião Salgado (1980–1996)." Research seminar. University of Glasgow Stirling Maxwell Centre, October 4, 2018.

———. *Fotografia Pública: Usos, funções e circuitos sociais no Brasil, séculos XIX e XX*. CNPq, 2015–2019.

———. "Fotograficamente Rio, a cidade e seus temas." Laboratório de História Oral e Imagem, http://www.labhoi.uff.br/fotograficamente-rio.

———. "Imagens em fuga: Considerações sobre espaço público visual no tempo presente." *Tempo e Argumento*, 10.23, 2018, pp. 252–85.

———. "O olhar engajado: Fotografia contemporânea e as dimensões políticas da cultura visual." *Artcultura*, 10.16, 2008, http://www.seer.ufu.br/index.php/artcultura/article/view/1495.

———. *O olhar engajado: Prática fotográfica e os sentidos da história, Brasil 1960–1990*. CNPq, 2011–2015.

———. "Por uma história fotográfica dos acontecimentos contemporâneos, Rio de Janeiro, 30 de junho de 1987." *Revista Tempo e Argumento*, 8.17, 2016, pp. 90–133.

———. *Poses e Flagrantes: Ensaios sobre história e fotografias*. EDUFF, 2008.

———. *Sob o signo da imagen: A Produção da Fotografia e o Controle dos Códigos de representação Social da Classe Dominante, no Rio de Janeiro, na Primeira Metade do Século XX*. Universidade Federal Fluminense, 1990, http://www.labhoi.uff.br/sites/default/files/dssam.pdf.

Mauad, Ana Maria, and Charles Monteiro, guest editors. *Estudos Ibero Americanos:*

Dossiê Fotografia. Cultura Visual e História: perspectivas teóricas e metodológicas, 44.1, 2018.

Maud, Ana Maria, and Marcos Felipe de Brum Lopes, guest editors. "Imagen, História e ciencia." *Ciencias Humanas: Dossiê*, 9.2, 2014, pp. 283–86.

McCormick, Susan. *Early Peruvian Photography: A Critical Case Study*. UMI Research Press, 1985.

———. "Oral History and Photography Review." *Oral History Review*, 40.2, 2013, pp. 422–26.

McElroy, Keith. *The History of Photography in Peru in the Nineteenth Century, 1839–1876*. University of New Mexico, 1977.

Medina, Cuauthémoc. "El ojo breve: Mundos privados, ilusiones públicas." *Reforma*, 11, September 2002.

Meiselas, Susan. *Susan Meiselas: In History*. International Center of Photography, 2008.

Meléndez, Carlos. "Notas acerca de la Historia de la Fotografía en Costa Rica." *Revista de Artes y Letras*, 1.5, 1968, pp. 3–6.

Meneses, Ulpiano Bezerra de. "Fontes visuais, cultura visual: Balanço provisório, propostas cautelares." *Revista Brasileira de História*, 23.45, 2003, pp. 11–36.

———. "Rumo a uma 'história visual.'" *O imaginário e o poético nas ciências sociais*, edited by José de Souza Martins et al., EDUSC, 2005.

Meyer, Eugenia. *Imagen histórica de la fotografía en México*. INAH/SEP, 1978.

Mitchell, W. J. T. *Iconology: Image, Text, Ideology*. University of Chicago Press, 1987.

———. *Picture Theory: Essays on Verbal and Visual Representation*. University of Chicago Press, 1994.

———. *What Do Pictures Want? The Lives and Loves of Images*. University of Chicago Press, 2005.

Modotti, Tina. "Sobre la fotografía – On Photography." *Mexican Folkways*, 5.4, 1929, pp. 196–98.

Monroy Álvarez, Roberto Carlos, and Laksmi Adyani de Mora Martínez. "La imagen del desecho: Hacia un análisis de la estética del cadáver, el desaparecido y el cuerpo como basura." *Las Torres de Lucca: Revista Internacional de Filosofía*, 4.7, 2015, pp. 71–109.

Monroy Nasr, Rebeca. *Con el deseo en la piel: Un episodio de fotografía documental mexicana a fines del siglo XX*. Universidad Autónoma Metropolitana Unidad Xochimilco, 2017.

———. "Conversation with Nathanial Gardner." November 2018.

———. *De luz y plata: Apuntes sobre tecnología alternativa en la fotografía*. México/INAH, 1998.

———. *Historias para ver: Enrique Díaz fotorreportero*. IIE-UNAM and INAH, 2003.

———. *Revista de Revistas: Ezequiel Carrasco, De las balas de bronce a las de plata*. México/INAH, 2010.

Monroy Nasr, Rebeca, and Alberto del Castillo Troncoso. *Caminar entre Fotones: Formas y Estilos de la Mirada Documental*. Instituto Nacional de Antropología e Historia, 2013.

Mora, Giles. "Introduction: Weston the Magnificent." *Edward Weston: Forms of Passion*, edited by Giles Mora, Thames & Hudson, 1995, pp. 9–25.

Moyle, Iván. "2 de octubre de 1968: Todos callaron menos una revista." *El mañana*, October 3, 2015, https://www.elmanana.com/2-octubre-1968-todos-callaron-menos-revista-2-octubre-matanza-tlatelolco-estudiantes/3047654.

Mraz, John. "'En calidad de esclavas': obreras en los molinos de nixtamal, México, diciembre, 1919." *Historia Obrera*, 6.24, 1982, pp. 2–14.

———. *History and Modern Media: A Personal Journey*. Vanderbilt University Press, 2021.

———. *Looking for Mexico: Modern Visual Culture and National Identity*. Duke University Press, 2009.

———. "Lucía: History and Film in Revolutionary Cuba." *Film and History: An Interdisciplinary Journal of Film and Television Studies*, 5.1, 1975, pp. 6–16.

———. "Mexican History in Photographs." *The Mexico Reader: History, Culture, Politics*, edited by Gilbert Joseph and Timothy Henderson, Duke University Press, 2002, pp. 295–331.

———. *Nacho López: Mexican Photographer*. Minnesota University Press, 2003.

———. *Photographing the Mexican Revolution: Commitments, Testimonies, Icons*. University of Texas Press, 2012.

———. "What's Documentary about Photography?" *Zone Zero*, January 2003, http://v1.zonezero.com/magazine/articles/mraz/mraz01.html.

Mraz, John, and Jaime Vélez Storey. *Uprooted: Braceros in the Hermanos Mayo Lens*. Arte Público, 1996.

Mraz, John, and Raymond Tracy. "Classroom Production of a Historical Film Essay: Reflections and Guidelines." *The History Teacher* 7.4, 1974, pp. 540–51.

Murra, John V. *On Inca Political Structure*. Bobbs-Merrill, 1958.

Nair, Parvati. *A Different Light: The Photography of Sebastião Salgado*. Duke University Press, 2011.

Naggar, Carole, and Fred, Ritchin. *Mexico Through Foreign Eyes: Visto por Ojos Extranjeros, 1880–1990*. W. W. Norton, 1996.

Nelson, Diane M. *Un dedo en la llaga*. Cholsamaj Fundacion, 2006.

Newhall, Beaumont. *The History of Photography: From 1839 to the Present*, 5th edition. Museum of Modern Art, 1982. First published in 1937.

———. *Supreme Instants: The Photography of Edward Weston*. Thames & Hudson, 1986.

Nietzsche, Friedrich. *The Gay Science*. Translated by Walter Kaufmann, Vintage Press, 1974.

Nochlin, Linda. "Foreword." *Photography at the Dock: Essays on Photographic History, Institutions, and Practices*, edited by Abigail Solomon-Godeau, University of Minnesota Press, 2002, xiii–xvi.

O'Bryen, Rory. "McOndo, Magic Realism and Latin American Identity." *Bulletin of Latin American Research*, 30.1, 2011, pp. 158–74.

Ortiz Monasterio, Pablo, Juan de La Cabada, and Héctor García. *Escribir con luz*. Fondo de la Cultura Económica, 1985.

Osborne, Peter. *Anywhere or Not at All: Philosophy of Contemporary Art.* Verso, 2013.

Otero Muñoz, Gustavo. "Monografía de Colombia." *Colombia: 200 grabados en cobre*, Paris: Braun & Cie Editors, 1951, pp. 7–34.

Ovalle, Manuel T. *Directorio del viajero en la República de Guatemala, América Central.* Imprenta El Porvenir, 1899.

Panofsky, Erwin. *Meaning in the Visual Arts.* University of Chicago Press, 1982.

Parkinson Zamora, Lois. "Quetzalcóatl's Mirror: Reflections on the Photographic Image in Latin America." *Image and Memory*, edited by Wendy Watriss and Lois Parkinson Zamora, University of Texas Press, 1998, pp. 293–375.

Pere, Carito. *La ciudad de los fotógrafos.* Estudios del Pez, 2006.

Pérez Fernández, Silvia, and Cora Gamarnik. "Artículos de Investigación sobre Fotografía." Uruguay: Centro Municipal de Fotografía de Montevideo, 2011. http://cdf.montevideo.gub.uy/fotografia/convocatorias/edicionescmdf/libros/investigacion_2011.html.

Pérez Montfort, Ricardo. *Estampas de nacionalismo popular mexicano: Ensayos sobre cultura popular y nacionalismo.* Centro de Investigaciones y Estudios Superiores en Antropología Social, 1994.

———. *Yerba, goma y polvo: Drogas, ambientes y policías en México, 1900–1940.* Ediciones Era, 1999.

Philips, Christopher. "The Judgement seat of Photography." *October (Journal)*, 22, 1982, pp. 27–63.

Pink, Sarah, editor. *Visual Interventions: Applied Visual Anthropology.* Berghanh Books, 2009.

Pinney, Christopher. *Camera Indica: The Social Life of Indian Photographs.* Reaktion Books, 1997.

———. "Seven Theses on Photography." *Thesis Eleven*, 113.1, 2012, pp. 141–56.

Pinney, Christopher, Nicolas Peterson, and Nicholas Thomas, editors. *Photography's Other Histories.* Duke University Press, 2003.

Plato. *The Republic*, edited by GRF Ferrari and translated by Tom Griffith, Cambridge University Press, 2000.

Poniatowska, Elena. "Letter to Nathanial Gardner." September 2009.

———. *Massacre in Mexico.* Translated by Helen R Lane, University of Missouri Press, 1984.

———. *La noche de Tlatelolco.* Ediciones Era, 1971.

———. *Tinísima.* Ediciones Era, 1992.

Poole, Deborah. "Figueroa Aznar and Cusco Indigenistas: Photography and Modernism in Early-Twentieth-Century Peru." *Photography's Other Histories*, edited by Christopher Pinney and Nicolas Peterson, Duke University Press, 2003, pp. 173–201.

———. *Vision, Race, and Modernity: A Visual Economy of the Andean World.* Princeton University Press, 1997.

Pratt, Mary Louise. "Arts of the Contact Zone." *Profession*, 1991, pp. 33–40.

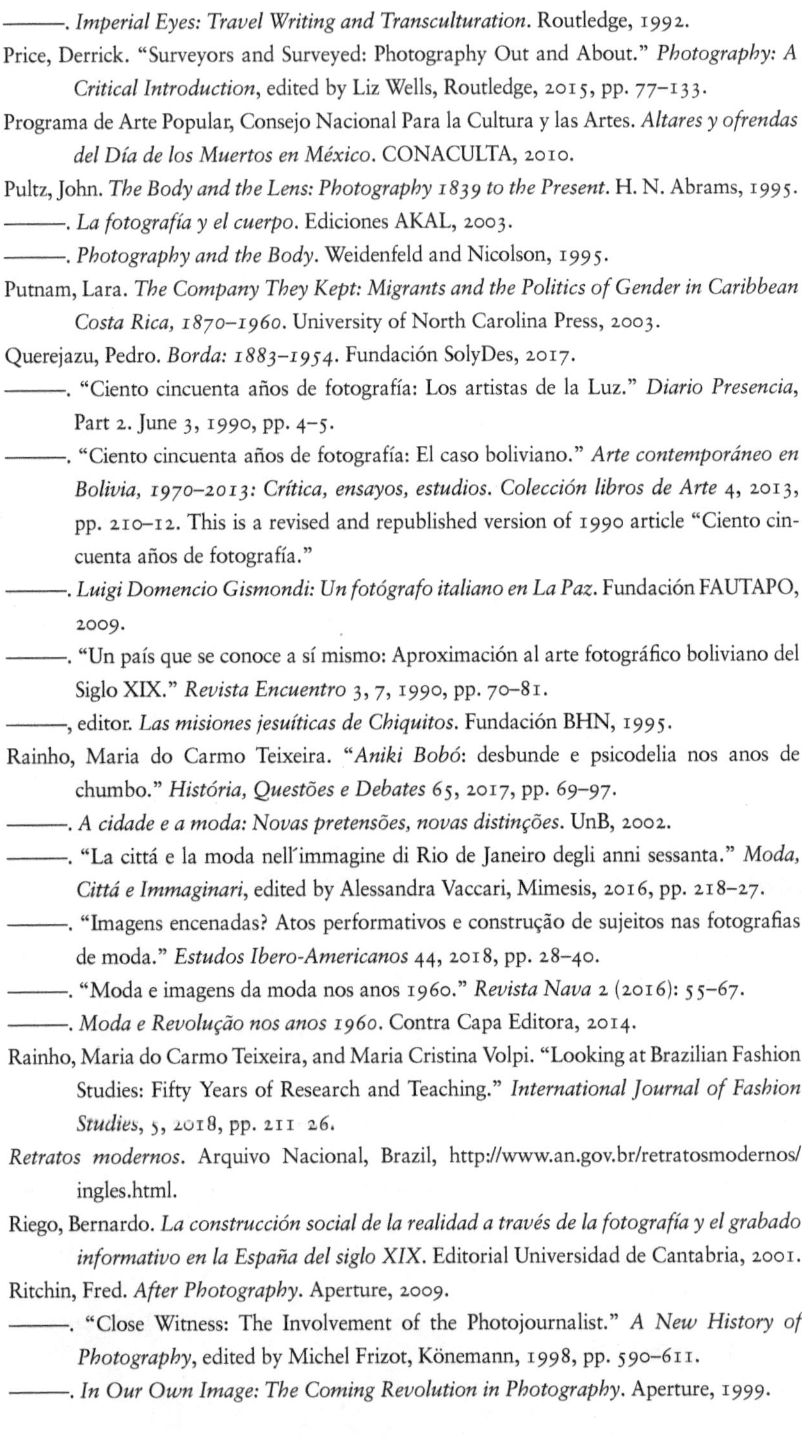

———. *Imperial Eyes: Travel Writing and Transculturation*. Routledge, 1992.

Price, Derrick. "Surveyors and Surveyed: Photography Out and About." *Photography: A Critical Introduction*, edited by Liz Wells, Routledge, 2015, pp. 77–133.

Programa de Arte Popular, Consejo Nacional Para la Cultura y las Artes. *Altares y ofrendas del Día de los Muertos en México*. CONACULTA, 2010.

Pultz, John. *The Body and the Lens: Photography 1839 to the Present*. H. N. Abrams, 1995.

———. *La fotografía y el cuerpo*. Ediciones AKAL, 2003.

———. *Photography and the Body*. Weidenfeld and Nicolson, 1995.

Putnam, Lara. *The Company They Kept: Migrants and the Politics of Gender in Caribbean Costa Rica, 1870–1960*. University of North Carolina Press, 2003.

Querejazu, Pedro. *Borda: 1883–1954*. Fundación SolyDes, 2017.

———. "Ciento cincuenta años de fotografía: Los artistas de la Luz." *Diario Presencia*, Part 2. June 3, 1990, pp. 4–5.

———. "Ciento cincuenta años de fotografía: El caso boliviano." *Arte contemporáneo en Bolivia, 1970–2013: Crítica, ensayos, estudios. Colección libros de Arte* 4, 2013, pp. 210–12. This is a revised and republished version of 1990 article "Ciento cincuenta años de fotografía."

———. *Luigi Domencio Gismondi: Un fotógrafo italiano en La Paz*. Fundación FAUTAPO, 2009.

———. "Un país que se conoce a sí mismo: Aproximación al arte fotográfico boliviano del Siglo XIX." *Revista Encuentro* 3, 7, 1990, pp. 70–81.

———, editor. *Las misiones jesuíticas de Chiquitos*. Fundación BHN, 1995.

Rainho, Maria do Carmo Teixeira. "*Aniki Bobó*: desbunde e psicodelia nos anos de chumbo." *História, Questões e Debates* 65, 2017, pp. 69–97.

———. *A cidade e a moda: Novas pretensões, novas distinções*. UnB, 2002.

———. "La cittá e la moda nell'immagine di Rio de Janeiro degli anni sessanta." *Moda, Cittá e Immaginari*, edited by Alessandra Vaccari, Mimesis, 2016, pp. 218–27.

———. "Imagens encenadas? Atos performativos e construção de sujeitos nas fotografias de moda." *Estudos Ibero-Americanos* 44, 2018, pp. 28–40.

———. "Moda e imagens da moda nos anos 1960." *Revista Nava* 2 (2016): 55–67.

———. *Moda e Revolução nos anos 1960*. Contra Capa Editora, 2014.

Rainho, Maria do Carmo Teixeira, and Maria Cristina Volpi. "Looking at Brazilian Fashion Studies: Fifty Years of Research and Teaching." *International Journal of Fashion Studies*, 5, 2018, pp. 211–26.

Retratos modernos. Arquivo Nacional, Brazil, http://www.an.gov.br/retratosmodernos/ingles.html.

Riego, Bernardo. *La construcción social de la realidad a través de la fotografía y el grabado informativo en la España del siglo XIX*. Editorial Universidad de Cantabria, 2001.

Ritchin, Fred. *After Photography*. Aperture, 2009.

———. "Close Witness: The Involvement of the Photojournalist." *A New History of Photography*, edited by Michel Frizot, Könemann, 1998, pp. 590–611.

———. *In Our Own Image: The Coming Revolution in Photography*. Aperture, 1999.

Robinson, William. *Latin American and Global Capitalism: A Critical Globalization Perspective*. John Hopkins University Press, 2008.

Roca, Lourdes Ortiz, and Fernando Aguayo. *Investigación con imágenes: Usos y retos metodológicos*. Instituto Mora/ CONACYT, 2012.

Rodríguez, José Antonio. *Fotógrafas en México, 1872–1960*. Turner, 2012.

Rodríguez Villegas, Hernán. *Historia de la fotografía: Fotógrafos en Chile 1900–1950*. Centro Nacional de Patrimonio Fotográfico, 2011.

———. *Historia de la fotografía: Fotógrafos en Chile durante el siglo XIX*. Centro Nacional de Patrimonio Fotográfico, 2001.

Roei, Noa. *Civic Aesthetics: Militarism, Israeli Art and Visual Culture*. Bloomsbury Publishing, 2016.

Rojo, Juan. *Revisiting the Mexican Student Movement of 1968: Shifting Perspectives in Literature and Culture since Tlatelolco*. Palgrave Macmillan, 2016.

Rose, Gillian. *Visual Methodologies: An Introduction to the Interpretation of Visual Materials*. Sage, 2007.

Rose, Nikolas. *Powers of Freedom: Reframing Political Thought*. Cambridge University Press, 1999.

Rosenblum, Naomi. *A World History of Photography*. Abbeville Press, 1984.

Rossell, Daniela. *Ricas y famosas*. Turner, 2002.

Rouillé André. *L'Empire de la photographie: Photographie et pouvoir bourgeois 1839–1870*. Le Sycomore, 1982.

———. *A fotografia: Entre documento e arte contemporânea*. Senac, 2009.

———. *Histoire de la photographie*. Bordas, 1986.

Said, Edward. *Culture and Imperialism*. Vintage, 1994.

Salgado, Sebastião. *Workers*. Aperture, 1993.

Salomon, Carlos Manuel. *The Routledge History of Latin American Culture*. Routledge, 2017.

Sampaio Barbosa, Carlos Alberto. *A fotografia a servico de Clio: Uma interpretação da história visual da Revolução Mexicana (1900–1940)*. Editora UNESP, 2006.

Sandeen, Eric J. "*The Family of Man* in Guatemala." *Visual Studies* 30.2, 2015, pp. 123–30.

———. "The International Reception of *The Family of Man*." *The History of Photography* 29.4, 2015, pp. 344–55.

———. *Picturing an Exhibition: The Family of Man and 1950s America*. University of New Mexico Press, 1995.

Sandweiss, Martha. *Print the Legend: Photography and the American West*. Yale University Press, 2002.

Santana, Andrés Isaac. *Nosotros, los más infieles: Narraciones críticas sobre el arte cubano (1993–2005)*. CENDEAC, 2007.

Schaedel, Richard Paul. *La etnografía muchik en las fotografías de H. Brüning, 1886–1925*. COFIDE, 1988.

Schwartz, Jorge. "Among Friends: Portraits of Writers an Interview with Sara Facio." *Photography and Writing in Latin America: Double Exposures*, edited by Marcy E. Schwartz and Mary Beth Tierney-Tello, University of New Mexico Press, 2006, pp. 251–58.

Sekula, Allan. *Mining Photographs and Other Pictures, 1948–1968*. Press of the Nova Scotia College of Art & Design, 1983.

———. *Photography Against the Grain: Essays and Photo Works, 1973–1983*. The Press of the Nova Scotia College of Art and Design, 1984.

Sekula, Allan, and Benjamin H. D. Buchloh. *Fish Story*. Richter Verlag, 2002.

Selejan, Ileana L. "Pictures in Dispute: Documentary Photography in Sandinista Nicaragua." *photographies* 10.3, 2017, pp. 283–302.

Serrano, Eduardo. *Historia de la fotografía en Colombia, 1840–1950*. Museo de arte Moderno de Bogotá, 1983.

———. *Historia de la fotografía en Colombia, 1950–2000*. Planeta/Museo Nacional de Colombia, 2006.

Sire, Agnès. *Sergio Larrain: Vagabond Photographer*. Thames & Hudson, 2003.

———. *Valparaíso*. Aperture, 2017.

Sloan, Julia L. "Talking Tlatelolco: The Power of a Collective Memory Suppressed but not Surrendered." *Projections of Power in the Americas*, edited by Niels Bjerre-Poulsen, et al., Routledge, 2012, pp. 61–88.

Smith, Graham. "François Aubert's Shirt of Emperor Maximilian of Mexico." *History of Photography*, 16.2, 1992, pp. 171–73.

———, editor. *History of Photography*, 29.4, 2005, pp. 313–95.

Solomon-Godeau, Abigail. *Photography at the Dock: Essays on Photographic History, Institutions, and Practices*. University of Minnesota Press, 1991.

Sontag, Susan. *Ensaios sobre fotografia*. Translated by Joaquim Paiva, Editora Arbor, 1981.

———. *On Photography*. Penguin, 2014. Originally published in 1977.

———. *Regarding the Pain of Others*. Picador, 2004.

Sougez, Marie-Loup. *Historia de la fotografía*. Cátedra, 2011.

Soutter, Lucy. "Notes on Photography and Cultural Translations." *photographies* 2.2–3, 2018, pp. 329–38.

Stack, Trudy Wilner. "An Appetite for the Thing Itself: Studio Vegetables and Female Nudes." *Edward Weston: Forms of Passion*, edited by Giles Mora, Thames & Hudson, 1995, pp. 134–227.

Steichen, Edward. *The Family of Man: 30th Anniversary Edition*. Museum of Modern Art, 1983.

Stein, Sally. *Official Images: New Deal Photography*. Smithsonian Institute, 1987.

Stern, Grete, and Sara Facio. *Fotografía en la Argentina, 1937–1981*. La Azotea Editorial Fotográfica, 1988.

Stoler, Ann Laura. "Colonial Archives and the Arts of Governance: On the Content in the Form." *Refiguring the Archive*, edited by Carolyn Hamilton, et al., *Springer Science & Business Media*, 2012, pp. 83–102.

Strauss, D. L. *Between the Eyes: Essays on Photography and Politics*. Aperture, 2003.

Szarkowski, John. *Photography Until Now*. Museum of Modern Art, 1990.

Taracena, Arturo, and Rosina Cazali. *Imágenes de Guatemala 1850–2005*. Cima, 2005.

Todorov, Tzvetan. *Symbolism and Interpretation*. Cornell University Press, 1986.

———. *Theories of the Symbol*. Cornell University Press, 1984.

Toomey Frost, Susan. *Timeless Mexico: The Photographs of Hugo Brehme*. University of Texas Press, 2011.

Toro, Hardy Alfredo. *Understanding Latin America: A Decoding Guide*. World Scientific, 2017.

Torrico, Zamudio, Rodolfo. *Bolivia pintoresca*. University Society, 1925.

Treviño, Estela. *160 años de fotografía en México*. Centro de la Imagen, 2004.

Turner, Fred. "*The Family of Man* and the Politics of Attention in Cold War America." *Public Culture*, 24.1, 2012, pp. 55–84.

Valdeavellano, Alberto G. *Los indígenas de Guatemala vistos por el fotógrafo Alberto G. Valdeavellano (1861–1928): Exhibición*. Instituto Guatemalteco de Turismo, 1987.

Vargas, Sussy. "*Breve historia de la taxonomía del cuerpo y del pecado en el arte en Costa Rica*." 2016, https://revistas.ucr.ac.cr/index.php/escena/article/view/25585.

———. *El caribe limonense a través de la mirada y la obra de Hans Wimmer 1903–1947*. Universidad Veritas, 2017.

———. "Francisco Valiente." *Artstudio*, 2006, http://www.artstudiomagazine.com/fotografia/francisco-valiente.html.

———, et al. "*Manuel Gómez Miralles – Fotografía y Memoria*." *Artstudio*, 2006. http://www.artstudiomagazine.com/fotografia/gomez-miralles.html.

———, et al. *La mirada del tiempo: Historia de la Fotografía en Costa Rica 1848–2003*. Fundación Museos del Banco Central/Universidad Veritas, 2004.

Vargas, Sussy, and Carolina Goodfellow. *Grafitica: Gráfica popular en Costa Rica*. Roger Union Printing, 2014.

Vargas, Sussy, and Roberto Guerrero, curators. *Detrás del portón rojo: Una visión de la erótica en el arte costarricense*. Museo de Arte Costarricense (MAC), November 2017–April 2018.

Vargas, Gaby. "Genio y figura: Ricas y famosas." *Reforma*, 1 September 2002.

Vicente, Filipa Lowndes, editor. *O Império da Visão: Fotografia no Contexto Colonial Português (1860–1960)*. Edition 70, 2014.

Vigarello, Georges. *The Silhouette: From the 18th Century to the Present Day*. Bloomsbury Publishing, 2016.

Villela, Samuel, and Sara Castrejón Reza. *Sara Castrejón: Fotógrafa de la Revolución*. INAH, 2010.

Villoro, Juan. "Ricas, famosas y excesivas." *El país semanal*, 341, June 9, 2002, pp. 42–50.

Volpi, Jorge. *La imaginación y el poder: Una historia intelectual de 1968*. Ediciones Era, 1998.

Vovelle, Michel. *Enlightenment Portraits*. Translated by Lydia G. Cochrane, University of Chicago Press, 1997.

Warren, Beth Gates. *Artful Lives: Edward Weston, Margrethe Mather, and the Bohemians of Los Angeles*. J. Paul Getty Museum, 2011.

Watriss, Wendy, and Lois Parkinson Zamora, editors. *Image and Memory*. University of Texas Press, 1998.

Weaver, Mike. *The Photographic Art: Pictorial Traditions in Britain and America*. Herbert, 1986.

Wells, Liz. *Photography: A Critical Introduction*. Routledge, 2015.

———. "Thinking About Photography: Debates, Historically and Now." *Photography: A Critical Introduction*, edited by Liz Wells, Routledge, 2015, pp. 9–76.

Weston, Edward. *The Daybooks of Edward Weston: California*. Aperture, 1973.

———. *The Daybooks of Edward Weston: Mexico*. Aperture, 1973.

White, Hayden. *Metahistory: The Historical Imagination in Nineteenth-Century Europe*. John Hopkins University Press, 1973.

Wilson, Charis, and Wendy Madar. *Through Another Lens: My Years with Edward Weston*. Farrar, Straus and Giroux, 1999.

Wolf, David, Mike Weaver, and the Royal Academy of Arts. *The Art of Photography: 1839–1939*. Yale University Press, 1989.

Yampolsky, Mariana, editor. *Bailes y balas: Ciudad de México 1921–1931*. Archivo General de la Nación, 1991.

Yas, Juan José de Jesús, and José Domingo Noriega. *La Antigua Guatemala: J.J. Yas, J.D. Noriega, 1880–1960*. La Azotea, 1990.

Yuyanapaq. Para recordar: 1980–2000 relato visual del conflicto armado interno en el Perú. Pontificia Universidad Católica del Perú (PUCP) Fondo Editorial, 2014.

Zelizer, Vivian. *Pricing the Priceless Child: The Changing Social Value of Children*. Princeton University Press, 1985.

Index

www.ingramcontent.com/pod-product-compliance
Lightning Source LLC
LaVergne TN
LVHW091032080826
845145LV00002B/468

* 9 7 8 0 8 2 6 3 6 8 1 0 2 *